Islamic Jurisprudence
(*Uṣūl al-Fiqh*)

ISLAMIC JURISPRUDENCE
(*Uṣūl al-Fiqh*)

Imran Ahsan Khan Nyazee

Center for Excellence in Research
Islamabad

Center for Excellence in Research,
Head Office: No. 103, Street 2, PTV Colony,
Shahpur, Islamabad,
Pakistan 44000

First Published: 2000
Revised Edition: 2007
Third Revised Edition: 2012, 2016

CENTER FOR EXCELLENCE IN RESEARCH

For My Wife

Table of Contents

PREFACE TO THE THIRD REVISED EDITION

Islamic jurisprudence or *uṣūl al-fiqh* provides the foundation for any meaningful study of Islamic law. The present book has been in the field for more than a decade and has received a positive response from many quarters. It is used as a textbook in a number of university courses. The information in the book was kept to a bare minimum; it was generally considered sufficient to understand the sources of Islamic law along with the basic methods of interpretation, also called *ijtihād*. Over the years, however, students have shown an eagerness to know more. They have raised many questions whose answers the book does not provide, because the book was not intended to answer those questions. Many of these students had recourse to the Internet and raised the questions in the hope of getting the right answers. Some of the answers given were, unfortunately, incorrect or misleading, primarily because they were not given by persons qualified to do so. The activity still continues and is gathering pace. It was also realized that there were several questions that had not been raised by the students and general readers, but these were questions that should have been asked. A catologue of the questions asked, and those not asked, gave rise to the need to revise the present book.

One main issue that was a cause of concern was that, even after reading the book, most readers fail to distinguish between the meaning of *uṣūl al-fiqh* as sources and *uṣūl al-fiqh* as a discipline. The phrase "*uṣūl al-fiqh* are four" has become embedded so deeply in minds that it is difficult to think about the meaning of the discipline itself, which is the real purpose of studying *uṣūl al-fiqh*.

The present, third, edition of the book has, therefore, been revised and three chapters at the end have been completely rewritten. The slight increase in the size of the book has been ignored keeping in view the significance of the issues involved. The book continues to have five parts as earlier.

It was originally planned to include a few topics that are very important from the comparative perspective and also from the perspective of the Islamization of laws. These issues have not been dealt with by any book or scholarly work. One such area is about the comparison of legal reasoning in Islamic law with legal reasoning in the Common law. This is important for a country like Pakistan where the Common law operates side by side with Islamic law. The comparison to be presented would also have been useful for Muslim majority countries where the Civil Law is applied in some form, because many of the comparisons are equally valid for both legal systems. Another area that has been dealt with by hundreds, if not thousands, of books and research projects is that of the *qawā'id fiqhiyyah*. The Islamic Fiqh Academy, Jeddah had even planned an encyclopedia on the subject. Despite such attention by scholars, it has never been sufficiently elaborated how these *qawā'id* are to be employed within the legal system, and what is their significance within such system. A separate part or book needs to be devoted to this subject, with explanations that will not only enhance understanding of the *qawā'id*, but also lead to further research. Other important topics like, human rights, justice, nature of the Islamic state, and so on also need to be discussed. All these have not been included in this book as these have been discussed in our book *Outlines of Islamic Jurisprudence*. The important issues, mentioned and, left out of both books will be discussed in a separate volume called the "Secrets of *Uṣūl al-Fiqh*." One important question that has been taken up is about following a single school of Islamic law. This question has not been answered adequately by writers, therefore, it has been taken up in the last part. As the issue of *fatwās* is becoming increasingly important, the last chapter has been devoted to this topic.

Imran Ahsan Khan Nyazee
Islamabad
December, 2012

1 Introduction

1.1 The Problem With the Meaning of Jurisprudence

The study of Islamic law and jurisprudence in English brings with it some problems that need to be resolved before the subject is approached in earnest. These problems pertain to terminology and are imported into Islamic disciplines from Western Jurisprudence simply by the use of Western terms. The term "Islamic Jurisprudence," for example, cannot be assigned a clear meaning if the meaning of the term "Jurisprudence" itself is not clear in Western law. According to Dias, one of the most difficult problems of jurisprudence has been, and perhaps still is, to determine the exact meaning of "jurisprudence" as well as to determine its province and scope.[1] This is so despite the fact that "jurisprudence was the first of the social sciences to be

1. R. W. M. Dias, *Jurisprudence* (London: Butterworths, 1985), 3.

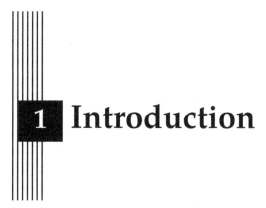

born."[2] Explaining the problem of the meaning and scope of jurisprudence, Dias says:

> Its province has been determined and re-determined because the nature of the subject is such that no delineation of its scope can be regarded as final. On torts and contracts, for example, a student may be recommended to read any of the standard textbooks with assurance that, whichever book he does read, he will derive much the same idea as to what the subject is about. With jurisprudence this is not so. Books called "jurisprudence" vary so widely in subject matter and treatment that the answer to the question, what is "jurisprudence"?, is that it means pretty much whatever anyone wants it to mean—a depressing start indeed.[3]

A possible reason, in our view, is that Western jurisprudence has not been developed systematically within one legal system; it has been subject to diverse influences from various legal systems in the Western world. While we use the terms Western law and Western legal system, there are different approaches to the law in different jurisdictions and even the word jurisprudence does not have the same meaning.

For Western law, the term "jurisprudence" was first used by the Roman jurists, but they never developed an independent subject called *jurisprudentia*.[4] Since then its "province has been determined and re-determined," as Dias says.[5] In the last few decades, this activity has increased and the study of jurisprudence has changed radically.[6] The result of this activity has influenced even the titles used to study the subject: "Jurisprudence," "Legal

2. Wurzel, "Methods of Judicial Thinking," in *Science of Legal Method: Selected Essays*, 289, as quoted in Dias, *Jurisprudence*, 3.
3. Dias, *Jurisprudence*, 3.
4. Ibid.
5. Ibid.
6. In Pakistan, we still cling to the old method, perhaps, oblivious to the changes that are taking place in the rest of the legal world.

Theory," "Theories of Law," "Legal Philosophy" and "General Theory of Law."

The modern format for the study of jurisprudence—we feel and it will be obvious to whoever compares the two systems—is gradually heading towards the format that was developed by Muslim jurists for *uṣūl al-fiqh* more than a thousand years ago. This, of course, is true for the general format and there are differences too that spring from the fundamental distinctions between the two legal systems. To understand the similarities and differences, we shall briefly examine the meanings of jurisprudence recorded by Roscoe Pound and then look at the format of the "general theory of law" provided by Ronald Dworkin.[7]

1.2 A Format for the General Theory of Law

Roscoe Pound identified three uses of the word jurisprudence.[8] Two of these uses, he thought, were justified, while the third was wholly unjustifiable.[9] The two relevant uses are as follows:

1. The first use, he said, was peculiar to England, British dominions, and the United States. This meaning was assigned to jurisprudence by Austin in his *Province of Jurisprudence Determined* (1832). As Austin's method was exclusively analytical, a narrower meaning of jurisprudence became current in English speaking countries.[10] "It [this concept of jurisprudence] thinks of law as an aggregate of laws and of laws as rules, and this narrow definition of law gives a narrower limitation of the science of law."[11] In this

7. Ronald Dworkin is the leading legal philosopher in the Western world today.
8. Roscoe Pound, *Jurisprudence*, vol. 1 (St. Paul, MN, 1958), 7.
9. For example, "medical jurisprudence," "dental jurisprudence," "engineering jurisprudence" and so on could not really be considered within the subject-matter of jurisprudence.
10. As well as in the dominions we may add.
11. Ibid. 8.

sense jurisprudence might be called *the comparative anatomy of developed systems of law.* Pound says: "This is one side of the science of law (jurisprudence). I shall call it *analytical jurisprudence.*"[12]

2. The second use he mentions is French, and to some extent American. The French use the word *jurisprudence* to mean the course of decisions in courts.[13] The French term for jurisprudence in the English sense is called *théorie générale du droit.*[14] Roscoe Pound elaborating the use of the French term says something that appears to be very important; it

---

12. Ibid. 9. Pound says:

> Holland uses the term in this sense when he defines Jurisprudence as the "formal science of positive law." Holland, *Jurisprudence* (13th ed., 1924) 13, as quoted by Pound, *Jurisprudence,* 8. This definition proceeds on the Aristotelian distinction between substance and form. To give an old-time illustration, a smith has in his hand the raw material, the substance, steel and wood. He has in his mind the idea, that is, the picture of a saw. He fashions the substance to that mental picture and so gives to the substance the form of a saw. Hence the maxim *forma dat esse rei.* Accordingly, by saying that Jurisprudence is a formal science, Holland means that it has to do with systems of legal precepts but not with legal precepts, the substance given form in those systems. It does not criticise the content of a body of laws except for being out of line with the analytical system. It arranges and systematises that content. By "positive law" he means the body of legal precepts which actually obtain as authoritative legal materials for decision and authoritative bases of predicting decisions in a given time and in given places; not the received ideals of legal systems, and the ideal precepts which philosophical or economic or sociological considerations might dictate or indicate.

13. Ibid. 9. According to Lloyd, the word "jurisprudence" is not generally used in other languages in the English sense. Thus, in French it refers to something like English "case-law." Lloyd, *Introduction to Jurisprudence* (1979), 1, fn. 1.
14. Ibid.

may help in understanding modern developments. He says:

> In America the word "jurisprudence" has been used to some extent in the French sense. Thus the phrase "equity jurisprudence," meaning the course of decision in Anglo-American courts of equity, has been fixed in good usage by the classical work of judge Story.[15]

The second meaning throws some light on the nature of American jurisprudence with its emphasis on the nature of the judicial process and theories of adjudication. When the judge is faced with hard cases, the question arises as to where does he get his law from when the statutes or existing decisions do not help? This is where the theories of law, and the political philosophy of the judge, whether he has one or not, become relevant.

In Britain today, the study of analytical jurisprudence, as represented by Salmond's book,[16] has been given up completely. The emphasis now is entirely on legal theories. The true importance of the theories of law will not be realized, however, unless the emphasis shifts from the study of the concept of law to the nature of the judicial process.

The positivists have consistently maintained that the judge uses his "discretion" in hard cases, and this is where philosophers like Dworkin have opposed them. These philosophers maintain that the "discretion" of the judge is not uncontrolled and he is bound by a body of "general principles," which are law as well, and he is also bound by a determined methodology.[17]

---

15. Pound, *Jurisprudence,* 8.
16. Sir John Salmond's book, *Jurisprudence* written in 1902 has dominated the field for a long time and is still used in Pakistan. It was revised, among others, by Glanville Williams and then by Fitzgerald.
17. As law is the adjudication of pre-existing rights, if we maintain that the judge is using his discretion, he is not only creating new law, but also applying it retrospectively.

In addition to the judge, the legislators exercise the power to grant and take away rights from the public. What guides them in determining these rights? What are the limits on the authority that they exercise? What are the sources of this authority and of the rights that they lay down in the law? The legislators too are bound, or should be bound, by some methodology. Their power is not absolute. Here too the theories of law become relevant.[18]

As a result of the identification of a methodology for the judge and the legislator, the study of the theories of law has assumed significance even in England. The British jurists can no longer ignore the theories of law as "mere theory." In fact, it is the study of analytical jurisprudence that has now been given up.[19] In short, the nature of the study of jurisprudence has changed. In many former colonies of Britain, however, the focus is still on analytical jurisprudence. The importance of legal theories and general jurisprudence has not been realized so far.

Jurisprudence today is, therefore, viewed as a general theory of law. What is the format of this theory? The best format for the study of jurisprudence has been provided by Ronald Dworkin as

---

18. In Britain, Bentham has reigned supreme and it has been maintained that it is the law that grants rights and it is the law that takes them away. The public interest is usually in the forefront. The independent existence of natural rights outside the ambit of law is not firmly rooted. It is also for this reason that in countries like Pakistan, where the ideas of Bentham still exist unconsciously in their pure form, the idea of natural rights and human rights in the American sense has not been fully comprehended.
19. Lloyd has a theory that the study of "theories of law" was ignored in Britain because of the apprenticeship system prevalent in England for the teaching of law, there being no regular university teaching. In addition to this, there was the hard-headed, practice oriented, attitude of the British lawyer, who was not interested in "mere theory." Lloyd, *Introduction to Jurisprudence,* 3. The truth appears to be that British positivist theories and the use of "discretion" by the judge have been subjected to severe criticism by American jurists like Dworkin. The change in the study of jurisprudence in Britain appears to be the result of this criticism.

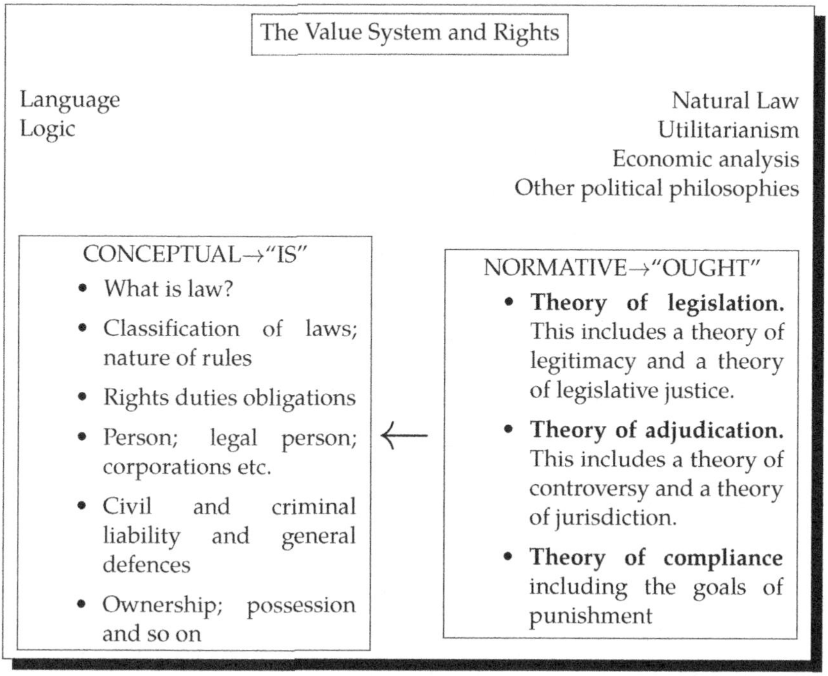
The Value System and Rights
Language
Logic
Natural Law
Utilitarianism
Economic analysis
Other political philosophies
CONCEPTUAL→"IS"
• What is law?
• Classification of laws; nature of rules
• Rights duties obligations
• Person; legal person; corporations etc.
• Civil and criminal liability and general defences
• Ownership; possession and so on
NORMATIVE→"OUGHT"
• Theory of legislation. This includes a theory of legitimacy and a theory of legislative justice.
• Theory of adjudication. This includes a theory of controversy and a theory of jurisdiction.
• Theory of compliance including the goals of punishment

the "General Theory of Law" a title that is obviously influenced by the second meaning of jurisprudence given above. Dworkin describes the structure of a general theory of law, in his book, *Taking Rights Seriously*. This has been amended slightly for our purposes, but is described below in Dworkin's own words:[20]

1. A general theory of law, says Dworkin, must be normative as well as conceptual.

2. The conceptual part should deal with law as it is, while the normative part should deal with the law as it ought to be.

3. Its normative part must have a theory of legislation, a theory of adjudication and a theory of compliance. These three theories look at the normative part of the law (or the law

20. Ronald Dworkin, *Taking Rights Seriously*, iv.

as it ought to be) from the standpoint of the lawmaker, the judge and the ordinary citizen.

4. The theory of legislation must contain a theory of legitimacy, which describes the circumstances under which a particular person or group of persons is entitled to make law. It should also contain a theory of legislative justice, which describes the law they are entitled or obliged to make.

5. The theory of adjudication must contain a theory of controversy, which sets out standards that judges should use to decide hard cases at law.[21] It should also contain a theory of jurisdiction, which explains why judges, rather than other groups or institutions, should make the decisions required by the theory of controversy.

6. The theory of compliance must contrast and discuss two roles. It must contain a theory of deference, which discusses the nature and limits of the citizen's duty to obey the law in different forms of state and under different circumstances. It should also contain a theory of enforcement, which identifies the goals of enforcement and punishment and describes how officials should respond to different kinds of crime or fault.

7. The categories described above are not watertight compartments and a subject described in one may fall in another.[22]

---

21. By "hard cases" Dworkin means those in which no clear statute or rule governs the problem. H.L.A.Hart calls it the "open texture of the law." H.L.A.Hart, *The Concept of Law* (Oxford: Clarendon Press, 1961), 120, 14–32.
22. For example, says Dworkin, we may raise the question whether the most fundamental principles of the constitution, which define who is competent to make law and how, themselves be considered part of the law? The question concerns the theories of legitimacy as well as that of jurisdiction. Further, if these are law then the right of the judges to decide what the constitution requires appears to be confirmed. This question, therefore, affects the conceptual part of the theory as well. Ronald Dworkin, *Taking Rights Seriously,* iv.

8. A general theory of law will have many connections with other departments of philosophy. The normative part of the general theory will be embedded in a more general political and moral philosophy which may in turn depend upon philosophical theories about human nature and morality.

9. The conceptual part will draw upon the philosophy of language and upon logic.

We are indebted to Dworkin for providing such a clear picture of the general theory of law, a picture that helps us elaborate the scope of *uṣūl al-fiqh* as it has always existed in the past and as it should be viewed in the modern context.

To expand this general format, we may add that in the present century there has been a revival of natural law. This has led to what is called a value-oriented jurisprudence. Values are seen in the shape of interests that need to be secured by society.[23] These are: (1) national and social safety; (2) sanctity of the person; (3) sanctity of property; (4) social welfare; (5) equality; (6) consistency and fidelity to rules, principles, doctrine and tradition; (7) morality; (8) administrative convenience; and (9) international comity.[24] Each dispute or issue is seen as a clash between two or more interests and the decision involves preference of one interest over the other. This is achieved through the concept of justice prevailing in society.[25] In other words, these values provide the highest general principles, which may also be

23. Jurists like Roscoe Pound do not consider these interests to be mere values, but individual and social wants that need to be satisfied and reconciled. See Edgar Bodenheimer, *Jurisprudence: The Philosophy and Method of the Law* (Cambridge, Massachusetts: Harvard University Press, 1974), 118. [hereinafter referred to as Bodenheimer, *Jurisprudence*]. Further, Ronald Dworkin himself does not subscribe to the use of values.
24. Dias, *Jurisprudence*, 197–213.
25. Some Western jurists, like Kelsen and Alf Ross, have rejected the use of values as a reliable guide for justice. These jurists maintain that the use of these values leads to irrationality. Bodenheimer, *Jurisprudence*, 203.

considered a part of law. For Dworkin himself, the judge enforces some rights. These rights lie outside the ambit of the law, so to say. His ideas are to be viewed in the context of what is called "Dworkin's Rights Thesis."[26]

1.3 A Model for the Study of the General Theory of Islamic Law or *Uṣūl al-Fiqh*

It has been stated that in the United States the emphasis has been more on the French meaning of *theorie generale* or general theory. Accordingly, Ronald Dworkin has used the format of a general theory for understanding jurisprudence. This format, it is suggested here, would be suitable for a comparison not only of Western jurisprudence with Islamic Jurisprudence, but also for identifying a format for the study of *uṣūl al-fiqh* in the modern age.

The format, in our view, will not only facilitate the understanding of *uṣūl al-fiqh,* but lead to its further development. Yet, there cannot be one model or format for such a study. The needs of Muslims in an Islamic state are different from those living as minorities in non-Muslim countries or even for those living in states with a Muslim population, but which have a more or less secular ideological orientation. We, therefore, have to adopt a flexible model that can be adjusted to the needs of Muslims wherever they are and whatever system they are living under. The model adopted here is one for an Islamic state, but it can be adjusted to meet the needs of those living in non-Muslim states. The figure given above for law is now adapted to the structure of the Islamic legal system and *uṣūl al-fiqh.*

On the left side is the framework in which the *mujtahid* arranges or places his law after he has derived it from the sources. The *mujtahid* usually discovers the law for the first time. In this sense, his task is akin to that of the modern

26. A detailed study of the Islamic legal system shows that some of Dworkin's ideas may fit in perfectly with the system.

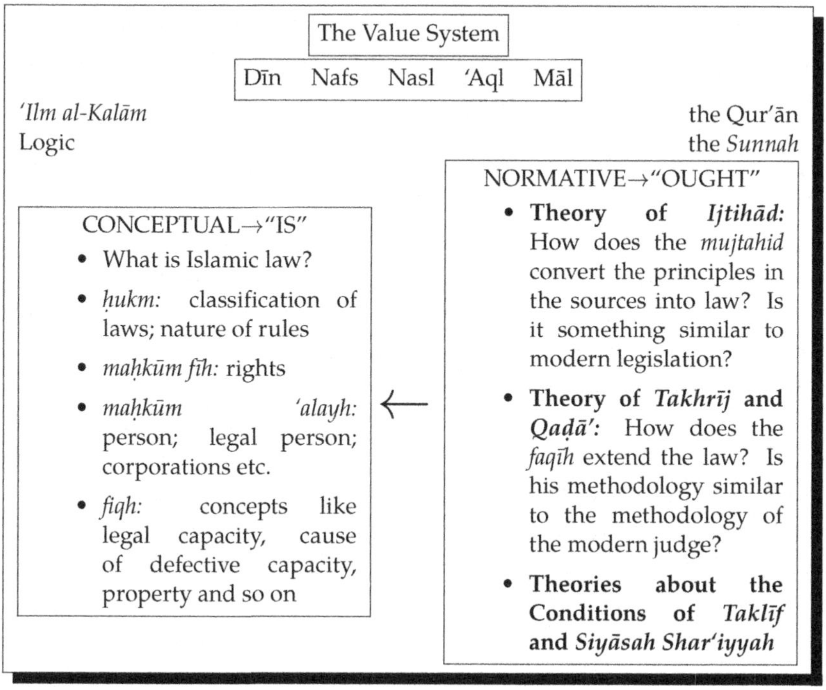

legislature. His primary task is to see what "is" the existing law and then to examine what "ought" to be the law in the light of the primary sources—the Qur'ān and the *Sunnah.* The *mujtahid* is always converting the "ought" into the "is" in case of deviation, but invariably according to a prescribed methodology. This methodology is called *ijtihād* and is necessary for legislation in a modern Islamic state. ***Ijtihād*, therefore, is a legislative function.**[27]

27. In Islamic law, as in other legal systems, there is not one, but several theories of legislation or *ijtihād.* These theories have been developed by what are called schools of Islamic law. The theories of some of the schools may appear identical, yet they have their distinctive features. For an examination of some of these theories and for the methodology of *ijtihād,* traditional and as it may be practised in the modern world, see Imran Ahsan Nyazee, *Theories of Islamic Law: The Methodology of Ijtihād* (Islamabad: Federal Law House, 2007).

The word *faqīh* was originally applied to mean a *mujtahid,* as will be explained in the next chapter, but is now used for an expert who is not a full or independent *mujtahid.*[28] The *faqīh* makes use of the reasoning adopted by the *mujtahid* in the past. Through the help of such reasoning and past decisions rendered by the *mujtahid,* or rules laid down by him, he formulates broad general principles. As a very simple example, we may cite a principle formulated by al-Dabbūsī after studying the decisions of the Ḥanafī school and the Shāf'ī school and comparing them. The principle is: "The world according to our jurists (Ḥanafīs) is divided into two worlds, while the world according to Imām al-Shāfi'ī is one world." The principle is based on the jurisdiction of the Islamic state and the protection afforded by its law.[29] This principle helps the *faqīh* to decide cases correctly in line with the legal reasoning of his school. Even if there is nothing else but this principle to guide the jurist, he will arrive at a reasonably correct and an analytically consistent opinion. Of course, there are many other techniques and standards that the *faqīh* uses to arrive at a decision, but we are focusing here on his search for the law to see what is valid law in a particular case.

The above figure shows that Islamic legal theory has a theory of legislation, a theory of adjudication and even a theory of compliance. *Uṣūl al-fiqh* deals with legislation through its theory

28. A full or independent *mujtahid* is called a *mujtahid muṭlaq,* a title usually reserved for the founder of the famous schools. These jurists are responsible for formulating theories of *ijtihād,* which are adopted and followed by the jurists of the school. As compared to the *mujtahid,* there are many grades for the *faqīh.* One such grade is that allocated to the *aṣḥāb al-takhrīj.* These are jurists who extend the law, if needed, by reasoning from general principles. For details see p. 187 below.
29. Thus, an offence committed by a person in the *dār al-ḥarb* (enemy territory) may not be punishable under the Ḥanafī law, because the Ḥanafīs give importance to the protection afforded to a citizen by the Islamic state. This protection is lacking in enemy lands. Al-Shāfi'ī, on the other hand, would consider the offence punishable as he does not make a distinction between the two *dārs* for this purpose. See al-Dabbūsī, *Ta'sīs al-Naẓar,* 58.

of *ijtihād*. It deals with adjudication through its methodology of *takhrīj*.[30] The theories of compliance are covered by what are called the conditions of *taklīf*, which define the limits within which the subject is obliged to obey the law. The theory of enforcement is included in the well known doctrine of *siyāsah shar'iyyah*.

The top of the structure shows that the Islamic legal system is trying to achieve or secure certain goals or values. These are known as the *maqāṣid al-sharī'ah*. They are quite similar to the modern interests or values that the legal system seeks to preserve and implement.[31] These interests were discussed in detail and finalised by the Muslim jurists a thousand years ago.[32] These purposes are vital for the methodology called *takhrīj* and equally important for *ijtihād*.

The format described exists already within *uṣūl al-fiqh*. In fact, the whole material has been arranged accordingly by the earlier jurists. All that is needed is to find a modern expression for it. It is in this context, then, that *uṣūl al-fiqh* is to be studied. Accordingly, wherever possible, the various theories pertaining to legislation, adjudication and compliance will be referred to in this book in the context of Islamic law. The model described above, it will be seen, can be adjusted with ease for Muslims who do not have courts adjudicating their rights according to Islamic law. This means that a theory of adjudication is not needed in such a model. Yet this

30. The word *takhrīj* as used here is not to be confused with the sense in which it has been conveyed in books by jurists like al-Zanjānī called *Takhrīj al-Furū' 'alā al-Uṣūl*. The methodology described in such books is the same as *ijtihād*. What we mean by *takhrīj* is the method of legal reasoning from general principles and this is to be derived from manuals of well known jurists. As an example of this method see generally Imran Ahsan Nyazee, *Partnerships in Islam* (Islamabad: Federal Law House, 2007). The companion volume to this book on corporations—*Corporations in Islam*—by the same publisher may also be examined.
31. In fact, the natural rights recognised by the *sharī'ah* are also linked to these purposes.
32. As compared to this, the first Western theory of the purposes or ends of law was developed by Jhering in the late nineteenth century. See Bodenheimer, *Jurisprudence*, 88–90; Dias, *Jurisprudence*, 423–25.

should not mean that the methodology of *takhrīj* is not useful in this environment.

We may now turn to the description of the contents of *uṣūl al-fiqh* in a more traditional method. In accordance with the format above, however, *uṣūl al-fiqh* has been called "the general theory of Islamic law" in this book. The term "Islamic Jurisprudence" also covers the general principles of Islamic law and *fiqh;* these will be studied in separate volumes.

1.4 The Subject-matter of *Uṣūl al-Fiqh*

Islamic jurisprudence, when viewed in the meaning of *uṣūl al-fiqh,* covers three things:

- **The Formal Structure of Islamic law:**[33] The formal structure of Islamic law is studied by the Muslim jurists under the title "the *ḥukm shar'ī.*" This study of the conceptual structure of Islamic law attempts to answer the following questions: What is Islamic law? What is the nature of rules in this legal system? How many kinds of rules are there and how do they unite with each other to give rise to the Islamic legal system? What is legal capacity and how does it interact with the operation of the rules? What kind of rights underlie the various kinds of rules? How are these rights secured through the legal framework and machinery of Islamic law? This area is shown on the left side of the figure above. This will be studied in part 1 of the book.

- **The Sources of Islamic law and the Methodology of the *Mujtahid:*** The *mujtahid* is an independent jurist who

33. The term formal pertains to the distinction made by Aristotle between "form" and "substance" as referred to above. If a carpenter is trying to make a chair, the picture of the chair in his mind is called the form, while the material, like wood, he will use is the substance. In prayer, bowing and prostrating pertain to form, while the verses recited are the substance or content. In jurisprudence, the distinction between form and content is often used.

is qualified to derive the law directly from the sources of Islamic law, like the Qur'ān and the *Sunnah.* Under this heading the following questions are raised and answered: What are the sources of Islamic law? How does the *mujtahid* interpret the textual sources? How does he employ the rational sources? What kind of methodology is employed by the *mujtahid?* The *mujtahid,* as stated earlier, performs the legislative function within the Islamic legal system. Parts 2 and 3 are devoted to these topics. This area deals with the theory of legislation described in the figure above. While this part deals with the methodology of the *mujtahid,* it will not be possible for us to study the theory of Islamic justice on which modern legislation must be based and which is linked to human rights under Islam. The topic requires comprehensive treatment in an independent study.[34]

- **The Methodology of the *Faqīh* and the Sources employed by him:** The *faqīh* is not an independent jurist, as he is dependent upon the work of the *mujtahid.* This area of Islamic jurisprudence is seldom discussed in books on the subject. A study of *uṣūl al-fiqh* cannot be complete without a study of the methodology of the *faqīh.* It is for this reason that it has been included in this book. Under this heading, we try to understand the meaning of the term "sources" for the *faqīh* as distinguished from the sources for the *mujtahid.* In addition to this, we try to answer the following questions: How does the *faqīh* settle legal issues? How does he extend the law for new cases? How far is the *faqīh* dependent upon the *mujtahid?* What, according to the *faqīh,* is the art of distinguishing cases, that is, *al-furūq?* In short, the *faqīh* performs the judicial function in Islamic law. The modern judge and lawyer must both master the methodology of the *faqīh* and acquire the ability to extend

34. In our view, this topic is very important for each Muslim country. Not only does it entail the development of a theory of justice, but also a theory of rights. The theory of legislation in Islam cannot be complete without an exposition of these topics.

the law through reasoning from Islamic legal principles. It may be mentioned here that the works of jurists like al-Dabbūsī (d. 430 A.H./1039 C.E.), al-Sarakhsī (d. 483 A.H./1090 C.E.) and others are outstanding models. Part 4 of this book deals with the methodology of the *faqīh*. As compared to the earlier editions, Part 4 now includes brief explanations about why it is necessary to follow a single school, what is the meaning of *fatwā* and how is it issued. A sample *fatwā* has also been included, which is intended to serve as an example of how a modern *muftī* is to reason when he issues a ruling. The additional topics have become essential due to the questions that are frequently raised by readers. The topics have also become necessary to the increasing interest in the methodology and field of *fatwās*.

1.5 The Scope of This Book

This book seeks to provide a broad introduction to Islamic legal theory. It also seeks to impart some basic skills that can be developed by the reader through further study. Being an introduction to Islamic Jurisprudence, the book also attempts to present an outline of the Islamic legal system as it existed in the past and as it is being developed today.

This book has also been written for two other reasons. First, there is a need for a comprehensive treatment of the subject. Secondly, in an attempt to oversimplify the subject, certain works contain statements that are creating conceptual problems for readers.

The book that has been used for a long time in law courses, at least in Pakistan, is by Sir Abdur Rahim. This is a good book that was written in 1905. There has, however, been extensive research in Islamic law and jurisprudence in this century, and this book is no longer considered sufficient. The need of the student has increased further with the new three year law programme in Pakistan.[35] The old course on Islamic jurisprudence has been split

35. And now a five year course has been designed, which has

into two courses, which means that the part that dealt with Islamic jurisprudence has increased. A book that deals comprehensively with the subject is, therefore, needed. In addition to this, and perhaps more important, is the increase in readers all over the world who require material on *uṣūl al-fiqh* in English.

The second reason for writing this book may be explained through examples. One example is that some writers, following 'Alī Ḥasab Allāh,[36] have stated in their books written either in English or in Urdu that *ijtihād* is a source of Islamic law. They make this statement while talking about the methodology of the *mujtahid.* Does this mean that after a jurist has undertaken *ijtihād,* his own *ijtihād* becomes a source of law for him? Nothing could be farther from the truth. Again, the statement may imply that *ijtihād* is something outside or independent of the sources of Islamic law, the Qur'ān and the *Sunnah,* as if the *mujtahid* is exercising his independent "discretion" or "judgement" through his *ijtihād* and adding something to what is contained in the sources. If this is the implication, then, the statement is not only incorrect it is downright ludicrous.[37] There is no *ijtihād* outside the Qur'ān and the *Sunnah.* The truth is that *ijtihād,* or the output of *ijtihād* to be exact, is a source of law for the *faqīh,* and not for the *mujtahid.* The reason is that the *faqīh* is dependent on the *mujtahid.*

In addition to this, some writers may condemn *taqlīd* (that is, following the opinion of another jurist). This condemnation comes without making a distinction between the functions of the *mujtahid* and the *faqīh,* and also without understanding the true meaning of *taqlīd. Taqlīd* is prohibited in general, but an exemption has been made by the *sharī'ah* in certain cases, and these cases

---

commenced in a few law schools. The five year course has added an introductory course on Islamic jurisprudence in addition to the existing course.

36. See generally 'Alī Ḥasab Allāh, *Uṣūl al-Tashrī' al-Islāmī* (Cairo: Dār al-Ma'ārif, 1971).

37. It is in this meaning that the term *ijtihād* is translated as "independent reasoning," which is an incorrect translation. It also shows that a proper appreciation of the meaning of *ijtihād* is not found in some works.

include those of the *faqīh* and the layman.[38]

Examples of such misconceptions can be multiplied with ease. In other words, some books have completely ignored the methodology of the *faqīh*. While both types of methodology are important, an understanding of the methodology of the *faqīh* is considered more important for the present age. The reason is that it is expected to be employed by the judges of the superior courts in an Islamic state and, therefore, by the lawyers who help the courts. It should also be employed by the *muftī* in the present age, if his *fatwās* are to have any persuasive force. Even in non-Muslim countries with Muslim minorities, the methodology of *takhrīj* will prove more useful for dealing with local problems.

After the introductory chapters, the book has been divided into four parts. The first part deals with the concept and structure of Islamic law. The second part describes the sources of law, while the third part shows how they are used by the *mujtahid*. The fourth part deals with the sources and methodology of the *faqīh*, who is a jurist in his own right, but is not a full *mujtahid*.

An attempt has been made to use examples that are general and apply to all Muslim countries or communities. Yet, in many places Pakistan specific examples have been used. This is natural for this writer, however, the examples are such that the reader can easily adapt them to his own country or situation as most of the basic issues are common.

I would like to acknowledge here that whatever little knowledge I have acquired of *uṣūl al-fiqh* and *fiqh* is primarily because of my two teachers: Dr. Ḥusayn Ḥāmid Ḥassān and Dr. Ḥasan 'Abd al-Laṭīf al-Shāfi'ie. I have spent countless hours with them not only as a student in their classes, more than three decades ago, but also as an evening student when I used to impose myself on their generous hospitality. An earlier work that has been published (*Islamic Law of Business Organization*) has as much to do with Dr. Shāfi'ie's brilliant guidance as with Mrs. Shāfi'ie's delightful cooking. I have also been taught by the late Dr. Ahmad Hasan and by Dr. 'Abd al-Hādī Sirāj. Their guidance,

38. See p. 420 in this book for details.

especially during detailed discussions with them on difficult questions, has been very beneficial for me. I have not been taught, formally, by Dr. Zafar Ishaq Ansari, but I have learned much from him through my association with him during the last many years. He has also edited most of the books that I have written and his help, in his kind and gentle ways, has immense value for me. Finally, my adventure into the fascinating world of *uṣūl al-fiqh* and *fiqh* would not have been possible without my wife's help and understanding. I dedicate this book to her.

Review Questions

1. The theory of *ijtihād* is similar to the theory of legislation. Elaborate.
2. What do you understand by the terms *takhrīj* and "the Islamic theory of adjudication"?
3. What is the subject-matter of *uṣūl al-fiqh*?
4. Is the term "Islamic Jurisprudence" the equivalent of *Uṣūl al-Fiqh*?
5. The "General Theory of Law" has now acquired a structure that is quite similar to that laid out, centuries ago, by the earlier jurists for *Uṣūl al-Fiqh*. Elaborate and describe the two structures.

2 *Uṣūl al-Fiqh* as Sources of Islamic Law and *Uṣūl al-Fiqh* as a Discipline

2.1 Distinguishing Between *Uṣūl al-Fiqh* as Sources of Islamic Law and *Uṣūl al-Fiqh* as an Independent Discipline is Crucial to the Understanding of Islamic Jurisprudence

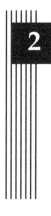

Islamic law is a religious law based on the texts of the Qur'ān and the *Sunnah*. The discipline that tells us how this law is derived from these texts, and how it is classified, understood and applied, is called *uṣūl al-fiqh*. A study of Islamic law, therefore, begins with the definition of *uṣūl al-fiqh*. It must be emphasised in the strongest terms that a failure to distinguish between the meaning of *uṣūl al-fiqh* as sources of Islamic law and *uṣūl al-fiqh* as an independent discipline has been a cause of tremendous confusion both in the minds of the readers, and also in the minds of the scholars who have contributed works on the subject, because most or all of them fail to make this distinction. The earlier jurists have always made this distinction, but the distinction has not been appreciated in modern times. The reason most probably is that the earlier jurists had a unique way of describing the sources. They would first say, "*Uṣūl al-fiqh* are four," and by this they meant "four sources." After this, they had their special method of deriving the meaning of *uṣūl al-fiqh* as a discipline from this statement about sources. This method used in the earlier edition of this book has not been appreciated, and it is felt that the earlier form of presentation was not sufficient to convey this distinction.

The failure to make the distinction is the cause of the failure to understand how *uṣūl al-fiqh* really works as well as the failure to understand other questions like why it is important to follow a school. We are now adopting a different method of explaining these vital meanings so that there is no confusion about the distinction.

2.2 Describing *Uṣūl al-Fiqh* as Sources of Islamic Law

The term is broken up into its two components: *uṣūl* and *fiqh*. These two components are defined separately and then combined. This separation of the components and relinking establishes the separate meanings of the two terms and their relationship. It thus becomes a useful device for elaborating the meaning of this discipline.

Defining these terms, however, is not intended to tell us what we mean by Islamic law, even if that knowledge is acquired as a by-product.[39] The definitions of these two terms help us identify the role and function of the specialists within the Islamic legal system. The terms also elaborate the relationship that exists between the fully empowered jurist and the person who is a pure layman. In

39. The meaning of Islamic law is understood through an examination of the *ḥukm sharʿī*. See p. 69 below.

other words, the definitions indicate the levels at which different experts operate within the Islamic legal system.

The definitions of the two components also inform us about the nature of the rules of Islamic law, and the nature of the sources from which the laws are derived. Understanding these definitions is, therefore, very important. The reader who does not comprehend their exact implications is likely to miss much during the rest of the study.

According to the method of study preferred by the jurists, a reader embarking upon the study of Islamic law must first understand the meaning of essential terms like *fiqh*, *sharīʿah*, *ijtihād*, *mujtahid*, *faqīh*, *taqlīd*, and *muqallid*. These terms have to be understood in the precise meanings that the jurists assigned them, that is, their legal or technical meanings. An understanding of Islamic law will otherwise be considerably hampered. What, for example, is the meaning of *fiqh* as distinguished from the meaning of *sharīʿah*? If the reader cannot define these two terms with precision or identify a difference between them, then he needs to read this chapter. By the end of this chapter, he will hopefully be able to define each of the terms listed above and a few more that will come up during the discussion. This chapter is, therefore, of crucial importance for those who do not already have a knowledge of Islamic law.

Uṣūl al-fiqh then is composed of two terms: *fiqh* and *uṣūl. Once these constituent parts are defined, the jurists combine the two parts to arrive at the final definition.*[40] The jurists define the term *fiqh* first.

40. The mode of definition used by the *fuqahā'* (plural of *faqīh*: jurist) is what we call genus-species definition, a method that originated with Plato and Aristotle. There is an elementary distinction in philosophy between the definition of a word and that of an entity. Definitions of words are called nominal definitions, while those of entities, that is, concepts and objects, are called real definitions. Such definitions are not considered very effective in modern times, but to understand what the *fuqahā'* said we must use the method they wanted us to. This method, which is one of the most common in Islamic law, consists in the selection of a word called *definiendum*. This word is first set into its genus (class) and then distinguished from the other

2.2.1 The Literal Meaning of *Fiqh*

The term *fiqh* is used in the literal sense to mean "understanding" and "discernment." In this sense the words *fiqh* and *fahm* are synonymous. It implies an understanding of Islam in a general way. It may also mean what a prudent person is likely to conclude from obvious evidences. The word has been used in the Qur'ān, in this sense, on several occasions:

فمال هؤلآء القوم لا يكادون يفقهون حديثا

> What hath come to these people that they fail to understand a simple statement. [Qur'ān 4 : 78];

لهم قلوب لا يفقهون بها

> They have hearts wherewith they understand not. [Qur'ān 7 : 179]

The same meaning is reflected in the words of the Prophet (pbuh):

من يرد الله به خيرا يفقهه في الدين

He for whom Allah wills His blessings is granted the understanding of *dīn*.

2.2.2 Earlier General Meaning of *Fiqh*

The term *'ilm* (knowledge) also has the same literal meaning as *fiqh*. During the time of the Prophet (pbuh) there appears to be no difference in the two terms. Later, as sophistication crept in, the term *'ilm* came to be applied in a narrow sense to mean knowledge that comes through reports, that is, traditions: *aḥadīth* and *āthār*.[41]

The term *fiqh*, on the other hand, came to be used exclusively for a knowledge of the law. Thus, the concepts *'ilm* and *fiqh* were separated when specialisation in law and traditions came

members of the class.

41. *Aḥadīth* is the plural of *ḥadīth*. The term *ḥadīth* is used for reports from the Prophet, while *athar* is a report about a precedent laid down by a Companion. The detailed meanings will be provided later in this book.

into existence toward the end of the first century of the Hijrah.[42] During this period the word *fiqh* also included the meaning of the term *kalām* within it. These two terms were not separated till the time of al-Ma'mūn (d. 218 A.H.). *Fiqh* till such time embraced both theological problems and legal issues.[43] It is for this reason that Abū Ḥanīfah (d. 150 A.H.) defined *fiqh* as:

معرفة النّفس ما لها و ما عليها

A person's knowledge of his rights and duties.[44]

The definition is very wide and includes elements that are part of the subject of *kalām*, like the tenets of faith (*'aqā'id*).

This definition was formulated to mean *al-fiqh al-akbar* or *fiqh* in its wider sense. When the subject of *kalām* was introduced by the Mu'tazilah during the time of al-Ma'mūn, the term *fiqh* came to be restricted to the corpus of Islamic law alone. *Fiqh* in this restricted meaning is sometimes called *al-fiqh al-aṣghar* in order to distinguish it from the wider definition given by Imām Abū Ḥanīfah. It is in this restricted sense that we use the term *fiqh* today, as will be obvious from the definition given below.

2.2.3 Later Definition of *Fiqh*

The term *fiqh* was not defined in precise terms in the first three centuries of the Hijrah.[45] The first attempt appears to have been made by Abū al-Ḥusayn al-Baṣrī followed by al-Juwaynī, al-Ghazālī and others. Some crucial additions were made by Ibn al-Ḥājib, and we finally find the definition, in the form that we

42. *See, e.g.*, Ahmad Hasan, *The Early Development of Islamic Jurisprudence* (Islamabad, 1970) 4. "It is to be noted that *'ilm* from the very beginning carried the sense of knowledge that came through an authority—it may be God or the Prophet." Ibid. 5.
43. Ibid. 3.
44. *See* Ṣadr al-Sharī'ah (d. 747 A.H./1346 C.E.), *al-Tawḍīḥ fī Ḥall Jawāmid al-Tanqīḥ* (Karachi, 1979), 22. He adds the word *'amalan* (for conduct) to this definition to make it conform to the narrower meaning.
45. The law, or *fiqh*, itself had grown to maturity during this period, which shows that for growth and development we do not need precise definitions.

are about to discuss, in the work of the Ḥanafī jurist Ṣadr al-Sharī'ah, who criticised the definition and finally came up with his own definition as he found the definition provided to be a very narrow definition. The definition is attributed by some to al-Shāfi'ī himself,[46] but this is obviously not true. *Fiqh* in its technical sense, then, is defined as follows:

العلم بالاحكام الشرعيّة العمليّة المكتسبة من أدلّتها التفصيليّة[47]

> It is the knowledge of the *shar'ī aḥkām* (legal rules), pertaining to conduct, that have been derived from their specific evidences.[48]

This definition carries within it a number of meanings and concepts. It needs to be analysed at some length for a proper understanding.

2.2.4 Analysis of the Definition of *Fiqh*

Each word used in the definition affects the required meaning and sharpens our understanding of the term defined—by excluding categories from the specified genus.[49]

It is knowledge. The first segment "*fiqh* is knowledge" identifies the genus (*jins*) we are dealing with. The use of the term *al-'ilm*

46. See Wahbah al-Zuhaylī, *Uṣūl al-Fiqh al-Islāmī,* vol. 1 (Tehran: Dār Iḥsān, 1997), 19.
47. Badr al-Dīn al-Zarkashī, *al-Baḥr al-Muḥīṭ fī Uṣūl al-Fiqh,* vol. 1 (Kuwait: Dār al-Ṣafwah, 1992), 21; Nāṣir al-Dīn al-Bayḍāwī, *Minhāj al-Wuṣūl ilā 'Ilm al-Uṣūl* (Cairo: Maṭba'at Kurdistān al-'Ilmiyyah, n.d.), 3; See Ṣadr al-Sharī'ah, *al-Tawḍīḥ,* vol. 1, 26 for a somewhat altered form of the definition. He does not use the word *al-muktasabah,* but reproduces the rest of the definition. Ibid.
48. The term *adillah tafṣīliyyah* has been intentionally translated here to mean specific evidences rather than the usual translation—"detailed proofs,"—which is likely to confuse the reader. It is the specific evidences that are referred to in the definition, as distinguished from the general evidences or the *adillah ijmāliyyah.*
49. For an analysis of the definition see Ṣadr al-Sharī'ah, *al-Tawḍīḥ,* vol. 1, 26–28; see also Al-Zarkashī, *al-Baḥr al-Muḥīṭ fī Uṣūl al-Fiqh,* vol. 1, 21–23.

(knowledge) brings into our vision the entire field of knowledge, whatever its source or origin. If the definition were restricted to this segment alone, *fiqh* would mean all and any kind of knowledge. In this sense the meaning would conform with its literal application.

Knowledge of *aḥkām*. The wide meaning of knowledge is qualified or restricted by the use of the word *aḥkām* (rules), which excludes from the definition of *fiqh* all kinds of knowledge that do not pertain to *aḥkām* or rules.

Knowledge of the *shar'ī aḥkām*. This meaning is narrowed down further by the term *shar'ī* and the domain of *fiqh* is confined to the knowledge of the *shar'ī aḥkām* alone, that is, legal rules. Here we must distinguish between the *shar'ī aḥkām* and the *ghayr shar'ī aḥkām*, that is between legal rules and rules that do not pertain to the law.[50] The *ghayr shar'ī aḥkām* are of three types:

1. Those that are rational, like 2+2=4, or the rule that the sum is greater than its parts;
2. Those that are perceived by the senses, like fire burns or wood floats on water; and
3. Those that are discovered through experience, like aspirin cures headache.

These rules, and their like, are not *shar'ī aḥkām*. In other words, they are the *ghayr shar'ī aḥkām* (non-legal rules) that do not form part of the *sharī'ah*. As compared to this, the *shar'ī aḥkām* are of two types:

1. The *aḥkām* relating to belief (*i'tiqād*), like the existence of Allāh, His oneness, the truth of the mission of the Prophet (peace be on him), belief in the Day of Judgement, and so on;

50. The term *ghayr shar'ī* does not necessarily mean illegal, as it might sometimes imply in Urdu, but those rules which do not fall within the ambit of *fiqh* or *sharī'ah*.

2. The *aḥkām* relating to acts (*a'māl*). These are divisible further into three types:

   - those that pertain to physical acts, like the acts of prayer (*ṣalāh*), or those constituting wilful homicide (*qatl 'amd*);
   - those that take place within the *qalb*, like intention, love, hate, or jealousy; and
   - those that pertain to speech, like recitation during prayers, or offer and acceptance in a contract.

Aḥkām 'amaliyyah. The word used next in our definition is *al-'amaliyyah.* It qualifies the meaning of *aḥkām* and restricts it to those that pertain to acts (physical, of the *qalb*, or speech). The use of this word excludes, from the meaning of *fiqh,* the knowledge of the *aḥkām* with respect to belief. This excluded knowledge is confined to the discipline known as *'ilm al-kalām.*[51]

Fiqh, then, is *knowledge of the shar'ī aḥkām that pertain to conduct.* This includes physical acts, acts of the *qalb,* and acts arising out of the spoken word, that is, the three types of *'amal* mentioned above. This qualification also distinguishes the technical meaning of *fiqh* from the meaning of *al-fiqh al-akbar* defined by Imām Abū Ḥanīfah, and mentioned above.

***Aḥkām muktasabah*—derived rules**. The definition is further qualified by the use of the word *al-muktasabah,* which means derived or acquired. The employment of this word excludes from the definition of *fiqh* the following types of knowledge about the *shar'ī aḥkām*:

1. Knowledge of these *aḥkām* that rests with Allāh Almighty;

2. Knowledge of the *aḥkām* granted to the Prophet;[52]

---

51. Al-Zarkashī, *al-Baḥr al-Muḥīṭ fī Uṣūl al-Fiqh,* vol. 1, 22.
52. The jurists discuss a situation where the Prophet (pbuh) may be considered to have exercised *ijtihād.* This, in their view, may affect the binding force of such a ruling. It does not appear to be a very useful distinction, as it would be difficult to separate it from the *Sunnah.*

3. Knowledge of the *aḥkām* granted to Jibrīl (Gabriel).

These three types of knowledge are not acquired or derived (their source is different) and, therefore, are not included in the definition of *fiqh*. On the other hand, there are two types of knowledge that are acquired: the knowledge of the jurist (*faqīh*) and the knowledge of the layman (*muqallid*).

Acquired from the *adillah tafṣīliyyah*. At this stage the definition is qualified further with the phrase *adillah tafṣīliyah* or specific evidences. The specific evidences are primarily individual texts, whether of the Qur'ān or of the *Sunnah*. As stated above, the definition so far, includes two kinds of derived or acquired knowledge: the acquired knowledge of the *faqīh* and the acquired knowledge of the *muqallid* (layman). The use of the term *adillah tafṣīliyah* excludes, from the definition of *fiqh*, the knowledge of the layman or *muqallid*. The reason is that the layman does not acquire his knowledge of *fiqh* directly from specific evidences in the Qur'ān and the *Sunnah*, as does the *faqīh*; the *muqallid* acquires his knowledge of *fiqh* from the *faqīh*, just as in the law, the layman gets his knowledge of the law from the legal expert.

What about reasoning from general evidences? This definition insists that law or *fiqh* be derived from specific evidences. Does this meaning exclude general principles? A general principle is a general evidence and includes within it a number of specific evidences. This problem is explained below (see page 51). Here it is pertinent to note that this definition has been provided by the Shāfi'ī jurists (mostly) and is in line with their somewhat strict methodology.[53]

Conclusion: The definition of *fiqh* explained above began by first encompassing all knowledge within it, and then systematically excluded those types of knowledge that do not form part of *fiqh*, to give us a precise definition of *fiqh*. The final form of the definition declares *fiqh* to be the knowledge of the rules of conduct that have been derived by the jurist from *specific evidences* found in the

53. For the details of this methodology and its comparison with other types, see the author's *Theories of Islamic Law* mentioned earlier, chapter on "Strict Theories of Interpretation".

Qur'ān and the *Sunnah* as well as other *specific evidences* in *ijmā'* and *qiyās*. In other words, ***fiqh* is a knowledge or understanding of Islamic law; it is not the law itself.** From this it should not be concluded that *fiqh* is one thing and *sharī'ah* another, or *fiqh* is something that has been developed by the jurists independently of the texts of the Qur'ān and the *Sunnah*. There is no way of knowing the *sharī'ah* without *fiqh* as it is fully entrenched in the sources.

2.2.5 Distinctions Based on the Definition

The definition leads to the following distinctions:

2.2.5.1 Distinction between *sharī'ah* and *fiqh*

There is a difference between the meaning of the terms *sharī'ah* and *fiqh*. Yet, these two terms are often used interchangeably. The definition, however, indicates that the term *sharī'ah* has a wider meaning than *fiqh*. The term *sharī'ah* includes both law and the tenets of faith, that is, the *'aqā'id*. The real distinction between *sharī'ah* and *fiqh*, however, is that *sharī'ah* is the law itself, while *fiqh* is a knowledge of that law—its jurisprudence.

2.2.5.2 Distinction between *mujtahid* and *faqīh*

In later times a distinction was drawn between the terms *mujtahid* and *faqīh*.[54] In the definition both terms are applied to mean the jurist who derives the *aḥkām* directly from specific evidences.[55] The term *faqīh* came to be applied later to the jurist who derived his

54. For the meaning of *faqīh* see Ṣadr al-Sharī'ah, *al-Tawḍīḥ*, vol. 1, 34.
55. This again is a statement that conforms with the Shāfi'ite methodology. The *mujtahid* according to the Ḥanafīs and Mālikīs use general principles to derive laws. General principles are not specific evidences or *adillah tafṣīliyyah*.

knowledge from the manuals of *fiqh*.[56] These manuals contained the opinions of the *mujtahids*. The laws derived by the *mujtahid* become a source of law for the *faqīh*. Although the *faqīh* is a qualified jurist, he is still classified as a *muqallid*. He follows some *mujtahid*, who has derived the law directly from the specific evidences.

In reality, the term *faqīh* cannot be applied to a single type of specialist. There are various grades of the jurists according to their skills and levels of ability. This may be compared with the legal profession as it exists today. Some lawyers practice in the lower courts dealing mostly with questions of fact, while others appear before higher courts where the questions facing the court are usually those of law. These grades have been explained in part 4 of this book. Today, judges, lawyers and law teachers should be classified as *faqīhs*.

2.2.5.3 Distinction between *ijtihād* and *taqlīd*

Ijtihād and *taqlīd* are somewhat complex concepts. It would, therefore, not be possible for us to go into details at the preliminary stage of our study, yet we may indicate the basic distinction. *Ijtihād* is the name for the activity of the *mujtahid* that makes use of all the sources to derive the law. This activity is indicated in the definition above. The output of the *mujtahid* is the substantive as well as procedural law, a knowledge of which is called *fiqh*. In addition to this, the absolute *mujtahid* lays down the principles of interpretation as well as the general principles of the substantive and procedural law.

Taqlīd, on the other hand, is the activity of the layman (which term includes the modern day *faqīh* as explained above). *Taqlīd* in the legal sense means following the opinion of another. When a legal justification is found, *taqlīd* is permitted. Permitted *taqlīd* is similar in its logic to following the opinion of a doctor prescribing

56. Here again the meaning suits Shāfi'ite methodology and not that of others. Al-Karkhī, al-Dabbūsī, al-Jaṣṣāṣ, al-Sarakhsī as well as others have all used general principles to derive the law. They require the *faqīh* to focus on general principles rather than the manuals alone.

medicine, a lawyer pointing out the law, or the opinion of any other specialist, or even the following of precedents. *Taqlīd* as a judicial method is permitted in Islamic law.

The topics of *ijtihād* and *taqlīd* are dealt with in detail in parts 3 and 4 of this book. Here, the purpose is to show their relationship with the concept of *fiqh* in Islamic law.

2.2.5.4 Distinction between a *muqallid* and a *faqīh*

As stated above, the term *faqīh* came to be applied to a person who was not able to undertake independent *ijtihād*, because he lacked the requisite qualifications or skills. Technically, then, he was a *muqallid*, that is, the person who was following the opinion of the *mujtahid*. As compared to him, the ordinary person who does not have any knowledge of *fiqh* also follows the opinion of the *mujtahid* in the daily performance of his duties or in other matters of the law. This person too is a *muqallid*. What, then, is the difference between an ordinary *muqallid* and a *muqallid* who is a *faqīh*? The difference lies in understanding the texts in which the opinions of the *mujtahids* are recorded. If an ordinary person reads these books he will find himself facing a number of opinions on a single issue and he will not be able to determine what the law is on the issue. He will have to go to the *faqīh*, who will be able to state which opinion is upheld by the school at a certain time or which one is preferred. Thus, the position of an ordinary *muqallid* is the same as that of a client with respect to his lawyer.

The *faqīh*, besides having a knowledge of Islamic law, is sometimes able to extend the law through reasoning from principles, on the basis of a methodology called *takhrīj*. A *faqīh*, who has the ability to perform *takhrīj*, may be compared with a judge of the superior court dealing with questions of law; he lays down the law, but is not legislating (according to the accepted theory).

2.2.6 A Wider Definition of *Fiqh*: Criticising the Narrow Definition

A number of objections can be raised against the definition of *fiqh* mentioned above. Before some objections are noted it would be pertinent to analyze the meaning of the term *dalīl tafsīlī.*

2.2.6.1 What in reality is the *dalīl tafṣīlī*?

The term *dalīl tafṣīlī* has been translated as a specific evidence. It is sometimes translated as "detailed proof." It has been assumed in what has preceded that *dalīl tafṣīlī* or specific evidence is an individual verse of the Qur'ān or an individual *sunnah.* As compared to this a *dalīl kullī* is a general evidence; it contains within it a number of specific evidences. Accordingly, each of the four sources of law is considered a *dalīl kullī,* also called *dalīl ijmālī.* This is not the only meaning in which the term *dalīl kullī* is used. A general principle is also referred to as a *dalīl kullī.* Thus, the principle *al-amr li al-wujūb* (the command gives rise to an obligation) is a general evidence as it covers all the individual commands that are deemed to be specific evidences.[57] This is a rule of interpretation and not that of *fiqh.*

It may happen that a verse of the Qur'ān or an individual *sunnah* is in itself a general principle or evidence. Many examples may be quoted, the most outstanding being the verse dealing with the prohibition of *ribā* as well as the tradition *al-kharāj bi al-ḍamān.* The principle *al-kharāj bi al-ḍamān* or "entitlement to profit (or

57. We do not wish to make the discussion too technical, especially when the reader has not reached the discussion about the different rules of interpretation. For those who would like to analyse the matter in greater depth a few questions may be raised. The *amr* is considered to be a category of the *khāṣṣ* (specific word). Does this mean that every *dalīl tafṣīlī* has to be in the category of the *khāṣṣ,* whether it gives rise to a demand or to a choice? If this is not the case, then, will the meaning of *dalīl tafṣīlī* apply to all texts whether or not they contain the *amr*? While considering such questions it is important to remember that meanings of *amr* and *nahy* would cover all cases of the *ḥukm taklīfī* and the *ḥukm waḍ'ī.*

earning) is based on a corresponding liability for bearing loss" is the source of numerous rules in many areas of Islamic law. In this sense it is a true *dalīl kullī.* The definition of *fiqh* analysed above would, however, treat it as a *dalīl tafṣīlī,* because it is found in a tradition. If this principle under which many rules are classified is treated as a *dalīl tafṣīlī,* the definition of *fiqh* provided by the (later) Shāfi'ī school would no longer be very helpful.

In addition to this, a number of individual cases that have been derived from the Qur'ān and the *Sunnah* may imply the existence of a general principle. For example, the principle *al-ajr wa al-ḍamān lā yajtami'ān* (wages and compensation cannot be combined). This principle governs a number of cases relating to damages. It has been derived from a large number of settled cases and is supported by texts from the *Sunnah.* In this meaning, the principle too is a *dalīl kullī* and has a link extending back to the texts.

If all these meanings are to be included in the term *dalīl tafṣīlī,* then, it covers the following meanings:

1. an individual text from which a single rule is derived;
2. a general principle that is stated explicitly in the texts and that is a source for a number of other sub-principles and finally individual rules; and
3. a general principle that is implied by a number of texts or individual cases.[58]

The meaning of the term *dalīl tafṣīlī* covering all these meanings is difficult to accept as it would make the definition highly confusing. There are other difficulties too and these are linked to the resulting methodology. Some of these reasons are discussed

58. The reader should not assume that we are talking about legal maxims here, some of which are nothing more than presumptions of law. Presumptions of law are arbitrary inferences which the law expressly directs a judge to draw from particular facts. A general principle, on the other hand, gives rise to a number of legal rules and points in a direction that the law should take.

in the following paragraphs, especially the section dealing with the *qawā'id fiqhiyyah.* It would be helpful, however, to understand the legal structure of the evidences after the preceding discussion.

2.2.6.2 The legal structure of the evidences (*adillah*)

The structure of the legal norms has been discussed by al-Ghazālī and reproduced by us elsewhere.[59] We propose to explain this in simple terms here. The evidences are structured in a hierarchy. It is something similar to the hierarchical structure of norms in a legal system elaborated by Hans Kelsen for his pure theory of law.

At the top is the *dalīl kullī* or *dalīl ijmālī.* In the figure below, it has been shown as the Qur'ān, however, the same would apply to the *Sunnah.* Primarily, the reader will come across two types of texts. The first type may be a text directly giving rise to a rule. By rule we mean something that attaches specific consequences to a specific set of facts. For example, the text pertaining to theft says that the hands of the thieves, both male and female, are to be cut. As compared to this, the other type of text may not directly attach such consequences, but point in a certain direction. Thus, the verse of the Qur'ān telling us in a general way that "all sales are permitted except those bearing *ribā*" is laying down a broad general principle. This text does not spell out the individual transactions, but applies to all in a general way. Such a general principle may give rise to specific rules and also to other general principles controlled by it. The principle quoted above about the legality of earning being based on risk (*al-kharāj bi al-ḍamān*) has settled many specific cases (laid down rules) and has also given rise to the principle that "wages and compensation cannot be combined" as well as several others like it. Such principles, it is important to note, have not been stated explicitly in the texts, but have been derived by the jurists either from general principles or a number of specific evidences taken together. These principles may, therefore, be called second-level principles. Needless to say that each specific evidence and specific rule derives authority from the general evidence above it as we move along the hierarchy.

59. See Imran Ahsan Nyazee, *Theories of Islamic Law,* 203–208.

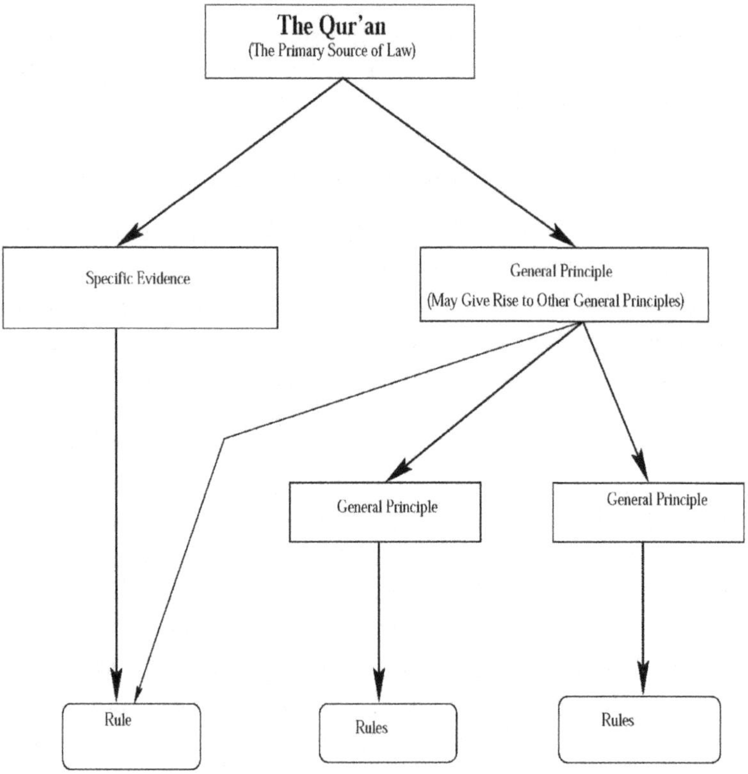

The question that we wish to raise at this stage is: which type of evidence do we classify as the *dalīl tafṣīlī* in order to satisfy our definition of *fiqh*?

There are further questions of methodology here too. For example, in the case of a clash between a general principle and a specific evidence, which one is to be preferred? or how are they to be reconciled? or if the specific evidence is from the *Sunnah* and the general evidence is from the Qur'ān, how is the reconciliation to take place? The answers to these questions are so fundamental that they give rise to different theories, or schools of interpretation, of Islamic law. We will have little more to say about this within this chapter.

2.2.6.3 Identifying the defects of the narrow definition

The definition of *fiqh* provided by the Shāfi'ī school focuses on the meaning of *dalīl tafṣīlī* by including both the specific evidences as well as the general principle if it is mentioned explicitly in the text. This suits the literalist methodology. Such an approach cannot grant the status of the *dalīl tafṣīlī* to the second-level principles discussed above. Keeping this in view, the follow observations are to be noted.

1. **The definition is too narrow and confines the activity of the jurist to a very strict method of interpretation.** The definition is built around the Shāfi'ī methodology of interpretation and does not conform completely with the methodology of the other schools. This may be observed from the remaining points.

2. **The narrow definition focuses on the specific evidences (*adillah tafṣīliyah*) and, therefore, prevents the use of the *maqāṣid al-sharī'ah,* which are general evidences, but second-level principles.** If the above definition is used to determine the meaning of *fiqh,* the principle of *maṣlaḥah* (reasoning through general evidences or the purposes of law) cannot be used to derive the *aḥkām.*

3. **The definition prevents the use of broad general principles, which are not detailed evidences, unless they have been specifically mentioned in the texts.** It is well known that Ḥanafī, and even the Mālikī methodology, is based on the use of general principles. The definition, therefore, excludes the use of the *qawā'd fiqhiyyah,* unless these principles are explicitly mentioned in the texts of the Qur'ān and the *Sunnah.*

4. **The Shāfi'ī definition also excludes the use of the principle of *istiḥsān,*** which in many cases is based on the preference of a wider form of analogy, using general principles, over strict analogy called *qiyās.* This will be

obvious when we study *istiḥsān*. The Ḥanafīs and Mālikīs both employ *istiḥsān*.

Despite these problems, we find some of the later Ḥanafī jurists and most Malikīs, probably under pressure from the Shāfi'īs, adopting this definition in their books. Ṣadr al-Sharī'ah, for example, quotes this definition among others, and after subjecting it to analysis restates the meaning of *fiqh* as:

> The knowledge of the *shar'ī aḥkām*—laid down by revelation and settled by *ijmā'*—as derived from their evidences, along with the requisite skill of deriving them from such evidences."[60]

This definition, however, is intended to take into account a number of objections that its author has raised against the Shāfi'ite definition. For example, the words "skill of deriving them" are intended to exclude the knowledge of the ordinary subject who does have knowledge of the *aḥkām* due to necessity, like prayers, fasting, and so on.

The earlier Ḥanafī jurists, who were not employing comparative methods of the later jurists, do not define *fiqh* in the way the later Shāfi'īs have defined it. Al-Sarakhsī, for example, quotes Ibn 'Abbās (R), who equates *fiqh* with *ḥikmah*, to define *fiqh* as follows: "Wisdom (*ḥikmah*) is the knowledge of the *aḥkām* with the *ḥalāl* distinguished from the *ḥarām*."[61] A similar meaning is given in the books of other Ḥanafī jurists as well.[62] Al-Ghazālī, who advocates the use of *maṣlaḥah*, does not accept the Shāfi'ī definition stated here although he belonged to the Shāfi'ī school.[63]

2.2.6.4 Redefining *fiqh*

It is to be noted that in the modern age, with many writers promoting the principle of *maṣlaḥah* as well as the use of general

60. Ṣadr al-Sharī'ah, *al-Tawḍīḥ*, vol. 1, 36.
61. Al-Sarakhsī, *al-Mabsūṭ*, vol. 1 (Beirut: Dār al-Ma'rifah, 1989), 2.
62. See, e.g., al-Kāsānī, *Badā'i' al-Ṣanā'i'*, vol. 1, 2.
63. See al-Ghazālī, *al-Mustaṣfā min 'Ilm al-Uṣūl*, vol. 1, 3–4. See also the excerpt, from the pages cited, at the end of this chapter.

principles, the narrow or strict definition of *fiqh* provided by the Shāfiʿī jurists is not very useful. A broad and general definition of *fiqh* may be employed and is formulated as follows, by way of example:

> *Fiqh* is the knowledge of the *sharʿī aḥkām* derived directly from the specific evidences in the texts or extended through reasoning from general propositions of the *sharīʿah* in the light of its *maqāṣid*.

By "general propositions" here we mean all those general principles that are laid down or supported by the *sharīʿah* whether directly or indirectly. In fact, the definitions of *fiqh* preferred by two famous Shāfiʿī jurists, al-Ghazālī and al-Rāzī are much wider, and we would prefer those to the one we have given. Al-Ghazālī states the definition of *fiqh* as follows:

> عبارة عن العلم بالاحكام الشرعية الثابتة لأفعال المكلفين خاصة
>
> An expression for the knowledge of legal rules established specifically for human conduct.[64]

This, indeed, is a very general and wide definition. Imām al-Rāzī gives a more precise definition. He states it as follows:

> العلم بالاحكام الشرعية، العملية، المستدلّ على أعيانها، بحيث لا يعلم كونها من الدين ضرورة.
>
> The knowledge of the legal rules, pertaining to conduct with reference to their sources, when this knowledge is not obtained by way of necessity (in religion).[65]

It is to be noted that some scholars may understand even this definition in terms of the specific evidences,[66] but that meaning is not to be found here as will be seen in the definition of *uṣūl al-fiqh* stated below. The words "not obtained by way of necessity" mean that every subject is supposed to have knowledge of some

64. Ibid., 3.
65. Al-Rāzī, *al-Maḥṣūl fī ʿIlm Uṣūl al-Fiqh*, vol. 1, 78.
66. See, e.g., ibid., f.n. 7 at 79, where Ṭāha Jābir al-ʿAlwānī interprets it in the meaning of *juzʾī*.

aḥkām by necessity, because without such knowledge he will not be able to perform certain obligatory acts, or abstain from those prohibited. The knowledge of a follower is not *fiqh* as it has not been derived from the sources; it is necessary for him to possess this knowledge and he gets it from the jurist.

2.2.7 Rejection of the Narrow Definition of *Fiqh* and its Impact

What difference, one may ask, will a narrow or wider definition of *fiqh* make? The response is that the wider definition of *fiqh* takes into account the methodology of *ijtihād* followed by the Ḥanafī and the Mālikī schools as well. This enables reasoning from general principles and the use of principles like *istiḥsān* and *maṣlaḥah mursalah.* The narrow definition accommodates the Shāfiʿī and Ḥanbalī methodologies alone.

2.2.7.1 The Meaning of *Aṣl*

The literal meaning of the term *aṣl* is "something from which another thing originates." Thus, the origin of a thing is its *aṣl.* That is the reason for translating the word *aṣl* as "root." The term *aṣl* also means "something upon which another thing is constructed,"[67] and here it gives the meaning of "foundation." In certain cases, the term *aṣl* is used in the sense of the Arabic word "*maṣdar*,"[68] which means "source." All these are the literal applications of the word *aṣl.* For purposes of Islamic law we are interested in the technical use of the term.

There are several technical applications of the word *aṣl.* Some of these are listed below. It is the fourth meaning that is needed to complete the definition of *uṣūl al-fiqh.*

1. **The word *aṣl* is used to mean *dalīl.*** The word *dalīl* is applied to mean a guide leading a caravan, or scout finding the trail.

67. Ṣadr al-Sharīʿah, *al-Tawḍīḥ,* vol. 1, 20.
68. The word *maṣdar* is rarely used by the earlier jurists; it is a term borrowed from Arab law.

In this sense, a directory, like a telephone directory, is called a *dalīl*, because it leads us to a number or an address. In Islamic law, in this context, the word *dalīl* is used in two ways: *dalīl tafṣīlī* and *dalīl kullī* also called *dalīl ijmālī*. The former, that is, *dalīl tafṣīlī*, may be an individual verse of the Qur'ān or an individual *sunnah* in a *ḥadīth*. We may refer to it as a "specific evidence," though it is sometimes translated as "detailed proof." For example, the verse, "Verily prayers are enjoined on believers at stated times," [Qur'ān 4 : 103] is a specific evidence in the Qur'ān that points to a *ḥukm* of Allah about the obligation of prayer. As compared to this, the *dalīl ijmālī* or *kullī* is a general evidence, because it contains within it a large number of specific evidences. The Qur'ān is a general evidence: it contains a large number of specific verses within it. So is the *Sunnah*, which contains within it a large number of individual *sunan*. The same applies to *qiyās* and to *ijmā'*. This use of the term *dalīl* conforms with the meaning of "source." Thus, we usually say there are four sources of Islamic law, meaning thereby the four *adillah ijmāliyyah*: the Qur'ān, the *Sunnah*, *ijmā'* and *qiyās*. In the previous section, we observed that focusing on the *dalīl tafṣīlī* alone caused the narrowing down of the meaning of *fiqh*. With *uṣūl* the position is different; the focus in *uṣūl* is on the *dalīl ijmālī* (general evidence) and that includes general principles.

2. **The word *aṣl* is also used to indicate the foundation upon which analogy is constructed.** Thus, *khamr* is an *aṣl* or basis for the extension of the prohibition to the *nabīdh* (mead) of dates, as the common cause (*'illah*) of intoxication is found in both.[69] The meaning of intoxication is extended from *khamr*, which is the *aṣl*. This meaning of *aṣl* will be explained in detail when we take up the study of *qiyās*.

69. This is the opinion of the majority and not that of the Ḥanafī school. In their view, the meaning and prohibition of *khamr* are not extendible.

3. ***Aṣl* is sometimes used in the sense of the original rule.** Thus, the maxim says:

   الأصل في الأشياء الإباحة

   The original rule for all things is permissibility.[70]

   The principle implies that all things are permissible, unless specifically prohibited by the *sharī'ah*. In other words, if no rule can be found in the *sharī'ah*, the case under examination will be considered permitted, which is presumed to be its previous or original *ḥukm*. This meaning of *aṣl* forms the foundation of the principle of *istiṣḥāb*, as we shall understand later. In this sense it is a presumption of continuity.

4. **Finally, the term *aṣl* is used in the meaning of a general principle.** General principles are of two kinds. Those that govern the law and those that govern interpretation. The former are sometimes called *qawā'id fiqhiyyah* or general principles of *fiqh*, while the latter are referred to as *qawā'id uṣūliyyah*. Examples of the *qawā'id fiqhiyyah* have been provided in part 4 of this book under the methodology of the *faqīh*.

2.2.7.2 The Final Meaning of *Uṣūl al-Fiqh* as sources of law

To arrive at this meaning, we focus on the meaning of the term *dalīl* or source assigned to the word *aṣl* in the previous paragraphs. In this sense then the meaning of *uṣūl al-fiqh* is arrived at by combining the meanings of the two components: *uṣūl* and *fiqh*, that is, the first meaning of *aṣl* discussed above in the sense of source. The meaning derived is simple: "It is a knowledge of

70. In reality, this is not a general principle. It has so many exceptions that its generality is eroded. Thus, sex activity is prohibited, unless permitted by law, so is shedding of blood, the taking of another's property and so on. Accordingly, some Ḥanafīs and several others maintain that the original rule for all things is prohibition; things become lawful when they are permitted by the *sharī'ah*.

the *aḥkām* (legal rules) that is derived from the sources or the *adillah*." This has led many of the earlier jurists to say that "*uṣūl al-fiqh* or the sources are four." By this they mean the Qur'ān, the *Sunnah*, *ijmā'* and *qiyās*. Some jurists, like Imām al-Ghazāli, deem this statement to be sufficient, because they consider sources like *istiḥsān*, *istiṣlāḥ* and others to be offshoots of *qiyās*. Others would consider sources like the Opinion of a Companion, or the practice of the people of Medina to be acknowledged by the *Sunnah*. In modern times the trend is to consider the first four sources as the agreed upon sources and the rest as disputed, that is, acceptable to some schools and not to others.

Those who focus on this meaning of *uṣūl al-fiqh*, and confine themselves to such meaning, begin with the description of the *adillah* or the sources. Thus, they define and study the meaning of the Qur'ān and the *Sunnah* as sources. They do the same with *ijmā'* and *qiyās*. To the description these four sources, and of sources linked with them, they add the description of the *aḥkām*, because it is the *aḥkām* that are the legal effect of the sources or they are what is established by the sources. Some texts also describe the meaning of *ijtihād* and *taqlīd* and their related issues.

This type of description is undertaken by the later classical jurists and almost all modern scholars, by emphasising the meaning of *uṣūl al-fiqh* as sources of Islamic law. A study of the *adillah* or the sources is vital for the understanding of Islamic jurisprudence, but such a description is not enough for a complete understanding of Islamic jurisprudence or for becoming a jurist or ultimately for becoming a *mujtahid* or the independent jurist. Something more is needed, and for this we turn to the next section.

2.3 Describing the Meaning of *Uṣūl al-Fiqh* as a Discipline

The true masters, or real jurists, or the *mujtahids*, while keeping the study of the *adillah* in mind, focus on the meaning of the discipline of *uṣūl al-fiqh*. To do so they employ a different meaning of the term *aṣl*, a meaning different from the term "source." They use the last meaning of the term *aṣl* described in a previous section. This is the meaning of "general principle," "*qā'idah*," "*qānūn*," "rule" or "presumption." This meaning is then used to arrive at the meaning of the title "Discipline of *Uṣūl al-Fiqh*."

2.3.1 *'Ilm Uṣūl al-Fiqh* (the Discipline of *Uṣūl al-Fiqh*) Defined

The meaning of *uṣūl al-fiqh*, as we have said, is arrived at by understanding the meanings of *uṣūl* and *fiqh* separately and then combining them. When the meaning of *qawā'id uṣūliyyah* is combined with the meaning of *fiqh* explained earlier, we arrive at the definition of *'ilm uṣūl al-fiqh* or the discipline of *uṣūl al-fiqh*. This is stated very simply as:

هي القواعد التي يتوصل بها المجتهد الى الأحكام الشرعية
العملية من الأدلة التفصيلية

> They are the principles (or rules or *qawānīn*) by the use of which the *mujtahid* derives the legal rules of conduct from the specific evidences.[71]

This definition states that the *uṣūl al-fiqh* are a body of principles of interpretation by the help of which the *mujtahid* is able to derive the law from the detailed evidences in the Qur'ān, the *Sunnah*, *ijmā'* and *qiyās*.

We face the same problem with this definition as we faced with that of *fiqh*. This definition of *uṣūl al-fiqh* does not enable us to use principles like *maṣlaḥah* and *istiḥsān* insofar as these methods are based on the *qawā'id fiqhiyyah*. To understand this problem, we have to probe the nature of the *qawā'id fiqhiyyah* and to identify their relationship with the *qawā'id uṣūliyyah*.[72] Here, however, it is sufficient to form an idea about the nature of these rules or *qawā'id* or *qawnīn*.

---

71. Ibn al-Ḥājib, *Mukhtaṣar al-Muntahā*, vol. 1, 4.
72. This we will do in a separate work called *Secrets of Uṣūl*.

2.3.2 Examples of the *Qawā'id Uṣūliyyah*

For the jurist, the term *uṣūl* implies "a body of principles" that he uses to interpret the texts.[73]

These principles of interpretation are formulated by the Muslim jurists in the form of general propositions. The major premiss of these propositions serves as the principle. Such a principle is referred to as a *qā'idah uṣūliyah*. A few examples of such *uṣūl* are given below:

1. Each time a *ḥukm* is discovered in the Qur'ān it is said to be proved. [Unanimous]

2. Each time a *ḥukm* is discovered in the *Sunnah* it is said to be proved. [Unanimous]

3. Each time a *ḥukm* is discovered through *ijmā'* it is said to be proved. [Unanimous, though al-Shāfi'ī had some reservations]

4. Each time a *ḥukm* is discovered through *qiyās* it is said to be proved. [Unanimous for the existing Sunnī schools]

5. Each time a *ḥukm* is discovered through the opinion of a Companion it is said to be proved. [Not unanimous; the Ḥanafīs consider it binding, but the Shāfi'īs do not]

6. Each time a command (*amr*) is found in the texts it conveys an obligation, unless another evidence indicates the contrary. [Not unanimous]

7. Each time a proscription (*nahy*) is found in the texts it conveys a prohibition, unless another evidence indicates the contrary. [Not unanimous]

8. Each time a *ḥukm* is expressed in general terms it applies to all its categories with a certainty, unless restricted by an equally strong evidence. [Not unanimous]

73. For a discussion on the nature of these rules see Ṣadr al-Sharī'ah, *al-Tawḍīḥ*, vol. 1, 41–45.

9. The *ḥukm* is proved through the persuasive power of the *dalīl* and not through the number of evidences. [Not unanimous]

2.3.3 The Subject-matter of *'Ilm Uṣūl al-Fiqh*

The rules listed above are only a few out of a large body of rules called the *qawānīn uṣūliyyah*. They have been stated so that the reader may form a basic idea.[74] Such rules are the subject-matter of *'ilm uṣūl al-fiqh* or the discipline of *uṣūl al-fiqh*. It is important not to conclude that the meaning of *uṣūl al-fiqh* as sources is not relevant here. In fact, the discipline and the sources cannot be kept apart; both taken together form the subject-matter of the discipline. Thus, taken together, the *uṣūl al-fiqh* as a discipline deals with both the sources and with the *qawā'id* or rules used to interpret the sources. Those who, while studying the sources or the *adillah*, forget or neglect the meaning of *'ilm uṣūl al-fiqh* are bound to get lost on the way. Further, anyone who wishes to acquire the true knowledge of Islamic jurisprudence, and to be able to derive the rules through the method of *takhrīj*, must become proficient in the discipline of *uṣūl al-fiqh* in this meaning. Understanding this meaning is also crucial for the modern *muftī* if his *fatwās* are to have some meaning and persuasive force.

Review Questions

1. Why is the definition of *fiqh* given by Imām Abū Ḥanīfah too wide? How can it be narrowed down to apply to *fiqh* alone?

2. Define *fiqh* as preferred by the Shāfi'ī school and then list the defects of this narrow definition.

3. Which definition of *fiqh* prevents the use of general principles and *maṣlaḥah mursalah*, and why? How would you include them in your definition of *fiqh*?

4. What is the meaning of the term *dalīl tafṣīlī*? Does it include general principles within its meaning? If not, why?

74. The details will be provided in our work *Secrets of Uṣūl*.

5. To remedy the defects of the narrow definition of *fiqh*, give a wider definition of *fiqh* and then criticise this definition.

6. What is the meaning of the term *dalīl*? How many types of *adillah* can you identify and how are they employed?

7. How many meanings of the term *aṣl* can you identify and which meaning is directly relevant to the discipline of *uṣūl al-fiqh*?

8. Combine the narrow meaning of the term *fiqh* with the term *uṣūl* to arrive at the meaning of *uṣūl al-fiqh*. Try to find defects in the definition so derived.

9. What is the relationship between the term *uṣūl* and a school of law?

10. If each school of law has a different set of *uṣūl* (other than the first four unanimous *uṣūl*), what impact can this have on the interpretation of the texts?

11. What do you understand by the term *qawā'id fiqhiyyah*? How are these different from the *qawānīn uṣūliyyah*?

12. Are the *qawā'id fiqhiyyah* evidences (*adillah*) for the derivation of the *aḥkām*? If not, what is their nature?

13. What is the relationship between the *qawā'id fiqhiyyah* and the *maqāṣid al-sharī'ah* (purposes of the *sharī'ah*)?

14. Try to criticise the narrow definition of *uṣūl al-fiqh* (based upon the narrow meaning of *fiqh*) and then provide a wider defintion of *uṣūl al-fiqh*.

15. How is the meaning of *uṣūl al-fiqh* as sources of Islamic law to be distinguished from *uṣūl al-fiqh* as a discipline?

16. Will you apply the term Islamic jurisprudence to *uṣūl al-fiqh* as sources of Islamic law or to *uṣūl al-fiqh* as a discipline?

Part I

The *Ḥukm Shar'ī*

﴿الحكم الشرعى﴾

3 The *Ḥukm*: What is Islamic Law?

The purpose of studying the *ḥukm shar'ī* is to understand the conceptual part of Islamic law. This study provides the framework within which the meaning of Islamic law is understood, the nature of its rules is grasped, and the operation of the legal system is seen. In the figure of the general format of the theory of Islamic law, described earlier, this part is shown on the left side. (See p. 29 above).

3.1 The Three Elements of the *Ḥukm Shar'ī*

The *ḥukm shar'ī* in its literal sense conveys the meaning of a rule of Islamic law.[75] It comes into being through the operation of its

75. The term *ḥukm* (plural *aḥkām*) has been translated into English in different ways: injunction, command, prescription, and *sharī'ah*-value. None of these terms conveys completely the comprehensive meaning of the term, as will be obvious in the discussions to follow. It is preferable to retain such terms in their untranslated forms.

three elements (*arkān*).[76] These elements are:

1. **The Lawgiver (*Ḥākim*).** The true source from which the *ḥukm* originates. The original source for Islamic law is the *Ḥākim* or the Lawgiver, that is, Allah Almighty;
2. **The Act (*Maḥkūm Fīh*).** The *maḥkūm fīh* or the act on which the *ḥukm* operates—also called the *maḥkūm bih;* and
3. **The Subject (*Maḥkm̄ 'Alayh*).** The *maḥkūm 'alayh* or the subject (legal person) for whose conduct the *ḥukm* is stipulated.

A discussion of the meaning of the *ḥukm shar'ī* in Islamic law amounts to asking the question: what is Islamic law? The response deals with Islamic law as a system as well as with individual rules. The study of the *ḥukm shar'ī*, when it deals with the nature of rules, reveals the types of legal obligation created by the rule. It tells us that all the rules may not create an obligation and that some rules are laid down by the Lawgiver to facilitate the operation of other rules.[77] A classification of the various types of rules or *aḥkām* becomes necessary to grasp these meanings.

The first of the three *arkān* (elements) of the *ḥukm shar'ī* mentioned above is the Lawgiver (the *Ḥākim*). In the study of this element, it is shown that Allah is the Ultimate and True Source of all laws in Islam. Further, the implication of this statement is examined, that is, what do we mean by saying that Allah is the source of all laws? The second element deals with the act on which the *ḥukm* operates and the legal rights that are affected. The third element deals with the types of subjects who are affected by a *ḥukm*, that is, those who possess full legal capacity and those who do not. It also deals with cases in which the legal capacity of the subject is restricted or becomes defective.

76. *Arkān* is the plural of *rukn*. A *rukn* may be conceived as a pillar on which a thing is erected. If we pull out the pillar the structure on top of it will collapse. A *rukn*, therefore, is an essential element of a thing without which it cannot stand.
77. This is where Islamic law differs with the approach adopted by John Austin for law: the imperative theory of law. See below.

3.2 The Meaning of the *Ḥukm Shar'ī* or the Meaning of Islamic Law

The Arabic word *ḥukm* (pl. *aḥkām*) in its literal sense means a command. In its technical sense it means a "rule" This may be a rule of any kind. Thus, it may be a rational rule, like 2 + 2 = 4, or the rule that the whole is greater than its parts. It may be a rule perceived by the senses, like fire burns. Again, it may be based upon experience or experiment, like aspirin is good for headache. Here, however, we are concerned with the legal rule, which is called the *ḥukm shar'ī*.

The Muslim jurists give us a definition of the *ḥukm shar'ī* when they attempt to answer the question: What is Islamic law? They define it as:

خطاب الله تعالى المتعلق بأفعال المكلفين بالاقتضاء أو التخيير أو الوضع

> A communication from Allah, the Exalted, related to the acts of the subjects through a demand or option or through a declaration.[78]

This definition highlights the following important points:[79]

1. **The *ḥukm* or a rule of law (to be referred to as *ḥukm* from now on) is a communication from Allah.** This means that it is not treated merely as a command.[80] It also means that a communication from anyone else cannot be considered as a *ḥukm*, be he a ruler or someone else in authority.

2. **The communication is related to the acts of the subjects.** The communication invariably gives rise to a rule of some kind and enables the jurist to understand whether the requirement is for the commission of an act or its omission, or whether a choice has been granted for the commission or

78. Ṣadr al-Sharī'ah, *al-Tawḍīḥ*, vol. 1, 28.
79. For an analysis see ibid., 28–32.
80. The method is, therefore, different from the one adopted by John Austin for law in his well known imperative theory or the command theory of law.

omission of such act. While every *ḥukm* is related, directly or indirectly, to the act of the subject, the declaratory *ḥukm* may address situations or sets of facts. For example, the *ḥukm* may tell us that the time for the evening prayer is related to the setting of the sun. Now, this is not an act of the subject, but an act (the evening prayer) is indirectly addressed. The words "acts of the subjects" in the definition are, therefore, to be read with this qualification. Thus, the words of Allah, "Do not go near unlawful sexual intercourse (*zinā*)," [Qur'ān 17 : 32] contain a *ḥukm* that requires omission and affects conduct. Some jurists divide the *khiṭāb* into two types: *khiṭāb jinā'ī* and the *khiṭāb* of *muu'āmalāt* (criminal and civil liability).

3. **The *ḥukm* may be expressed through a demand.** The demand in this case may be for the commission of an act or its omission. In each case, the demand may be expressed in binding terms or otherwise. When the demand is expressed in binding terms and requires the commission of an act, the *ḥukm* creates an obligation (*ījāb*). When the terms used are not binding or absolute, the *ḥukm* gives rise to a recommendation (*nadb*) for the commission of the act. The jurists use various rules to decide when a demand has been expressed in binding terms.

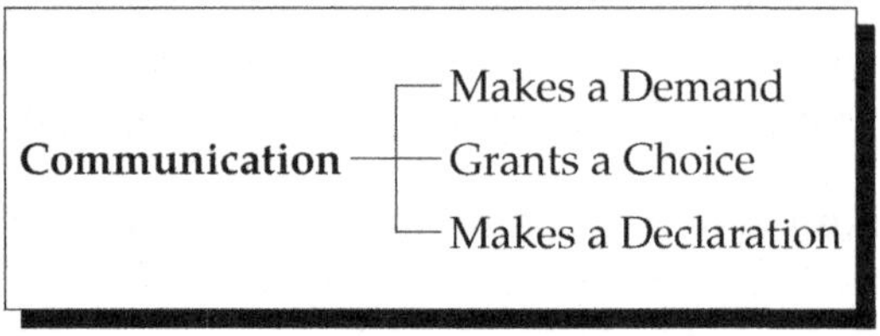

When the demand in the *ḥukm* is for abstention from or omission of an act and is expressed in binding or absolute terms, the *ḥukm* conveys a prohibition (*taḥrīm*). If the demand, for omission, is not expressed in binding terms the act is looked down upon and conveys disapproval (*karāhah*).

Al-Ghazālī describing the division of commission and omission and the resulting *rules*, says: When there is a demand for the commission of an act, we conclude that there is a command (*amr*), but when this command is accompanied by additional evidence about a consequential penalty for omission the act is obligatory *wājib*. In case we do not find such evidence, the act is recommended. In the case of a demand for the omission of an act, if there is accompanying evidence entailing punishment for the omission, the act is *ḥarām*; if not, the act is *makrūh*.[81]

In any case, we have four categories of obligations arising from a demand: obligation, recommendation, disapproval, and prohibition. These obligations are mostly associated with sanctions. When the obligations relate to ritual or worship the sanctions pertain to the hereafter or to censure through public opinion, and when the obligations relate to mundane affairs they invoke sanctions in the form of punishment in this world.

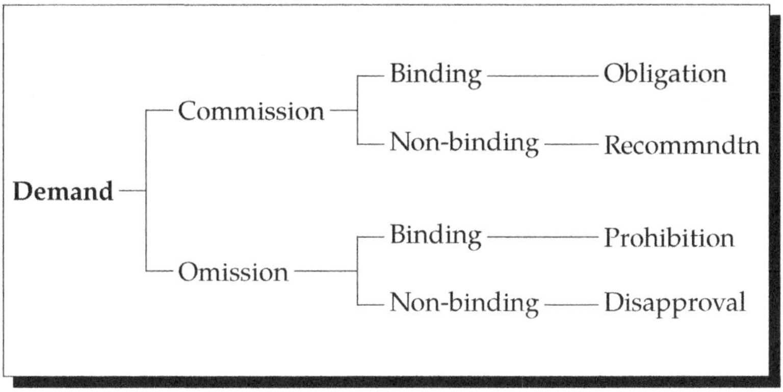

4. **The *ḥukm* may grant a choice or option to the subject for the commission or omission of an act.** If a text tells the subject to "eat and drink," a choice is offered to him that he may exercise when he likes. In other words, the subject is free to perform the act at his discretion. The bulk of the Islamic laws fall under this category and include all kinds

81. Al-Ghazālī, *al-Mustaṣfā min 'Ilm al-Uṣūl,* vol. 1, 42. See also al-Rāzī, *al-Maḥṣūl,* vol. 1, 93–104.

of contracts and transactions. The Lawgiver, it is sometimes said, is indifferent to the performance of such acts.[82]

5. **The communication may be expressed through a declaration.** In this case, the communication declares or determines the relationship of an act, or set of facts, with the *ḥukm*. The communication, therefore, declares that an act or set of facts is the cause (*sabab*), condition (*sharṭ*), or an impediment (*māni'*) for the application of the *ḥukm*. For example, in the *ḥukm* of the payment of *zakāt* (obligatory religious contribution), the possession of a minimum amount of wealth (*niṣāb*) is the cause for the application of the *ḥukm*, having retained this wealth for a year (*ḥawl*) is a condition for the *ḥukm*, and the existence of debts against the subject may be the impediment or obstacle in the way of fixing liability for *zakāt*. The declaratory communication explains the relationship of all these categories. Further, the declaratory communication tells us whether an act has been performed properly (*ṣaḥīḥ*), with some removable defect (*fāsid*), or has been done in a totally incorrect way (*bāṭil*).

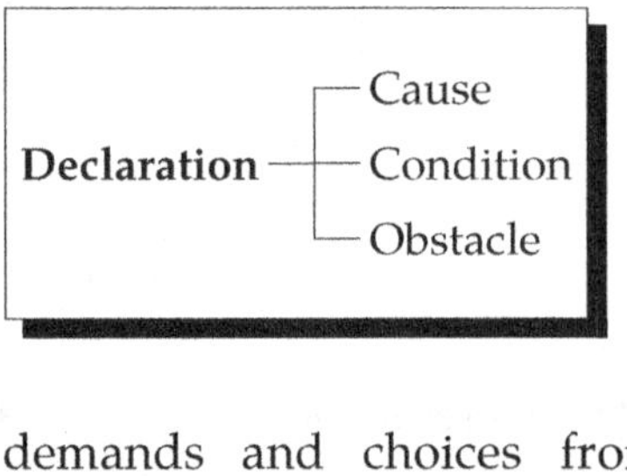

If we separate demands and choices from declaratory communications, we have two main categories for the *ḥukm*. The first is called the *ḥukm taklīfī* or the obligation-creating *ḥukm*. The second category is called the *ḥukm waḍ'ī* or the declaratory *ḥukm*. We shall first take up the discussion of the obligation creating rule or the *ḥukm taklīfī*.

82. In the discussion of the *mubāḥ*, see p. 100 below, we will see that this indifference is not absolute. For example, eating and drinking is permissible, but a person cannot give up eating altogether. If he does so, the rule will convert itself from indifference to one of obligation.

3.3 The *Ḥukm Taklīfī*—Obligations and Duties

The *ḥukm taklīfī* or the obligation-creating rule is viewed from two perspectives in Islamic law. It is viewed from the point of view of the *uṣūlī*, who is a specialist in *uṣūl al-fiqh*, and from the point of view of the *faqīh*, who is a specialist in *fiqh* or the substantive law.[83] It is possible, though, that one jurist may be performing both functions. The definition of the obligation-creating rule from the point of view of the *uṣūlī* is: "The demand of the Lawgiver requiring the subject to perform or omit an act or to have a choice between commission and omission." The definition from the point of view of the *faqīh* is: "The legal attribute of the acts of the subject after the demand of the Lawgiver requiring its commission or omission or to His granting a choice between commission and omission."

It is obvious that the earlier jurists were not providing different definitions to satisfy the requirements of their individual perspectives. There is a legal basis for the two views. When we look at these categories from the point of view of the jurist who is concerned with derivation of the *ḥukm* (that is, the *usūlī*), we call them obligations. The *uṣūlī* is concerned with the question as to whether the *ḥukm* has created an obligation. On the other hand, the *faqīh* is more concerned with the performance of the acts and he, therefore, looks at the duties that are created. The two perspectives are, thus, complementary. The *uṣūlī* is looking at the obligations that are created by the *ḥukm shar'ī*, while the *faqīh* is looking at the corresponding duties that arise. A similar distinction is made with respect to the *ḥukm waḍ'ī* as well.

These two perspectives have an effect on the terminology employed in *uṣūl al-fiqh*. Let us list the different categories from both perspectives to see the difference in the terminology.

83. In reality, the two perspectives are those of the legislature and the judiciary: the laying down of the law and its implementation.

3.3.1 The *ḥukm taklīfī* from the perspective of the *uṣūlī*

The *uṣūlī*, who is emphasising the obligations created by the *ḥukm*, uses the following terminology for the five categories:[84]

1. Obligation (*ījāb* — إيجاب)
2. Recommendation (*nadb* — ندب)
3. Disapproval (*karāhah* — كراهة)
4. Prohibition (*taḥrīm* — تحريم)
5. Permissibility (*ibāḥah* — إباحة)

The *uṣūlī* is saying that **the *ḥukm* to be derived from the texts** is creating an obligation, or a recommendation and so on.

3.3.2 The *ḥukm taklīfī* from the perspective of the *faqīh*

The *faqīh*, who is emphasising the performance of duties created by the *ḥukm*, states the five categories in the following terminology:[85]

1. Obligatory (*Wājib* — واجب)
2. Recommended (*Mandūb* — مندوب)
3. Reprehensible, Disapproved (*Makrūh* — مكروه)
4. Prohibited (*Ḥarām* — حرام)
5. Permissible (*Mubāḥ* — مباح)

The *faqīh* is saying that **the *act* to which the derived *ḥukm* is related** is obligatory, recommended and so on. He will be focusing on duties and their performance all the time.

84. Ṣadr al-Sharī'ah, *al-Tawḍīḥ*, vol. 1, 30; vol. 2, 678.
85. Ibid., vol. 2, 678.

3.3.3 The *ḥukm taklīfī* according to the Ḥanafīs

These five categories of obligations and duties emerge from the operation of laws in the opinion of the majority of the Sunnī schools. The Ḥanafīs derive seven categories from the same definition. Let us view the categories derived by the Ḥanafīs in terms of duties, that is, from the perspective of the *faqīh*, who is concerned more about the performance of duties.

1. *Farḍ*: Obligatory. This duty arises from an evidence or source that is definitive[86] with respect to the authenticity of its transmission.

2. *Wājib*: Obligatory. This duty is slightly weaker than the first in its demand for commission. It arises from a source that is probable with respect to its authenticity. The demand, however, has been expressed in binding terms.

3. *Mandūb*: Recommended. The difference between recommendation and the two kinds of obligation above, it should be recalled, is based on the binding nature of the

86. The meanings of the terms "definitive" and "probable" are explained later on (see section 9.2.3). The words "with respect to the authenticity of its transmission" have been used intentionally to protect against the use of vague terms. The allusion here is to a distinction drawn by some modern writers aiming to simplify the understanding of texts. This is the distinction between *qaṭʿī al-thubūt* (definitive by way of transmission) and *qatʿī al-dalālah* (definitive by way of implication). This classification appears to have originated with al-Rāzī and was picked up by al-Shāṭibī and other later writers, but it is not to be found with the earlier jurists and rightly so. The reason is that a text cannot be deemed definitive or probable in its implication in a general way. There are detailed categories for analysing this according to the system of the Mutakallimūn as well as the Ḥanafīs. When the earlier jurists use the term *qaṭʿī* or *ẓannī*, they always refer to the strength of the transmission, that is, *mutawātir, mashhūr* or *āḥād*. It has been felt necessary to point this out because this vague and somewhat inaccurate terminology has taken hold in modern writings. We do acknowledge, however, that in certain cases it does serve as a very instructive device.

command. The source is probable here, but the demand is expressed in non-binding terms.

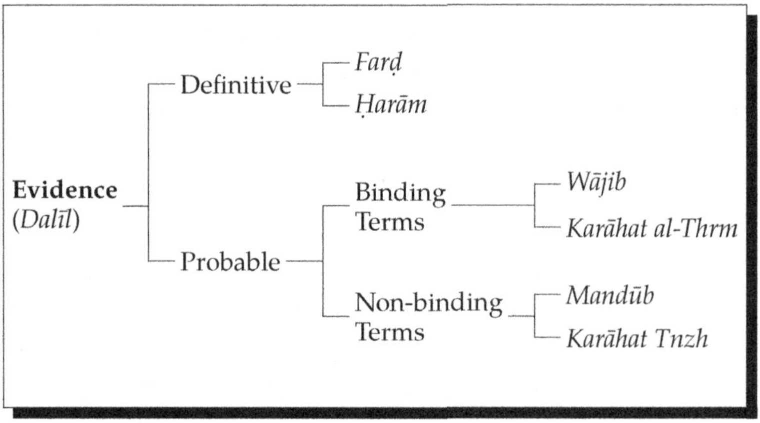

4. *Makrūh karāhat al-tanzīh*: Disapproved. It is an act whose omission is demanded by the Lawgiver through a probable evidence *expressed in non-binding terms.*

5. *Makrūh karāhat al-taḥrīm*: Reprehensible. This category arises from a probable evidence *expressed in binding terms.* It is close to prohibition.

6. *Ḥarām*: Prohibited or duty not to commit an act. This arises from a definitive evidence.

7. *Mubāḥ*: Permissible. No duty is created and the subject is given a choice to perform the act or not to perform it. We may also say here that the subject is sometimes given the power to create obligations and duties with respect to other individuals. This may occur, for example, in the case of a person appointing another his agent or concluding a contract with him.

Some modern writers try to ignore this division by saying that the addition of two categories by the Ḥanafīs has no practical significance. This seems questionable for there are some practical consequences though they relate mostly to ritual and in one case to apostasy.[87]

Let us now examine the classification of the declaratory rules that flows from the definition provided by Muslim jurists.

3.4 The *Ḥukm Waḍʿī*—Declaratory Rules

The definition of the *ḥukm sharʿī* provided above stated that the communication from Allah may be related to the acts of the subjects in a manner that is declaratory. This is stated in order to accommodate rules that cannot be classified under the obligation creating rules. The following classifications are made:

1. Classification of secondary rules into *sabab, sharṭ* and *māniʿ*. The *uṣūlī* is concerned more with this classification.

2. Classification into *ṣiḥḥah, buṭlān,* and *fasād* (validity, nullity and vitiation). This classification is more important for the *faqīh,* because it pertains to the performance of acts.[88]

3. Classification into *ʿazīmah* and *rukhṣah* (general rules and exemptions). This classification helps the jurists identify the general principles of the law or initial rules and the exceptions to these rules. It is used as a tool for achieving analytical consistency.[89]

87. For a discussion see Ṣadr al-Sharīʿah, *al-Tawḍīḥ,* vol. 2, 682.
88. Ṣadr al-Sharīʿah, *al-Tawḍīḥ,* vol. 2, 679–80.
89. It is sometimes stated that all the injunctions of the *sharīʿah* are of two types: broad general principles and exceptions to these principles. See, e.g., Amīn al-Iḥsān Mujaddadī, *Qawāʿid al-Fiqh* (Karachi: al-Ṣadaf Publishers, 1986), 5. In terms of our explanation of evidences as general principles and specific evidences, it would mean that the specific evidences sometimes provide exceptions to the general principles. It is the task of the jurist, for the sake of analytical consistency, to relate the general principles and the exceptions. Another aspect of this view is the laying down of an initial rule, called *ʿazīmah* and then providing an exception to it, called *rukhṣah.* (See p. 105 below.)

3.5 The Distinction Between the *Ḥukm Taklīfī* and the *Ḥukm Waḍʿī*

1. The aim of the *ḥukm taklīfī* is to create an obligation for the commission or omission of an act or to grant a choice between the commission or omission of the act. The *ḥukm waḍʿī* has no such aim. Its purpose is to either inform the subject that a certain thing is a cause of, condition for or obstacle to a *ḥukm* or it is to explain the relationship that exists between two rules or to provide the criterion for judging whether an act performed is valid or void.

2. The act or event that is affected by the *ḥukm taklīfī* is within the ability of the subject with respect to its commission or omission. The act affected by the *ḥukm waḍʿī* may or may not be within the ability of the subject with respect to commission or omission. In other words, it is always possible for the subject to commit or omit an act affected by the *ḥukm taklīfī*, but it may not be possible for him to commit or omit all acts that fall within the domain of the *ḥukm waḍʿī*. Thus, theft is an act the omission of which is required and it is possible for the subject to avoid it, but the setting of the sun is the legal cause for the evening prayer, and it is not possible for the subject to bring it about. *Rushd* (discretion) is a necessary condition for contracts, but it is a condition that is beyond the power of the subject to create. Insanity is a defence against criminal liability, that is, it is an obstacle (*mānīʿ*) for the *ḥukm* to take effect, but it is beyond the power of the subject (he can only feign it for some time).

It is not to be assumed that the *ḥukm taklīfī* and the *ḥukm waḍʿī* are always stated in separate texts. It is possible for them to exist in the same text. For example, the verse about theft states: "The thief, male and female, cut off their hands." Here the *ḥukm* is the obligation to cut off the hand, the cause for it is *sariqah* (theft), thus, both occur in the same text.

Review Questions

1. What are the elements (*arkān*) of the *ḥukm shar'ī*? Describe them briefly indicating the topics covered under each element.

2. Define the *ḥukm shar'ī* and analyse the definition into its various implications.

3. Is the *ḥukm shar'ī* always "related to the acts of the subjects" as stated in the definition?

4. How many differences can you point out between the definition of the *ḥukm shar'ī* and the definition of law as the command of the sovereign?

5. Analyse the word "communication" giving the reasons due to which the jurists divide it into obligation, prohibition, recommendation and disapproval. How does the method of the Ḥanafīs differ from the other schools in this respect?

6. Give the classification of the *ḥukm shar'ī* on the basis of obligations and duties. Does the distinction between obligations and duties have some advantage?

7. Describe the various ways in which the *ḥukm waḍ'ī* is classified. What is the benefit of the classification of the *aḥkām* into *'azīmah* and *rukhṣah*?

8. What is the distinction between the *ḥukm taklīfī* and the *ḥukm waḍ'ī*?

9. How would you compare the classification of the *ḥukm shar'ī* by the Muslim jurists with the classification of the law into primary and secondary rules given by H.L.A. Hart?

4 Classification of Rules in Islamic Law

The main categories of rules emerging from the definition of the *ḥukm shar'ī* have been identified in the previous chapter, both in terms of obligations and in terms of duties. The details of these categories will be taken up in this chapter. The discussion of *wājib, mandūb, mubāḥ, makrūh* and *ḥarām* will be taken up first. This will be followed by the discussion of the types of *ḥukm waḍ'ī*.[90]

4.1 The Meaning of *Wājib* (Obligatory Act) and its Different Types

The term *wājib* means an act the performance of which is obligatory for the subject. In its technical sense, it is an act whose commission is demanded by the Lawgiver in certain and binding

90. The discussions that follow are based on the work of Ṣadr al-Sharī'ah and the commentary on this work by al-Taftāzānī. See Ṣadr al-Sharī'ah, *al-Tawḍīḥ,* vol. 2, 677 passim.

terms.[91] The binding and certain nature of the demand may be inferred from the syntax of the statement in which the demand is expressed. It may also be inferred from an evidence external to the syntax, for example, the existence of a consequential punishment for omission. Examples of these are: the performance of *ṣalāt*, the payment of *zakāt*, pilgrimage to the Ka'bah, the fulfilling of promises and many other acts that are required by the Lawgiver from His subjects. The Lawgiver has determined penalties for the omission of such acts.

4.1.1 The *ḥukm* or rule for the *wājib*

The rule for the *wājib* is that it must be brought about by the subject and for doing so there is reward (*thawāb*) for him, while omitting it, without a legal excuse, entails a penalty.[92] The rule further says that a person who denies the legality of a *wājib* when it is based upon a definitive (*qaṭ'ī*) evidence is to be imputed with *kufr* (infidelity).[93] This is the rule according to the Sunnī majority. The rules according to the Ḥanafīs for the *farḍ* and for the *wājib* are as follows:

- The *wājib*, according to the Ḥanafīs, is what has been made binding for the subject by the Lawgiver, but which has been established through a probable (*ẓannī*) evidence, whose strength is not that of a definitive evidence. The examples are: *ṣadaqat al-fiṭr*, *witr* prayers, prayers of the two *'Īd*s and reciting *sūrat al-Fātiḥah* in prayers. These cases have

91. Ṣadr al-Sharī'ah, *Tawḍīḥ*, vol. 2, 680–81. Al-Ghazālī states the meaning of *wājib* in simpler terms. He says: When there is a demand for the commission of an act, we conclude that there is a command (*amr*), but when this command is accompanied by additional evidence about a consequential penalty for omission the act is obligatory *wājib*. In case we do not find such evidence, the act is recommended. Al-Ghazālī, *al-Mustaṣfā min 'Ilm al-Uṣūl*, vol. 1, 42.
92. Ṣadr al-Sharī'ah, *Tawḍīḥ*, vol. 2, 680–81; Al-Ghazālī, *al-Mustaṣfā min 'Ilm al-Uṣūl*, vol. 1, 42.
93. Ṣadr al-Sharī'ah, *Tawḍīḥ*, vol. 2, 681.

been established, according to the Ḥanafīs, through a *khabar wāḥid*, which is a probable evidence.[94]

- The *farḍ*, on the other hand, has been made binding for the subject and is established through a definitive (*qaṭ'ī*) evidence. By *qaṭ'ī* in this sense, we mean *qaṭ'ī al-thubūt* and not *qaṭ'ī al-dalālah*. The evidence may be a verse of the Qur'ān or a *mutawātir* or *mashhūr* tradition. Examples of the *farḍ* are: the five daily prayers, *zakāt*, *ḥajj*, recitation of the Qur'ān in prayer and so on.[95]

- The rules for *farḍ* and *wājib* are different in their view. The rule for *farḍ* is the obligation of performance and liability for punishment on omission as well as imputation of *kufr* for denying its legal validity. The rule for the *wājib* is the obligation of performance and liability for punishment for omission, but of a lesser gravity as compared to the *farḍ*. They also do not impute with *kufr* the person who denies the *wājib*.[96]

- This distinction, drawn by the Ḥanafīs, has an effect on the opinions derived in *fiqh*. For example, they say, if one forgets to recite the Qur'ān in prayer, the prayer is a nullity (*bāṭil*), because this is noncompliance with a definitive evidence in the Qur'ān requiring such recitation: "Then recite what is easy from the Qur'ān." On the other hand, if one forgets to recite *sūrat al-Fātiḥah*, but does recite something else, it does not invalidate the prayer, although this is noncompliance with a tradition that says: "There is no prayer for one who does not recite the *Fātiḥah* of the Book." This, however, is a *khabar wāḥid*.[97]

94. Ibid., 680, 682.
95. Ibid., 681.
96. Ibid., 681.
97. See al-Sarakhsī, *Kitāb al-Uṣūl*, vol. 1, 133.

4.2 The Classifications of the *Wājib* (Obligatory Act)

There are several classifications for the *wājib* (obligatory act)[98] based upon different criteria. These are described below:[99]

4.2.1 Classification based on the time available for performance: *muṭlaq* and *muqayyad*

On the basis of the time of its performance the *wājib* is divided into *wājib muṭlaq*, which is absolute or unrestricted by time, and into *wājib muqayyad* or *wājib* with a time limitation.

4.2.1.1 *Wājib muṭlaq* (obligatory act independent of time)

Wājib muṭlaq is an act whose performance has been demanded by the Lawgiver, but He has not fixed a definite time for its performance. An example is the payment of expiation (*kaffārah*) and the *nadhr* for fasting sometime in the future.

The rule for *wājib muṭlaq* is that the subject may perform the act whenever he likes. For example, if he took an oath to do something and then broke his oath, he may pay the *kaffārah*, for which he is liable, anytime he wishes to do so.

4.2.1.2 *Wājib muqayyad* also called *wājib muwaqqat* (obligatory act limited by time)

It is an obligatory act demanded by the Lawgiver from the subject for which a time period is also determined having a beginning and an end. Examples are: the five daily prayers, fasting during Ramaḍān, and Ḥajj.

98. A question may be raised as to why the term "obligatory act" is being used and not "obligation". The basic reason is that the term for "obligation" is *wujūb*. Further, the focus here is on the duties created and their performance rather than on creation of the obligation.
99. For the divisions below, see Ṣadr al-Sharī'ah, *al-Tawḍīḥ*, vol. 2, 682; al-Sarakhsī, *Kitāb al-Uṣūl*, vol. 1, 26–30; al-Ghazālī, *al-Mustaṣfā min 'Ilm al-Uṣūl*, vol. 1, 42–44.

The *wājib muqayyad* or *muwaqqat* gives rise to two further subdivisions depending on the performance of the act within time and depending on the time available for the performance of the act, that is, whether the time is just enough for the act or exceeds the time required. Let us look at both divisions.

First subdivision of the *wājib muwaqqat:* early, timely and delayed performance or *ta'jīl, adā'* and *qaḍā'*. The three types are as follows:[100]

1. *Ta'jīl* or early performance of an obligatory act, if permitted by the Lawgiver, amounts to performance in time, like the early payment of the *ṣadaqat al-fiṭr*.

2. *Adā'* is the timely performance of the act, that is, the time that the Lawgiver has fixed for it, without there being any shortfall in such performance. In case the act has not been properly performed and is repeated within time and is performed properly, it is called *i'ādah* (repetition), like a person praying with *tayammum* finds water, performs ablution and prays again within time. There are some fine distinctions about the term *i'ādah* among the majority and the Ḥanafīs, that is, when a repetition is called *i'ādah* and when *adā'*.

3. *Qaḍā'* is the performance of an obligatory act after the time fixed for it by the Lawgiver, like offering the morning prayer after the sun has risen or like offering *ẓuhr* in the time of *'aṣr*. The jurists agree that one who misses the determined time is obliged to offer the act as *qaḍā'* and if the delay was without a valid excuse, he is liable for blame. The Ẓāhirī jurists confine the excuse to one who forgot or one who missed the act while he was asleep, thus, it is obligatory only for these two cases in their view and not for one who misses it intentionally.

100. See al-Sarakhsī, *Kitāb al-Uṣūl*, vol. 1, 44–59.

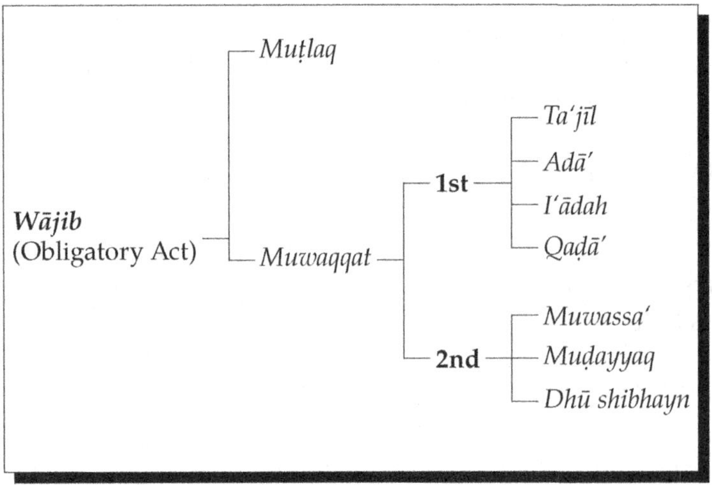

Second subdivision of the *wājib muwaqqat:* wide, narrow and dual duration for the performance of the act or *muwassa'*, *muḍayyaq* and *dhū shibhayn*. The three types are as follows:

1. *Wājib muwassa'* (Obligatory act with extra time) is an act for which the time given by the Lawgiver is enough for this act and others like it. The time for the act is called *ẓarf* according to the Ḥanafīs. An example is the time for the *ẓuhr* prayer. The subject is permitted to perform the required act in any part of this time period. After agreeing on this, the jurists disagreed as to which part is the *wujūb* (obligation) connected to: the beginning or the end of the period. Supposing a woman starts menstruating in the middle of the period for the *ẓuhr* prayer, when she has not offered the prayer. Is she liable for *qaḍā'*? This problem is actually related to the issue in *uṣūl* whether a command necessitates immediate or delayed compliance. It is somewhat complex and lengthy to discuss here.[101]

101. For the details see al-Sarakhsī, *Kitāb al-Uṣūl,* vol. 1, 26–59. He discusses these details under the topic of *amr* (command) and all these categories are dealt with as types of commands.

2. *Wājib muḍayyaq* (Obligatory act with time sufficient for a single performance) is an act for which the time granted by the Lawgiver is just enough for its performance and for no other, like the fasts of Ramaḍān or like the evening prayer. The time granted itself becomes the standard (*mi'yār*) for the validity of this act.

3. *Wājib dhū shibhayn* (Obligatory act with extra time from one aspect and sufficient time from another) or the act that can be performed once in a time period, yet it permits other acts. An example is *ḥajj*. It can be performed once in a year in known months, but it permits the subject to perform acts like *ṭawāf* a number of times during this period.

A major reason for this distinction is that the *wājib muwassa'* is not valid if the subject does not form a *niyyah* required for it, because the time available may include other acts and the act has to be identified. As compared to this the *wājib muḍayyaq* is valid with a general *niyyah* or even a *niyyah* for another act of the same kind. The *niyyah* will be redirected, so to say, toward the act for which the time is just sufficient.

4.2.2 Classification based on the extent of the required act

The *wājib* is classified according to the extent or amount of the act required into *wājib muḥaddad* and *wājib ghayr muḥaddad*.

4.2.2.1 *Wājib muḥaddad* (determinate obligatory act)

It is an act whose amount or extent has been determined by the Lawgiver, like the five daily prayers and the amount of *zakāt*. The rule for this type of *wājib* is that it becomes due as a liability as soon as its cause is found. A demand for its performance or payment is valid without waiting for a judicial verdict or on the willingness of the subject to perform the act. The subject is not absolved from the liability to perform or pay unless he does so in the way determined by the Lawgiver and in the amount fixed by Him.

4.2.2.2 *Wājib ghayr muḥaddad* (indeterminate obligatory act)

It is an act whose amount or extent has not been fixed by the Lawgiver, like spending in the way of Allāh, feeding the needy or hospitality for guests. These things depend upon the need and capacity of the individual and thus vary. The rule for this kind of *wājib* is that it does not become a liability, unless it is imposed by a judicial decision or through willingness and acceptance.

The jurists have differed as to which act is to be attached to which type of *wājib*. For example, maintenance of wife and children, or support for the next of kin: are these to be linked to *wājib muḥaddad* or *wājib ghayr muḥaddad?* According to some Ḥanafī scholars these are to be linked to the *ghayr muḥaddad*, because there is no fixed amount for them. A court decision would, therefore, be required or it will become obligatory through an agreement between the parties. The majority link these to the *muḥaddad* and no court decision is required in their view for a claim.[102]

4.2.3 Classification based on the subjects who are required to perform

Depending on who is required to perform the act, the *wājib* is divided into the universal obligation and the communal obligation or the *wājib 'aynī* and the *wājib kifā'ī*.

4.2.3.1 *Wājib 'aynī* (the universal obligatory act)

Wājib 'aynī or the universal obligation is a demand by the Lawgiver from each subject, or each subject with legal capacity for the act, to perform the act, like prayers, fasting, *ḥajj* and *zakāt*. The rule for this type of obligation is that it is to be performed by each person from whom it is demanded. The individual is not absolved of the liability even if some other persons have performed the act.

102. Perhaps, the opinion of the majority would be preferable today as it will provide a less cumbersome procedure for implementation. In other words, the rights of the neglected women and children can be secured more easily if this decision is followed.

4.2.3.2 *Wājib kifā'ī* (the communal obligatory act)

The *wājib kifā'ī* is an act whose performance is required from the whole community and not from each individual, like *jihād*, answering the *salām*, and rendering testimony.

The rule for the *wājib kifā'ī* is that if it is performed by some individuals in the community, the rest are no longer liable for it, as the required act stands performed. The communal obligation may turn into a universal obligation, however, in certain cases. For example, if there is only one doctor in the community, it will be his personal obligation to look after a patient.

4.2.4 Classification based on the identification of the object of the required act

The obligatory act is divided into two types on the basis of the determination of the object of the act. The types are *wājib mu'ayyan* and *wājib mukhayyar*.

4.2.4.1 *Wājib mu'ayyan* (the specified obligatory act)

The *wājib mu'ayyan* is an act that is required by the Lawgiver specifically; there is no choice in it with respect to the act to be performed. The examples are prayer, fasting, payment of due wages and so on. The rule is that the subject is not free of the liability without specific performance.

4.2.4.2 *Wājib mukhayyar* (the unspecified obligatory act or obligatory act with an option as to its performance)

This type of act is required by the Lawgiver not as a specific act, but as one out of several determined acts, like the *kaffārah* (expiation) for breaking the oath: feeding ten needy persons, or clothing them, or the freeing of a slave. If the subject is not able to perform one act, he may perform the other. Each of these three acts, however, are required by way of a choice. When one is performed, the subject is absolved of liability.

4.3 The Meaning of *Mandūb* (Recommended Act) and its Different Types

Mandūb or the *mandūb ilayh* is defined as "a demand by the Lawgiver for the commission of an act without making it binding and without assigning any blame for its omission."[103] The non-binding nature of the demand can be inferred from the syntax. Sometimes the syntax may indicate that the demand is binding, but there may be related evidence showing that the demand is non-binding. The related evidence may be a text or a general principle of the *sharī'ah* or some other indication, like the absence of a penalty for non-performance.

For example, in the verse,

إذا تداينتم بدين الى أجل مسمّى فاكتبوه

> O ye who believe, when you enter into a transaction involving a *dayn* (debt), write it down. [Qur'ān 2 : 282]

the demand for the recording of the debt is a recommendation and is non-binding, because of an associated evidence that indicates this. The evidence is found in the following verse:

فإن أمن بعضكم بعضا فليؤد الّذي أوتمن امانته

> And if one of you deposits a thing on trust with another, let the trustee faithfully discharge his trust. [Qur'ān 2 : 283]

This indicates to the creditor that he may trust the debtor without the writing down of the debt. Likewise in the verse

والّذين يبتغون الكتاب ممّا ملكت أيمانكم فكاتبوهم إن علمتم فيهم خيرا

> And if any of your slaves ask for a deed in writing (to enable them to earn their freedom for a certain sum) give them such a deed, if ye know any good in them. [Qur'ān 24 : 33]

The command requires the agreement of *mukātabah* with the slave (in which the slave pays for his freedom in installments). It is,

103. Ṣadr al-Sharī'ah, *al-Tawḍīḥ*, vol. 2, 682.

however, not binding on the owner. This is inferred from the established principle of the *sharī'ah* that an owner of property is free to dispose of it as he likes. It is not permitted to coerce him into a specific transaction, unless there is a legal necessity for doing so.[104]

4.3.1 Types of *Mandūb*

The recommended act (*mandūb*) sometimes has some additional legal emphasis behind it for persistent or continued performance. On this criterion, it has been divided into three broad types:

Mandūb
(Recommended Act)
- *Sunnah Mu'akkadah*
- *Sunnah Ghayr Mu'akkadah*
- *Sunnat Zawā'id*

4.3.1.1 *Sunnah mu'akkadah* (the emphatic recommended act)

Sunnah mu'akkadah is a recommended act that was persistently performed by the Prophet (pbuh). He did not give up its persistent performance, except on some occasions. This again is of two types:

- ***Sunnah mu'akkadah* that complements and completes a *wājib*,** like *adhān* and congregational prayers. The rule for this category is that the person who gives up such acts is liable to some blame, though this does not reach the level of punishment. The person who performs them is entitled to reward in the hereafter. If an individual gives up such

104. Although writers use this example as an evidence to show that writing down of an agreement is not necessary and is merely recommended, the verse as translated appears to be talking about the agreement itself and not the act of writing down of the agreement. This would be the view if the word *al-kitāb* is translated as a "deed in writing". If the word *al-kitāb* is translated as "the agreement of *mukātabah*", the example is in order.

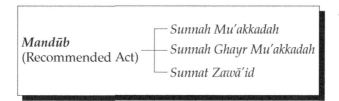

acts totally, he is liable to lose his *'adālah* (moral probity), which may in turn result in the rejection of his testimony. If a township collectively decides to give up these recommended acts, it exposes itself to legal and military action. The reason is that these acts are part of the fundamental practice (*sha'ā'ir*) of Islam. (ما لا يتم الواجب الّا به فهو واجب —An act essential for completing an obligatory act becomes an obligation in itself).

- ***Sunnah mu'akkadah* that does not complement or complete a *wājib*,** though it is generally supportive of it, like praying two *rak'as* before the *fajr* prayer, or after *ẓuhr*, *maghrib* and *'ishā'*. There is reward for the performance of such an act and blame for giving it up, however, the person giving it up totally does not lose his *'adālah*. If a township gives them up, it does not become liable for civil or military action, because these acts are not considered part of the *sha'ā'ir* of Islam.

4.3.1.2 *Sunnah ghayr mu'akkadah* (non-emphatic recommended act)—*nafl, mustaḥabb*

The recommended act that is not emphatic is called *sunnah ghayr mu'akkadah* or *nafl* or *mustaḥabb*. It is an act that was not performed persistently by the Prophet (pbuh), that is, he performed it several times and did not do so at other times. Examples of this type are the four *rak'ah*s before *'aṣr* and *'ishā'* and giving *ṣadaqah* to the poor. The rule for this type of act is that one who performs it is entitled to *thawāb*, but one who does not, is not subject to blame.

4.3.1.3 *Sunnat zawā'id*

This term is used by some jurists for the acts of the Prophet (pbuh) pertaining to ordinary daily tasks as a human being, like his dress, food and drink, as well as his dealings with his family members.[105] The rule for such acts is that one who adopts them

105. Ṣadr al-Sharī'ah, *al-Tawḍīḥ*, vol. 2, 682.

seeking to follow the Prophet's example, out of love for him, is to be rewarded. The person who does not adopt them is not blameworthy in any way.

4.4 The Meaning of *Ḥarām* (Prohibited Act) and its Different Types

The prohibited act (*ḥarām*) is one whose omission is required by the Lawgiver in binding and certain terms. According to the majority of the jurists (*jumhūr*), it does not matter whether the evidence informing us of this omission is definitive or probable. According to the Ḥanafīs, however, the act that is *ḥarām* is based upon a definitive evidence.[106] The prohibited act that is based on a probable evidence expressed in binding terms, falls within the category of the abominable act that is closer to prohibition (*makrūh karāhat al-taḥrīm*). The rule for the prohibited act in their view is the imputation of *kufr* for the person who denies its legal validity. The rule according to the majority is also the same, that is, the imputation of *kufr* is applicable when the prohibition arises from a definitive evidence.

The binding and certain terms in which the demand is expressed are understood either from the syntax of the text alone or from other supporting evidence. Some examples of the prohibited act (*ḥarām*) are: 1) Eating of carrion; 2) infanticide; 3) marriage with mothers or step mothers; 4) false evidence; 5) the misappropriation of another's wealth; 6) murder and 7) unlawful sexual intercourse. The texts on which these are based are:

(١) حرّمت عليكم الميتة

Forbidden to you (for food) is dead meat. [Qur'ān 5 : 3]

(٢) ولا تقتلوا أولادكم من إملاق

Do not kill your children on plea of want. [Qur'ān 6 : 151]

106. That is, with respect to its transmission.

(٣) حرّمت عليكم أمّهاتكم

Prohibited to you (for marriage) are your mothers. [Qur'ān 4 : 23]

(٤) لا تنكحوا ما نكح آباؤكم من النساء

And marry not women whom your fathers married. [Qur'ān 4 : 22]

(٥) واجتنبوا قول الزور

And shun the word that is false (perjury). [Qur'ān 22 : 30]

(٦) ولا تأكلوا أموالكم بينكم بالباطل

And do not eat up your property among yourselves for vanities. [Qur'ān 2 : 188]

(٧) من يقتل مؤمنا متعمّدا فجزاؤه جهنم خالدا فيها

If a man kills a believer intentionally, his recompense is Hell, to abide therein (for ever). [Qur'ān 4 : 93]

(٨) لا تقربوا الزنا إنّه كان فاحشة وساء سبيلا

Nor come nigh to unlawful sexual intercourse, for it is a shameful deed. [Qur'ān 17 : 32]

The communication in all the above texts is expressed in binding terms, and this is obvious either from the word prohibition or from the negation of permissibility or from the demand for the avoidance of the act.

4.4.1 The types of *ḥarām*

The prohibited act is divided into two types: prohibited for itself and prohibited due to an external factor.[107]

107. Ṣadr al-Sharī'ah, *al-Tawḍīḥ,* vol. 2, 683.

Ḥarām (Prohibited Act)
- *Ḥarām li-dhātihi* (prohibited for itself)
- *Ḥarām li-ghayrihi* (prohibited for an external factor)

4.4.1.1 *Ḥarām li-dhātihi* (prohibited for itself)

The act that is prohibited for itself is one that was declared prohibited for itself *ab initio* and right from the start, and not for an external category. Examples of this type are: unlawful sexual intercourse, theft, and selling of carrion.

The rule for this category is that it is not permissible *ab initio* and if the subject commits such an act, there will be no beneficial legal effects or the gains desired. Thus, unlawful sexual intercourse cannot lead to the establishing of paternity or claims of inheritance,[108] while theft cannot be a reason for the claim of ownership, nor can the selling of carrion lead to ownership.

4.4.1.2 *Ḥarām li-ghayrihi* (prohibited for an external factor)

The act that is prohibited due to an external factor was not prohibited initially, and was legal in itself, but an external factor intervened and led to its prohibition, like fasting on *'Īd* day. Fasting is legal otherwise, but the Lawgiver prohibited it on the day of *'Īd*, because the subjects that day are the guests of Allāh, and fasting becomes a hurdle for this hospitality. Another example is the sale that involves *ribā*. Sale is legal in itself, but a condition stipulated in it that requires the charging and giving of interest leads to its prohibition.

The rule for this type is that as the act is valid in itself, if it is possible to remove the obstructing factor the act may be declared valid. Thus, according to the Ḥanafīs, if the condition of *ribā* is

108. Some people argue that the unlawful act here has been committed by the parents, while the denial of benefits is for the illegitimate offspring, who is innocent.

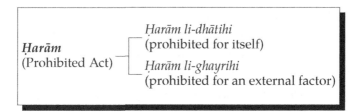

removed from the *ribā* based sale, the sale may be declared valid. It is for this reason that they place this type of contract in the category of *fāsid* (vitiated; unenforceable) and not *bāṭil* (void).

4.4.1.3 Distinction between the two types

There are two basic distinctions between acts that are prohibited for themselves and those that are prohibited due to an external factor:

1. When an act prohibited for itself becomes the subject-matter of a contract, the contract is void, that is, it will have no legal effects. As compared to this, when the act prohibited for an external factor becomes the subject of a contract, it is not void, but is valid or is vitiated with partial or suspended legal effects, according to the varying opinions of jurists on this. Thus, if the sale pertains to carrion or to wine, the contract is void having no legal effects. Likewise, a contract of marriage within the prohibited degree is void and has no legal effects. As for the contract of *ribā* mentioned above, it is vitiated.

   The reader will come across many examples that are said to fall in the category prohibited for an external factor. However, in most examples one finds that they fall in this category according to the majority of the jurists; the Ḥanafīs would place them in the category of *makrūh* that is closer to prohibition. Thus, some care is to be exercised in studying the examples.

2. The act prohibited for itself cannot be permitted, except in the case of duress (*iḍṭirār*). For example, wine is prohibited for itself and cannot be permitted, unless the person affected is dying of thirst and there is nothing else available. The reason is that preservation of life is a vital interest secured by the *sharī'ah*. As compared to this, an act prohibited for an external factor may be permitted in case of dire need to the extent of the need. Thus, the covering of private body parts is prohibited not for itself, but for what it leads to. It is,

therefore, permitted to uncover these parts in case of need, as when it is necessary for medical treatment.

4.5 The Meaning of *Makrūh* (Disapproved Act) and its Different Types

The *makrūh* (disapproved act) is a single category according to the majority of the jurists, but is divided by the Ḥanafīs into two types: *makrūh taḥrīman* and *makrūh tanzīhan.*[109] The first is what has been called reprehensible as it is closer to the category of *ḥarām.* This type of act is the opposite of *wājib,* according to the Ḥanafīs. It is an act whose omission has been demanded by the Lawgiver in certain terms through a probable evidence, like making a proposal for marriage where the proposal of another is awaiting response or even making an offer for sale where the offer of another is pending. Each of these has been established through a *khabar wāḥid.* The *ḥukm* or rule for this type of *makrūh* is punishment for the person denying it, though he is not imputed with *kufr.*

The simple *makrūh* (disapproved) act is one whose omission is demanded by the Lawgiver in non-binding terms whatever the type of evidence from which it arises. It is one for which omission is better than commission. For example, a verse of the Qur'ān proscribes sale at the time of the Friday congregational prayer, and asks the believers to avoid it at that time. This, however, may be interpreted as *makrūh* rather than prohibited; and even if it is interpreted as prohibited due to an external factor, the result is the same.

The above division of *makrūh* into two types is based on the Ḥanafī opinion. The majority of the jurists place *makrūh taḥrīman* into the category of *ḥarām* insofar as it is a demand for omission expressed in binding terms.

Al-Shāṭibī, the Mālikī jurist, explains that something that is considered disapproved in an individual case may be deemed prohibited as a whole. This means that a person should not make a habit of indulging in disapproved acts.

109. Ṣadr al-Sharī'ah, *al-Tawḍīḥ,* vol. 2, 685.

4.6 The Meaning of *Mubāḥ* (Permitted Act) and its Different Types

The *mubāḥ* or permissible act is one in which the Lawgiver has granted a choice of commission or omission, without blame or praise for omission or commission. It is also called *ḥalāl.*

The *mubāḥ* that is mentioned in the texts is usually expressed in words like "There is no harm for you...," or "It is no sin for you" and so on. The *mubāḥ* is also understood through the principle of *istiṣḥāb,* which states that anything that is not expressly prohibited or considered abominable by the *sharī'ah* is permissible. According to the above rule, all contracts and transactions are permissible, unless there is an evidence indicating that they are not. This principle emphasises the fact that underlying rule for all things is permissibility. It will be explained, however, in detail in the sources for the *mujtahid.*

There is an interesting discussion in *uṣūl al-fiqh* about the *ḥukm* of *mubāḥ.* It is generally maintained by the jurists that once an act is established as *mubāḥ,* the Lawgiver cannot be assumed to have an intention of omission or commission related to it, and the performance or non-performance cannot be deemed an act of worship or required obedience.

On the other hand, there are certain groups, like a section of the Ṣūfīs, who are attributed with the statement that the omission of *mubāḥ* is a required act. They rely for this on certain verses and texts of the traditions in which the temporal world and its pleasures have been looked down upon by the Lawgiver. They also argue that indulging in the permitted pleasures of this world leads to the commission of the disapproved and the forbidden. The jurists, however, reject such opinions and maintain that omission of the *mubāḥ* is not a required act.

There have been other jurists who insist that as the commission of a *mubāḥ* act amounts to the non-performance of a prohibited act, the commission of *mubāḥ* becomes *wājib.* Al-Shāṭibī, thinking in different terms, has explained in great detail how the *mubāḥ* may be permitted for individual cases, but taken as a whole may be considered obligatory or permitted. For example, eating and drinking is permitted and the subject has a choice in eating or not eating, but overeating may destroy his health and not eating at all may kill him too; a balance, therefore, has to be maintained. He calls such an act *wājib bi al-kullī* and *mubāḥ bi al-juz'ī.* This means that at the level of a specific evidence it is permitted, but when it attacks a purpose of the law it becomes obligatory or prohibited, as the case may be.

We may raise the question here as to whether the *mubāḥ* is permitted by itself or whether it becomes permitted with the approval of the *sharī'ah*? For example, whether eating and drinking was permitted anyway or only when the texts said "eat and drink". This question is directly concerned with the principle of *istiṣḥāb.* The answer will, therefore, be provided there (see p. 295 below).

4.7 The *Ḥukm Waḍ'ī* or the Declaratory Rule

The declaratory rule or the *ḥukm waḍ'ī* does not create an obligation; it is a rule that facilitates the operation of the obligation-creating rule or it explains the relationship between different obligation-creating rules. The major classifications are:

1. *sabab, sharṭ* and *māni'*;
2. *ṣiḥḥaḥ, fasād* and *buṭlān*; and
3. *'azīmah* and *rukhṣah.*

4.7.1 *Sabab, sharṭ* and *māni'*

The secondary or declaratory rules primarily include the causes of, conditions for, and obstacles to the *ḥukm.* These may be described very briefly.[110]

110. For the details see Ṣadr al-Sharī'ah, *al-Tawḍīḥ,* vol. 2, 705–20. For an even more detailed explanation see al-Sarakhsī, *Kitāb al-Uṣūl,* vol. 2, 301 passim.

4.7.1.1 *Sabab* (Cause).

Sabab is the cause on the basis of which a primary rule or *ḥukm taklīfī* is invoked or is established. The literal meaning of *sabab* is the means to a thing. In its technical meaning it is what the Lawgiver has determined to be the identifier of a legal rule so that its existence means the presence of the rule, while its absence means the absence of the rule.[111] Thus, it is each entity or incident whose existence the Lawgiver has determined to be the prerequisite for the existence of the *ḥukm,* and its absence an indication of the absence of the *ḥukm.* Unlawful sexual intercourse, for example, is a cause for the obligation of implementing *ḥadd,* while *safah* and insanity are the causes for interdiction, but when these causes are missing there is no obligation to impose *ḥadd* or interdiction.

The cause (*sabab*) is divided with respect to the act of the subject into two types. The first is not dependent on the act of the subject, nor is it within his power to bring it about. Yet, when such a cause is found the *ḥukm* exists, like the setting of the sun as a cause for the obligation of the evening prayer, and the beginning of the month of Ramaḍān as a cause for the obligation of fasting, and like *safah* for the obligation of interdiction.

The second type is an act of the subject and is within his power to bring about, like journey for the permissibility of not fasting, or murder (*qatl 'amd*) for the obligation of *qiṣāṣ,* or the formation of contracts as a cause for enforcing their performance. Such an act may itself be the subject of a *taklīfī* rule, that is, it would be required or prohibited or recommended, and it may fall under the category of declaratory rules.[112] Thus, marriage is a cause for the permissibility of marital relations, but it becomes obligatory when there is fear of falling prey to unlawful sexual intercourse.

The distinction between a *sabab,* that is, a *sabab* alone and a *sabab* that amounts to an *'illah* for a *ḥukm* is important and must be understood. The simplest way to understand this distinction is to say that when a cause can be rationally perceived to be the reason

111. See al-Ghazālī, *al-Mustaṣfā,* vol. 1, 93-94.
112. See al-Shāṭibī, *al-Muwāfaqāt,* vol. 1, 188.

for the existence of the *ḥukm* it is an *'illah,* but when the cause is obscure for human reason and it is not possible to understand why the cause has been associated with a *ḥukm,* the cause is simply a cause and not an *'illah.* For example, human reason can comprehend why journey has been determined to be the cause for the permissibility of not fasting, but it may not understand why the month of Ramaḍān has been fixed for fasting.[113] Another way of looking at it would be to say that the *'illah* is a *sabab* that can be rationalised.

4.7.1.2 *Sharṭ* (Condition).

The Lawgiver may declare that a set of facts must exist or an act must take place before the cause can take effect and invoke the related *ḥukm.*[114] The existence of such a set of facts is called a *sharṭ* or condition for the *ḥukm.* A *sharṭ* or condition then is a sign or an indication on which the existence of another thing depends, but the existence of this sign does not necessarily mean the existence of that thing; however, its absence does mean the non-existence of the other thing. By existence and non-existence of the *ḥukm* here is meant something of which the *sharī'ah* will take cognisance and to which it will also assign legal effects.

In its technical sense, however, it implies a necessary condition for a *ḥukm.* Ablution is a condition for prayer and the presence of witnesses a condition for the marriage contract. The existence of witnesses, however, does not necessarily mean that a marriage has taken place, yet without witnesses a marriage would not be valid.

The meaning of *sharṭ* is understood clearly by distinguishing its meaning from those of other attributes. There are similarities and differences between a *sharṭ* and a *rukn.* The similarity is that the legal existence of a thing depends on both; if either is missing the act is not valid or the *ḥukm* does not exist. The difference between the two is that a *rukn* (element) is always part of the act, while a *sharṭ* is external to it. For example, bowing is a *rukn*

113. For further details see al-Sarakhsī, *Kitāb al-Uṣūl,* vol. 2, 301.
114. Ibid., vol. 2, 320.

of prayer and is a part of it, while ablution is a condition and is external to prayer.

There are similar distinctions between *sabab* and *sharṭ*. The similarity is that both are external to the act and on both depends the existence of the *ḥukm*. The difference is that the existence of the cause necessarily leads to the existence of the *ḥukm*, but the existence of a *sharṭ* does not necessarily mean the existence of the *ḥukm*, as in the case of witnesses to a marriage contract.

A *sharṭ* is divided into two types by the jurists: *sharṭ shar'ī* and *sharṭ ja'alī*. These are conditions imposed by the Lawgiver and conditions imposed by the subjects, as in contracts that accept them.

4.7.1.3 *Māni'* (Obstacle).

A condition or set of facts may exist that prevent the *ḥukm* from being applied even if the cause is found and the condition is met. The obstacle or *māni'* is a factor whose existence indicates the negation of a *ḥukm* or its *sabab*. This implies that an obstacle is of two types. The first type negates the *ḥukm* or prevents it from coming into operation, like the negation of the *ḥukm* of retaliation when the accused is the father of the victim. The other type is the obstacle that affects the cause and prevents it from coming into being. The majority of the obstacles are of this type. Those who will study Islamic criminal law should understand that the first kind of *māni'* constitutes the doctrines of criminal law also called general defences. The principle is the same as in Western criminal law where the definition of the crime is not constituted unless the doctrines are read in with them, that is, the general defences are implied in the definition. We shall be discussing some of these general defences under the heading of legal capacity of the *mukallaf* (subject).

4.7.2 *Ṣiḥḥah, fasād* and *buṭlān* (validity, vititation and nullity)

An act that is obligatory, recommended, or permissible may be required to be performed in a certain manner by the Lawgiver.[115] When the act is performed properly it is deemed as valid (*ṣaḥīḥ*) otherwise it is null and void (*bāṭil*). Here too the Ḥanafites add another category called irregular or vitiated (*fāsid*). Such an act can become valid if the cause of the irregularity is removed, otherwise it stays suspended. It may, however, have some legal effects. An example is a contract involving *ribā*. Under Ḥanafī law such a contract is considered vitiated (*fāsid*). This means that it can become a valid contract if the offending condition is removed. Such a contract is to be distinguished from the voidable contract under law. A voidable contract is dependent upon the option of the parties, while in a *fāsid* contract the offending condition must be removed; the parties have no option in this.

4.7.3 *'Azīmah* and *rukhṣah* (initial rules and exemptions)

The Lawgiver may indicate that one *ḥukm* is to be considered as an obligation imposed initially as a general rule (*'azīmah*).[116] This may be followed by another rule that is an exemption (*rukhṣah*) from the general rule. Drinking of wine is prohibited as a general rule. In cases of duress (*iḍṭirār*), however, one is allowed to consume it, if it saves one from dying of thirst. This is a *rukhṣah*. According to some jurists, the entire law may be classified into general rules and related exemptions. This division has important methodological consequences and helps the jurist achieve analytical consistency. One important significance is that analogy (*qiyās*) cannot proceed from an exemption, it must be based on a general rule. Thus, if the contract of *salam* is an exemption from the rules of *ribā*, it cannot be used as a basis for constructing further analogies to obtain exemptions.

115. Ṣadr al-Sharī'ah, *al-Tawḍīḥ*, vol. 1, 30.
116. Ibid., vol. 2, 686.

This provision, considered with other strict conditions, further narrows down the operation of *qiyās*.

4.8 The Purpose of the Classification

The primary purpose for Muslim jurists in classifying the *ḥukm shar'ī* into obligation-creating rules and into declaratory or rules was to show that by the term law we mean not merely the command of the Lawgiver, but also categories like *mubāḥ* and the declaratory communications that include secondary rules. This gives us a meaning that is much wider than the simple literal meaning of the word "command." John Austin, in his imperative theory of law, had defined law as a "command" for which he has been taken to task by legal philosophers like H.L.A. Hart, because it cannot explain the power-conferring rules that are not really commands. Such rules under the Islamic legal system fall within the category of *mubāḥ*. It is also for this reason that the *ḥukm shar'ī* cannot be translated as a "command."

In addition to this, the classification helps us understand how the *taklīfī* and *waḍ'ī* rules interact to create obligations and determine the operation of law. The declaratory rules facilitate, so to say, the application of the obligation-creating or *taklīfī* rules.

Review Questions

1. Why is an act considered *wājib* (obligatory)?

2. What is the *ḥukm* for the *wājib*? Compare the position taken by the ḥanafīs with that of the majority schools.

3. Define *wājib muqayyad* or *wājib* limited by time and then describe its various divisions. What practical advantage does such a classification have?

4. Is *ḥajj* a *wājib muṭlaq* or *muqayyad*? Give reasons for your answer.

5. Whaere would you place *nafaqah* (maintenance) for wife and children: *muḥaddad* or *ghayr muḥaddad*?

6. How does an act become *mandūb*? Explain through examples.

7. Link the *mandūb* with different types of *Sunnah*. Elaborate through examples.

8. Elaborate the meaning of the term *ḥarām* and then explain its different types making distinctions between them.

9. How do the Ḥanafīs differ with the majority schools with respect to the *makrūh* category of rules?

10. How do the jurists differ with the sufis with respect to the *mubāḥ*?

11. Why does al-Shāṭibī maintain that the *mubāḥ* sometimes becomes a *wājib*?

12. Explain the meaning of *sabab* (cause) and show how it differs from the *'illah*.

13. How does the *sharṭ* differ from *rukn*?

14. Elaborate the term *māni'* through examples from the criminal law.

5 The Lawgiver (*Ḥākim*)

5.1 Allah is the True Source of all Laws

The source of all laws in Islam is Allah and Allah alone. The verse of the Qur'ān, "The *ḥukm* belongs to Allah alone," [Qur'ān 6:57] is often cited in support of this. This basic rule determines the character of Islamic law and gives direction to all interpretation and *ijtihād*. The rule says that it is Allah's laws alone that are acceptable to the Muslim. No temporal authority can command a Muslim's obedience, unless the authority is based on the commands of Allah. This is the essence of social contract[117] within a Muslim community.

Each Muslim is a Muslim not only because he believes in

117. By social contract we mean the basis upon which Muslims, acting upon the commands of Allah, have agreed to cooperate with each other and to live together in the form of an organized Muslim society. It exists in the form of a covenant (*ahd*) and is directly related to Man's personality *dhimmah*.

the existence of one God and the truth of the mission of His Messenger, but also because the laws are prescribed by the Wise and Just Lord. It is these laws that grant him security from oppression and ensure justice and fair play in all dealings. A Muslim surrenders his will to Islam so that his life may be regulated in accordance with the *ḥukm* of Allah.

What, then, do we mean when we say that Allah is the True and Ultimate Sovereign? What is the general nature of the laws laid down by Allah? In other words, can we see a broad intention of the Lawgiver when we look at all the laws? We, therefore, ask the question: Are these laws laid down in the interest of Man? Thus, if we make a law that serves the interest of humanity (say based upon utilitarian principles), can this law be assumed to be valid and in accordance with the dictates of the *sharī'ah*?

Further, an extension of the above inquiry pertains to the independent use of reason. If the assumption is that Allah's laws are always in conformity with human reason, then, can we also assume that all laws that appear reasonable to humans must be in conformity with the *sharī'ah*?

There are a number of other questions that pertain to the methodology to be adopted to ensure that laws conform with the injunctions of the Qur'ān and the *Sunnah*, but these require exhaustive analysis and will not be taken up in this chapter.

5.2 The Fundamental Norm of the Legal System

The fact that ultimately Allah alone is the source of all laws indicates to us the fundamental rule or norm of the Islamic legal system.[118] The other rules of the legal system are all referred to,

118. The idea of the fundamental norm or *grundnorm* was introduced into legal philosophy by Hans Kelsen, the German legal philosopher. He tried to present a concept of law that was different from the one presented by John Austin. Austin had stated that law is the command of the sovereign enforced under threat of sanctions. In other words, a valid law is a command of the sovereign. Kelsen,

or checked against, this norm for their validity. The fundamental norm is repeated several times each day by every Muslim. It is contained in the declaration: "There is no god, but Allah, and Muḥammad is the Messenger of Allah." As the Muslim is ready to accept the laws of Allah, he will accept only those laws that were revealed through His Messenger. The revelation granted to the Messenger is in the form of the Qur'ān. Once this is accepted, we find that the Qur'ān itself declares the *Sunnah* of the Messenger of Allah to be a source of laws. Some say that the *Sunnah* is itself a form of revelation, that is, revelation in meaning alone as compared to the Qur'ān, which is revelation in both word and meaning. Starting from the other end, the Muslim may say:

- I am ready to obey such and such law as it has been communicated to me by a qualified jurist.
- I follow the opinion of the jurist as it is in conformity with the sources of Islamic law.
- I obey a law based on the sources as they are the sources revealed to Muḥammad. I obey Muḥammad for he is the Messenger of Allah, and
- I believe in Allah.

In this way the validity of all laws is traced to Allah. This basic norm or rule does two things. First, it provides a standard or criterion with which we can judge whether or not a law is valid

on the other hand, stated that each law in a state, in order to be valid, must conform with a basic rule or norm, and in a modern state, he said, such a a norm is provided by the constitution. Thus, the fundamental norm is that each law must conform with the constitution in order to be valid. Kelsen's theory was employed in Pakistan in cases related to the imposition of martial law as well as other matters related to the Objectives Resolution. The idea of the *grundnorm* has, therefore, figured prominently in case law. The Objectives Resolution is now part of the Constitution of Pakistan as article 2A. The impact of this article is that all laws must conform with the injunctions of the Qur'ān and the *Sunnah.*

law. Second, it creates for each Muslim an obligation or duty to obey the law. A subject of an Islamic state does not have to look for some external rule of morality or justice for his duty to obey the law.

5.3 The Law and the Interest of Man

Has the Lawgiver laid down laws in the interest (*maṣlaḥah*) of Man? If this is true, can the interest of Man be an independent source of laws? Is Man free to determine his own interest, or is it predetermined by the Lawgiver? These questions have always been at the forefront of Islamic legal theory. The answers form the basis of the principle of *istiṣlāḥ* that seeks to secure the interests (*maṣāliḥ*) preserved and protected by the Islamic legal system. This issue is extremely important for *ijtihād* and the framing of new laws in the present times. The reason is that in the absence of a direct and express evidence in the Qur'ān and the *Sunnah*, laws are to be framed in the light of the interest (*maṣlaḥah*) of Man as determined by the Lawgiver.

The majority of the Muslim jurists agreed that the Lawgiver lays down laws in the interest of Man. There have been some voices against it too, notable among them being the objections of the illustrious Imām al-Rāzī (d. 606 A.H./1210 C.E.). He gave extremely powerful arguments against this idea.[119] Al-Rāzī did concede though that whenever we consider the laws and the interests of Man, we find them lying side by side, or existing together, yet we cannot establish a causal relationship between them, that is, the laws are laid down because they serve the interest of Man. The problem may be explained in a simple way.

5.3.1 Is Man the sole purpose of creation?

Take the case of a factory producing something. The sole purpose of the existence of this factory is the creation of a product. Every directive that is issued to the workers is intended to enhance the

119. See al-Rāzī, *al-Maḥṣūl fī 'Ilm Uṣūl al-Fiqh,* vol. 5, 168–180.

quality of this product or to create it on time, or to create a product that is more useful. The factory does not exist for the workers, but for the creation of that product. The effective production of goods, however, requires that the interest and welfare of the workers be kept in view, for that will lead to a better product. If the worker performs well he is rewarded or promoted, because he is in harmony with the process leading to the ultimate product. If he does not perform well, he will not be rewarded and may also be penalised for a breach of discipline. The factory does have laws to regulate the activity of the workers. These laws are laid down primarily to ensure an effective production of goods, though the laws may indirectly serve the interest of the worker.

Is Man the final product of this universe created by Allah, or is the purpose of this universe something larger, larger than Man?

أ أنتم أشدّ خلقا أم السّمآء بنٰها

> What! Are ye the more difficult to create or the heaven (above); (Allah) hath constructed it. [Qur'ān 79 : 27]

If Man is the sole purpose, then, all laws must have been made to serve his interest. On the other hand, if the purpose of the creation of the universe is something other than Man as may be understood from the above verse, then, is Man in the position of the worker, a servant of Allah (*'abd Allah*), who is to be rewarded if he performs well and punished if he misbehaves? The laws in this case would appear to be lying side by side with the interest of Man, as al-Rāzī maintains, because they are actually serving some larger purpose. Again, if Man is the sole purpose of the universe, the laws would be laid down to serve his interest alone. Thus, there would be a causal relationship between the laws and the interest of Man. In such a case, would he be called the vicegerent of Allah (*khalīfat Allah*)? Some jurists have conceded that it is proper to assign this title to Man, for the Qur'ān mentions it too, while others consider it as heresy and maintain that the reference in the Qur'ān is to some previous creation to which Man is a successor (*khalīfah*).[120] The

120. See e.g., Qamaruddin Khan *The Political Thought of Ibn Taymiyyah* (Islamabad, 1973) 78 for a discussion of Ibn Taymiyyah's views on

latter jurists prefer to use the title "vicegerent of the Messenger" or *khalīfat al-Rasūl*. The answers to these questions are known to Allah alone. That is where the jurists leave the discussion, and we should do the same.

5.3.2 Can we employ *maṣlaḥah* (interest) for new laws?

Whichever approach we take on this issue it does not alter the decision on the interest of Man. There is some relationship between the interest of Man and the *ḥukm* of Allah. It does not matter if this is a causal relationship. The majority of the jurists, therefore, agree that *maṣlaḥah* or the interest of Man may be employed for the derivation of new laws. This in no case means that the Muslims are free to make laws in accordance with whatever they deem to be their interest. The interest of Man is determined by the Lawgiver Himself, and there is a determined methodology for identifying this. The jurists have taken great pains to lay down this methodology in a way that the laws derived through it may still be termed as the *aḥkām* of Allah. It would not be an exaggeration to say that the key to the future development of Islamic law is through the doctrine of *maṣlaḥah*,[121] as will be shown later in this book.

5.4 Are the *Sharī'ah* and Natural Law Compatible?

Can the *aḥkām* (legal rules) be discovered by human reason independent of the sources of Islamic law? This is a question that pertains to natural law or to the use of reason independent of the *sharī'ah*. There have been heated debates among the early Muslim jurists over this issue, though the terminology used by them was

---

the subject.

121. The intention behind the use of the word "doctrine" is to distinguish it from the narrower principle of *maṣlaḥah*, which is a form of extended analogy.

different. The terms they used were *ḥasan* (good) and *qabīḥ* (bad or evil).[122]

Natural law has a very long history beginning in ancient thought and continuing right up to our times. The classical theory of natural law, as Hart puts it, is that "there are certain principles of human conduct, awaiting discovery by human reason, with which man-made law must conform if it is to be valid."[123] It should be made clear that natural law has not always been associated with God, and even when it has been its basic assumptions have not been dependent upon a belief in God. Our discussion, however, pertains to a much restricted version of natural law in which belief in Allah as the Lawgiver and Master of the Universe is essential. Even in the West, the real developments in natural law came through the writings of Thomas Aquinas. Some of his views, it is acknowledged in the West, were based on the works of Ibn Sīnā and the Spanish jurist-philosopher Ibn Rushd (Averröes), especially his commentaries on Aristotle. To describe what we mean by natural law in this context, let us borrow a definition provided by John Austin. He says:

> Of the Divine laws, or the laws of God, some are *revealed* or promulgated, and others are *unrevealed*. Such of the laws of God as are unrevealed are not unfrequently denoted by following names or phrases: 'the law of nature;' 'natural law;' 'the law manifested to man by the light of nature or reason.'
>
> ...Paley and other divines have proved beyond a doubt, that it was not the purpose of Revelation to disclose the *whole* of those duties. Some we could not know, without the help of Revelation; and these the revealed law has stated distinctly and precisely. The rest we may know, if we will, by the light of nature or reason; and these the revealed law supposes or assumes. It passes them over in silence, or with a brief and incidental notice.[124]

Austin also says that these "unrevealed" laws are the only laws which God makes for that portion of mankind who are excluded from the light of revelation.[125] We may qualify Austin's

122. Ṣadr al-Sharī'ah, *al-Tawḍīḥ*, vol. 1, 32–33.
123. H.L.A. Hart, *The Concept of Law* (Oxford, 1961), 182.
124. John Austin, *Lectures on Jurisprudence* (London, 1911) vol 1, 104. (Emphasis in the original).
125. Austin, *Lectures*, vol. 1, 104.

description of natural law by saying that these are laws that are to be discovered by mankind through reason prior to revelation, that is, before the arrival of the light of revelation amidst a particular community. Once revelation has come, such laws may only be discovered in the light of revelation, because revelation does not pass them over in silence; it indicates them through general principles. We are now ready to look briefly at some of the discussions of Muslim jurists.

There was complete agreement among Muslim jurists about the meaning of the words of the Exalted, "The *ḥukm* belongs to Allah alone." [Qur'ān 6 : 57] The Mu'tazilah agreed with the majority that the source of all laws is Allah, but they disagreed with them about the identification and discovery of these laws prior to revelation. They maintained that reason can discover the laws of Allah, that is, the *shar'ī aḥkām*, in the absence of revelation. The Mu'tazilah were not alone in holding these views and there were other sects who held the same or similar views, especially the Māturīdīs, some of whom were Ḥanafīs, though their views were slightly different. Ṣadr al-Sharī'ah has the following to say:

> The term *shar'iyyah* (legal according to Islamic law) includes all that would not have been known had the communication from the Law not been issued. This is irrespective of whether this communication pertained directly to a particular *ḥukm* or was issued in a manner that the *ḥukm* was dependent upon it, as in the issues based on analogical deduction. The rules for these too would be legal for had the communication not been issued for the original case, the rule extended for analogy would not have been known either. This stipulation (of the term *shar'iyyah*), therefore, includes the goodness (*ḥusn*) and badness (*qubḥ*) of all acts according to those who deny that this can be discovered through reason.
>
> Know that, in our view (Ḥanafī), and that of the majority of the Mu'tazilah, the goodness of some acts as well as their badness can be discovered through reason, but in certain acts they cannot be discovered and are dependent upon the communication from the Lawgiver. The first type of acts are not part of *fiqh;* they belong to the domain of ethics. The second type are part of *fiqh* and the definition of *fiqh* remains

> sound, comprehensive and precise (with the stipulation of the term *shar'iyyah*) according to this view.
>
> According to al-Ash'arī and his followers, on the other hand, the goodness and badness of every act is known through the *sharī'ah* (even those of purely moral acts) and all these acts would, therefore, be part of *fiqh* (according to the definition under discussion).[126]

The Ash'arites held the view that the laws of Allah can be discovered through revelation alone and there is no way in which reason can discover these laws. The basis of this disagreement is the debate over *ḥusn* and *qubḥ* or good and evil or right and wrong.

The basic question was whether an act recognised by reason as good or right in itself became binding on the subject? Was he to act upon it even in the absence of revelation or prior to it? The Ash'arites maintained that even if reason could identify such an act there was no obligation to obey it or act according to it, the sole criterion for right and wrong being revelation. An extreme view of the Mu'tazilah appears to be that the laws of Allah must conform with reason, in fact, some of them appear to have gone so far as to say that it is binding upon Allah to lay down laws that conformed with reason. This was objected to by many as it amounted to restricting the attributes of Allah.[127]

The essential point in all this is whether reason can be used as a source of law for those things on which the *sharī'ah* is silent? In other words, if something is not expressly prohibited or commanded by the Qur'ān and the *Sunnah*, can the law for such a thing be discovered through reason? The answer of the majority appears to be a clear "No!"

This, however, does not mean that reason has no part to play in the discovery of laws in Islam. The requirement is that all reason and reasoning must proceed from the principles in the Qur'ān and the *Sunnah*. The process is the same in many other legal systems and judges are required to apply the general principles of law rather than those of natural law. The fundamental position

126. Ṣadr al-Sharī'ah, *al-Tawḍīḥ*, vol. 1, 32–33.
127. See ibid., 345-47.

of Muslim jurists is that there is no such thing as natural law outside the realm of the *sharī'ah* on which we can rely as soon as we discover that a rule of law is not directly discoverable from the texts. Such a rule, they insist, needs to be discovered directly or indirectly from the principles of Islamic law, and not from some "ominous brooding in the sky."[128]

In the few issues discussed above, we have tried to examine some factors that can intrude upon the concept that the *ḥukm* belongs to Allah alone. This is a very important, interesting, and fertile area. Many conceptions of, and misconceptions about, Islamic law can be cleared up if they are discussed in the light of this concept. The conclusion we may draw is that a *hukm* or a rule of law in an Islamic state is only that injunction that has either been directly stated in the texts of the Qur'ān or the *Sunnah* or in which the intention of the Lawgiver has been ascertained and verified through methods accepted as valid in Islamic law.

Review Questions

1. What is the fundamental norm of the Islamic legal system?
2. Can the interest or welfare of Man be used independently to make laws in an Islamic state?
3. Compare Islamic law and its methodology with natural law.
4. What position do the Ḥanafīs take with respect to the role of reason in Islamic law?
5. A law that emerges from the texts is called the *ḥukm* of Allah. Can all the laws made by an Islamic state be designated as such? If not, why?
6. In your opinion, is there some conflict between revelation and reason? Elaborate with the help of examples.

128. A phrase used by Oliver Wendell Holmes for natural law.

6 The Act (*Maḥkūm Fīh*)

The *ḥukm shar'ī*, as stated earlier, has three elements, which interact with each other to give rise to liability and to the obligation to obey the law. The three elements of the *ḥukm* or a rule of law in the Islamic legal system are: the Lawgiver (*Ḥākim*); the act to which the *ḥukm* is related (*maḥkūm fīh*, also referred to as *maḥkūm bih*); and the subject who performs the act (*maḥkūm 'alayh*), that is, the person who is under an obligation to obey the law. The first element has already been discussed. In this chapter, the second element will be examined briefly.

6.1 Defining the *Maḥkūm Fīh*

The *maḥkūm fīh* is the act to which the *ḥukm* is related. The act is always the act of the subject if the communication from Allāh is related to this act by way of *taklīf*, that is, when it creates an obligation. If the communication (*khiṭāb*) is related to an act by way of declaration, that is, through a secondary rule, the act may or may not be the act of the subject.[129] For example, when there is a command to pay the *zakāt*, the obligation it creates is linked to the act of the subject. On the other hand, when there is a command to fix the minimum *niṣāb* for *zakāt*, there is an obligation to obey a secondary rule (*ḥukm waḍʿī*), which is in the nature of a declaration supporting the imposition of *zakāt*.

Muslim jurists discuss the *maḥkūm fīh* from two aspects: the conditions of *taklīf* and the nature of the act.

6.2 The Conditions for the Creation of Obligation (*Taklīf*)

The jurists mention a number of conditions for the existence of obligation (*taklīf*). A person acquires an obligation, and is placed under some kind of duty, when all these conditions are met. Two important conditions are noted here.[130]

6.2.1 The act to be performed or avoided must be known

The first condition for the creation of an obligation is that the subject must be asked to perform a known act. There is no obligation to perform an unknown or uncertain act. The reason is that the subject has to conceive the act in his mind and usually formulate an intention for its performance. There is a tradition to the effect that the performance of acts is determined by the nature of the intention (Verily the (nature) of acts is determined by intentions). The knowledge of the subject about the act here implies either actual knowledge or at least potential knowledge, that is, he should either be aware of the nature of the act or be in a position to find out about it either directly or indirectly. For knowledge about the nature of the act, the existence of the subject within the Islamic territory (*dār al-Islām*) is considered sufficient. Thus, the rule within the *dār al-Islām* is the same as

129. Ṣadr al-Sharīʿah, *al-Tawḍīḥ*, vol. 2, 715.
130. For a systematic exposition of the conditions of obligation, see al-Ghazālī, *al-Mustaṣfā*, vol. 1, 53-54.

that in law: "ignorance of law is no excuse even in a layman." Islamic law, however, makes an exception in the cases of *shubhah fī al-dalīl* (doubt in the case of conflicting evidences).[131] These are equivalent to mistake of law and mistake of fact in the positive law.

There is a disagreement among the Ḥanafīs and the Shāfi'īs about the presence of the subject within the *dār al-Islām* for acquiring a legal obligation. It rests on whether the world is one with respect to the *aḥkām* of Allah or is divided into two worlds, that is, obligation exists where the Islamic state has jurisdiction.[132]

6.2.2 The subject should be able to perform the act

The second condition is that the act should be such that it can be performed by the subject; it should not be an impossible act. The purpose of creating an obligation is to command the obedience of the subject. If the subject is not able to perform the act, the creation of the obligation becomes futile. This condition is split up into two sub-conditions: (1) there is no obligation to perform an impossible act; and (2) the performance of the act should be dependent on the will of the subject.

The former case is obvious. The latter includes such acts that involve the subject's inner emotions over which he may have little control. Thus, the tradition that requires the subject not to feel angry is not in the nature of an absolute command creating a binding obligation. It is more in the nature of a recommendation or an advice. The same would apply to a father loving some of his children more than the others, though he is not permitted to let this love interfere with his other legal obligations towards his children whom he is supposed to treat equally.

Further, the ability to perform the act may be relative to the nature of the act. What, then, about acts in which hardship is excessive? The answer depends upon the act itself. For example, hardship involved during a journey while fasting is more than

131. See Ṣadr al-Sharī'ah, *al-Tawḍīḥ*, vol. 2, 784–97.
132. See al-Dabbūsī, *Ta'sīs al-Naẓar*, 67.

normal, and here the Lawgiver has provided relief. In other cases, where the act relates to a communal or collective obligation and has to be met by some persons and not everyone, the act must be performed even with the accompanying hardship, as in the case of *jihād*. There are cases where the subject invokes the hardship himself, because of his eagerness to please the Lawgiver or for some other reason. Consider the case of the person who used to stand constantly under the sun while fasting. He was ordered to stay in the shade and to sit down to complete his fast. There were several other incidents like this during the period of the Prophet (pbuh).[133]

6.3 The Nature of the Act (*Maḥkūm Fīh*)

The structure of Islamic law, its classification, and the consequential obligations and duties, revolve around a set of rights. The classification of laws in Islam can generally be gleaned from the writings of Ḥanafī jurists.

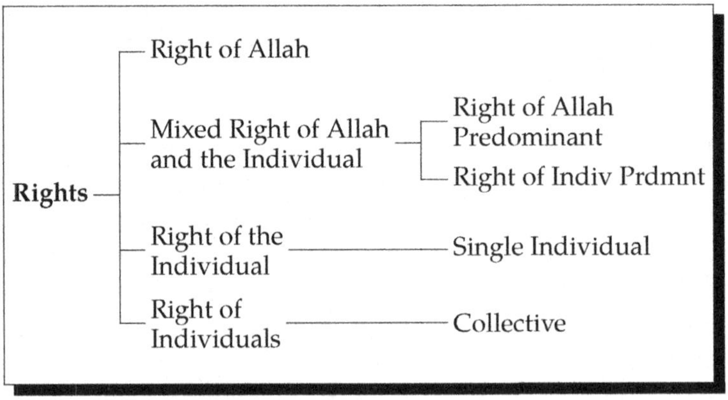

Each act affected by an obligation creating rule (*ḥukm taklīfī*) is based on a right. There are three kinds of basic rights in Islamic law: the right of Allah, the right of the individual, and the rights of the individuals collectively or the right of the state. The third

133. Al-Ghazālī, *al-Mustaṣfā*, vol. 1, 53-54.

category of rights is mentioned rarely by jurists, because it relates to the area of law with which they did not deal directly. This is the area left to the ruler (*imām*). This kind of right is sometimes designated as the right of the ruler (*ḥaqq al-sulṭān*)[134] or as the right of the state (*ḥaqq al-salṭanah*).[135] Modern writers consider the right of Allah and the right of the state or that of the *salṭanah* to be the same thing, because both are related to social interests. A thorough analysis of the Islamic legal system shows, however, that THE RIGHT OF ALLAH IS DISTINCT AND INDEPENDENT OF THE RIGHT OF THE STATE. This is of crucial significance in understanding the structure of Islamic law. In fact, when we use the term *ḥuqūq al-'ibād* in the plural we may mean the rights of individuals generally, or we may mean the collective rights of the individuals, that is, the rights of the community as a whole. In this latter sense, that is, the rights of the community, the implication should be the same as the rights of the state or *salṭanah*. Again, the rights of the state should not be merged with the rights of Allah.

Once this has been understood, we may say that sometimes the right of Allah may coexist with the right of the individual. In these cases, it is either the right of Allah that is predominant or it is the right of the individual that is at the forefront. This gives rise, in all, to the following kinds of rights:

1. The right of Allah (*ḥaqq Allah*—حقّ الله).
2. The right of the individual (*ḥaqq al-'abd*—حقّ العبد).
3. The right of Allah lying side by side with the right of the individual. These are of two types:
   (a) Those in which the right of Allah is predominant.
   (b) Those in which the right of the individual is predominant.
4. The collective rights of the individuals or of the community, also referred to as *ḥaqq al-salṭanah* or *ḥaqq al-sulṭān*.

134. See Ibn Rushd, *Bidāyat al-Mujtahid*, vol. 2, 303.
135. See al-Māwardī, *al-Aḥkām al-Sulṭāniyyah*, 237–38.

The classification of rights is of great significance in understanding the structure and operation of Islamic law. There are many practical consequences attached to these rights. It is said that where there is a right there is a corresponding duty. The Muslim jurists also deal with duties with reference to rights. The classification of laws on the basis of rights is explained below.

6.4 Classification of the *Ḥukm Taklīfī* on the Basis of Rights

The proper classification of laws, perhaps, was first provided by the Ḥanafī jurist al-Sarakhsī.[136] The majority of the jurists classified laws under the heading of *maḥkūm fīh* or the act to which the *ḥukm* is related. Under the heading of the *ḥukm sharʻī*, they give an account of the obligations arising from the operation of the act in relation to the *ḥukm*. Al-Sarakshsī combined the two. It is in this combined form that the subject is approached here.

Al-Sarakshsī says that all *aḥkām* are divided into four kinds of rights.[137] These are further subdivided as follows:

136. Al-Sarakhsī, *Kitāb al-Uṣūl*. See the last chapter in vol. 2. The classification of the rules within the category of the right of the state is left by the jurists for the *imām*, who is theoretically a full *mujtahid*. The ruler may decide how the rights of the state are to be classified in accordance with his *ijtihād* and his times. The classification of the right of state may, therefore, vary in different ages.

137. Al-Sarakhsī, *Uṣūl*, vol. 2, 332; Ṣadr al-Sharī'ah, *al-Tawḍīḥ*, vol. 2, 729 passim. We also find this classification in al-Bazdawī's book on *uṣūl al-fiqh*. See its commentary 'Abd al-'Azīz al-Bukhārī, *Kashf al-Asrār*. When we examine the two books, that is, al-Sarakhsī's book and al-Bazdawī's book, it becomes obvious that al-Bazdawī's book is a highly systematic arrangement of al-Sarakhsī's book with additions and with its own merits (Al-Bazdawī is reported to have died in 482A.H., while al-Sarakhsī is reported to have died in 483 or in 490A.H.—so the dates do not tell us much). Many of the sentences (and definitions) are the same too. We are not implying here that al-Bazdawī was relying upon al-Sarakhsī's work or vice versa. This is something that a researcher will have to unravel taking into account that al-Sarakhsī is reported to have written his book in jail, as he

1. Rules that relate to the *right of Allah* alone. These are of eight kinds:

    - *Pure Worship.* The first of these is belief in Allah or *īmān*. The second is prayer. The third is *zakāh*. The fourth is fasting (*ṣawm*). The fifth is *ḥajj*. The sixth is *jihād*. There are other acts of worship associated with the above like *'umrā* and *i'tikāf* (seclusion in a mosque for worship).
    - *Pure punishments.* These are the *ḥudūd* penalties that have been instituted as deterrents, as a pure right of Allah.
    - *Imperfect punishments.* The example of this type is prevention from inheritance in case of murder, that is, the murderer cannot inherit from the victim.

---

was imprisoned from the year 466A.H. onwards for a considerable period and was released close to the end of his life although reports vary. The researcher should also take into account that al-Bazdawī is also reported to have written a book in eleven volumes on *fiqh*, and this book was also called *al-Mabsūṭ*. He is also reported to have written commentaries on most of the books on which al-Sarakhsī has written commentaries. Nevertheless, both books on *uṣūl* are outstanding in their own ways and both jurists are well aware of many delicate points of the law, an awareness that we do not find in many other well known books. Nevertheless, we cannot ignore the fact that according to some al-Bazdawī was Imām al-Sarakhsī's student.

It is possible that both were relying on an earlier authentic work. The practice of Muslim jurist's has been to improve earlier texts and elaborate or abridge them for their own work. It is possible that both were relying, for example, on a work by al-Ḥalwānī, who was al-Sarakhsī's teacher. The book that we think may have been used, however, was al-Dabbūsī's *Taqwīm al-Adillah*. 'Abd al-'Azīz al-Bukhārī refers to it on occasions while clarifying difficult points in al-Bazdawī's book. Al-Bazdawī is reported to have written a commentary on this book. *Taqwīm al-Adillah* has now been published. An examination of the book confirms our belief that al-Bazdawī was relying mostly on the work of his teacher al-Sarakhsī, while al-Sarakhsī was relying on al-Bazdawī.

- *Those vacillating between a worship and a penalty.* These are the *kaffārāt*, that is, acts of expiation made for different reasons.
- *Worship in which there is an element of a financial liability.* The example for this is *ṣadaqat al-fiṭr*, which is a payment made before the *'Īd* following Ramaḍān.
- *Financial liability in which there is an element of worship.* This is like *'ushr*, the ten percent charge levied on the produce of land.
- *Financial liability in which there is an element of a punishment.* The example given by al-Sarakhsī is that of the *kharāj* tax.[138]
- *Those that exist independently.* These are three: those laid down initially as a rule; those that are imposed as an addition to a rule; and those that are associated with the initial rule. The examples of these are the *khums* levied on cattle, minerals, and treasure-troves.

2. Rules in which the *right of Allah and the right of the individual* lie side by side, but the *right of Allah is predominant.* These are like the the *ḥadd* of *qadhf*.[139] It is to be noted that for the Shāfi'ī jurists this is a pure right of the individual.

3. Rules in which the *right of Allah and the right of the individual* lie side by side, but it is the *right of the individual that is predominant.* For this category the example is *qiṣāṣ* or retaliation for bodily injuries or culpable homicide amounting to murder.

4. The last category is that of rules affecting the *right of the individual.* This category includes almost everything that is not included in the above categories and is beyond reckoning. The important point to consider is that al-Sarakshsī does not mention *ta'zīr* or discretionary penalties.

138. Tax on land left with the non-Muslim subjects after conquest or annexation.
139. False accusation of illicit sexual relations.

> The reason is that the discretionary penalties fall within the category of the right of the individuals, when these are considered collectively, that is, they are the right of the state. The Ḥanafī jurist al-Kāsānī clearly states that all *ta'zīr* relates to the right of the individual.[140] The Shāfi'ī jurist al-Māwardī has caused some confusion by stating that some *ta'zīr* penalties fall under the right of Allah.[141] Al-Māwardī's statement leads to analytical inconsistencies. Some later Ḥanafī jurists have also given confusing opinions on the issue. For our purposes, we adopt the more detailed Ḥanafī view.

The classification given above pertains to obligation-creating rules and shows how each type of law is linked with a right, which is either a right of Allah, or the right of the individual, or the right of both. The most important thing to remember, however, is that each act to which a *ḥukm* is related must be assigned a specific right or combination of rights. Each act, therefore, must be a right of Allāh, or the right of the individual, or a combination of the two. In the classification provided by jurists, the right of the *salṭanah* is not mentioned, because the further sub-classification of this right is left to the ruler. It should be obvious, however, that all acts related to *ta'zīr* offences, to taxes other than *zakāt*, and a host of other areas will all be affected by the right of the state, as distinct from the right of Allāh. Acts affecting the right of Allāh involve duties owed to Allāh alone, while the right of the state relates to obligations created by the state. Even the ruler or the state owes some rights to Allah. As the causes, consequences, and conditions affecting the right of state vary with the passage of time, the *fuqahā'* saw no need to issue permanent rulings for them.

140. Al-Kāsānī, *Badā'i' al-Ṣanā'i'*, vol. 7, 65. He makes this statement while explaining how *ta'zīr* is proved.

141. Al-Māwardī, *al-Aḥkām al-Sulṭāniyyah,* 236. This is not to say that his statement is incorrect. In fact, in the Shāfi'ī school to which he belongs, even the *ḥadd* of *qadhf* is a right of the individual. He includes other penalties within the *ḥudūd*, like the refusal to pay debts, and considers them the right of the individual. Ibid. 223.

6.5 Classification of Duties: Original and Substitutory

Each right has a corresponding duty. A right is secured when the subject who owes the duty brings about the required act, that is, performs the duty owed by him. Muslim jurists say that each duty has an original form (*aṣl*) and a substitutory form (*khalaf*). For example, performance of prayer is a duty that flows out of a right of Allah requiring it. The condition for its performance is ablution (*wuḍū'*) with water, which also becomes a duty as it completes a *wājib*. If the subject fails to perform this duty, because he cannot find water, the Lawgiver provides a substitute in the form of clean soil. In the case of *qiṣāṣ* (retaliation), it is the duty of the ruler or the state to subject the offender to *qiṣāṣ*. If this is not possible for some reason, the state has to ensure the recovery of compensation in money as a substitute (*badal sulḥ* or *diyah*).

Some writers, following Abdur Rahim, have called this a classification of rights: original and substitutory rights. This is possible, because where there is a right there is a duty. It is suggested, however, that it is better to focus on performance and duties, otherwise some confusion may be created. This can be seen from the example of retaliation above. *Qiṣāṣ* is claimed by the state as a mixed right of Allah and the individual (the heirs of the victim). When *qiṣāṣ* is not possible monetary compensation is substituted. Is the right of Allah replaced by the right of the individual here during substitution? The question is answered when we think in terms of duties. Thus, when we speak of original and substitutory rights, we may not be speaking of the original claimants of these rights.

The rule for substitutory duties is that they cannot be performed unless the original duty has been created and is not possible to perform.

6.6 The Importance of the Classification of Rights for Islamic Criminal Law

There are many ways in which the classification of the *maḥkm fīh* into various kinds of rights and their related acts is employed in Islamic law. The explanation of the above classification will remain incomplete if we do not indicate some area of the law with respect to the operation of different rights. We have chosen the criminal law to do so, though we can deal with the topic very briefly here.[142]

Muslim jurists classified crimes on basis of the right violated. The classification on the basis of rights is linked directly with procedure. The kind of right violated determines the procedure to be followed in courts. If the right of Allah is violated, the procedure followed is that for *ḥudūd* and *qiṣāṣ*. When the right of the individual is violated, the procedure followed is that prescribed for *ta'zīr,* which maintains the *nisāb* in evidence of two females for one male. When the right of the state is violated, the procedure followed is that of *siyāsah.*

Jurists like al-Sarakhsī placed *ḥudūd* penalties, excluding the *ḥadd* of *qadhf* in the category of the pure right of Allah. The *ḥadd* of *qadhf* is classified as a mixture of the right of Allah and the right of the individual, in which the right of Allah is predominant. The offence of murder liable to *qiṣāṣ* is classified as a mixture of the right of Allah and the right of the individual, but here it is the right of the individual that is predominant. It is because of the existence of the right of Allah in these categories that the procedure adopted is that determined for the pure right of Allah. *Ta'zīr* and *diyah* are classified by most Ḥanafī jurists as belonging to the area of the right of the individual. The *fuqahā'* do not mention the *siyāsah* penalties, yet we know that the ruler exercised this jurisdiction right from the first century of the Hijrah onwards. The *maẓālim*

142. For an explanation in a little more detail see Imran Ahsan Nyazee, *General Principles of Criminal Law: Islamic and Western* (Islamabad: Advanced Legal Studies Institute, 1998), 59–69; *Theories of Islamic Law* (Islamabad: Federal Law House, 2007), the chapter on "The Spheres of Islamic Law".

courts, the institution of the *'āmil al-sūq*, and the institution of the *muḥtasib* belong to this jurisdiction. This was the area of the right of the state, and the procedure was determined by the state to ensure flexibility and ease of implementation. This classification led to the following legal rules and distinctions:

1. **Commuting the sentence and pardon:** The penalty for an offence against the right of Allah cannot be waived or commuted after apprehension and conviction. However, the penalty for an offence against the right of an individual alone or against the rights of individuals, that is, the right of the state, can be commuted. The important point to be made here is that if the right of Allah and the right of the state (or the right of the community as a whole) were the same thing, the state would not be able to commute any sentence according to the system developed by the jurists, whether awarded as *ḥadd, ta'zīr*, or as *siyāsah*. We know very well that the state can pardon any sentence that is not a *ḥadd*. The reason is that sentences other than *ḥadd* are not awarded and applied as a right of Allah.

2. **The operation of *shubhāt* (mistakes) in *ḥudūd*:**[143] *Shubhah* (lit. doubt) in the right of Allah has the effect of waiving the penalty of *ḥadd*, while it does not have the same effect in *ta'zīr*. *Qiṣāṣ* (retaliation) has been assigned an element of the right of Allah as it is waived due to *shubhah*. This kind of doubt is not to be confused with the benefit of a doubt that goes to the accused in positive law, which is a doubt in the mind of the judge as to whether the crime has been proved beyond doubt. Islamic law has no objections to this, as proving an offence beyond doubt is a requirement

143. One jurist who states clearly that the *shubhāt* mentioned in the traditions and operative in the *ḥudūd* are actually mistakes is al-Bazdawī. He also goes into details of why these *shubhāt* do not operate in *ta'zīr*. His discussion is not confined to the *ḥudūd* alone and he establishes the link between *shubhāt* and mistakes in general. See al-Bazdawī, *Uṣūl* on the margin of 'Abd al-'Azīz al-Bukhārī, *Kashf al-Asrār*, vol. 4, 534 passim.

in Islamic law. *Shubhah* mentioned here exists in the mind of the accused at the time of the commission of the act on the basis of conflicting opinions about the *ḥukm* or because of a particular set of facts.[144] An example of *shubhat al-milk* is, in the opinion of Mālik, when the offender steals (or takes by way of stealth) the property of the *bayt al-māl* (treasury) under the impression that he is part owner of the property.[145] In law the *shubhāt* are referred to as mistakes: mistake or ignorance of fact and mistake or ignorance of law.

3. ***Shubhah* and *ta'zīr:*** All *ta'zīr* is the right of the individual and it is for this reason that *shubhah* does not operate in it. This is the claim made by al-Kāsānī. Some jurists, mostly Shāfi'ites,[146] have said that *ta'zīr* can also be a right of Allah. This is an inconsistent statement, for *ta'zīr* as a right of Allah

---

144. Ibid.
145. If a man steals from the *bayt al-māl* there is no *ḥadd* penalty for him. The reason is based on *shubhat al-milk*. The *bayt al-māl* is the common property of the Muslims and for purposes of *ḥadd* the offender is considered to have committed a theft from his own property that is jointly owned with the Muslims. *Ḥadd* is waived due to the doubt, actual or legal, in the mind of the offender arising from joint ownership of the property. In other words, there was a mistake of law and fact. This person, however, is not allowed to go scot free. He is awarded punishment under the rights of the state, as *shubhat al-milk* is not operative against these rights, but it is effective in the waiver of punishment in the right of Allah. If *ta'zīr* is declared as a right of Allah, this particular offender will go scot free on the basis of the same *shubhah*, as the right of Allah is to be waived in such a case, which would defeat the purposes of the law and those of social control. To state it differently, if both *ḥadd* and *ta'zīr* are considered the right of Allah, the doubt or *shubhah* related to ownership would operate in both.
146. Al-Māwardī is one of the first to have said this. See *al-Aḥkām al-Sulṭāniyyah*, 237. There are some later Ḥanafī jurists too who have maintained that *ta'zīr* may be a right of Allah or the right of the individual. One such Hanafī jurist is Ibn 'Ābidīn. He does, however, realize the inconsistency and is forced to say that when *ta'zīr* is a right of Allah, it cannot be commuted, that is, it will not accept *'afw* (pardon). See *Ḥāshiyat Ibn 'Ābidīn*, vol. 3, 192.

would prevent pardon (*'afw*), which is an acknowledged attribute of *ta'zīr*.

4. **Criminal proceedings and evidence:** The evidence of women is not admissible in the right of Allah, that is, in *ḥudūd*, while it is in the case of *ta'zīr*, which is the right of the individual, but the *niṣāb* of one man and two women has to be maintained, as in the case of other rights of the individual. No such restriction is applicable to the right of the state and a single woman can furnish evidence that is admissible in cases falling under *siyāsah*, just as circumstantial evidence is admissible whenever the *ḥaqq al-salṭanah* is in issue.[147] In other words, the criminal proceedings and requirements of evidence change according to the right involved. In modern Muslim writings and in the application of the law in Pakistan today, *ta'zīr* and *siyāsah* are both classified under the heading of *ta'zīr*.

If one ponders over these classifications of crimes and the statements of the jurists about the various associated rules, the only conclusion that can be drawn is that the right of the state is distinct from the right of Allah. The main point that we wish to make here is that one use of the classification of acts into rights is that it governs the rules of evidence and procedure in the criminal law.

Modern jurists have ignored the significance of *siyāsah* in crimes, and they appear to have merged the two areas of *ta'zīr* and *siyāsah*. This is a wise step, but only if the contradictions resulting from this merger are resolved. For example, after the

147. In the case of murder or *qatl 'amd* the penalty is *qiṣāṣ*, but only when the offence is proved through the testimony of two male *'adl* witnesses. If the offence is not proved in a certain case, but there is sufficient circumstantial evidence to convict the offender, will the state try this person under *ta'zīr* or under *siyāsah*? Under *ta'zīr*, the system of the *fuqahā'* requires two witnesses again, with one male being replaced with two females, that is, almost the same kind of testimony. In *siyāsah* the standards of testimony are lowered and the case can be proved more easily.

merger, they appear to have forgotten that according to the earlier jurists the *niṣāb* of witnesses has to be maintained in *ta'zīr*.[148] The second point that needs to be emphasised here with respect to contradiction is that this area, whatever the name chosen for it, *cannot be designated as a right of Allah,* as this would invoke *shubhah* and its consequences along with the other rules that operate exclusively within the right of Allah.

Finally, if the condition of the *niṣāb* of witnesses imposed by the jurists has been removed arbitrarily for *ta'zīr* and a single woman is permitted to testify in such crimes, a logical problem pertaining to the evidence of women in commercial law is raised. The question is: If the *nisāb* of two female witnesses for one male witness can be eliminated in the case of *ta'zīr,* which is the right of the individual, should it not be waived in the case of other rights of the individual, i.e., commercial transactions? A solution would be to interpret the Qur'ānic text as a recommendation (*nadb*) rather than as an obligation (*wujūb*). In short, these are not matters for picking and choosing according to convenience; the whole system has to be checked for analytical consistency.

6.7 Human Rights and Other Classifications

It is possible to classify rights in other ways in Islamic law. One such classification can be seen in the public and private interests into which the *maqāṣid al-sharī'ah* or the purposes of Islamic law are divided. It is from this classification that human rights recognised by Islamic law are also derived. The division into public and private interests is discussed briefly under the topic of *maṣlaḥah* in the next part of this book.

148. Thus, for example, the *Ḥudūd* Ordinances applied in Pakistan do not require the testimony of two male witnesses in offences other than *ḥadd*. An offence classified as *ta'zīr* can be proved through the testimony of one witness, even when the witness is a female. According to the jurists, this is only possible in the area of *siyāsah* where the standards of proof and modes of procedure are at the discretion of the *imām*.

6.7.1 Developing the Islamic Theory of Rights and Duties

After having discussed rights and duties in the traditional sense, it must be pointed out that these concepts need to be elaborated and analysed further so as to enable the modern legal system and the members of the legal profession to make use of them. Here we can only briefly indicate the areas in which research is required by Muslim jurists and scholars. Some ideas from the works of different thinkers and writers are given below to indicate the different issues that may need to be given importance. The purpose is to show that while there are some jurists who have criticised the very idea of rights and their utility for the legal system, others have deemed rights to be essential for the smooth functioning of the legal machinery and the protection of interests. What is clear, however, is that there is scope for such discussions within the area of rights called the right of the state and the area that is purely the right of the individual. The category designated as the right of God is clearly settled by the *sharī'ah*, yet the relationship of such rights with individual and public interests needs to be developed in greater detail.

According to Dias, conduct is regulated by the imposition of duties.

> Claims [or rights in the strict sense] may assist in achieving this end, but if it can be otherwise achieved, there is no reason why the mere fact that Y is under a duty with regard to X should confer upon X, or anyone else for that matter, a corresponding claim. There is nothing to prevent it being the law that every breach of duty, of whatsoever sort, shall be dealt with by the machinery of the state. Such a state of affairs, though possible, would be inconvenient, for it would stretch state machinery to breaking point. Where duties are of private concern, the remedies are best left to individuals to pursue in the event of their breach. Above all, it is expedient to give aggrieved persons some satisfaction, usually by way of compensation. Every system of law has to decide which breaches of duties shall be taken up by the public authorities on their own motion; and which shall be left to private persons to take up or not as they please.

> The distinction between "public" and "private" law is quite arbitrary. It would seem, therefore, that there is no intrinsic reason why claims should be a necessary concomitant of duties. Indeed, some modern writers, for different reasons reject the whole idea of claims or rights as redundant.[149]

One such writer was Leon Duguit (1859–1928), although similar ideas in a somewhat altered form may be found in the writings of Scandinavian jurists as well. According to Edgar Bodenheimer, Duguit, a French jurist, presented a new type of natural law theory. This doctrine was diametrically opposed to other natural law doctrines.

> Duguit repudiated any natural or inalienable rights of individuals. His objective was to supplant the traditional system of legal rights by a system which would recognise only legal duties. Every individual has a certain task to perform in society, Duguit said, and his obligation to perform this function may be enforced by the law. The only right any man might be said to possess under this theory is the right always to do his duty. As Corwin has aptly said, "this theory is that of Locke stood on its head."
>
> Notwithstanding his emphasis on social duties, Duguit rejected any absolutist conception of state power. He proposed to strip the state and its organs of all sovereign rights and other attributes of sovereignty with which the traditional doctrine of public law had endowed it. Duguit taught that the governing authorities, like citizens, have only duties, and no rights. Their activity is to be confined to the performance of certain social functions, and the most important of these functions is the organisation and maintenance of public services. It is the duty of governmental officials to guarantee a continuous and uninterrupted operation of the public services. This aim, Duguit believed, would be most effectively realised by a far-reaching decentralisation and technical autonomy of the public utilities under a syndicalist structure of the state. [150]

149. Dias, *Jurisprudence*, 27 (Footnotes omitted).
150. Bodenheimer, *Jurisprudence*, 147 (footnotes omitted)

According to J.W. Harris, on the other hand, correlativity is essential:

> Correlativity is essential, as part of the law's lowest common denominators, because every judicial question concerns two people. The notion of tax law imposing duties without correlative rights does not arise because, in court, someone or the other (some revenue officer perhaps) must be claiming that a man ought to have paid so much tax. The only question the court has to decide is: Did this defendant owe a duty to this plaintiff?[151]

Thus, in accordance with this reasoning, the answer would be that if there is someone in court to claim the breach of a duty, a correlative right exists. As long as there is someone to enforce the performance of a duty, a right exists; the right vests in the person undertaking the enforcement. The idea of rights in Islamic law clearly includes this function, because the function of the legal system is the adjudication of rights, and this makes it necessary that there be someone to claim the right.

It is obvious that the concept of rights in Islamic law is much wider than this. First, there are certain duties that the state owes to God. An example is the implementation of *ḥudūd* (*iqāmat al-ḥudūd*). Such duties of the state emerge from the negative or defensive component of the purposes of law. Further, there are the duties of the state that emerge from the positive component of the *maqāṣid:* the establishing of *dīn,* the creating of conditions for the healthy flourishing of life, the strengthening of the family system, the creation of conditions for the development of the mind, and the striving for the growth of communal and individual wealth. All these duties are justiciable. Any Muslim can go to a court of law and seek the enforcement of these duties of the state. The right belongs to God, but the claimant is an individual. All this will conform with what Harris has said above, but the idea needs to be developed in detail along with a discussion of fundamental rights.

Besides these there are duties owed to God by individuals: like praying, fasting, paying *zakāt* and the like. Out of these

151. Harris, *Legal Philosophies* (London: Butterworths, 1980), 81.

the payment of *zakāt* is justiciable and the claimant will be the community or the state. The other rights may become justiciable when neglected by the entire community.

In Islamic law the idea of rights has another important dimension, a dimension that is usually overlooked.[152] Different classes of rights in Islamic law determine the procedure to be adopted even within categories like criminal procedure, for example. Each matter brought before the court is adjudicated on the basis of the right claimed. This is evident in the criminal law and should be explained through its procedure. We have already discussed this above.

6.7.2 The analysis of rights

Western jurists have contributed tremendously to the analysis of rights. Their efforts sharpen our understanding of the idea of rights and help us identify certain jural relations. The word "right" in ordinary speech or in a "wider sense" includes the following terms: claims, liberties, powers and immunities. It is only the word "claim" that conveys the meaning of right in the strict sense. For example, when we speak of having a right to appoint an agent or to enter into a contract, it is not a right we are speaking of but a power given to us by the law. At other times the term right is used to convey the meaning of liberty to act or not to act. This type of analysis of rights has led to what is called the Hoffeldian scheme. The subjection of the idea of rights in Islamic law to such a scheme would lead to a better understanding of jural relations within this legal system. Such an understanding in turn will lead to a better adjudication of rights.

6.7.3 The nature of duties in Islamic law

The analysis of duties within Islamic law is no less important. A duty is an obligation to do something. In other words, it is better to view it from the point of view of performance, as compared to obligation, which may be viewed from the perspective of

152. It is the same idea that helps us distinguish crimes from torts in law.

acceptance and imposition. We have already stated that the jurists attempt to make this distinction by treating *ījāb* in a different sense from *wujūb*. The analysis of duties in Islamic law must answer the fundamental question: why does a duty continue to exist, that is, continue to be law? The answer lies in the examination of the changing purposes of duties. We have to examine the issue whether "[t]he morality of yesterday has perpetuated itself as an anachronism in legal form. Or it may be that considerations other than morality gave rise to a duty, in which case the duty is independent of morality."[153] Is there something binding in the sources and morality must conform to it? For example, how is it that the earlier jurists could perceive such wide rights for the guardian (*walī*), but modern jurists may be inclined to be lenient today, especially when the system of tribal morality has collapsed? How is it that the earlier jurists could see a duty on would-be spouses to observe the rules of proportionality in status and modern writers do not see such a duty? The same can be said about slavery and other matters.

These questions require that the nature of duties be analysed in depth. The broad general features of duties in Islamic law must be identified, features that help us identify the law as well as accommodate the changes in the environment.

6.7.4 Natural rights and rights given by the law

Above all, the question has to be answered whether Islamic law recognises certain natural rights or whether it looks at rights granted by the *sharī'ah* alone. These two types of rights would be different from the rights granted and taken away by the state. In fact, the state it appears has a limited role to play in the granting of rights. This means that if the rights are given by the *sharī'ah*, they can only be taken away by the *sharī'ah*. In such a case, the rights will exist whether or not they are stated in the constitution of a Muslim state. The courts will have to enforce these rights under all circumstances and no emergency can justify the suspension of such rights. The Cairo Declaration on Human Rights upholds

153. Dias, *Jurisprudence*, 229.

this view. Yet, more research is needed to develop the theory of these rights. In our view, however, a deeper research may reveal that such rights are not only individual rights guaranteed by the *sharī'ah*, but they may turn out to be rights that have been guaranteed to the individuals and are claimed as the right of God.

Review Questions

1. Define the *maḥkūm fīh*. What is its relationship with rights?
2. What are the conditions of *taklīf*? Do they differ with the change of the *dār*?
3. The act should be dependent on the will of the subject. Elaborate.
4. How far does hardship (*mashaqqah*) affect the nature of acts?
5. The right of Allah is distinct and independent of the right of the state. Evaluate this statement with reasons.
6. There are two theories of rights in law: the interest theory and the will theory. Does Islamic law have its independent theory of rights? If so what is this theory, and if not, which of these two theories does Islamic law support?
7. How do rights affect the nature of acts in Islamic law? Use the idea of *ḥudūd* penalties to answer this question.
8. How does Imām al-Sarakhsī classify the *ḥukm taklīfī* on the basis of rights? Should this classification include the right of the state? If so, how will it be accommodated?
9. What are substitutory duties?
10. What impact does the classification of rights have on the Islamic criminal law?
11. Is the idea of rights necessary in Islamic law? If so, why?

7 The Subject (*Maḥkūm 'Alayh*)

The subject or the *maḥkūm 'alayh* forms the third element of the *ḥukm shar'ī*. He is the person whose act invokes a *ḥukm*, or a *ḥukm* requires him to act in a prescribed manner. In legal parlance, he is known as the *mukallaf* (subject). A *mukallaf* is a person who possesses legal capacity, whether he acts directly or through delegated authority.

The first requirement for legal capacity is the ability to understand the communication that creates the obligation.[154] In addition to this, there are a number of other conditions that must be fulfilled before the law can operate against or for a person. These conditions are all related to legal capacity, known as *ahliyyah* in juristic terminology. This topic is important for understanding Islamic law generally, but it has special significance for criminal law and the law of contract. All the

154. This does not mean understanding the texts directly. The subject should be able to understand the meaning of the *ḥukm* communicated to him by the *mujtahid* or the *faqīh*.

general defences, for example, under criminal law are covered under this topic. Further, possession of contractual capacity is an essential element of each contract.

7.1 *Ahliyyah* or Legal Capacity

7.1.1 The two parts of legal capacity

The literal meaning of the word *ahliyyah* is absolute fitness or ability.[155] *Ahliyyah* is "the ability or fitness to acquire rights and exercise them and to accept duties and perform them."[156] This meaning indicates two parts for capacity: the first is based on the acceptance or acquisition of rights and the other on the performance of duties. These are called *ahliyyat al-wujūb* and *ahliyyat al-adā'* or **the capacity for acquisition (of rights) and the capacity for execution or performance of duties.**[157] Capacity for acquisition enables a person to acquire both rights and obligations, while capacity for execution gives him the ability to exercise such rights and perform his duties.

7.1.2 *Dhimmah* and legal capacity

In the opinion of some jurists, the term *dhimmah* also means the ability to acquire rights and obligations. The majority of the jurists consider *dhimmah* to be an imaginary container or receptacle that holds both the capacity for acquisition and the capacity for execution. It is the location or place of residence for the two kinds of capacity. In short, *dhimmah* is the balance-sheet of a person showing his assets and liabilities, in terms of his rights and obligations.

155. For a lucid discussion of legal capacity see al-Sarakhsī, *Uṣūl,* vol. 2, 232 passim; see also Ṣadr al-Sharī'ah, *al-Tawḍīḥ,* vol. 2, 751 passim; al-Ghazālī, *al-Mustaṣfā,* vol. 1, 53–54.

156. 'Abd al-'Azīz al-Bukhārī, *Kashf al-Asrār 'an Uṣūl Fakhr al-Islām al-Bazdawī,* vol. 4 (Beirut: Dār al-Kutub al-'Ilmiyyah, 1997), 335.

157. Ibid.; al-Sarakhsī, *Uṣūl,* vol. 2, 233; Ṣadr al-Sharī'ah, *al-Tawḍīḥ,* vol. 2, 751.

In Islamic law, *dhimmah* is deemed a requisite condition for the existence of *ahliyyah*. According to al-Sarakhsī, *dhimmah* is the "trust" that was offered to the mountains, but they refused; Man accepted it.[158] Thus, *dhimmah* is an attribute conferred by the Lawgiver. It is a trust resulting from a covenant (*'ahd*).[159] The fact that *dhimmah* is a covenant between the Lawgiver and the *'abd* (subject) means that *dhimmah* can be assigned to a natural person alone. In Western law, the term *dhimmah* conforms with "personality," which is an attribute conferred on a natural person[160] as well as an artificial person.

7.2 The Underlying Bases of Legal Capacity

7.2.1 *Insāniyyah* and *'Aql*

Legal capacity, as stated, is of two types: *ahliyyat al-wujūb* and *ahliyyat al-adā'*. *Ahliyyat al-wujūb* is defined as the ability of a human being to acquire rights and obligations.[161] It may, therefore, be referred to as the capacity for acquisition.

Manāṭ is a thing from which another thing is suspended. The *manāṭ* or basis for the existence of the capacity for acquisition is the

158. Al-Sarakhsī, *al-Uṣūl,* vol. 2, 333; 'Abd al-'Azīz al-Bukhārī, *Kashf al-Asrār,* vol. 4, 335–38.

159. Al-Sarakhsī, *al-Uṣūl,* vol. 2, 333; Ṣadr al-Sharī'ah, *al-Tawḍīḥ,* vol. 2, 751–53.

160. For a detailed discussion of this issue, see Imran Ahsan Khan Nyazee, *Corporations in Islam* (Islamabad: Federal Law House, 2007). 'Abd al-'Azīz al-Bukhārī says something similar: "If we enter into a compact with those who do not believe and grant them a *dhimmah,* they can have rights and duties like those of the Muslims." Thus, the term Ahl al-Dhimmah is applied to the non-Muslim citizens who have an agreement with the Muslims. 'Abd al-'Azīz al-Bukhārī, *Kashf al-Asrār,* vol. 4, 336. It follows that *dhimmah* is a restricted form of legal personality granted to the *dhimmī.*

161. "It is the capacity to follow the obligation (*wujūb*) in a *ḥukm.*" 'Abd al-'Azīz al-Bukhārī, *Kashf al-Asrār,* vol. 4, 335–38.

attribute of being a human or natural person (*insāniyyah*).[162] There is complete agreement among jurists that this form of capacity is possessed by each human being irrespective of his being a *mukallaf*.

Capacity for execution, on the other hand, is defined as the "capability of a human being to issue statements and perform acts to which the Lawgiver has assigned certain legal effects."[163] The *manāṭ* or basis of the capacity for execution is *'aql* (intellect) and (*rushd*) discretion. *'Aql* here implies the full development of the mental faculty. As there is no definitive method for checking whether this faculty is fully developed, the Lawgiver has associated it with *bulūgh* or puberty. Thus, the presumption is that a pubescent person is assumed to possess *'aql* necessary for the existence of the capacity for execution. This presumption, however, is rebuttable, and if it is proved that though a person has attained puberty, he does not yet possess *'aql*, capacity for execution cannot be assigned to such a person. This is the view of the majority of the jurists.

7.2.2 Mental maturity

The Ḥanafīs acknowledge a deficient capacity for execution for purposes of some transactions for a person who has attained a degree of discretion, even if his mental faculties are not yet fully developed. Thus, a minor (*ṣabī*) who possesses discretion, or exhibits "mental maturity" may be assigned such a capacity, for the *khiṭāb* of *mu'āmalāt*.[164] Again, there is no way here of determining whether the minor has attained discretion. The Ḥanafī jurists have, therefore, fixed the minimum age of seven years for assigning such a capacity; anyone over seven years of age who has not yet attained puberty may be assigned such a capacity, but the law makes this dependent on the guardian's will and discretion.

162. Al-Sarakhsī, *al-Uṣūl,* vol. 2, 333; Ṣadr al-Sharī'ah, *al-Tawḍīḥ,* vol. 2, 751.
163. Ṣadr al-Sharī'ah, *al-Tawḍīḥ,* vol. 2, 755.
164. See the next paragraph for its meaning.

7.2.3 Legal capacity and liability

Accordingly, this type of capacity is divided into three kinds on the basis of the type of liability associated with an act:

1. **Capacity for the *khiṭāb jinā'ī*** or legal capacity for criminal liability. It is based on the ability to comprehend the *khiṭāb jinā'ī*, i.e., the communication pertaining to criminal acts.

2. **Capacity for the *khiṭāb* of *'ibādāt*** or legal capacity for *'ibādāt*. It is based on the ability to understand the *khiṭāb* of *'ibādāt*, i.e., the communication from the Lawgiver pertaining to acts of worship.

3. **Capacity for the *khiṭāb* of *mu'āmalāt*** or legal capacity for transactions. It is based on the ability to understand the *khiṭāb* of *mu'āmalāt*, i.e., the communication from the Lawgiver pertaining to the *mu'āmalāt*.

Two of these are civil and criminal liability, while the third is an addition because of religious law. The reason for separating the capacity for execution into these three types is to indicate that a person may, for example, be in possession of the capacity for transactions, but not the capacity for punishments. To put it differently, all three kinds of capacity may be found in the person who is sane and a major, but one or more of these may be lacking in other persons.

7.3 Complete Capacity

Muslim jurists divide legal capacity into three types: complete, deficient and imperfect. The terms *kāmilah*, *nāqiṣah* and *qāṣirah* are used to distinguish such capacities.[165]

165. Ṣadr al-Sharī'ah, *al-Tawḍīḥ*, vol. 2, 755; al-Bukhārī, *Kashf al-Asrār*, vol. 4, 335.

7.3.1 Legal effects of complete capacity

Complete capacity for acquisition is found in a human being after his birth. This makes him eligible for the acquisition of all kinds of rights and obligations. Complete capacity for execution is established for a human being when he or she attains full mental development, and acquires the ability to discriminate. This stage is associated with the external standard of puberty. The physical signs indicating the attainment of puberty are the commencement of ejaculation in a male and menstruation in a female. In the absence of these signs, puberty is presumed at the age of fifteen in both males and females according to the majority of the jurists, and at the age of eighteen for males and seventeen for females according to Abū Ḥanīfah.

Attaining *bulūgh* (puberty) alone is not sufficient, however. For a person to acquire complete capacity for execution, in addition to puberty, the possession of *rushd* (discrimination; maturity of actions) is stipulated as well. The *dalīl*, or legal evidence, for this is the verse of the Qur'ān:

> Make trial of orphans until they reach the age of marriage; then if ye find sound judgement in them, release their property to them; but consume it not wastefully, nor in haste against their growing up. [Qur'ān 4 : 6]

This verse lays down clearly that there are two conditions that must be fulfilled before the wealth of orphans can be handed over to them. These are *bulūgh al-nikāḥ* and *rushd*.

The term *rushd*, according to the majority, signifies the handling of financial matters in accordance with the dictates of reason. The *rashīd* is a person who can identify avenues of profit as well as loss, and act accordingly to preserve his wealth. *Rushd* is the opposite of *safah* (foolishness), which implies waste and prodigality. Shāfi'ī jurists define *rushd* as maturity of actions in matters of finance as well as of *dīn*. In their view, a person who has attained puberty and is adept in dealing with financial matters cannot be called *rashīd*, unless he obeys the *aḥkām* of the *sharī'ah* in matters of *'ibādāt* as well.

A person, then, is eligible for taking over his wealth if he is both a *bāligh* and a *rashīd*. This is the general view. Abū Ḥanīfah, however, maintains that a person who attains the age of twenty-five years, must be delivered his property irrespective of his attaining *rushd*. In addition to this, he maintains that if a person attains *bulūgh* and *rushd* and is given his property, but subsequently loses his *rushd*, while yet under twenty-five, he cannot be subjected to interdiction (*ḥajr*). Abū Ḥanīfah appears to be giving preference to life and freedom of the individual over his wealth in these cases.[166] The majority of the jurists (*jumhūr*) subject a person to interdiction if he has not attained *rushd* or even when he loses it subsequently, irrespective of his age.

On attaining complete capacity, an individual comes within the purview of all the different kinds of *khiṭāb* (communication from the Lawgiver). He, therefore, becomes liable to punishments because of the *khiṭāb jinā'ī* being directed towards him, just as he becomes liable because of the *khiṭāb* of transactions and *ibādāt*.

7.3.2 The stages leading to complete legal capacity

The conditions laid down by the Ḥanafī jurists indicate that there are three stages through which an individual passes with respect to his capacity for execution.

1. The first stage is from birth till the attainment of partial discretion, which is considered to be the age of seven years. During this period, the child is assumed to lack *'aql* and discretion completely, and is ineligible for the assignment of a capacity for execution.

2. The second stage commences from the age of seven and continues up to actual puberty or the legal age of puberty, whichever is earlier. Deficient capacity for execution is normally assigned during this stage, as the individual possesses a certain amount of *'aql* and discretion.

166. This view appears to be in line with the priorities determined within the *maqāṣid al-sharī'ah*.

3. The final stage commences from actual physical puberty or the legal age determined for it, whichever is earlier. On reaching this age the individual is assigned complete capacity for execution, and becomes eligible for each kind of *khiṭāb*. An exception arises in the case of *safah* and the individual may be placed under interdiction for some time. *Rushd* (discretion) is a condition for attaining this stage, in addition to puberty.

7.4 Deficient and Imperfect Capacity

Deficient capacity is assigned in cases where the *manāṭ* or basis of legal capacity is not fully developed. Thus, a person may not have been born as yet or he may not have reached full mental development. In other cases, the attribute of being a human may be missing altogether.

Imperfect capacity is assigned in cases where the bases of capacity, being a human and possession of discretion, are present, but an external attribute has been introduced that does not permit the recognition of the legal validity of certain acts.

Deficient and imperfect capacity is understood through the study of different cases falling under each. A brief look at these cases follows.

7.4.1 Cases of deficient legal capacity

7.4.1.1 The unborn child (*janīn*)

Deficient or incomplete capacity is established for an unborn child or the foetus (*janīn*).[167] Deficient capacity implies that only some rights are established for the *janīn* and no obligations are imposed on it. The reason is that the *janīn* is considered part of the mother in some respects. Thus, it is set free with the mother and is also sold as a part of her (in the case of the *umm al-walad*). An independent personality is, therefore, not assigned to it.

167. Al-Sarakhsī, *al-Uṣūl*, vol. 2, 333–34.

In other respects, the *janīn* enjoys a separate life and is preparing for separation from the womb. Its personality is, therefore, considered deficient or incomplete. By virtue of this deficient capacity, the *janīn* acquires certain rights: freedom from slavery, inheritance, bequest, and parentage. On the other hand, the *janīn* cannot be made liable for the satisfaction of rights owed to others. A purchase made by the would-be *walī* (guardian) on behalf of the *janīn* cannot make the *janīn* liable for the payment of the price. Likewise, the maintenance of close relatives and the membership of the *'āqilah* cannot be enforced against the *janīn*. Once the child is born, these rights can be enforced against it, but not when the obligations were acquired during the gestation period.

7.4.1.2 Capacity of a dead person

A deficient capacity for acquisition is also assigned to a *dead man or to a corpse*. Thus, amounts due on account of debts, bequest, and funeral expenses are taken from the wealth of the dead man. For example, if a person had thrown a net into the water immediately before his death, the fish caught in the net after the person's death belong to him. Likewise, if he had dug a pit before his death with the intention of trapping someone in it, then the *diyah* due as a result of someone falling in it is to be recovered from such a person's wealth. Further, any compensation due for property destroyed by acts commencing before his death shall be recovered from his property. As in English law, the estate of the deceased is not assigned legal personality. The Roman law and the French law do assign a personality to the estate.[168]

7.4.1.3 Capacity of a fictitious person.

Modern Muslim writers being faced with the need to acknowledge the existence of a fictitious personality, as it forms the basis of the present socio-legal structure, have claimed that such a concept does exist in Islamic law. They rely for this on

168. See Salmond, *Jurisprudence*, 351.

instances like *waqf, bayt al-māl,* and the estate of the deceased. These assertions seem to be misplaced. Islamic law as expounded by the jurists does not acknowledge the concept of a fictitious person.[169] It will be found to clash with the provisions of this law, whether the area is that of contracts, *ḥudūd,* or constitutional law. In other words, the idea of a fictitious person is incompatible with Islamic law as expounded by the jurists.

This does not mean that the jurists were not aware of the concept. They were aware of it, but did not acknowledge it for Islamic law. The main reason appears to be that *dhimmah* is an *'ahd* (covenant) with the Lawgiver (see p. 143 above), and a fictitious person cannot be expected to enter into such a covenant **primarily because it cannot perform religious duties.**[170] In other words, the law derived by the jurists does not need this concept and will reject it. Nevertheless, the modern world is organized around the concept of the corporation or the fictitious personality. Modern scholars will, therefore, have to work hard to accommodate this concept into the fold of Islamic law. This means that adjustments will have to be made in the law wherever this concept clashes with it. The fictitious person may be deemed to have deficient capacity that is not fit for the performance of religious duties, like the payment of *zakāt.*

It is important to note that justifying the legal validity of a fictitious legal personality under Islamic law may not be very difficult if the general principles of this law are applied. It is what comes after such justification that is important. Take the case of the state. When we admit the state as a person within Islamic law a number of traditional concepts prevalent within Islamic constitutional law appear to need alteration. For instance, the state owns all the land within its territory. The stipulations regarding revival of barren land (*iḥyā' al-mawāt*) become meaningless, because the primary condition is that only

169. This issue has been discussed at great length in the author's *Islamic Law of Business Organization: Corporations* (Islamabad: Federal Law House, 2007). We, therefore, do not feel the need to go into the details here.

170. This is true in English law as well for corporations.

that land can be revived that is not owned by anyone. Here all the land is owned by the state as a person, and this excludes the possibility of any revival. Yes, the state may grant land to landless peasants, but that is not the issue here; here we are talking about the clash of concepts. Further, Islamic law contemplates a personal relationship between the head of the state or the chief executive and between the members of the community, that is, the relationship is governed by the contract of *wakālah* (agency) where the head of state is an agent of the citizens. When the state intervenes, these relationships are altered. In the case of corporations, when the juristic person steps in, the traditional concepts of *sharikah* lose their significance. In short, what we mean is that accepting this concept is not a question of saying "yes" or "no"; a number of changes will have to be made to the existing Islamic law of contract, changes that may wreck its whole structure and violate the fundamental principles upon which it is based.

7.4.1.4 Capacity of the minor (*ṣabī*)

A child possesses a complete capacity for acquisition of rights and obligations, but until he attains the age of actual or legal puberty, he lacks the capacity for execution. To facilitate matters, this child is made liable by the *sharī'ah* only for those obligations that he can meet.

Deficient capacity for execution is assigned to a non-pubescent who possesses some discretion, or to a *ma'tūh* (idiot) who has attained puberty yet lacks complete mental development.

The person who possesses deficient capacity is not subject to the *khiṭāb jinā'ī;* he cannot, therefore, be held criminally liable. The minor, however, is subjected to *ta'dīb* (discipline)—the reason being that the *khiṭāb jinā'ī* is applicable to that person alone who comprehends the *khiṭāb* fully. This is based on the principle of legality in Islamic law.

With respect to the *'ibādāt*, there are detailed discussions whether the *khiṭāb* is addressed to the *ṣabī* and *ma'tūh* by way of *nadb* (recommendation) or *khiyār* (choice), or whether it is addressed to them at all. There is no dispute that there is reward (*thawāb*) for such a person for the performance of the *'ibādāt*.

The Ḥanafīs treat the issue of legal capacity of the minor in a somewhat different way. Our major concern here is for the capacity of such a person for the purpose of transactions.

1. Financial transactions are established against the *dhimmah* of the *ṣabī*. Though he cannot meet them personally due to the absence of the capacity for execution, the Lawgiver allows his *walī* (guardian) to stand in his place and represent him through a substitutory duty. The *ṣabī* is also liable for any damage caused to another's property, and for the maintenance of his wives and near relatives. He is also liable, except in the opinion of the Ḥanafī school, for the payment of *zakāt*. All financial transactions are divided into three types for determining the liability of the discriminating minor.[171]

    a) **Purely beneficial transactions.** The transactions falling under this category are the acceptance of a gift or of *ṣadaqah*. These are allowed to the person who has not attained puberty, but who can discriminate and has been permitted by his *walī* (guardian) to exercise such acceptance.

    b) **Purely harmful transactions.** The granting of divorce, manumission (*'itq*), charity (*ṣadaqah*), loan (*qarḍ*),[172] and gift (*hibah*), as well as the making of a trust (*waqf*) and bequest (*waṣiyyah*) are considered transactions resulting in pure financial loss. These are not permitted to the *ṣabī mumayyiz* (discriminating minor).

171. Al-Sarakhsī, *Uṣūl*, vol. 2, 335; Ṣadr al-Sharī'ah, *al-Tawḍīḥ*, vol. 2, 762.
172. Ṣadr al-Sharī'ah states that a *qarḍ* may be given to a *qāḍī* in his official capacity. Ṣadr al-Sharī'ah, *al-Tawḍīḥ*, vol. 2, 757. This may be interpreted to mean that a minor's wealth may be invested in government securities. The reason why a *qarḍ* is considered a financial loss is because the minor will be deprived of the benefit of its use during the loan period. In *qarḍ ḥasan* this use is gifted to the beneficiary, and gift by a minor is not valid.

c) **Transactions vacillating between profit and loss.** Sale, hire, partnership, and other such transactions are considered valid if ratified by the *walī.*

2. Criminal liability does not exist in the case of a person who has not attained puberty, because he is not a *mukallaf*, and the *walī* cannot stand in his place for criminal offences: punishments being deterrents for the offender himself and not for those who represent them. This, however, holds true as far as *ḥudūd* and *qiṣāṣ* penalties are concerned; a child over seven may be liable to some suitable form of *ta'dīb*. Yet, this may not be interpreted to mean that a minor can be awarded penalties other than the *ḥudūd* if he is over seven, as is done in the law.

3. The *'ibādāt* are not obligatory on the *ṣabī*, as he does not possess the capacity for execution.

The deficient capacity granted to the discriminating minor by the Ḥanafīs is also granted to the *ma'tūh* (idiot). The majority of the jurists (*jumhūr*) oppose the Ḥanafīs and refuse to acknowledge any kind of capacity for the discriminating minor. They maintain that the communication (*khiṭāb*) is not directed toward such a minor at all, and it is of no consequence whether the transactions are beneficial or harmful. In practice, however, we find young boys minding stores on behalf of their fathers, and often handling the transactions exceptionally well.

7.4.2 Cases of Imperfect Capacity

Capacity for acquisition may be perfect or imperfect. Imperfect capacity is attributed to women and slaves.

7.4.2.1 Legal Capacity of a Woman

A woman is said to possess imperfect legal capacity. Those who hold this view deny her the right to be the head of state, the right to be a *qāḍī* (judge), and the right to testify in cases being tried under *ḥudūd* and *qiṣāṣ* provisions (that is, duties where the right of God is involved). In addition to this, she does not have the right to divorce, like the right given to a man, she is given a share in inheritance that is equal to half the share of male heirs, and the *diyah* paid in compensation of her death is half that of a man. These provisions have led certain Orientalists, like Joseph Schacht, to observe that in Islamic law "a woman is half a man." Women who are struggling for the emancipation and acceptance of their rights in Muslim countries have objected seriously to such a status granted to them. Demanding equality with men, they maintain that the status of women should be the same as that of men, by which they mean that their legal capacity should not be considered imperfect or deficient in any way. The purpose here is not to argue from one side or the other, but to identify the legal issues involved. Reasons or solutions will become obvious once these issues are grasped.

Evidence of women. The most important issue appears to be that of the evidence of women. This is split into two sub-issues. The first is whether the evidence of women is excluded by the texts of the Qur'ān and *Sunnah* in cases of *ḥudūd?* The usual answer given in reply is that the evidence of women is excluded in such cases on the basis of the *Sunnah,* which is also a source of law. These are cases involving the right of Allāh. The approach to this issue is that somehow women have been deprived of a right. This is incorrect. Evidence in these cases, and in others too, is a duty and not a right. Women have been spared the burden of this duty. The purpose is to waive the penalty of *ḥadd,* which is usually an extreme punishment, and to show mercy to the accused in an indirect way. This, perhaps, is the intention of the Lawgiver. Related to this is a misconception that the offence of rape cannot be proved and punished with the evidence of one woman. It is true that *ḥadd* cannot be awarded upon the testimony of one woman, but that does not mean that no other punishment can be awarded to the rapist on the basis of such testimony. The ruler or the state has wide powers under the doctrine of *siyāsah* to award an equally stiff penalty. The Federal Shariat Court of Pakistan has ruled that this will be possible.[173]

The second sub-issue is about the evidence of two women being equal to that of one man. This requirement is derived from a verse of the Qur'ān, and is supported by the *Sunnah*. The details of this problem cannot be discussed here. It is suggested, however, that the scholars of this age may try to interpret the relevant verse of the Qur'ān as implying a recommendation rather than an obligation. It should be remembered again that rendering testimony is primarily a duty and not a right, though it leads to the protection of rights.

A woman's share in inheritance. The next issue is whether it is justified in the present times to give a woman half the share of a man. The answer is that the Qur'ān has laid down the law on this in explicit terms. The justification provided by scholars is that the Islamic legal system places a much greater financial burden on the male in terms of maintenance of his family and near ones. Such a burden has not been placed on a woman. Further, a woman is paid dower upon her marriage by the husband. This increases the financial liability for males. The argument from the other side may be that Islamic law, like any comprehensive legal system, especially one that is a complete code of life, is to be applied as a whole, in toto, not in pieces. In such a situation, is it possible for a woman who is left all alone to go to a court of law and enforcing her rights ask her brother, uncle, or cousin to support her? It is obvious that many such rights that the law provides her may not be enforceable today.

Right to divorce. As to the question of a woman not having a right to divorce the husband, the jurists unanimously agree that such a right has not been granted to her directly. There are, however, provisions in the law like *tafwīḍ*, *takhyīr* and *tamlīk* through which she may be granted such a right at the time of the marriage contract, if she so desires. Perhaps, the rulers exercising their *siyāsah* jurisdiction may make this provision mandatory.

173. *Rashida Patel v Federation of Pakistan*, PLD 1989 FSC 89.

Diyah. In the case of *diyah*, the majority of the jurists hold that the *diyah* of a woman is half that of a man. This view is based on some traditions and a number of reports from the Companions. Taking into account the number of reports from the Companions, some of the jurists consider it to be a case of *ijmā'* (consensus of opinion). There are a few jurists, however, like Ibn 'Ulayyah and Abū Bakr al-Aṣamm who maintain that the *diyah* of a male is equal to that of a female. They base their opinion upon the generality of a tradition from the Prophet (pbuh) reported by 'Amr ibn Ḥazm: "For a believing person (نفس مؤمنة) a hundred camels." The generality of this tradition treats men and women equally. Few will disagree with the statement that women are working today and are equally efficient working members of the society. In fact, some of them may be earning more than men. In this issue, it is not the right of a woman that is involved, because the right to *diyah* belongs to the heirs, but it is a question of her status. The new law of *qiṣāṣ* and *diyah* in Pakistan, therefore, makes no distinction between a male and female for purposes of *diyah*.

Judicial office and being head of state. According to the jurists, the reason why a woman cannot become a *qāḍī* or judge is linked to the question of evidence. A *qāḍī* can only hear cases in which he or she can also be an eligible witness. This is a qualification for the *qāḍī*. As a woman cannot be a witness in cases of *ḥadd*, she cannot be a *qāḍī* for hearing the cases and passing sentence. The question of being a head of state depends on the same reasoning. The primary duty of a head of state is the implementation of *ḥudūd* (*iqāmat al-ḥudūd*), which again requires the qualification of a witness for such cases. A woman is, therefore, considered ineligible for the job. In Pakistan, women judges today are deciding cases under the *ḥudūd* laws.

7.4.2.2 Slaves

The slave does not possess the right of ownership, but he does have a capacity for acquiring obligations pertaining to *'ibādāt*, and for criminal offences.[174]

Review Questions

1. Describe the two parts of legal capacity and compare legal capacity with the *dhimmah* of a person.

2. What are the underlying attributes for assigning legal capacity? What role does mental maturity play in the case of a minor?

3. Describe the legal effects on attaining complete legal capacity. What role does *rushd* (discretion) play in the attainment of complete capacity.

4. What are the stages leading to complete capacity.

5. Does the unborn child have rights under Islamic law?

6. Explain in some detail the position taken by Islamic law with respect to the fictitious person.

7. Under what circumstances are the acts of the minor valid for financial transactions? Compare this with the acts of the minor in law.

8. Do you agree with the position taken in *uṣūl al-fiqh* that a woman has deficient legal capacity?

9. "In Islam a woman is half a man."—Joseph Schacht. Argue against this statement in the light of the evidence of women, their right to inheritance, *diyah* and their right to be *qāḍīs*.

---

174. Some might observe that slavery no longer exists, so why do we have to study examples that mention slaves? The answer is that a number of legal principles explained by the jurists may fall under this topic. To understand these principles, the discussions of issues related to slavery are sometimes unavoidable. Some of these issues may pertain to human rights.

8 Causes of Defective Legal Capacity

The causes affecting capacity are found in those factors that prevent *capacity for acquisition* and *capacity for execution* from taking full effect. The existence of these factors may result in the total absence of capacity or in deficient or incomplete capacity. For purposes of the present discussion, we may refer to all such forms as defective capacity.

The *manāṭ* (legal basis) for the capacity for acquisition, as we have said, is being a natural person (*insāniyyah*), and it is death alone that can cause a change in this kind of capacity. We have seen, however, that under certain circumstances a corpse may have such a capacity. Reason (*'aql*) and discretion (*rushd*), on the other hand, are the bases for the capacity for execution, and each factor that has the power to influence and affect the normal functioning of the human mind can become a cause for defective capacity.

It is pertinent to note that many of the causes of defective capacity mentioned here will appear to the reader to be the same as the general defences in criminal law, or as other grounds for waiver of liability in civil or ritual matters.

The jurists divide the causes of defective capacity into two kinds: natural causes (*samāwiyyah*) and acquired causes (*muktasabah*). We may designate these as natural and acquired causes. Some of these causes have already been explained in the previous chapter, while discussing deficient and imperfect capacities of various persons: women, slaves, *janīn* (foetus), corpse, and fictitious persons. Some of these will not be repeated here, but can be classified under natural or acquired causes.

8.1 Natural Causes of Defective Capacity

These are causes that are beyond the control of the subject (*mukallaf*), and result from an act of the Lawgiver and Creator. Under this heading, the jurists list ten causes: *ṣighar* (minority); *junūn* (insanity); *'atah* (idiocy); *nisyān* (forgetfulness); *nawm* (sleep); *ighmā'* (unconsciousness; fainting; epilepsy); *riqq* (slavery); *maraḍ* (illness); *ḥayḍ* (menstruation); *nifās* (puerperium; post-natal state of woman); and *mawt* (death). We shall discuss a few of these here, the rest are either obvious or have a greater bearing on *'ibādāt*.

8.1.1 Minority (*ṣighar*)

It is the state or condition of a human being after birth and before puberty. This, in fact, is not a cause of defective capacity or even an obstacle in its way, but a necessary stage in the growth of the human being. It is considered as a cause for noting its effect upon capacity or *ahliyyah*.

- Minority does not affect capacity for acquisition or *ahliyyat al-wujūb*. All rights and obligations are acquired as their establishment requires merely a *dhimmah* and the *manāṭ* (being a natural person), which is the basis for the capacity for acquisition. Minority does not oppose this *manāṭ*. The jurists, therefore, maintain that the minor is liable for compensation of property destroyed by him, for goods and services bought, for maintenance of relatives, and also for *zakāt* according to some.

- Capacity for execution or *ahliyyat al-adā'* requires *'aql* (reason) for its fulfilment, and this the non-discriminating minor (*ṣabī ghayr mumayyiz*) lacks, because he does not understand the *khiṭāb*. He is, therefore, not liable for the *'ibādāt*, for financial transactions, or for punishments. The Ḥanafīs make an exception in the case of the *ṣabī mumayyiz* or one who has attained some discretion. The *'ibādāt* of such a minor are rewarded in the Hereafter, and it is a matter of controversy whether the *khiṭāb* of *targhīb* or recommendation is addressed to him. He is not liable for punishments, but financial transactions undertaken by him are valid in certain cases. Transactions that are purely harmful for such a minor, like donating his property, have no legal effect. Transactions that are purely beneficial or those that are evenly balanced between profit and loss are allowed, with the prior permission of the guardian or his subsequent ratification. The position of the *ṣabī mumayyiz* may be compared with the contract for necessaries by a minor under sections 11 and 68 of the Pakistan Contract Act. The freedom allowed to the *ṣabī mumayyiz* by the Ḥanafīs is much wider than that under the law. In other countries, the contracts of a minor may be considered valid with an option for the minor to rescind the contract and return the property.

8.1.2 Insanity (*junūn*)

Junūn has no effect on *ahliyyat al-wujūb,* because rights and obligations are established for and against an insane person, who is deemed liable for *itlāf* (destruction of property), payment of *diyah*, and the like.[175] The *manāṭ* of such a capacity is *insāniyyah,* and the *majnūn* is a human being. *Junūn,* however, completely negates the *ahliyyat al-adā'*, because of lack of *'aql*. The insane person, therefore, has no liability for *'ibādāt* or punishments, and all his transactions are void.

While the *fuqahā'* consider insanity as effective in negating the capacity for performance they do not describe the meaning of

175. Ṣadr al-Sharī'ah, *al-Tawḍīḥ*, vol. 2, 760.

insanity in detail. In Pakistan, section 84 of the Pakistan Penal Code appears to follow what are called the M'Naghten Rules for insanity in England. These rules have been criticised by lawyers as well as doctors as being inadequate. A number of other tests have also been devised, like the "irresistible impulse test," the "Durham test," and the "American Law Institute or Model Penal Code test." It is suggested here that Muslim scholars need to explore these issues in some depth. They may either accept the tests devised in different countries or devise some new tests. The same holds true for idiocy and death illness. Such questions must be answered on the basis of empirical evidence.

8.1.3 Idiocy (*'atah*)

It is a state in which a person at times speaks like a sane and normal person, while at others he is like a madman.[176] It is also described as a state in which a grown-up has the mind of a child. The capacity of an idiot is deemed equivalent to that of a *ṣabī mumayyiz,* who can be permitted by his guardian to undertake some transactions.

8.1.4 Sleep and fits of fainting (*nawm, ighmā'*)

Sleep and fits of fainting have relevance for purposes of *'ibādāt,* as well as for crimes and torts.[177] They do not affect *ahliyyat al-wujūb,* because the attribute of *insāniyyah* is intact. Persons in such a condition, however, do not understand the *khiṭāb.* Their capacity to understand things is temporarily affected and prevented from normal functioning. The liability for missed *'ibādāt* lingers against such a person and these have to be performed as *qaḍā'* (delayed performance). There is no liability for punishments and transactions. If a person, while sleeping, falls on a child during sleep and kills it, there is no liability for punishment,

176. Ibid., vol. 2, 762.
177. Ibid., vol. 2, 763–64.

but compensation is another matter for which there may be strict liability.[178]

8.1.5 Forgetfulness (*nisyān*)

This is a state in which a person is not very careful about things though he has full knowledge of them, as distinguished from sleep and fits of fainting in which such knowledge is lacking. Forgetfulness does not affect *ahliyyat al-wujūb* nor does it affect the capacity for execution. The *khiṭāb*, however, becomes operative as soon as the person remembers. Transactions undertaken by such a person are valid and enforceable against him.

8.1.6 Death-illness (*maraḍ al-mawt*)

This is a condition in which the mind of a sick person is dominated by the fact that he will die because of his illness.[179] It is of no consequence whether the person actually dies from this illness or from something else and whether the illness is in fact a terminal illness. Two conditions must be met before an illness may be declared a death-illness:

- The deceased person must be convinced that he is approaching death, irrespective of the nature of the disease. Diseases like common colds and headaches, however, are not taken into account for such purposes. Some jurists associate other circumstances with this state, like a person on a ship that is caught in a storm, or like a person facing a death sentence.

- Death should follow such a conviction, even if it is not caused by the feared illness.

178. This means that loss of life has to be compensated anyway, irrespective of intention to harm. In traditional Islamic law, the burden in such cases is placed upon the *'āqilah*, which is the tribe or group with which an individual is considered to be associated.
179. For the details see Ṣadr al-Sharī'ah, *al-Tawḍīḥ*, vol. 2, 778 passim.

- Some jurists stipulate a third condition here by saying that death must occur within one year of the commencement of illness, because any period above this would mean that the person is accustomed to his illness and that the fear of death is remote.

Maraḍ al-mawt (death-illness) has no effect on the capacity for acquisition or on the capacity for execution, and it is in fact a condition of *taklīf*, because it is the capacity to perform an act that is affected here and not the capacity to understand it.

A person suffering from such an illness is prohibited from entering into transactions that are in excess of one-third of his wealth. In other words, it takes the *ḥukm* of *waṣiyyah*. This condition is stipulated to protect the rights of the heirs. The reason assigned is that the rights of the heirs get linked to the estate as soon as *maraḍ al-mawt* takes hold. The Lawgiver has laid down that such rights are to come into play after the death of the person, but to protect the rights of the heirs and creditors it is assumed that death has already occurred. The justification provided is that the transactions of such a person are not those of one who wishes to live, but of one who is ready to depart.

The following rights are attached to the estate of the person suffering from *maraḍ al-mawt*:

- *Rights of creditors.* The creditors have a right prior to all, even if the debts consume all the estate.

- *Rights of beneficiaries.* The rights of beneficiaries restrict the transactions to one-third of the estate, however, amounts in excess of one-third will be valid if permitted by the heirs.

- *Rights of the heirs.* These rights are linked to the estate from the time of the commencement of illness, and any transactions undertaken by the sick person will be assigned *aḥkām* as follows:

    1. *Transactions with a counter-value.* If the person suffering from death-illness concludes a contract of sale with no apparent loss in it, that is, at the market value, then the

creditors or the heirs cannot have it set aside. It is to be assumed that such a sale was undertaken to fulfil his genuine needs and not with the intention to deprive his creditors or heirs. Abū Ḥanīfah maintains that if such a sale is made to one of the heirs, it is to be declared as void even if it is at market value. The two disciples maintain that the sale is valid. The difference of opinion is due to the question whether the right of the heirs is linked to the *'ayn* (substance) of the thing or to its value.

2. *Transactions without a counter-value.* If the transaction is a *hibah, waqf, ṣadaqah,* or a sale at less than the market value, or a purchase at more than the market value, then such a transaction will be restricted to one-third of the value of the estate, after the creditors have been satisfied.

Three conditions must be fulfilled before the rights of the creditors can come into play:

(a) That the transaction was without a counter-value or without adequate counter-value. This would cover transactions like gift, charity, *waqf,* sale at a discount, or purchase at a premium.

(b) That the transaction involves the transfer of a thing (*'ayn*) itself and not its use, provided that the benefit conferred through use will terminate upon the death of the owner. Some Ḥanafīs do not consider the benefits arising from the use of a thing as *māl.* The use of land, or of a house, or of an animal are examples that explain this case. The majority (*jumhūr*), however, consider the use of benefits as *māl.*

(c) That the transaction must be in *a'yān* (substance of things) and not in the revenue or profit derived from them. Any assignment of profits arising from a *sharikah* or *muḍārabah* will not be affected by this condition.

Besides transactions, any admission or acknowledgement of debts by the person suffering from *maraḍ al-mawt* may also invoke the rights of creditors and heirs. Al-Shāfi'ī is of the opinion that acknowledgement by a person suffering from death-illness is valid and is not affected by the rights of the creditors or the heirs. The reason he assigns is that a person approaching death would normally tell the truth, even if he is a habitual liar. The Ḥanafīs, on the other hand, make a distinction between two cases:

(a) **Acknowledgement of debt in favour of an heir:** An acknowledgement in favour of an heir can have legal effects if the rest of the heirs permit it. This is due to the apprehension that one heir may have been preferred over the others.

(b) **Acknowledgement of debt in favour of a stranger:** An acknowledgement favouring a stranger is valid. These debts are called *duyūn al-maraḍ* and are to be paid after all other debts, called debts of health, have been satisfied.

The Mālikīs distinguish between cases where an allegation of a "bond of affection" can be made, that is, where a possibility of undue influence is likely. For example in the case of a wife, close relative, or friend. The basis is the bond existing between them and not the blood relationship.[180]

8.2 Acquired Causes of Defective Capacity

Acquired causes are those that are created by Man or in which human will and choice are the basic factors. Muslim jurists list seven such causes: ignorance (*jahl*), intoxication (*sukr*), jest (*hazl*), indiscretion (*safah*), journey (*safar*), mistake (*khaṭa', shubhah*), and coercion (*ikrāh*). We will discuss some of the important causes, noting their effects on the capacity for acquisition and on the capacity for execution.

180. See Ibn Rushd, *Bidāyat al-Mujtahid*, vol. 2, 44.

8.2.1 Intoxication (*sukr*)

Drunkenness is a state caused in a human being due to the use of an intoxicant, which temporarily suspends the proper functioning of the mental faculty.

Intoxication does not cause a change in the capacity for acquisition, as its basis is the attribute of being a human.[181] Thus, a drunken person possesses a *dhimmah* (legal personality) with a complete capacity for acquisition, and he is held liable for destruction of life and property, and also for all obligations, for maintenance, and even for *zakāt*. All these duties and obligations require the existence of the capacity for acquisition alone, and intoxication does not negate it.

The basis for the capacity for execution, on the other hand, is *'aql* (reason) and *rushd* (discretion); these are negated in the case of the drunken person by the state of drunkenness. The *khiṭāb* is not addressed to the drunken person, because he does not comprehend it. The state of such a person is worse than that of one who is asleep, for the latter can be awakened; it is worse than that of an idiot, who may understand parts of the speech addressed to him.

The jurists agree unanimously that the *khiṭāb* is not directed toward the intoxicated person if such intoxication has been caused by the legal use of intoxicants. For example, the person who has consumed liquor without knowing what it is or when he has done so under coercion or under duress to save his life. In such cases, the *ḥukm* for this person will be the same as that of the person under a spell of fainting.

Muslim jurists disagree about the person who is intoxicated when such intoxication is caused by prohibited means. The Ḥanafīs and some other jurists do not consider such a cause to have any effect on the capacity for execution and on the understanding of the *khiṭāb*. Thus, the *'ibādāt* are established against such a person and he will be held liable for delayed performance (*qaḍā'*), along with the accompanying sin. Any transaction or acknowledgement he makes is valid and

181. Ṣadr al-Sharī'ah, *al-Tawḍīḥ*, vol. 2, 798.

enforceable against him. He acquires criminal liability for acts committed in such a state, though he can retract his confession made in this state regarding a case of *ḥudūd,* as these are pure rights of Allāh.

The argument provided by the Ḥanafīs is that intoxication is a crime and as such cannot be an excuse for waiving punishments. Further, one reason why intoxication has been prohibited is that it leads to other *khabā'ith.* Moreover, if the acts of the drunken person are to be exempted from liability, it will become a means for the commission of offences, and for evading liability. Relying on the verse, "O ye believers, approach not prayer when you are intoxicated, until you know what you say," [Qur'ān 4 : 43] they maintain that it is obvious that the *khiṭāb* is addressed to the drunken person and he is expected to understand the meaning and import of the verse even when he is intoxicated. If this is not the interpretation, it would amount to saying to a person under a spell of madness, "Do not commit such an act when you are insane." It is for this reason that the drunken person is held liable for his acts.

Some jurists are of the opinion that an intoxicated person has no capacity for execution, because his *'aql* (reason) is completely impaired by the state of intoxication. They maintain that the Lawgiver has already provided a penalty for the offence of intoxication and holding him liable for his transactions as well, that is, those undertaken in such a state, would amount to punishing him twice for the same offence, a kind of double jeopardy. They argue that the verse about avoiding prayers in an intoxicated state is actually addressed to a sober person telling him to avoid becoming intoxicated before the time of prayer, an act over which he has control, as compared to the person subject to fits of madness over which he has no control.

Modern jurists try to prefer the second opinion as it may be closer to some forms of Western law. It must be noted, however, that consuming liquor is an offence in Islamic law and it may not be so in the law.

8.2.2 Jest (*hazl*)

When a person uses words without intending to convey either their primary or their secondary meanings, that is, their denotations or their connotations, he is said to speak in jest (*hazl*). Such a person may, for instance, use words employed for the contract of marriage, but does not intend the *ḥukm* (effect) of such a contract.

Speaking in jest has no effect on the capacity for acquisition; rights as well as obligations will, therefore, be acquired. The basis of *insāniyyah* required for this kind of capacity is not altered by jokes.

Hazl or jest cannot negate the capacity for execution either, because such a person has not lost his intellect or discretion. Contracts, on the other hand, require consent and willingness to give rise to legal effects. The person speaking in jest does bring about the apparent form (*ṣīghah*) of the contract, but has not given his consent in reality. The Ḥanafīs, therefore, consider the transactions of such a person as invalid, except transactions like marriage, divorce, manumission, *rujū'* (retraction), and the like. This is based on the tradition that says, "Three things intended seriously are taken seriously, and if intended in jest are also taken seriously: marriage, divorce, and the freeing of a slave." Some jurists do not maintain this exemption, and treat all statements made in jest as being ineffective. The Shāfi'īs maintain that statements made in jest are to be considered valid at all times, because the person has brought about the cause—the *ṣīghah* (form)—and must, therefore, bear the consequences. This is based on the objective theory of contracts that is followed in Islamic law by most schools.[182]

182. It is followed in English common law as well and, therefore, in most countries that adopted this law. For example, it is a view taken by American law that contracting parties shall only be bound by terms that can be inferred from promises made. Contract law does not examine a contracting party's subjective intent or underlying motive. Judge Learned Hand said that the court will give words their usual meaning even if "it were proved by twenty bishops that [the] party

8.2.3 Indiscretion (*safah*)

This defect concerns financial transactions, that is, transactions undertaken carelessly and in a manner that a prudent person is likely to avoid. The result is foolish waste and squandering of property.

The tendency in a person to waste his property affects neither his capacity for acquisition nor his capacity for execution. The effect of *safah* is that a person, who has attained puberty, is subjected to interdiction (*ḥajr*) till such time that he mends his ways. This view is upheld by the majority. It is based upon the necessity (*ḍarūrah*) of preserving his wealth, because preservation of wealth is an acknowledged purpose of the law. Abū Ḥanīfah maintains that interdiction can last only till the age of twenty-five, after which the property of the individual is to be delivered to him, because at this age the individual is to be preferred over property.

8.2.4 Coercion and duress (*ikrāh*)

Ikrāh is a situation in which one is forced to do something without his willingness.[183] It has no effect either on the capacity for acquisition or the capacity for execution, because this state does not affect life or reason and discretion. It does, however, negate free consent and willingness.

Effect on free will. The jurists disagree about the extent to which *ikrāh* can affect free will. The views of these jurists may be classified into two opinions:

1. The first opinion maintains that *ikrāh* is an obstacle in the way of *taklīf* (creation of an obligation). Thus, the *khiṭāb* is not directed toward a person under coercion

...intended something else." *Hotchkiss v. National City Bank of New York*, 200 F. 287 (2d Cir. 1911). It appears that in France the subjective theory is followed, because of which some Muslim countries that have been influenced by that law are inclined towards the subjective theory.

183. For the details see Ṣadr al-Sharī'ah, *al-Tawḍīḥ*, vol. 2, 820.

or under duress, because this person is prevented from understanding the *khiṭāb*. Among those who hold this opinion are Shāfi'ī jurists, who maintain that free will is a condition of *taklīf*. *Ikrāh*, according to the Shāfi'īs, arises under a threat of death, hurt, perpetual confinement, and the like. It does not arise for causes of a lesser gravity, like a threat to property. *Ikrāh* defined this way is, in their view, divided into two kinds:

a. *Justified coercion*. This is like the order of a *qāḍī* directing a debtor to pay his debts to his creditors, or his command to a man to divorce his wife after the passage of the period of *īlā'*, as required by Shāfi'ī law. This kind of *ikrāh* does not affect the free will of a person, as the duty is imposed by the Lawgiver. Thus, any transaction in property undertaken under coercion for paying off creditors shall not be declared void.

b. *Unjustified coercion*. Coercion without justification is again of two types. The first type is where acts committed are legally permissible under coercion. Such acts, if committed through words or deeds, have no legal effect and are considered void. If these acts can be attributed to a third person, then, they are attributed to the person coercing or threatening another. For example, compensation for property destroyed through coercion shall be paid by the person who coerces the other. The second type are acts that are legally prohibited, like murder and rape. In such cases the person coerced shall be fully liable along with the person who coerced him.

2. The second opinion is held by the Ḥanafīs, who divide *ikrāh* into three types:

   a. First is coercion that negates free will or choice. This is coercion under threat of death or loss of limb.

   b. The second type is coercion that negates consent, but makes free will irregular or *fāsid*. This is brought about by confinement for a long period or by beating and torture that does not lead to loss of life or limb.

c. The third type is *ikrāh* that does not negate consent nor does it make free will *fāsid*. The example is confinement of close relatives. Some Ḥanafī jurists do not accept this third category, and link it with one of the categories above, depending upon the nature of the threat to dear ones.

Effect of coercion on legal capacity. The Ḥanafīs maintain that the condition of *taklīf* is the existence of the right to choose and not its validity (*ṣiḥḥah*). Irregular or *fāsid* free will, they say, is sufficient for the existence of *taklīf*. In all the above cases of *ikrāh*, free will is not invalid (*bāṭil*) though it may be irregular. *Taklīf*, therefore, may accompany *ikrāh*.

To facilitate the understanding of the act, for which coercion is taking place, the Ḥanafīs divide it into three types:

1. *Transactions.* These are divided into two kinds, on the basis of the effect of *ikrāh*:

   a. First are transactions that do not accept rescission, and do not depend upon consent, for example, divorce, manumission, marriage, retraction of divorce, *ẓihār, īlā', 'afw* (forgiveness) in intentional murder, and oath (*yamīn*.) All these transactions are valid under coercion, because they amount to a termination (*isqāṭ*) or relinquishment of a right, and relinquishment cannot be reverted, because these transactions are not dependent on consent.

   b. Second are transactions that accept rescission or revocation and depend upon consent. These are like sale, mortgage, hire, and other commutative contracts. These contracts accept rescission and depend upon the existence of free consent. The *ḥukm* of such contracts concluded under coercion is that they are irregular (*fāsid*.) They can be ratified by the coerced party, after coercion has ceased to exist, in which case they are declared as valid (*ṣaḥīḥ*).

2. *Admissions and confessions.* All admissions and confessions, in order to be valid, must be accompanied by free will.

3. *Acts in general.* Acts, for this purpose, are divided into two kinds by the Ḥanafī jurists.

   a. First is the case when the coerced is a mere instrument in the hands of another, like a person picking up another and throwing him upon another thereby causing death, or hurt, or causing damage to property. If A causes B to fire at a bush knowing that C is hiding behind it, thus, causing the death of C, then, A shall be guilty of murder, while B will be an instrument in his hand. Other cases can be imagined. In such cases the act is attributed not to the instrument, but to one who caused him to move.

   b. Second is the case when the coerced cannot become an instrument in the hands of another, for example, in the commission of *zinā* or eating of food. In such a case, the person coerced is fully aware of his actions. Here the person coerced is guilty of *zinā* or for compensating property consumed. In the case of drinking of *khamr*, however, *ḥadd* is waived on grounds of *shubhah.*

8.2.5 Mistake and ignorance (*khaṭa'*, *shubhah*, and *jahl*)

The topics of *jahl* and *khaṭa'* are usually discussed separately, while the topic of *shubhāt* is not discussed under defective legal capacity. All three are interrelated and deal with concepts that are similar to what in Western law are called mistake of law and mistake of fact.

The word *shubhah* is usually translated as doubt. The most important evidence in this respect is the tradition of the Prophet (peace be on him) in which it has been said that the *ḥudūd* penalties are to be waived in case of *shubhah.* This is usually taken to mean "benefit of doubt" given to the accused. While this meaning may be covered by the tradition it is not its primary concern. The rule of giving benefit of doubt to the accused is generally accepted as a rule of evidence in Islamic law. Further, this rule deals with the doubt in the mind of the judge as to whether an offence has been proved beyond doubt. The tradition, according to the jurists, deals with doubts in the mind of the subject at the time of commission or omission of an act. These are of several types: *shubhah fī al-dalīl* (mistake of law); *shubah fī al-milk* (mistake as to ownership); *shubhah fī al-fi'l* (mistake in the commission of the act); and *shubhah fī al-'aqd* (mistake as to the governing law in the contract).

For example, assuming that in the early days there was a person who was under the impression that temporary marriage is permitted, that is, he may not be aware of the abrogating evidence. If he entered into a temporary marriage under this impression, the marriage contract was declared void, but the law would waive the *ḥadd* penalty in such a case (this does not mean that *ta'zīr* was also waived). There could have been a possibility of the occurrence of such a case in the early days when people were not aware of the law. Today it is unlikely to happen. In any case, it is an example of *shubhah fī al-dalīl* as well as *shubhah fī al-'aqd.* If some of the heirs pardon the murderer, but some of the other heirs, who have not pardoned him, execute him, they will not be subjected to retaliation due to *shubhah fī al-dalīl* (mistake of law). They may be awarded *ta'zīr*. Today, these heirs are not permitted to take the law into their own hands. It should be obvious that exemptions for mistakes of law are given where the issue is subject to *ijtihād.* Where the matter is not subject to *ijtihād,* and is clearly known, or is supposed to be known to Muslims by necessity, there can be no exemption.

In the early days, when slavery was permitted, a husband may be under the impression that his wife's slave girl is also within his ownership. Under this wrong impression if he were to consider her *milk yamīn* and act upon it he would be under *shubhah fī al-milk.* The *ḥadd* penalty would be waived in such a case (though not *ta'zīr*). If a man aiming at an animal were to hit a human being, he would be guilty of manslaughter (*qatl khaṭa'*) and not murder.

This is an example of *shubhah fī al-fi'l.*

The law gives some exemption in such cases and lays down principles that may be applied to new cases. It can be seen with ease, however, that ignorance or mistake does not affect the capacity of acquisition at all. It does not affect the capacity for execution either, the basis for which is understanding or *'aql.* The only problem here is that the understanding of the subject is hampered somewhat, but the law takes notice even of this. This shows that ignorance and mistake are not causes of defective capacity at all, but statutory grounds of defence or exemptions.

Jahl (ignorance) may, thus, be that of law or of fact. In general, ignorance of law is no excuse for a subject present within the *dār al-Islām.* This, however, should not be confused with the acts of a Muslim residing in the *dār al-ḥarb.* The Ḥanafīs make an exemption for some of the unlawful acts of such an individual, because he is not enjoying the protection of the Islamic state during his stay abroad. Submission to the Islamic state and being subject to its jurisdiction is also stated as a condition of *taklīf* by some jurists. The issue of jurisdiction of the Muslim state is expressed as a principle by the Ḥanafī jurist al-Dabbūsī:

> The principle according to our jurists is that the world is divided into two *dārs*: *dār al-Islām* and *dār al-ḥarb.* According to Imām al-Shāfi'ī the entire world is a single *dār.*[184]

In other words, al-Shāfi'ī does not grant the same exemptions to an individual residing in enemy territory.

Review Questions

1. How does minority affect legal capacity?

2. What position does Islamic law take with respect to the defence of insanity?

3. Explain in detail the rules pertaining to *maraḍ al-mawt.*

4. When can intoxication be a defence?

184. Al-Dabbūsī, *Ta'sīs al-Naẓar* (Cairo, 1320 A.H./1902 C.E.), 58.

5. Islamic law follows the objective theory of contracts. Elaborate.

6. Distinguish between coercion and duress. When are these valid defences?

7. Explain the meaning of the term *shubhah*. How is this meaning related to the concept of mistake in Islamic law?

Part II

The Primary Sources of Islamic Law

9 The Meaning of Primary and Secondary Sources

The true source for the *aḥkām* of Islamic law, as already stated in the first part, is Allāh Almighty. The *aḥkām* of Allāh, however, are discovered through evidences leading to the *aḥkām*. These evidences are the sources of Islamic law. The meaning of the term source as used in Islamic law does not differ much from its use in positive law, but there are subtle differences that must be appreciated. The obvious difference between the two systems is that the material sources of Islamic law are divine in origin, while those of positive law are not. As regards the sources that are constructed upon human mental processes like analogy, there may be much that is common. To appreciate some of the differences and similarities we need to examine the meaning of the term *source* as used in Islamic law and, in addition, to examine the different ways in which the sources are classified by Muslim jurists.

9.1 The Meaning of "Source" in Islamic Law

In Islamic law, the term used for source is *dalīl* (pl. *adillah*).[185] The word *dalīl* means guide. The person leading a caravan is called *dalīl*, and so is a telephone directory, because it leads to a number. The Qur'ān, in this sense, is a *dalīl* for the *aḥkām* of Allāh, because it leads us to the *khiṭāb*[186] of Allāh that contains the *aḥkām* related to the acts of the subjects.[187] Thus, an examination of the contents of the Qur'ān yields the information required about a *ḥukm*. This is how some jurists describe the technical meaning of *dalīl*: "A valid examination of which yields transmitted information[, which is the *ḥukm*]" (ما يمكن التوصل بصحيح النظر فيه إلى مطلوب خبري)[188]

The term *dalīl* in this meaning is also considered equivalent to the terms *uṣūl al-aḥkām* (the roots of the *aḥkām*) and *al-maṣādir al-shar'iyyah li al-aḥkām* (legal sources of the *aḥkām*). As all these terms are considered synonymous, it would be helpful to understand the classification of the sources from various perspectives.

9.2 The Classification of the Sources

The jurists state that the sources of Islamic law are: the Qur'ān, the *Sunnah*, *ijmā'* (consensus of legal opinion), *qiyās* (analogy), *istiḥsān* (juristic preference), *qawl al-ṣaḥābī* (the opinion of a Companion), *maṣlaḥah mursalah* (jurisprudential interest), *sadd al-dharī'ah* (blocking lawful means to an unlawful end), *istiṣḥāb*

185. This term has been used throughout this book and the reader is already familiar with it.
186. The term *khiṭāb* is described by some as the personal and eternal communication of Allah, an indication or evidence (*dalīl*) of which is His *khiṭāb* in words, that is, the words of the Qur'ān.
187. This was explained earlier, while discussing the definition of *ḥukm*. See page 69
188. Al-Āmidī, *al-Iḥkām fī Uṣūl al-Aḥkām*, vol. 3, 11. Some of the jurists say that a *dalīl* is a source that indicates the *ḥukm* in a definitive manner, while the source that indicates it in a probable manner is a sign, but this analysis is rejected by the majority.

al-ḥāl (presumption of continuity of a rule), *'urf* (custom), and earlier scriptural laws. These sources are classified from different perspectives to facilitate study.

9.2.1 Agreed upon and disputed sources

The jurists classify some of the sources as being agreed upon unanimously. These are the Qur'ān and the *Sunnah*. Some of the other sources are agreed upon by the majority of the schools. These are *ijmā'* and *qiyās*. It is said that the principle of *ijmā'* was not accepted by al-Naẓẓām from the Mu'tazilah and some of the Khawārij. *Qiyās*, on the other hand, was rejected by the Ẓāhirī school and the Ja'farī school. There is another category of sources that are not accepted by all jurists. These are *istiḥsān* (juristic preference), *qawl al-ṣaḥābī* (the opinion of a Companion), *maṣlaḥah mursalah* (jurisprudential interest), *istiṣḥāb al-ḥāl* (presumption of continuity), *sadd al-dharī'ah* (plugging the lawful means to an unlawful end), *'urf* (custom), and earlier scriptural laws.

The reader should note that many of the differences, though not all, between the opinions and methodologies of the schools are based upon the acceptance and rejection of the disputed sources.

9.2.2 Transmitted and rational sources

The sources of Islamic law are divided into those that are transmitted and those that are rational, that is, those that relate to legal reasoning. The transmitted sources are the Qur'ān, the *Sunnah*, and *ijmā'*. To these are also linked the opinion of a Companion, and the laws of the earlier scriptures. These are the transmitted sources, for the legal validity of which reason has little role to play, though it does affect the legal reasoning that proceeds from them.[189] The other kind are analogy (*qiyās*), *maṣlaḥah*, *istiḥsān*, and *istiṣḥāb*. These sources pertain to the mental processes of human beings and are not transmitted, though their acceptance as legally valid and persuasive proofs does rely upon

189. In fact, reason plays a major role before *ijmā'* on a legal issue becomes a source.

the transmitted evidences. Thus, *qiyās* is the assigning of the *ḥukm* taken from a transmitted evidence to a set of facts about which there is no express provision in the transmitted evidences. This is a mental process. The acceptance of *qiyās* as a valid method of reasoning is derived from the transmitted evidences, the Qur'ān as well as the *Sunnah*. In short, the transmitted sources themselves identify the modes of legal reasoning that may be accepted as valid and persuasive proofs.

The transmitted sources, therefore, become sources from three aspects.

- First, by indicating the detailed rules of law, like those of prayer, *zakāt*, and inheritance.
- Second, by providing legal justification for the use of methods of reasoning like analogy and *maslaḥah*. In fact, all the transmitted evidences themselves find support for their acceptance in the Qur'ān. As an example we may state that the following verses provide the evidence for the *Sunnah* as a valid source:

> O ye who believe! Obey Allah and obey the Apostle, and those charged with authority among you. [Qur'ān 4 : 59]
>
> So take what the Apostle assigns to you, and deny yourselves that which he withholds from you. [Qur'ān 59 : 7]
>
> Then let those beware who withstand the Apostle's order lest some trial befall them, or a grievous penalty be inflicted upon them. [Qur'ān 24 : 63]

In addition to this, the function of the *Sunnah* is also indicated; namely, that it works as an elaboration and commentary on the Qur'ān:

> And we have sent down unto thee (also) the Message; that thou mayest explain clearly to men what is sent for them, and that they may give thought. [Qur'ān 16 : 44]
>
> O Apostle! proclaim the (Message) which hath been sent to thee from thy Lord. [Qur'ān 5 : 67]

In the study of the *Sunnah* in the next chapter, its close relationship with the Qur'ān will be examined in detail.

- A third characteristic of the transmitted sources is that they provide a basis for the extension of the law through the rational sources. Thus, a rule in the texts may be extended through analogy, but the basis or *aṣl* is provided by the texts or the transmitted sources.

9.2.3 Definitive and probable sources

The sources of Islamic law are also classified, by the majority of the jurists, as definitive (*qaṭʿī*) and probable (*ẓannī*). When we use the word definitive, we mean something about which we cannot have two opinions, while probable means something that does not reach this level of strength. From another perspective, the attribute of a source being definitive or probable refers to the strength of transmission of the source, that is, the way it has been transmitted by the first three generations. The classical jurists usually use the terms definitive and probable in the sense of transmission. Thus, when the Ḥanafīs say that the category of *farḍ* is proved by a definitive evidence, they are referring to an evidence that is definitive by way of transmission. Modern scholars, in their attempt to simplify things, have come up with an instructional device and have generalised the meaning of a text as definitive or probable in meaning. Thus, they refer to a source as *qaṭʿī al-thubūt* (definitive by way of transmission) and *qaṭʿī al-dalālah* (definitive in meaning). A closer examination shows that there is no such general category called *qaṭʿī al-dalālah* (definitive in meaning) in the systems followed by the classical jurists. When these jurists wanted to refer to such meanings, they listed separate individual categories: *muḥkam, naṣṣ, khafī, ẓāhir* and so on. All these categories were based upon the different strengths of meaning emerging from a word or a text. Nevertheless, we are retaining the broad category *qaṭʿī al-dalālah*, because of its instructional value. The reader is warned, however, to be careful about the distinctions. What follows is, therefore, based on the classification followed by modern scholars.

1. **With respect to transmission,** a source is *qaṭʿī al-sanad* if it has been reported by a large group of persons from a large

group of persons, when in practice a report of such a large group is not subject to suspicion, because they could not have assembled together to fabricate a falsehood. This type of transmission is called *tawātur.* Of this definitive category is the Qur'ān, because it has been transmitted to us, both in memorised and written forms, by way of *tawātur*. The same is the case with the *Sunnah* and *ijmā'* when they have been transmitted to us by way of *tawātur*. In the probable category fall individual narrations of the *Sunnah* and *ijmā'* when these have not been transmitted in a form that reaches the level of *tawātur*.

2. A source is definitive **with respect to the understood meaning** when the text of the transmitted evidence indicates something about which there can be only one opinion.[190] Thus, if the text of the Qur'ān says that you have "half" of what your deceased spouses left or when it says that for the fornicator are a "hundred" stripes, the words "half" and "hundred" cannot have dual meanings, because a "hundred" is a "hundred" any way we may read it or understand it. Probable means something that can have more than one meaning, and the examples are many.

   There are some texts of the Qur'ān and the *Sunnah* that convey definitive meanings and there are others that convey a probable meaning. As for *ijmā'*, it always indicates a definitive meaning, because having more than one meaning negates the very concept of *ijmā'*. The rest of the sources, like analogy and *istiḥsān* all convey probable meanings.

This division into definitive and probable gives us four combinations of the transmitted sources:

1. Sources that are definitive with respect to *sanad* (transmission) and definitive with respect to meaning. These would be the texts of the Qur'ān and the *Sunnah Mutawātirah* that convey single meanings.

190. As indicated above, this will be called *muḥkam* or *naṣṣ* and so on.

2. Sources that are definitive with respect to *sanad*, but are probable with respect to meaning. These would be the texts of the Qur'ān and the *Sunnah Mutawātirah* that convey more than one meaning, that is, they are subject to interpretation. When the Qur'ān says: "Rub your heads (*masḥ*) with water," [Qur'ān 5 : 6] it is probable that the meaning is the entire head or part of it, and both meanings have been upheld by jurists. The same is the case with the *Sunnah*.

3. Sources that are probable with respect to transmission and definitive with respect to the implied meaning. These would include traditions that were transmitted by one or two individuals in the first three generations. Examples would include those traditions that contain definitive words.

4. Sources that are probable with respect to *sanad* and probable with respect to meaning. An example is the tradition that says that "there is nothing out of the inheritance for the killer." The question is whether the killing here means *qatl 'amd* (murder), *shibh al-'amd* (culpable homicide not amounting to murder or voluntary manslaughter), *qatl khaṭa'* (manslaughter), or even homicide caused directly or indirectly. The opinions of the jurists, therefore, vary.

As for the sources that are not transmitted, they are not relevant to the discussion of the above four categories; in general they are considered as probable. It is only the opinion of a Companion that may be linked to the above four transmitted categories by some jurists.

9.2.4 Primary and secondary sources

The classification of the sources of Islamic law into primary and secondary is nothing more than a collection, and the combined effect, of the all the characteristics that have preceded in the previous classifications. Thus, when we view the previous characteristics, we distinguish the primary and secondary sources as follows:

1. **Primary sources are those that are unanimously agreed upon by the four Sunnī schools.** This would include analogy. When the range of schools is widened, analogy is excluded and so is *ijmā'*. Secondary sources are those that are not unanimously accepted.

2. **Primary sources are transmitted sources, while secondary sources are mostly rational sources.** This distinction would include the opinion of a Companion among the primary sources, but the previous criterion excludes it.

3. **Primary sources are definitive sources, while secondary sources are probable.** The *khabar wāhid,* we have said is probable, but here we are concerned with the *Sunnah* as a source of law on the whole. Likewise, this classification may be said to include only those types of *ijmā'* that are considered definitive, but again we are concerned with consensus as a source of law on the whole. Analogy and other types of rational sources would be classified as secondary sources.

4. **Laws discovered through the primary sources may be extended** through the rational sources or the secondary sources, while laws discovered through secondary sources cannot be further extended. This, perhaps, is the most important distinction between the primary and secondary sources.[191]

Primary sources, then, are at once agreed upon, transmitted, definitive on the whole, and those upon which further extension can be based. This would mean that the Qurān, the *Sunnah,* and *ijmā'* are the primary sources, while the rest are secondary sources.

191. A question may be raised here as to whether the law can be extended through broad general principles, especially when some of these are rational constructions or the result of systematisation? The discussion has preceded within the analysis of the *dalīl tafṣīlī*. See p. 51 above.

To describe the characteristics of secondary sources, just reverse the characteristics listed above. For example, secondary sources are mostly rational sources, or they are mostly disputed sources, or that they depend on the primary sources for their content.

9.3 Grades of the Sources

It is customary with writers to discuss the grades of the sources under a general and preliminary discussion such as this. By grades is meant the priority assigned to a source in the jurists' search for the *aḥkām*. This topic pertains to *ijtiḥād* and the *tarjīḥ*. It is, therefore, discussed briefly here.

Many writers maintain that the first source to be approached is the Qur'ān, the second is the *Sunnah*, the third is *ijmā'* (consensus of legal opinion) and the fourth is analogy. These writers also maintain, on the basis of this natural order, that it is not proper to move to another source unless the search in the prior source has been exhausted. Thus, the first search for a *ḥukm* is to be in the Qur'ān. The jurist should not move to the next source, the *Sunnah*, unless the search in the Qur'ān has been completed. Likewise, the jurist should not move to the consensus of jurists, unless the search in the *Sunnah* is exhausted. Analogy is to be resorted to only when the search in all three prior sources is completed. These scholars rely upon a number of evidences to strengthen this view.

For example, they rely upon the verse: "O ye who believe! Obey Allāh, and obey the Apostle, and those charged with authority among you. If ye differ in anything among yourselves, refer it to Allāh and His Apostle, if ye do believe in Allāh and the Last Day." [Qur'ān 4 : 59] In this verse, they maintain, obedience to Allāh means having recourse to the Book of Allāh, obedience to the Prophet (peace be on him) means having recourse to his *Sunnah* and obeying those in authority means having recourse to *ijmā'*. The order is, thus, prescribed in this verse.

Another source they rely upon is the well known tradition of Mu'ādh ibn Jabal:

> When the Apostle of Allāh intended to send Mu'ādh ibn Jabal to the Yemen, he asked: How will you judge when the occasion of deciding a case arises? He replied: I shall judge in accordance with Allāh's Book. He asked: (What will you do) if you do not find guidance in Allāh's Book? He replied: (I will act) in accordance with the *Sunnah* of the Messenger of Allāh. He asked: (What will you do) if you do not find guidance in the *Sunnah* of the Apostle of Allāh and in Allāh's Book? He replied: I shall do my best to form an opinion and spare no pains. The Apostle of Allāh then patted him on the breast and said: Praise be to Allāh Who helped the messenger of the Apostle of Allāh to find a thing which pleases the Apostle of Allāh.[192]

This tradition determines the order in which the sources are to be approached. It also indicates that analogy is to be resorted to when the search in the texts has been exhausted.

In addition to these two sources, these scholars mention the letter of 'Umar ibn al-Khaṭṭāb, may Allāh be pleased with him, written to the famous *qāḍī* Shurayḥ: "When you are faced with an issue, decide through what is laid down in the Book of Allah. If the issue you face relates to what is not in the Book of Allah, then decide by what is in the *Sunnah* of the Messenger of Allah (peace be on him)." In another version of this *athar* the words are: "If you find something in the Book of Allāh, decide through it and do not have recourse to anything else besides it." A third narration explains this meaning: "Examine what is evident for you in the Book of Allāh and do not ask anyone about it. If nothing is evident for you in the Book of Allāh, follow the *Sunnah* of the Messenger of Allah (peace be on him)."

All these evidences show, it is maintained, that there is a determined order for approaching the sources and that the jurist should not move to the next source, unless the first source has been searched thoroughly for a solution.

A closer examination of the issue reveals that the statement about the order in which the sources are to be examined needs to be qualified somewhat. This is obvious from the following points:

192. Abū Dāwūd, *Sunan Abū Dāwūd*, tr. Ahmad Hasan, vol. 3 (Lahore: Sh. Muhammad Ashraf, 1984), No. 3585 at 1019.

1. **Approaching the Qur'ān and the Sunnah together:** The first point to notice is that it is not possible for the jurist to understand the meaning of the text of the Qur'ān for the derivation of the *aḥkām,* unless he has recourse to the explanation and commentary of the Qur'ān. This explanation and commentary is the *Sunnah* itself. Thus, a jurist may not decide upon the basis of a general or absolute text in the Qur'ān, unless he has ascertained that the *Sunnah* has not restricted the general meaning or has not qualified the absolute text.[193]

   Take the case of the provisions for the thief (*sāriq*) in the Qur'ān. It provides that the hands of each thief are to be cut. The *Sunnah* restricts this general rule to the thief who steals wealth equivalent to the *niṣāb* (prescribed scale). It also restricts it to a person who steals something in protective custody (*ḥirz*). Likewise, the Qur'ān provides for the payment of *zakāt* in broad terms, that is, for all kinds of wealth, but the *Sunnah* excludes several categories of wealth from this wide provision.

   The *Sunnah* is, therefore, interlinked with the Qur'ān insofar as it restricts its general meaning or qualifies absolute texts or explains its difficult and unelaborated words. It would, thus, be inappropriate, if not incorrect, for the jurist to take the *ḥukm* directly from the Qur'ān without consulting the *Sunnah.* The statement, then, that the Qur'ān is to be consulted first and the *Sunnah* is to be consulted only if nothing is found in the Qur'ān, is to be qualified to mean that consulting the Qur'ān implies the consulting of the *Sunnah* along with it. In other words, there is a special bond between the *Qur'ān* and the *Sunnah* and this bond must never be severed.

2. In one classification above it is stated that a greater weight is attached to a definitive (*qaṭ'ī*) meaning arising from a

193. See the concept of *bayān* at page 341 for a deeper understanding of the issue.

mutawātir Sunnah as compared to a text in the Qur'ān that can be interpreted in more than one way. In technical terms, it means that such a *Sunnah* is definitive with respect to its transmission as well as its meaning, while a *ẓannī* text of the Qur'ān is definitive with respect to its transmission, but probable as regards the meaning. In such a case too, it would be inappropriate for the jurist to look at the text of the Qur'ān alone and not at the *Sunnah*.

3. ***Ijmā'* and the Texts:** *ḥukm* is sometimes established through consensus of opinion (*ijmā'*). *Ijmā'* is considered definitive by the jurists and the jurist is bound to follow its directives. According to the principles of *tarjīḥ* (precedence of evidences) it is required of a jurist that he first investigate whether the case he is examining has been settled by *ijmā'*. If it has been, he is to follow the settled rule and give up his own *ijtihād*. This process may be compared with the precedents laid down by higher courts. If the higher court has laid down a precedent and has interpreted a statute in a certain way, the lower court is bound to follow the precedent and construe the statute accordingly. It is obvious that consensus of legal opinion has assigned definitive meanings to texts in which the meanings were not very clear, therefore, *ijmā'* will have precedence over the unelaborated or multiple meanings in the texts.

4. **General principles derived from the texts:** According to the methodology of some jurists, especially the Ḥanafīs and Mālikīs, broad general principles that have been derived from the entire law through a process of juristic reasoning are to be preferred over the *khabar wāḥid* in certain cases. This is the view of the Ḥanafīs and Mālikīs.

The above discussion shows that the sources cannot be consulted in a simple order of priority advocated by some writers. The matter is much more complex, and it is one task of the subject of *uṣūl al-fiqh* to unravel these complexities for the student of Islamic law.

Review Questions

1. Rational sources are merely extensions of the transmitted sources. Comment.
2. Elaborate the characterstics of transmitted sources.
3. What is the significance of classifying sources into definitive and probable?
4. Distinguish primary sources from secondary sources.
5. What is the order in which the sources are to be approached during *ijtihād*?

10 The Qur'ān

The primary sources are the Qur'ān and the *Sunnah*, because these sources contain the law for many cases and also serve as the basis for the extension of the law. Consensus of legal opinion (*ijmā'*) also contains the law, and its provisions can be used for extending the law further, though some would prefer to have recourse to the basis or the *sanad* of *ijmā'* for the new case.[194] For this basis, we have to turn to the Qur'ān and the *Sunnah* again, therefore, some jurists maintain that the primary sources are the Qur'ān and the *Sunnah* alone, and *ijmā'* is a kind of secondary source. It is, however, associated with the primary sources for the purposes of this book on the basis of the reasons discussed earlier.

In this chapter the Qur'ān and the *Sunnah* will be studied as the two primary sources. This will be followed by a description of the close relationship between these two sources. Finally, the details of *ijmā'* as a source of law will be examined.

194. If the source on which the jurists have relied for *ijmā'* are mentioned, the binding force will come from this source rather than from *ijmā'*.

10.1 The Qur'ān as the Primary Source of Law

The words al-Qur'ān and *al-Kitāb* are used in the same meaning. The jurists who specialise in *uṣūl al-fiqh* (called *uṣūlīs*) are hesitant about providing a definition of the Qur'ān insofar as a definition means enclosing the defined thing within bounds.[195] Yet, many of them, in an attempt to grasp all its noble attributes and characteristics have provided definitions. They maintain that the purpose of the definition is not to enclose the nature of the Qur'ān in a definition, but to identify the book in response to the question: Which book do you mean? One such definition recorded here is from al-Bazdawī.

القرآن: هو الكتاب المنزل على رسول الله محمد صلى الله عليه وسلم المكتوب فى دفات المصاحف،
المنقول إلينا على الأحرف السبع المشهورة نقلا متواترا

This may be rendered into English as follows:

> The Qur'ān is the Book revealed to the Messenger of Allāh, Muḥammad (peace be on him) as written in the *maṣāḥif*[196] and transmitted to us from him through an authentic continuous narration (*tawātur*) without doubt.[197]

Some jurists add the words "revealed in Arabic" to emphasise that it cannot be translated, while others say that "the Qur'ān is the revealed and miraculous speech of Allāh ...," to emphasise the *i'jāz* (inimitable or miraculous nature) of the Book. Still others, like the Ḥanafīs, add that it is transmitted in its seven readings all of which are *mutawātir*.

The attempt in most of these definitions is to emphasise the following attributes:

1. *The Qur'ān is the speech of Allāh revealed to Muḥammd (peace be on him).* This attribute excludes other revealed books

195. See, e.g., Ṣadr al-Sharī'ah, *al-Tawḍīḥ*, vol. 1, 57.
196. This is used to indicate the order in which the Qur'ān is recorded as well as well as its syntax.
197. Al-Bazdawī, *Uṣūl al-Bazdawī* in 'Abd al-'Azīz al-Bukhārī, *Kashf al-Asrār 'an Uṣūl al-Bazdawī*, vol. 1, 23.

from the definition, that is, books that were not revealed to Muḥammad (peace be on him). These are like the Torah (التوراة) and the Evangel (الإنجيل). Some jurists maintain that the word Qur'ān applies to the eternal speech of the Almighty as well as to the written text that is recited. To refine their definition some insist that it is the recited text that is meant here, while others maintain that both meanings are included in the definition.[198]

2. *The Arabic words of the Qur'ān as well as their meanings are both revealed.* This attribute excludes the *Sunnah* from the definition, because the words of the *Sunnah* are not those of Allāh though its content is inspired and is considered to be revelation in meaning from Allāh.

   The attribute also excludes the *tafsīr* of the Qur'ān and the translation of the Qur'ān from this definition. It is said that Abū Ḥanīfah used to permit recitation in Fārsī during prayers for those who did not know Arabic, however, authentic reports in the Ḥanafī school confine such permission to converts to Islam for a period in which they are able to learn the Arabic text. Thus, the exemption was for necessity and need and was, therefore, limited. There has been an intense debate on the issue in Islamic legal literature.

   Translation of the Qur'ān is, therefore, not possible and what are termed translations are in fact translations of the *tafsīr* (interpretation) of the Qur'ān.

3. *The Qur'ān is transmitted to us by way of tawātur.* This means that the Qur'ān was transmitted to us both in its written and memorised form by such a large number of people in each generation starting with the first that any doubt about its not being the original text cannot be conceived rationally. This attribute is intended to exclude a few variant readings

198. 'Abd al-'Azīz al-Bukhārī, *Kashf al-Asrār*, vol. 1, 36–37.

of the Qur'ān that were not revealed by way of *tawātur*.[199] The Qur'ān cannot be communicated in what is less than *tawātur*.

4. *I'jāz of the Qur'ān.* *I'jāz* means the inability of human beings individually or collectively to imitate or bring about something similar to the Qur'ān. This inability was acknowledged by the Arabs during the period of the Prophet. The inability also confirms that the Qur'ān is the revealed word of Allāh, and is therefore a source of law.[200] In other words, for purposes of the jurist, *i'jāz* becomes an additional proof of the authenticity of the Qur'ān and the truth of the mission of the Prophet (peace be on him)

10.1.1 Justification of the Qur'ān as a source

The entire *ummah* agreed that the Qur'ān is the primary source for the *aḥkām* of Allāh. It is, therefore, binding upon the jurist to have recourse to it and to rely upon it for the discovery of the law in each case that he faces. They also agreed that the jurist will find each case provided for in the Qur'ān either expressly or by implication, that is, through derivation (*istinbāṭ*). In approaching the Qur'ān for the derivation of the laws, the jurist is also under an obligation to have recourse to its commentary and explanation, which is the *Sunnah* of the Prophet. The statement of al-Shāfi'ī recorded earlier that "there is no incident that befalls one of those who follow the *dīn* of Allāh without there being an evidence in the Book of Allāh providing guidance for it"[201] emphasises this meaning.

199. For the details of the seven readings transmitted by *tawātur* and three that are not so transmitted see Khuḍrī Bey, *Uṣūl al-Fiqh*, (Cairo: al-Maktabah al-Tijārīyah al-Kubrā, 1962), 251.

200. There is a discussion whether *i'jāz* pertains to individual verses or whole *sūrahs*.

201. Among the verses he quotes is verse 89 of Sūrah al-Naḥl: "And We have sent down to thee the Book explaining all things, a Guide, a Mercy, and glad tidings to Muslims." Al-Shāfi'ī, *al-Risālah* (Cairo, 1309/1891, Reprint Beirut: Dār al-Fikr, n.d.) 20, paras 48–52.

Considering the Qur'ān as *the primary source* means that all the other sources are secondary to it; even their legal validity and justification as sources is derived from the Qur'ān.

10.1.2 The recording and revelation of the Qur'ān

The compilation of the Qur'ān has a detailed and well documented history. These details can be gleaned elsewhere. The reason why it is studied under the title of the Qur'ān as a source of Islamic law is to provide further justification for its having been transmitted by way of *tawātur* and also to explain the reason for its unique arrangement.

The Qur'ān, as is well known, was not revealed all at once to the Messenger of Allāh (peace be on him), but in stages and in accordance with incidents faced by the Muslim community. The important aspect of the wisdom behind its revelation in this way is considered to be the ease in its memorisation by the Companions. Allāh, the Exalted, says: "(It is) a Qur'ān which We have divided (into parts from time to time) in order that thou mightest recite it to men at intervals: We have revealed it by stages," [Qur'ān 17 : 106] and "Those who reject faith say: 'Why is not the Qur'ān revealed to him all at once?' Thus (it is revealed), that We may strengthen thy heart thereby, and We have rehearsed it to thee in slow, well-arranged stages, gradually." [Qur'ān 25 : 32]

Another reason for the gradual revelation of the Qur'ān is considered to be the implementation of the law in stages. This has given rise to the abrogating and the abrogated verses.[202] The clearest example of the laying down of the law in phases is the case of the prohibition of *khamr* (wine).

The incidents, cases, and questions that often preceded the revelation of the verses help, those who came later, in understanding the meaning and import of the verses. These are called the *asbāb al-nuzūl* or occasions for the revelation. These reasons have facilitated to a great extent the application of the law in all ages.

202. For an explanation of the meaning of abrogation and its principles see the chapter on Abrogation and Preference at p. 390 below.

The Messenger of Allāh used to memorise a verse or verses of the Qur'ān after their revelation. He then recited these for his Companions who used to memorise them. There were also scribes with the Prophet (pbuh) who used to record the verses after their revelation and recitation. These written records were then preserved in the Prophet's house, while some of the scribes would record the verses for themselves and preserve them for their own use. Jibrīl used to inform the Prophet (pbuh) of the place and location of each verse within its chapter (*sūrah*). During each Ramaḍān, it is said, Jibrīl used to recite in its proper arrangement with the Prophet what had been revealed of the Qur'ān, and in the last year of his life Jibrīl recited the whole of it in its proper arrangement and the Prophet (pbuh) recited it twice after him. The Prophet, thus, memorised it and recited it for his Companions, who memorised it in this arrangement.

By the time of Abū Bakr, the Qur'ān was to be found in its complete form either memorised or recorded in *ṣuḥuf*. Zayd ibn Thābit, therefore, did not rely upon the memory of the Companions alone when he prepared the official copy; he relied upon both.

10.2 Legal strength and indication of *aḥkām* in the Qur'ān

As the Qur'ān has been transmitted to us by way of *tawātur*, its authenticity is definitive (*qaṭ'ī*). This is from the aspect of transmission. When we read the Qur'ān, however, some of its words convey a definitive meaning, which is not subject to interpretation, while others convey probable meanings, that is, there can be two or meanings for a word.[203] Taking both these

203. As indicated earlier, such a classification is used for illustrative purposes. The jurists have detailed and more precise categories for the different shades of meanings arising from the texts. A single category like "definitive" in meaning is not enough to explain the complexity.

aspects into account we say that the Qur'ān indicates the *aḥkām* in two grades of strength, as follows:

1. Indications that are definitive with respect to *sanad* (transmission) and definitive with respect to meaning. The examples of such meanings, as provided in the previous chapter, were the words "half" or "hundred." This type of text is also known as *naṣṣ* (explicit). The rule for such indications are: "There is no *ijtihād* in a *naṣṣ* (explicit meaning not subject to interpretation)." Some people mistakenly believe that this rule applies to all the texts of the Qur'ān and that *ijtihād* is not possible where a text exists. Accordingly they call *ijtihād* by names like "independent reasoning" and so on, as if *ijtihād* was something independent of the texts. It is for the same reason, probably, that the idea is advanced that *ijtihād* is a source of law.[204]

2. Indications that are definitive with respect to *sanad*, but are probable with respect to meaning. These would be the texts of the Qur'ān that convey more than one meaning, that is, they are subject to interpretation. When the Qur'ān says: "Rub your heads (*masḥ*) with water," [Qur'ān 5 : 6] it is probable that the meaning is the entire head or part of it, and both meanings have been upheld by jurists. The rule stated for the first category does not apply here. Thus, the texts of the Qur'ān that indicate such meanings are subject to interpretation, that is, *ijtihād*.

10.3 The kinds of *aḥkām* in the Qur'ān

There are approximately six hundred verses in the Qur'ān that indicate the *aḥkām* of Islamic law. Over four hundred of these pertain to the *'ibādāt* and the remaining to crimes, personal law,

204. For an elaboration of this point see p. 427 below.

and other *mu'āmalāt*.[205] A few of all these verses belong to the first of the two categories mentioned above, that is, they do not need further elaboration. The remaining verses require interpretation and elaboration. The primary means of such elaboration or the choosing of one meaning out of two or more probable meanings is through the *Sunnah*. This relationship of the *Sunnah* with the Qur'ān will be explained later in this chapter. The texts of the Qur'ān also require analysis through the tools and rules of literal interpretation, even when the *Sunnah* is being employed for elaboration, and these tools have been described in the part on *ijtihād*. The kinds of *aḥkām* that are contained in the six hundred or more verses of the Qur'ān cover a very wide range of *aḥkām*. These may be divided into the following categories:

1. ***Aḥkām* Pertaining to *Aqā'id* (Tenets of Faith)**. These are like belief in One God, His Angels, Books, Prophets, and the Day of Judgement. The discipline dealing with these is that of *Tawḥīd*.

2. ***Aḥkām* Pertaining to the Disciplining and Strengthening of the Self.** These rules deal with Qur'ānic ethics. The disciplines that deal with them are ethics and *taṣawwuf*. Many of the ethical norms of the Qur'ān are to be found clothed in the legal provisions.

3. **Rules of Conduct (Pertaining to the Words and Acts of the Subject)**. This category covers the entire field of *fiqh*. They are divided into two types:

   A. *Rules Related to Worship.* The purpose of these rules is to establish the relationship of the individual with his Creator.

   B. *All Those Rules that Relate to Conduct Other than Worship.* This area is called *mu'āmalāt* by the jurists. It regulates

205. According to one count, about 70 verses pertain to family law, 80 to trade and finance, 13 to oaths, 30 to crimes and sentencing, 10 to constitutional and administrative matters, 25 to international law and prisoners of war, while the rest, over 400, pertain to *'ibādāt*.

> the relationship of individuals among themselves, the relationship of individuals with states, and the relationship of the Islamic state with non-Muslim states. In short, it covers the entire are of substantive and procedural law or to put it differently, it includes private and public law.

It is to be remembered that though the particular cases mentioned in the Qur'ān are few, there are many broad and general principles that facilitate the derivation of countless *aḥkām*.

10.4 Can one text of the Qur'ān abrogate another?

This issue will be discussed in the part on *ijtihād* (see p. 390 below).

Review Questions

1. How does al-Bazdawī define the Qur'ān as a source of law? What attributes flow from this definition?
2. The Qur'ān has been communicated to us through a *mutawātir* transmission alone. Comment.
3. Write a short note on the recording an revelation of the Qur'ān.
4. How are the legal meanings in the Qur'ān indicated and with what strength?
5. What are the different types of *aḥkām* that are found in the Qur'ān? Also give some examples of general principles stated in the Qur'ān.
6. Give a classification of the legal verses indicating the number of verses dealing with the *'ibādāt* and with other matters.

11 The *Sunnah*

11.1 The *Sunnah* as a Primary Source

11.1.1 Definition of the *Sunnah*

The word *Sunnah* has a literal meaning and several technical meanings. An indiscriminate use of the term leads to confusion, therefore, it is necessary that most of the technical meanings be understood.[206]

11.1.1.1 Literal meaning

In its literal meaning the word *sunnah* stands for the "well-known path," or the "well-trodden path," which is followed again and

206. There are a number of terms whose meanings need to be understood in the precise meanings in which they are used by the jurists. Some of the important terms are: *sunnah, ḥadīth, khabar* and *athar.* In these pages we will try to identify the meanings of these and several other terms.

again. This may be the path on which people tread or it may be a practice. It is in this sense that the following saying of the Prophet (peace be on him) is understood: "He who establishes a good *sunnah* has its reward and the reward of whoever acts upon it till the Day of Judgement, and he who establishes a bad *sunnah* bears its burden and the burden of whoever acts upon it till the Day of Judgement." The *sunnah* of an individual is a practice that he considers binding for himself and that he attempts to protect and uphold.

11.1.1.2 Technical meanings

In its technical sense, the word *sunnah* is assigned the following meanings:

1. Some jurists apply it to mean recommended acts of worship, while others apply it to supererogatory acts (*nawāfil*).

2. The word *sunnah* as an antonym of *bid'ah* (innovation), that is, innovations in matters of religion. In this sense, it is said, "This act is a *sunnah*," that is, it is legal. The meaning of "legal" is assigned to it irrespective of the legality arising from the Qur'ān or the *Sunnah*. When it is said that such and such act is a *bid'ah* it means it is not legal according to the Qur'ān and the *Sunnah*.

3. The term *sunnah* is used to mean the practice of the Companions (*Ṣaḥābah*) irrespective of their relying in it on the Book, the *Sunnah*, or their own *ijtihād*. An example is the compilation of the Qur'ān for which there was no authorising text either in the Qur'ān or in the *Sunnah*, but it amounted to an interest (*maṣlaḥah*) indicated by all the texts; namely, the preservation of *Dīn*. The saying of the Prophet (peace be on him), "Hold on to my *sunnah* and the *sunnah* of the rightly guided caliphs after me," is understood in this sense.

4. Finally, it is defined as **"what was transmitted from the Messenger of Allāh (peace be on him) of his words, acts,**

and (tacit) approvals." It is in this sense that we shall be using the term *sunnah*, that is, as the *Sunnah* of the Prophet (peace be on him) and a source of Islamic laws.

11.1.2 Kinds of *Sunnah*

The question that arises here is whether every saying, act and approval of the Prophet (peace be on him) has the same status for purposes of acting upon it as a source of law. To be able to answer this question it is necessary to look at the types of the *Sunnah*. For this purpose, the *Sunnah* is classified in two ways:

1. The kinds of the *Sunnah* when we look at the channels through which the *aḥkām* are established. This is also called the classification of the *Sunnah* according to its nature.

2. The kinds of the *Sunnah* with respect to the channels through which it is transmitted to us. This may be called the classification of the *Sunnah* according to its written record, that is, the classification of *ḥadīth*, when this term is used not merely for the sayings of the Prophet (peace be on him), but for the entire written record.

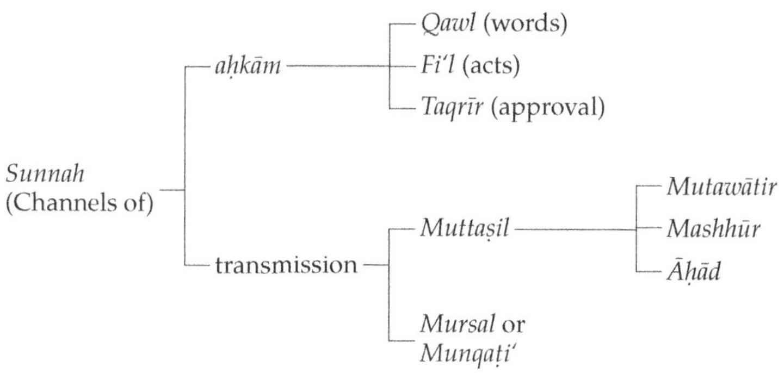

11.1.2.1 Kinds of the *Sunnah* with respect to the channels of the *aḥkām*

This type of the *Sunnah* is of three types: *sunnah qawliyyah* or the sayings of the Prophet (peace be on him); *sunnah fi'liyyah* or the acts of the Prophet (peace be on him); and *sunnah taqrīriyah* or the tacit approval given by the Prophet (peace be on him). Some jurists, like al-Shāṭibī, have discussed another subtype called *sunnat al-tark,* which is discussed briefly here along with *sunnah fi'liyyah.*

Al-Sunnah al-qawliyyah: It is defined as the sayings of the Prophet (peace be on him) through which he intended the laying down of the law or the explanation of the *aḥkām.* Generally, the word *ḥadīth* is used for this type of *sunnah* insofar as the word *ḥadīth* means "saying."[207] In this sense, the word *ḥadīth* has a

207. To avoid any confusion between the use of the terms *sunnah* and *ḥadīth,* we shall make a distinction between them for purposes of this book. The reason is that the terms are used interchangeably by authors and the result is a lack of precision.

The word *ḥadīth* means "saying." In this literal meaning it could stand for the sayings of the Prophet (peace be on him), that is, for one of the three types of *sunnah* mentioned in the definition above. Thus, it would exclude acts and tacit approvals. This, however, is not the meaning that we shall assign to the term *ḥadīth* here.

By *ḥadīth,* in this book, we mean the record of the *Sunnah* of the Prophet (peace be on him). This record may be written or in the form of an oral report. In this sense, one *ḥadīth* may contain more than one *sunnah.* A *ḥadīth* may report a saying, act, or approval of the Prophet (peace be on him). A single *sunnah* may be found in differently worded *aḥādīth.* When we say that a *sunnah* has been reported with a complete chain, what we mean is that it is contained in a *ḥadīth* with perfect *isnād. Hadīth* in this sense, then, is the bearer of the *Sunnah;* it is a report. It may also be added here that some jurists like Abū 'Ubayd ibn Sallām, the author of the well known book called *Kitāb al-Amwāl,* has used the term *ḥadīth* in a very wide sense of the word report. Thus, he includes in it reports from the Prophet (peace be on him), his Companions, and even their Followers. For our purposes here, the narrower meaning is intended: reports about the Prophet's

meaning narrower than that of *sunnah*. Some of the traditionists, however, use the term *ḥadīth* to mean all that is reported from the Prophet (peace be on him), that is, words, acts, and approvals. In this sense, the words *sunnah* and *ḥadīth* are synonyms. It is in this meaning that al-Bukhārī calls his book *al-Ṣaḥīḥ min al-Ḥadīth* when his book contains all three types.

There are a large number of sayings of the Prophet (peace be on him) that are considered as *sunnah qawliyyah*. Some well known examples are: الخراج بالضمان (Entitlement to revenue depends on a corresponding liability for loss); إنّما الاعمال بالنيّات (The nature of acts is dependent upon the underlying intentions); لا ضرر ولا ضرار (No injury is to be caused and none is to be borne); and العمد قود (Intentional murder leads to retaliation).

It is to be noted that not every saying of the Prophet (peace be on him) is a source of law. This is obvious from the definition stated above. To become a source of law, the purpose of the saying should be the laying down of the law or its elaboration.

Al-Sunnah al-fi'liyyah: It is defined as the acts of the Prophet (peace be on him) having a legal content, like his prayer, fasts and *ḥajj*. These acts or the method of their performance that he adopted are to be followed in the same way as his sayings. The acts that do not have a legal content do not become a source of law. This may be understood distinguishing between the following types of acts:

1. Ordinary physical acts performed by every human being, like eating, drinking, walking and sitting. Such acts are not meant to lay down laws, though some jurists consider them to be *mubāḥ*. This becomes clear when such acts are compared with acts that lay down the law. Jurists maintain that an act of the Prophet (peace be on him) pertaining to law indicates absolute or unqualified permission, which includes *wujūb, nadb,* and *ibāḥah,* till such time that another evidence fixes the meaning for one these. This means that

words, acts and approvals.

if no other evidence is available, the acts of the Prophet (peace be on him) will be interpreted to mean permissibility. As compared to this, the ordinary acts mentioned above, like eating and drinking, indicate *ibāḥah* or permissibility *ab initio;* they do not indicate recommendation or obligation.

In addition to this, there may be acts that pertain to his experience as a human being, like the organising of the army, war tactics, trading skills, and so on. These acts too do not become precedents of law, because their basis is skill and experience rather than revelation.[208]

Some jurists say that accepting evidence for proving facts in a trial or case cannot be considered as binding either. The reason is that they treat this as a skill. On the other hand, they would consider a decision rendered in a case as a binding precedent. He is reported to have said: "I am a human like you. When you come to me as litigants, some of you have better evidence than the others, and I decide according to what I hear. Thus, if I have given to one something that was due to the other, I have given him a piece of hellfire."

2. Acts that are specific to the Prophet (peace be on him) and the rest of the *ummah* is not to follow him in such acts. For example, in the case of the number of his marriages, which is based on a law specific to him.

3. Acts that are intended to be explanations of unelaborated rules in the texts. All such explanations have the status of law. The persuasive force of such explanations is the same as that of the text being elaborated. The explanation of a

208. During the Battle of Badr, when the Prophet (peace be on him) took up a position at a spot he selected a Companion asked him if the selection of the spot was based on guidance from Allah or it was based on his own tactical skill. The Prophet (peace be on him) told him that it was based on his own decision. The Companion selected a position close to a well and said: "O Messenger of Allah, we will drink from it and keep the enemy away."

mujmal (unelaborated) word will take the force of the *mujmal* on which it is based. The acts of his prayer, after his saying, "Pray as you see me praying," as well as his acts concerning the rites of *ḥajj* based on his saying, "Take (the knowledge of) your rites from me," are examples.[209]

4. Acts that establish new laws obviously have the force of law.

Intentional omissions (*sunnat al-tark*). Some jurists divide the *sunnah fi'liyyah* into acts and intentional omissions, and this leads to a further subtype:[210] *sunnat al-tark.* Omission or abstention from an act by the Prophet (peace be on him) indicates that the act he has given up is not permitted, and this includes disapproval and prohibition, and one of these will be determined by circumstantial or related evidence. The Prophet's omission of the act indicates that giving up the act is better than its performance. An example is the Prophet's refusal to become a witness for a person who had given most of his wealth to one child. He asked the man: "Have you treated each child like this." He said: "No." The Prophet (peace be on him) said: "Then get someone else as a witness. I will not be a witness to injustice."[211] The omission here indicates that the act is not legal. It covers both disapproval and prohibition, and the jurists have differed in determining one of these according to the evidences they have relied upon.

It may sometimes become obvious that the omission is not because of disapproval, but due to some other reason, like a natural aversion for a thing. The Prophet (peace be on him) refused to eat a *ḍabb* (a small animal of the rodent family) and then explained that he did not feel like having such food. As it was something personal to him, it means that it is not prohibited to eat such things.

209. For a discussion of this point see the section on *bayān* at p. 341 below.
210. See, e.g., al-Shāṭibī, *al-Muwāfaqāt,* vol. 4, 58 passim.
211. This in reality is a statement and will be construed as *sunnah qawliyyah,* but the idea is to explain the omission of the act.

Again, the omission may be for fear that the act may be construed as an obligation, when the act itself is required by law. Examples are the avoiding of *tarāwīḥ* prayer during Ramaḍān on certain occasions as well as his saying: "If I did not forsee hardship for my *ummah*, I would have ordered them to use the *siwāk* (brushing of teeth) before each prayer."

Sunnah taqrīriyyah: It is defined as the commission of certain acts, by word or deed, by some Companions and the maintenance of silence by the Prophet (peace be on him) without expressing disapproval. His silence in such a case is called *taqrīr* or tacit approval and is considered a *sunnah* that becomes a source for the permissibility of an act or a statement. An example of this type is the statement of Mu'ādh ibn Jabal when he was sent to Yemen and the Prophet (peace be on him) asked him how he will decide cases. This approval, however, was a little more emphatic than mere silence. A better example would be the contracts of *muḍārabah* and *sharikah*.

11.1.2.2 Kinds of *Sunnah* with respect to its modes of transmission

Aḥādīth (traditions) are divided, with respect to narration, into two types. First, the *aḥādīth* whose chain of narration is complete. These are the ones in which the narrators are mentioned from the beginning of the *sanad* upto the Messenger of Allāh, and no narrator is missing. Second, the *aḥādīth* from the chains of which one or more narrators are missing. The *ḥadīth* from which a narrator is missing is called *mursal* by the Ḥanafīs. The Traditionists (Muḥaddithūn) confine the term *mursal* to a tradition from the chain of which the name of the Companion is missing, while they term as *munqaṭi'* a tradition from the chain of which the name of a narrator other than a Companion is missing. Both types of *ḥadīth* will be discussed and within these the types of *Sunnah* they give rise to.

11.1.2.3 *Ḥadīth Muttaṣil*

The majority of the jurists divided the *muttaṣil aḥādīth* into two types: *mutawātir* and *āḥād*. In between these two, the Ḥanafī jurists added a third category called *mashhūr*. It is very important to note that for purposes of working out the number of narrators of a tradition, only the first three generations are taken into account. After their periods, the reports were compiled and all the reports became well-known.

Ḥadīth Mutawātir. The *mutawātir ḥadīth* is one that is related by such a large number of people that their agreement to propagate a falsehood cannot be conceived.[212] This applies to the narration from the beginning of its chain to its end, where it reaches the Prophet (peace be on him). An example of such a *ḥadīth* is:

إنما الأعمال بالنيّات، وإنما لكلّ امرئ ما نوى

> Acts are determined by intentions, and to each person belongs what he intends.[213]

In the same category are the reports about the number of daily prayers, number of *rak'ahs*, *diyāt* and the rates of *zakāt*.

Tawātur is of two types: *tawātur* in words and *tawātur* in meaning. When all the narrators are in agreement about the words as well as meaning, the *ḥadīth* indicates *tawātur* by its very words. An example are the words of the Prophet (peace be on him): "He who intentionally attributes a falsehood to me should prepare his abode in the Fire" (من كذب عليّ متعمدا فليتبوأ مقعده من النار). This tradition was related by a large number of Companions in these words. The narration was reproduced in great numbers

212. The term *khabar* means a report or news. If a single person, for instance, comes to your room and says that the building is on fire, you may or may not believe him. If he is followed by another person with the same report, you may be inclined to believe that the report is true. If more than two persons were to come to you with the same report, you are likely to be convinced that the report is true and all of them could not have agreed to fabricate the report.

213. This tradition is considered as *mashhūr* by some depending on who accepts *mashhūr* as a category in itself.

in the following generation when it was finally recorded. This makes it *tawātur lafẓī*. Some experts consider this tradition to be a true *mutawātir*, even stronger than the tradition about intentions above. The other kind is known as *tawātur ma'nawī*, which is a tradition that conveys the same meaning even if the words are not exactly the same. Most of the *mutawātir* traditions are of the latter category.[214]

The *mutawātir* tradition conveys definitive knowledge (*'ilm*) and is also definitive with respect to its authenticity. It is, therefore, said that a *mutawātir* tradition is *qaṭ'ī* with respect to *'ilm* as well as *thubūt*. In other words, it must be followed under all circumstances. *Qaṭ'ī al-thubūt* means that we are certain about its narration from the Prophet (peace be on him). It is to be noted, however, that the words of such a tradition may be subject to interpretation, in which case the meaning arising from such a tradition (its *dalālah*) will not be definitive, but will be probable.[215] Such a meaning will be definitive, of course, if only one meaning can be derived. For example, in the case of the tradition, mentioned above, saying that "acts are determined by intentions", some jurists may say that this means "for the purposes of the hereafter," while others may interpret it to mean acts in this world and thus apply it to contracts and other acts.

Ḥadīth Mashhūr. It has been stated above that the majority of the jurists classified the tradition with a complete chain into two types, but the Ḥanafī jurists added a third category called *mashhūr*.

The *mashhūr* tradition is one the number of whose reporters do not reach the level of *tawātur* in the first generation. Thus, if one or two Companions related the tradition from the Prophet (peace be on him), but in the next generation, that is, the generation of the

214. For example, there are a large number of reported cases where the sentence of *rajm* is said to have been awarded to the married (*muḥṣan*) offender. Some jurists looking at the common meaning emerging from all the individual reports may deem such meaning to be *mutawātir*.

215. See the division of the sources into definitive and probable in the previous chapter.

Tābi'ūn, a very large number narrated from them and so on till the end of the chain when the traditions were compiled, then, such a tradition is called *mashhūr*. The factor that makes such a tradition *mashhūr* (well-known) is the number of persons in the second and the third generation narrating it, because after this compilation started and all traditions became well-known.

The *mashhūr* tradition, according to the Ḥanīfīs, falls into a category that is lesser in strength than the *mutawātir* tradition, but is stronger than the *khabar wāḥid*. The majority of the jurists, however, consider such a tradition to be a *khabar wāḥid*. According to al-Sarakhsī, the tradition about the prohibition of marrying the maternal or paternal aunt of an existing wife belongs to this category.[216]

Ḥadīth al-Āḥād. The *ḥadīth al-āḥād* or the *khabar wāḥid* is reported by one or two persons from the beginning of its chain upto its end when all traditions were recorded. Thus, the narrators do not reach the level of *tawātur* in either of the first three periods: the period of the Companions, the Tābi'ūn, and the Tab' Tābi'ūn. After the third period, as stated above, the traditions were compiled and all became well known.

The *khabar wāḥid* is generally not relied upon by jurists in matters of faith (*aqā'id*), but it is accepted in matters of conduct, that is, in matters covered by the *mu'āmalāt*. In fact, there is generally an agreement of the Muslims about the acceptance of the *khabar wāḥid* in matters of *fiqh*.[217]

11.1.3 Justification of the *Sunnah* as a source of law

The *Sunnah* is unanimously accepted as a primary source of law and *aḥkām* can be derived from it independently of any

216. Al-Sarakhsī, *Uṣūl al-Sarakhsī,* vol. 1, 321.
217. 'Abd al-'Azīz al-Bukhārī has provided a detailed analysis, along with arguments of jurists, to show when and under what circumstances the *khabar wāḥid* may be accepted. 'Abd al-'Azīz al-Bukhārī, *Kashf al-Asrār,* vol. 2, 550–53.

other source. The jurists provide transmitted as well as rational arguments for its justification as a primary source of law.

1. **From the Book.** There are several ways in which this justification is understood:

   - The Book indicates that what the Prophet (peace be on him) lays down as law is based upon revelation. Allāh, the Exalted, says: "Nor does he say (aught) of (his own) desire. It is no less than inspiration sent down to him." (وما ينطق عن الهوٰى إن هو إلّا وحي يوّحى) [Qur'ān 53 : 3, 4] Thus, the words of the Prophet (peace be on him), being based upon revelation, are a valid source of law, except that the *Sunnah* is revelation in meaning alone, not in words.
   - Allāh granted the Prophet (peace be on him) the task of elaborating the meanings of the Qur'ān as well as the explanation of the unelaborated words. His elaboration, therefore, complements and completes the meanings in the Qur'ān and becomes a valid source or evidence for law. The verse of the Qur'ān supporting this is: "And We have sent down unto thee (also) the Message that thou mayest explain clearly to men what is sent down for them" (وأنزلنا إليك الذّكر لتبيّن للنّاس ما نزّل إليهم) [Qur'ān 16 : 44]
   - A number of verses in the Qur'ān that indicate definitively that the *Sunnah* is to be followed as a source of law:

     a) O ye who believe! Obey Allāh, and obey the Apostle, and those charged with authority among you. If ye differ in anything among yourselves, refer it to Allāh and His Apostle, if ye do believe in Allāh and the Last Day. [Qur'ān 4 : 59]

     b) He who obeys the Apostle, obeys Allāh. [Qur'ān 4 : 80]

     c) So take what the Apostle assigns to you, and deny yourselves that which he withholds from you. [Qur'ān 59 : 7]

d) But no, by thy Lord, they can have no (real) faith, until they make thee judge in all disputes between them, and find in their souls no resistance against they decisions, but accept them with the fullest conviction. [Qur'ān 4 : 65]

e) It is not fitting for a believer, man or woman, when a matter has been decided by Allāh and His Apostle, to have any option about their decision. [Qur'ān 4 : 65]

2. **On the Basis of *Ijmā'* (Consensus).** The Muslims all agreed during the period of the Prophet (peace be on him) upon the obligation of acting according to the *aḥkām* laid down by the *Sunnah* and upon the necessity of having recourse to it for the derivation and discovery of the *aḥkām*. There was no one among the Companions who disputed this, because the true source of these *aḥkām* was revelation.

3. **Rational Argument.** First, it is a part of a Muslim's faith that Muḥammad is the Messenger of Allāh charged with the mission of conveying the commands of Allāh. It is, therefore, obligatory to follow the Messenger of Allāh in all that he lays down by way *aḥkām*. Yet, the most powerful rational argument is to be found in the bond between the Qur'ān and the *Sunnah* and this is visible when we examine the relationship between the two. The rational argument for the necessity of the *Sunnah* can thus be seen in section 11.2 on page 219 dealing with the Status of the Qur'ān with respect to the *Sunnah*.

11.1.4 Justification of the different types of *Sunnah*

The Muslims agreed unanimously that the *Sunnah* is a source of the *sharī'ah*, as detailed above. It is an evidence to which recourse must be had for the derivation of the laws, if it meets the conditions that each Imām has laid down for it with respect to authenticity.

A group deviated from this unanimous agreement and denied the employment of the *khabar wāḥid* for establishing the *aḥkām*.

Imām al-Shāfiʿī gave detailed arguments in support of the *khabar wāḥid* with the intention that once this is established there can be no question about the validity of the (*mashhūr* and) *mutawātir*. A few of these arguments are provided below:

1. The Companions accepted the report of a single person when he informed them that *khamr*, which was hitherto permitted, had now been prohibited. In response to this report they broke the wine containers. This is proof that the report of an individual is valid.

2. The Messenger of Allāh ordered Unays to go to the married woman about whom an allegation of unlawful sexual intercourse had been made. He said to him, "If she confesses, subject her to *rajm*." Thus, his report alone about her confession would be sufficient for *rajm*.[218]

3. The Messenger of Allāh used to send his envoys on various missions. These envoys used to be alone.

11.1.4.1 Conditions for acting upon the *muttaṣil ḥadīth*

The traditions (*aḥadīth*) differ with respect to their narration and reporting. It is for this reason that the *mujtahids* laid down specific conditions for the acceptance of each category. The purpose of these conditions is to verify the strength of the authenticity of the report.

The *mutawātir ḥadīth* is considered certain proof of the *aḥkām* insofar as the conditions of *tawātur* are found in it according to all the jurists; so also the *mashhūr* tradition according to the Ḥanafīs, because it offers certain knowledge coming down from the Messenger of Allāh, even if the strength of this knowledge is a little less than that of the *mutawātir*.

With respect to the *khabar wāḥid*, each *mujtahid* has laid down specific conditions, when it is relied upon for the derivation of the law.

218. This means that the woman was to consider the word of Unays as authoritative, although it was based on his report alone.

Thus, **the Ḥanafīs stipulate** three conditions for the *khabar wāḥid*:

1. That the narrator should not have acted against the implication of the report. If he does act against it, the reliance will be upon his reported act rather than on the report. A narrator does not act against a report from the Prophet (peace be on him), unless he knows that the content of the report was abrogated. A deliberate act against the report would raise doubts about the *'adālah* of the narrator, and his report would not be acceptable, because the presumption is that the narrator is *'adl*.

2. That the report should not pertain to a matter of universal need, that is, something which is performed often and continuously repeated. Such an act requires that it be known to many people due to their need to know it prior to performance. An act that should be known to many people by necessity will push its report to the level of a report that is *mutawātir* or *mashhūr*, and it cannot be the subject-matter of a *khabar wāḥid*. The narration of an individual regarding such a matter provides circumstantial evidence of its not having been said or done by the Prophet (peace be on him).

3. That it should not oppose analogy (*qiyās*). By this is meant opposition to general and fundamental principles. If a report opposes a general principle it ceases to be a valid proof for the *aḥkām*. The reason is that the principle is usually not derived from a single text, but is based upon a number of texts, which together indicate a definitive meaning. As compared to this, a *khabar wāḥid* indicates a probable meaning that cannot be preferred over a definitive (*qaṭ'ī*) meaning. The Ḥanafīs made an exemption from this rule in the case of traditions reported or upheld by the Companions who were well known as jurists and *mujtahids*, like the first four caliphs, Ibn 'Abbās and Ibn Mas'ūd. A *khabr wāḥid*, however, will be preferred over an individual

qiyās, which is not in the meaning of a general principle. The distinction must be kept in mind.

Imām Mālik stipulates for the *khabar wāḥid* that it should not oppose the practice of the people of Medina.[219] If it does oppose it, the obligation is to follow the practice of the people of Medina and to forgo the requirement of the *khabar wāḥid*. The reason is that the practice of the people of Medina amounts to a *mutawātir* report, and the *mutawātir* being definitive is to be preferred over the *khabar wāḥid*, which is probable. It appears that he would also uphold the rule about analogy above.

Imām al-Shāfi'ī does not stipulate for the *khabar wāḥid* any other condition except that it have a sound and complete chain of narration. If this condition is met the report is to be accepted.

The condition stipulated by **Aḥmad ibn Ḥanbal** is similar to that laid down by Imām al-Shāfi'ī, however, he sometimes accepts traditions that do not strictly meet this condition. He is reported to have preferred even *mursal* traditions over analogy.

11.1.4.2 *Ḥadīth* that is not *muttaṣil*

A tradition that is not continuous (*muttaṣil*) is one that has the names of one or more narrators missing from the chain of narration. This is called a *mursal* report. It is like a reliable narrator from a later generation saying: "The Messenger of Allāh said that ...." As for the Traditionists, they apply the term *mursal* to a tradition from the chain of which the name of the Companion

219. In fact, some have attributed the opinion to Imām Mālik that the *khabar wāḥid* is not to be accepted if it opposes analogy (*qiyās*). 'Abd al-'Azīz al-Bukhārī has questioned the authenticity of this report from Mālik. He also quotes Abū al-Ḥusayn al-Baṣrī, who says that if the underlying cause of the analogy is found expressly stated in the text, the analogy is to be preferred, but if the cause has been derived by the jurist the report is to be preferred. Ibid., 451. An examination of some of the opinions of Imām Mālik shows that he may have subscribed to this view. Another reason advanced in favour of analogy is that analogy does not accept restriction (*takhṣīṣ*) whereas the *khabar wāḥid* does.

is missing. If the name of someone other than a Companion is missing, they term the tradition as *munqaṭi'*.

The jurists disagreed about the employment of a *mursal* tradition as proof for a *ḥukm*. Thus, al-Shāfi'ī does not rely upon it, unless its authenticity is supported by another tradition.

11.2 Status of the Sunnah With Respect to the Qur'ān

The jurists maintain that the *Sunnah* is the second source among the sources of Islamic law. If the *mujtahid* does not find a text in the Qur'ān for a case he has to settle, he has recourse to the *Sunnah* for the derivation of the *ḥukm*. The evidence for this is the well known tradition of Mu'ādh ibn Jabal who was sent to Yemen by the Prophet (peace be on him). The tradition has been quoted in the previous chapter.[220] In addition to this there is the letter of 'Umar ibn al-Khaṭṭāb to Qāḍī Shurayḥ in which he instructs him to follow the Qur'ān first and then the *Sunnah*.

As regards the status of the *Sunnah* being secondary to the Qur'ān for proof of the *aḥkām*, the jurists maintain that the Qur'ān is definitive (*qaṭ'ī*) with respect to its narration in its details and as a whole, while the *Sunnah* is definitive as a whole, but not in all its details, because many of the reports are of the status of *khabar wāḥid*.

The *Sunnah* being an elaboration and commentary on the Qur'ān, it is not required to have recourse to it unless a text requires elaboration and commentary. If the text of the Qur'ān is explicit (*naṣṣ*) in its meaning it is to be acted upon, but if it is apparent (*ẓāhir*) having more than one meaning it is necessary to have recourse to its commentary, which is the *Sunnah*.

220. *Sunan Abū Dāwūd*, tr. Ahmad Hasan (Lahore: Sh. Muhammad Ashraf, 1984), vol. 3, No. 3585 at 1019.

11.2.1 The manner in which the *Sunnah* lays down the *aḥkām*

As the *Sunnah* is a primary source of law, the jurist has recourse to it for the derivation of the *aḥkām*; it is secondary and complementary to the Qur'ān. The authority of the *Sunnah* as a source of law is derived from the Qur'ān. The *aḥkām* derived from the *Sunnah* are, therefore, considered an explanation of the meanings in the Qur'ān. Even when the *Sunnah* appears exclusively to be dealing with a *ḥukm*, a close examination reveals that the *aḥkām* so revealed are based upon principles found in the Qur'ān and the *Sunnah* is merely extending the meaning of these principles or is linking up the rule with the principle. This may be elaborated in the following points:[221]

1. **The Sunnah is a commentary of the Qur'ān.** The *aḥkām* are often found in the Qur'ān in general, undetermined, or unelaborated form. The *Sunnah* elaborates, restricts, or qualifies these *aḥkām*.

   Examples of the *Sunnah* elaborating the unelaborated are like (1) the timings of prayer and their number as well as their *rak'as*; (2) elaboration of the kinds of wealth in which *zakāt* is to be paid and the amount to be paid in each as well as the time of obligation; (3) the case of *ribā*.

   An example of the restriction of a general meaning is to be found in inheritance: "For the male two shares of the female." The *Sunnah* explains that the murderer will not inherit.

   The example of elaboration is in the case of theft where the *Sunnah* elaborates the meaning saying that the property must be removed from the *ḥirz* and that it is the right hand that is to be cut.

2. **The Sunnah links a vacillating case with a known principle.** The *Sunnah* sometimes lays down rules that

221. The details of this discussion can be gleaned from an excellent discussion by al-Shāṭibī, *al-Muwāfaqāt*, vol. 4, 32 passim.

are not mentioned in the Qur'ān. These rules appear to be additions over the meanings in the Qur'ān and cannot be considered as elaborations or qualifications within the categories explained in the previous section. Some jurists, however, are of the opinion that a closer examination reveals that these rules are an elaboration in the sense of classifying a rule under a principle. Often a case vacillates between two principles and the *Sunnah* links up the case with one of these principles.

For example, the Qur'ān has in a general way permitted all good things and has commanded the avoidance of *khabā'ith*. The *Sunnah* has linked with the *khabā'ith* the consumption of animals with molars and birds with claws, just as it has prohibited the consumption of domesticated donkeys.

The Qur'ān has permitted the consumption of seafood and prohibited carrion. The dead fish in the sea vacillated between these two principles. The *Sunnah* linked it with permitted food: "Its water is pure and its *maytah* (carrion) is permissible."

The Qur'ān permitted a slaughtered animal and prohibited carrion. The separated foetus of an animal after slaughter vacillated between the two principles. The *Sunnah* linked it with the slaughtered animal: "The slaughter of the foetus is the slaughter of its mother."

In these examples, we find that Qur'ān laid down two general principles, but there were certain cases that vacillated between them with the possibility of falling under either principle. The *Sunnah* attached the case to one of the general principles. Thus, the principle is mentioned in the Qur'ān and what appears to us as an additional rule laid down by the *Sunnah* is actually a category of the principle. The function of the *Sunnah* here is the analytical development of the law.

3. **The Sunnah performs analogy on the basis of a rule in the Qur'ān.** The Qur'ān sometimes lays down a principle

or a rule without elaborating all the categories falling under that principle or covered by the rule. The *Sunnah* links a resembling case with this rule, and this function appears to be similar to analogy.

The Qur'ān prohibits marriage of two sisters to one man and then says that what is besides this is permitted. The cases of a woman along with her maternal or paternal aunt are also similar because of a common underlying cause. The *Sunnah*, therefore, prohibits such marriages too.

The Qur'ān mentions that pure water descends from the sky and is preserved in the earth. The case of sea-water was not settled. The *Sunnah* declared that it is pure and even its carrion is lawful.

4. **The Sunnah lays down general principles.** The *Sunnah* sometimes lays down a general principle the individual categories of which have been mentioned by the Qur'ān. For example, the *Sunnah* lays down the principle: "No injury is to be caused or borne." The Qur'ān mentions a number of cases in which injury to others has been prohibited, like injury to a parents because of their child or injury to wives and so on. The prohibition of injury or harm is a general principle that is formulated by the *Sunnah*.

5. **The Sunnah elaborates the meaning of words in the Qur'ān.** An example of this the distinction of the white thread from the black thread during the month of Ramaḍān. The *Sunnah* explains that this is the light of day and the darkness of the night.

6. **The Sunnah abrogates the Qur'ān.** The jurists provide several examples of this that we shall have occasion to look at later (see page 390). Imām al-Shāfi'ī does not accept this and says that only the Qur'ān can abrogate the Qur'ān and the *Sunnah* can abrogate the *Sunnah*. Some modern scholars deny the theory of abrogation altogether.

11.2.2 Modern views about the relationship between the Qur'ān and the *Sunnah*

In the 20th century there have been a number of debates about the relationship of the Qur'ān and the *Sunnah*. It is not possible to record the various views expressed in these debates in this book. There is a huge amount of literature that the reader can access.[222] These debates have by no means come to an end.

While there are many types of views on the subject, a broad classification yields three types of trends.

1. The first is that of those people who wish to give greater prominence to the Qur'ān and wish to emphasise its coherence. Their view appears to be that only that *sunnah* is to be accepted as authentic that is compatible with the Qur'ān. This is an extreme view and if applied would demolish a greater part of the Islamic legal system as it exists today.

2. On the other extreme are those who maintain that the acceptance of a *sunnah* should be based on its chain of transmission. If the chain is sound the content of the tradition should be accepted and absorbed, whatever the consequences for the legal system. In other words, they relegate to the background the importance of examining the content (*matn*) of the traditions.

3. The third group consists of those who give importance to the *isnād* and also to the *matn*. This third group appears to represent a kind of a middle path, however, the situation here is somewhat complex. Within this group may be those who are inclined to check the *matn* against the Qur'ān alone, and this takes them closer to the first group. Then there are those who focus more on the chain of transmission and

222. For those interested in certain aspects of this debate should read Muḥammad al-Ghazālī's *al-Sunnah al-Nabawiyyah bayna Ahl al-Fiqh wa Ahl al-Ḥadīth* (Cairo, 1989) and Yūsuf al-Qardāwī's *Kayfa Nata'āmal ma' al-Sunnah al-Nabawiyyah* (El-Masur, 1990).

check the *matn* not against the Qur'ān alone, but also against the *Sunnah*, i.e., other traditions. In case of conflict, however, they accept the content of the conflicting tradition as an exemption from a broad rule, but then, following the Shāfi'ī rule, they consider the exemption as a broad principle in itself. This takes them closer to the second group.

To understand the problem, a few things have to be kept in mind. First, the *Sunnah*, like the Qur'ān, deals with life and not with the legal system alone. The meaning derived by a *sufi* from a tradition may not be same as that understood by a jurist. Second, a Muslim may be ready to follow any tradition in its literal sense out of his love for the Prophet (peace be on him) and his *Sunnah*, but the same person may understand the same tradition in a different way if he is asked to make law for the subjects to follow: his approach may be different.

Here we are concerned with what is binding and generates obligatory law. A sound method, therefore, has to be followed, a method that ensures that the intention of the Lawgiver is implemented and at the same time taking care that it will not upset or unduly disturb the functioning of the rest of the legal system.

Having said this, we notice that there has never been and, perhaps, there never will be a single system even for the law. Elsewhere,[223] we have discussed the methods followed by the jurists on their different approaches to the *Sunnah*. The two methods that emerged were as follows:

1. The method of the literalists, who gave more importance to the *isnād*. Once a sound chain was established, they tried to implement the content of the tradition even at the risk of losing analytical consistency.

2. The second method was followed by schools who preferred the analytical method based upon the general principles of the law, whether these principles had emerged out of the Qur'ān or the *Sunnah*.

223. See generally, the author's *Theories of Islamic Law*.

In that work, we had suggested that the first method may be more suitable for what we called the fixed part of the law, i.e., matters of *'ibādāt, ḥudūd, qiṣāṣ* as well as some other areas of the law that do not accept change and which deal with the relationship between the subject and the Creator (the right of Allah is involved). The second method, on the other hand, is more suitable for the rest of the *mu'āmalāt* where the relationship is either between individuals or between individuals and the community as a whole, i.e., the state. In the second area, reason has wider role to play and the examination of the *matn* for analytical consistency is essential.

The second method was refined further by al-Ghazālī (d. 505 A.H.) in his theory of the general purposes of the law. He suggested that any new principle made for the law must not only be checked against the *taṣarrufāt* of the *sharī'ah* (the established general propositions or principles of the law arising from the Qur'ān and the *Sunnah*), but also against the purposes of the law, the *maqāṣid al-sharī'ah,* which are taken to be the ultimate general principles. This method ensures the sound development of the law along with the implementation of the overall intention of the Lawgiver. The method is equally valid for the reconciliation of traditions. The method also explains why Abū Ḥanīfah would sometimes accept a tradition that did not have a sound chain of transmission. The reason was that a broad general principle, compatible with the tradition, was already present within the legal system, and the law would have still been the same even without the tradition. For the jurist, this may be the only method that can be followed.

Review Questions

1. What are the different meanings assigned to the word *Sunnah*? How does the meaning of the term *Sunnah* differ from the term *ḥadīth*?

2. State the classification of the *Sunnah* with respect to the channels of the *aḥkām*.

3. What do you understand by the term *sunnat al-tark*?

4. Give the classification of the *Sunnah* with respect to the modes of transmission.
5. Write a note on the concept of *tawātur* and give examples of the *ḥadīth mutawātir*.
6. What are the conditions for acting upon the *ḥadīth muttasil*?
7. What are the conditions stipulated by the jurists for accepting and acting upon the *khabar wāḥid*?
8. What is a *mursal* tradition? Is it accepted as a *ḥujjah*?
9. Describe in detail the status of the *Sunnah* with respect to the Qur'ān.
10. How does the *Sunnah* act as a commentary of the Qur'ān?
11. What are the different approaches to the *Sunnah* in the modern times? What approach would you adopt as a jurist?

12 Consensus of Legal Opinion (*Ijmāʻ*)

12.1 The Meaning of *Ijmāʻ*

The word *ijmāʻ* has literal meanings as well as a technical meaning. Literally, it is used in two senses. The first is determination and resolution (عزم وتصميم). The words of Allah, the Exalted: "**Determine** your plan and among your partners," (فأجمعوا أمركم وشركاءكم) [Qur'ān 10 : 71] convey this meaning, that is, decide and determine the matter. So also the words of the Prophet (peace be on him), "The person who has not **resolved** to fast prior to dawn has no fast," (من لم يجمع الصيام قبل الفجر فلا صيام له) convey the meaning of deciding and resolving. The second way in which the word is used is agreement upon a matter. It is said: "the people **agreed** upon such and such matter" (أجمع القوم علي كذا). The difference between the two literal meanings is that *ijmāʻ*, in the first meaning, is possible from one person, but in the second sense it requires two or more persons.

12.1.1 Technical or legal meaning

In the technical sense, *ijmāʿ* is defined as:

إتفاق المجتهدين من أمّة محمّد صلى الله عليه وسلّم بعد وفاته في عصر من العصور على حكم شرعي

> The consensus of *mujtahids* (independent jurists) from the *ummah* of Muḥammad (peace be on him), after his death, in a determined period upon a rule of Islamic law (*ḥukm sharʿī*).[224]

12.1.2 Conditions for the validity of *ijmāʿ*

The definition given above shows that there are seven conditions that must be met before *ijmāʿ* can be said to have taken place. These conditions are imposed by the majority of the jurists. Two more conditions (nos. 8 & 9 below) are imposed by some of the jurists; however, the majority do not follow them.[225]

1. **The agreement or consensus must take place among *mujtahids*, that is, those who have attained the status of *ijtihād*.** Thus, an agreement among those who have not reached this status or who are not qualified will not constitute *ijmāʿ*. This will exclude all non-*mujtahids*, the general public, the members of a modern legislature, unless all of them are *mujtahids*. As to the number of *mujtahids* agreeing upon a legal issue, there is a disagreement. Some say that this number must reach the level necessary for *tawātur*, while others say that three is enough. One thing is clear, though, that if there is a single *mujtahid* in a certain period, his view or verdict will not amount to *ijmāʿ*.

224. This definition is generally accepted and is found in most books. Al-Razī defines it as: "The consensus of the *ahl al-ḥall wa-al-ʿaqd …*," but he then interprets *ahl al-ḥall wa al-ʿaqd* to mean the *mujtahids*. Al-Rāzī, *al-Maḥṣūl*, vol. 4, 35 passim.
225. For a detailed account of these conditions, see ʿAbd al-ʿAzīz al-Bukhārī, *Kashf al-Asrār*, vol. 3, 360 passim.

2. **The agreement must be unanimous, that is, among all the *mujtahids*.** If the majority of them agree upon a *ḥukm sharʿī*, it will not amount to *ijmāʿ* according to most jurists, howsoever small the number of the opposing minority. The reason is that there is a possibility that the minority opinion may be correct.

   There are, however, those jurists who consider a consensus of the majority as valid *ijmāʿ* when they are being opposed by a minority. Some jurists, on the other hand, consider the agreement of the majority as persuasive, but would not call it *ijmāʿ*.[226]

3. **All the jurists participating in *ijmāʿ* must be from the *ummah* of Muḥammad (peace be on him).** Thus, an agreement of the jurist of another *ummah*, one of the earlier nations of the earlier prophets, will not be considered *ijmāʿ*. The reason is that there are textual evidences supporting the fact that it is only the *ummah* of Muḥammad (peace be on him) that is protected against error in collective agreements.

4. **The agreement or consensus must have taken place after the death of the Prophet (peace be on him).** Thus, an agreement during his lifetime is not considered *ijmāʿ*. If the Prophet (peace be on him) agreed with the Companions on an issue, then, he was the source of the rule and not *ijmāʿ*. If he went against their agreement, their agreement was not considered nor did it become a rule of law.

5. **The agreement must be among the *mujtahids* of a single determined period, even if some of the jurists of the following or subsequent period opposed them.** The reason is that the constitution of *ijmāʿ* depends upon the unanimous agreement of jurists and this is only possible in a determined period, like a generation. If the period were left open and the opinions of all the jurists of all periods were to be taken into account, the occurrence of *ijmāʿ* would become impossible.

226. Āmidī, *al-Iḥkām fī Uṣūl al-Aḥkām*, vol. 1, 140.

6. **The agreement must be upon a rule of law, the *ḥukm shar'ī*.** An agreement upon the rules of grammar in Arabic would not be *ijmā'* nor an agreement upon other rational propositions, like the creation of the universe. Thus, the rule must state that a certain thing is prohibited, permitted, valid, or void. All non-legal matters are excluded from the domain of *ijmā'*.

7. **That the *mujtahids* should have relied upon a *sanad* for deriving their opinion.** A *sanad* is an evidence in one of the accepted sources of law. This is dealt with in some detail below. Does this mean that every rule that is agreed upon must have some evidence as its basis in the Qur'ān and the *Sunnah*? If this is the case, the stipulation takes away something from the strength of *ijmā'* as an independent principle. While it is obvious that the jurist agreeing to a rule would be relying upon an evidence from the legal system, it cannot be a condition that the *sanad* must be found in a text. If it is, then, the *sanad* is the basis of the law. Yes, it can be said that the function of *ijmā'* is to make definitive an evidence that is probable and subject to interpretation. It should be noted that the strength of *ijmā'* lies in the agreement itself. Another reason for insisting on the *sanad* could be that those who stipulate this condition want to ensure that the jurist has undertaken proper *ijtihād* to arrive at his opinion.

8. **The death of those jurists who participated in the *ijmā'*, either explicitly or by silence, is not a condition for the validity of *ijmā'* according to the majority of the jurists.** *Ijmā'*, according to these jurists, becomes valid as soon as agreement is found. There are a few jurists who maintain that it is possible for a jurist to change his view and as long as a jurist is alive, this possibility exists. They quote the example of Ḥaḍrat 'Alī in the case of the sale of the *ummahāt al-awlād*. They maintain that *ijmā'* cannot be treated as final as long as the participating *mujtahids* are alive. The view of the majority in this case appears to be more practical,

otherwise one would have to wait for many years to finally benefit from a decision.

9. **That the *ijmāʿ* should have been transmitted to the later jurists by way of *tawātur*.** The argument is that as *ijmāʿ* is a definitive evidence, its mode of transmission should also be definitive. The majority of the jurists, however, do not accept this condition.

12.1.3 Types of *ijmāʿ*

Ijmāʿ is divided into two types on the basis of the way it is made known. These two types are: 1) *ijmāʿ ṣarīḥ* or *ijmāʿ qawlī* and 2) *ijmāʿ sukūtī* or tacit *ijmāʿ*.

12.1.3.1 Explicit *ijmāʿ* or *ijmāʿ qawlī*

Ṣarīḥ or explicit *ijmāʿ* is one in which the legal opinions of all the jurists of one period converge in relation to a legal issue, and each one of them states his opinion explicitly. This may happen when all of them are gathered in one session and an issue is presented to them and they collectively express a unanimous opinion. It may also take place when an issue is raised in a certain period and all the jurists, in turn, issue similar *fatwās* independently and at separate times.

12.1.3.2 Tacit *ijmāʿ* or *ijmāʿ sukūtī*

This form of *ijmāʿ* takes place when some *mujtahids*, one or more, issue a verdict on a legal issue and the rest of the *mujtahids* come to know of it during the same period, but they keep silent; they neither acknowledge it nor refute it expressly.

Conditions for tacit *ijmāʿ*. For the occurrence of tacit *ijmāʿ*, the following conditions must be met:[227]

227. Ibid.

1. The silence must be free of all external indications that point to agreement or disagreement. If an indication of some sort is found that conveys agreement, then, *ijmā'* is not tacit, rather it is explicit. If, however, an indication is found that points to disagreement, no *ijmā'* can be said to have taken place.

2. The silence of a *mujtahid* should be maintained for a considerable period of time. The duration, however, cannot be fixed, because the issues subject to *ijtihād* and the formulation of an opinion require time, which may vary for each *mujtahid*.

3. The issue must be one in which *ijtihād* is permitted. These are issues in which the available sources are probable (*ẓannī*).[228] If, however, the issue is one in which *ijtihād* is not permitted, that is, the controlling evidence is definitive (*qaṭ'ī*) having one meaning, then, the silence of some jurists cannot be considered tacit approval, because jurists are not supposed to open up these issues.

12.1.4 The legal force of *ijmā'* as a source

Ijmā', as we have said, is either explicit or it is tacit. Each has a rule (*ḥukm*) that differs from the other with respect to binding strength as a source of law. This distinction is presented below:

12.1.4.1 The binding strength of explicit *ijmā'*

The majority of the jurists agreed upon the rule that explicit *ijmā'* is a definitive source and it is obligatory to act upon it; its opposition is prohibited. Thus, if explicit *ijmā'* occurs on an issue and is published, then, the *ḥukm* upon which agreement is found stands established definitively (*qaṭ'an*) and it is not permitted to oppose it. Further, the issue that has been settled through such *ijmā'* can no longer be opened up again and subjected to *ijtihād*. In other words, the issue is no longer a moot point.

228. The meaning of *qaṭ'ī* and *ẓannī* has preceded in the previous chapter.

Al-Naẓẓām al-Baṣrī, a leading Mu'tazilite, and some of the Khawārij said that *ijmā'* is not a binding source. The majority, who upheld *ijmā'* as a binding source, as well as those who opposed them on this issue, argued on the basis of the Qur'ān and the *Sunnah*. Their arguments were as follows:

Arguments of the majority. The majority gave the following arguments:

1. The words of the Allah:

   ومن يشاقق الرّسول من بعد ما تبيّن له الهدي ويتّبع غير سبيل المؤمنين نوله ما تولّي ونصله جهنّم وساءت مصيرا

   "If anyone contends with the Messenger even after guidance has been plainly conveyed to him, and follows a path other than that of the believers, we shall leave him in the path he has chosen, and land him in hell. What an evil refuge."

   Allah has promised hell and a bad ending to those who follow a way different from that of the believers, and the way of the believers is determined by explicit and unanimous *ijtihād*. Thus, consensus after *ijtihād* is the true path to be followed, and it is not proper to go against it.

   This argument may be refuted in the following way. The intended meaning in this verse of the way of the believers is following the Prophet (peace be on him), helping him, and repelling his enemies. It does not mean following what the *mujtahids* have agreed upon with respect to the *aḥkām*. This is the apparent meaning of the verse, from its *sabab al-nuzūl*, and from the verse that follows, which says that Allah will not forgive *shirk* and may forgive what is less than that.

2. The tradition related from the Prophet (peace be on him) about the freedom from error when the *ummah* is unanimous about the matter, like his words: "My *ummah* will not collectively agree upon an error" (لا تجتمع أمّتي علي خطاء), "What the Muslims consider good is good in the eyes of Allah" (ما رآه المسلمون حسنا فهو عند الله حسنا) and "I asked Allah that my *ummah* not

> agree on an error and He granted it (this prayer) to me" (سألت الله أن لا تجتمع أمّتى علي الضّلالة فأعطانيها). They said that these traditions had been related by trustworthy narrators, and though they are not *mutawātir* in words, they are continuous (*mutawātir*) in the meaning they convey, and which is that my *ummah* is protected against falling into collective error.

It was on the basis of these evidences that the majority accepted *ijmā'* as a source of law and acted upon it as such.

Arguments of al-Naẓẓām al-Baṣrī Against *Ijmā'*. Al-Naẓẓām and those who supported him argued on the basis of the following evidences:[229]

1. In the words of the God, "O ye who believe, Obey Allah and obey the Prophet,...," Muslims have been commanded to refer each dispute to Allah and His Prophet, and the meaning of referring disputes to Allah and His Prophet is reference to the Qur'ān and the *Sunnah*. There is no command in this verse, he said, to refer the disputed matter to the agreement of the jurists.

   The response to this argument is that it is the Book of Allah and the *Sunnah* of His Prophet (peace be on him) that give us guidance about *ijmā'* as indicated in the arguments of the majority above.

2. When the Messenger of Allah (peace be on him) asked Mu'ādh ibn Jabal about the sources for his decision, he did not mention *ijmā'*. Had *ijmā'* been a valid source, it would not have been abrogated.

   This argument is considered weak because *ijmā'* is a source that comes into operation after the death of the Prophet (peace be on him) and Mu'ādh could not have possibly mentioned it.

---

229. See 'Abd al-'Azīz al-Bukhārī, *Kashf al-Asrār*, vol. 3, 351, for these arguments and also those of the majority. See also al-Rāzī, *al-Maḥṣūl*, vol. 4, 35 passim.

The reasoning and arguments of the majority, who accept *ijmā'* and act upon it as a source of law, are considered stronger than those of the opponents.

12.1.4.2 The binding strength of tacit *ijmā'*

As for tacit *ijmā'*, some of the jurists who upheld the binding strength of explicit *ijmā'*, objected to tacit *ijmā'* as a source of law. Some of them even refused to call it by the name of *ijmā'*. Among these jurists are Imām al-Shāfi'ī as well as Mālikites.

Those who object to it argue that silence on the part of some jurists could possibly mean that they agree with the opinions expressed explicitly. It could mean that they are not willing to express an opinion on the issue due to respect for the person who has done so or out of fear or some other reason. Silence, therefore, cannot be considered as an evidence of agreement.

The majority of the jurists, however, maintained that tacit *ijmā'* is a legally binding source, but they differed with respect to its strength. Some said that it is a definitive source, like explicit *ijmā'*, and these are the Ḥanafī jurists and Imām Aḥmad ibn Ḥanbal. Their argument is that evidences for *ijmā'* in the Qur'ān and the *Sunnah* do not differentiate between explicit *ijmā'* and tacit *ijmā'*. Some of the jurists said tacit *ijmā'* is a probable (*ẓannī*) source. Among these jurists is al-Karkhī, the well known Ḥanafī jurist and al-Āmidī, a later Shāfi'ī scholar.

It is well known that the Companions of the Prophet (peace be on him) used to speak out without fear whenever they felt that a decision could be improved. For example, when the mighty 'Umar ibn al-Khaṭṭāb decided to award the penalty of stripes to a pregnant woman for her offence, Mu'ādh ibn Jabal pointed out that he would be awarding the punishment to her as well as to what was in her womb. 'Umar said, "Had Mu'ādh not been here, 'Umar would have perished." There are many such examples. Further, one would expect from a person who has attained the status of a *mujtahid* to speak his mind whenever he feels that the truth is different. He should not remain silent because of fear or some other expediency, for he is no ordinary individual and it would be his duty to speak out if he disagrees. It is, therefore, felt that those who maintain that *ijmāʿ sukūtī* is equally binding as *ijmāʿ qawlī* are making a sound argument, and it appears better to consider both types of *ijmāʿ* as having equal strength.

12.1.5 The *sanad* of *ijmāʿ*

The *sanad* of *ijmāʿ* is the evidence upon which the jurists rely for arriving upon a consensus. The majority of the jurists agree that each *ijmāʿ* must have a *sanad* on which the jurist should rely, while arriving at the opinion, otherwise the resulting *ijmāʿ* would be based upon *ra'y* (personal opinion) and this is rejected by the *sharīʿah*.[230]

Evidences Qualifying as a *Sanad*. There is no disagreement among the jurists that evidences from the texts of the Qur'ān and the *Sunnah* are to be treated as valid *sanads* for *ijmāʿ*. Thus, for the *ijmāʿ* on marriage being unlawful with grandmothers, the *sanad* is the verse, "حرمت عليكم امهاتكم" (forbidden unto you (for marriage) are your mothers). For the *ijmāʿ* on the prohibition of sale of food prior to possession by the buyer, the *sanad* is the tradition: من ابتاع طعاما فلا تبعه حتي تقبضه (Whoever buys food should not sell it until he has taken possession of it).

As regards *qiyās* (analogy) being a *sanad* for *ijmāʿ*, there is disagreement among the jurists. Those who object to *qiyās* being a *sanad*, maintain that *qiyās* is a probable (*ẓannī*) evidence, while *ijmāʿ* is a definitive evidence, and it is not proper to construct a definitive evidence upon a probable evidence. The majority of the jurists, however, accept *qiyās* as a valid *sanad* for *ijmāʿ*. They argue that even a *khabar wāḥid* is a probable evidence, yet it is accepted as a valid *sanad* for *ijmāʿ* by agreement of the jurists. Further, they argue that even an analogy traces its logic back to an *aṣl* in the texts

230. We have already indicated that the stipulation of this condition may take away something from the strength of *ijmāʿ* as an independent principle. As mentioned below, some jurists even object to analogy being a supporting evidence for a rule based on consensus, the argument being that analogy is a probable evidence and it cannot support a definitive evidence.

of the Qur'ān and the *Sunnah*, so accepting *qiyās* as a *sanad* should not be a problem.

Similar arguments are advanced with respect to *maṣlaḥah mursalah* as a *sanad* for *ijmā'* and it has been used as a *sanad* in practice. The examples they cite are the collection of the Qur'ān into a *muṣḥaf*. All the Companions agreed on this in the interest (*maṣlaḥah*) of the *ummah*. Another example they cite is about the *kharāj* lands of Iraq, which were conquered during the period of 'Umar. These lands were not divided up as *ghanīmah*, but were left in the hands of those in possession as *kharāj* lands, again in the interest of the *ummah*. Those who upheld using *maṣlaḥah mursalah* as a *sanad* agree that an *ijmā'* based on it cannot be permanent, and will last as long as the *maṣlaḥah* persists. If the *maṣlaḥah* changes, the *ijmā'* will also have to be altered.

12.1.6 Likelihood of the occurrence of *ijmā'*

There is some disagreement about the possibility of consensus and its actual occurrence. The majority of the jurists maintained that such a consensus is possible and actually did take place. Al-Naẓẓām and his followers maintained that such a consensus is not possible. They argue that a condition for *ijmā'* is the participation of all the *mujtahids* of a particular period and this requires the identification of all *mujtahids* as well as the identification of their opinions. This they argue is not possible, because there is no criterion for distinguishing a *mujtahid* from a non-*mujtahid*, and even if there was such a criterion, the *mujtahids* are spread all over the Muslim lands and it is not possible to gather them in one place nor to ascertain where they are. They argue further that a *mujtahid* has to rely on an evidence in the sources for the formulation of his opinion. Now, such an evidence is either definitive or probable. A definitive evidence conveys a single meaning and there cannot be two views about it, therefore, there is no function that *ijmā'* can perform in this case. If, on the other hand, the evidence is probable, that is, it has more than one interpretation, getting all the *mujtahids* to agree upon a single meaning is an impossibility.

To these arguments, the majority respond by saying that there have been such agreements in Islamic history. The examples they quote pertain to the period of the Companions. For example, the granting of one-sixth share in the inheritance to the grandmother, the prohibition of sale of food before the buyer has taken possession, the prohibition of the marriage of a Muslim woman to a non-Muslim, and the validity of marriage (*nikāḥ*) when a dower has not been mentioned.

The objection to this argument may be that even if this were possible during the period of the Companions, when all the *mujtahids* were well known and easily accessible, it would be impossible today when the Muslim world is composed a large number of states. Some may respond, however, that the world is once again becoming a smaller place with the rapid advancements in technology, and we cannot call the possibility of the occurrence of *ijmā'* as impossible.

12.1.7 Cases of *ijmā'* transmitted in books of *fiqh*

For an agreement to constitute valid *ijmā'* it must be among all *mujtahids* in a determined period upon a legal issue. The jurists have argued in support of this concept of *ijmā'* on the basis of the texts of the Qur'ān and the *Sunnah*. The question is: Have the rules about *ijmā'* laid down in these texts, and formulated by the *fuqahā'*, been followed in books of *fiqh*?

Those who study these books notice that instances of *ijmā'* mentioned in the books of *fiqh* are either among the majority of the jurists or they are agreements pertaining to the jurists of one school. On a number of occasions, the cases cited are those of tacit rather than explicit *ijmā'*. Thus, for example, we may find, in the Ḥanafī books, statements to the effect that such and such jurist upheld such an opinion and no one opposed him, thus it constitutes *ijmā'*. It is obvious that such claims of *ijmā'* do not meet all the conditions that the *fuqahā'* have themselves laid down for valid *ijmā'*.

In addition to this, there is no compiled source for cases of *ijmā'*. There are a few books, like the one by Ibn Ḥazm, who belonged to the Ẓāhirī school, which is now extinct. The name of the book is *Marātib al-Ijmā'*.

12.1.8 Role of *ijmā'* in the modern world

In the preceding discussion, it has been stated that there are various objections against the principle of *ijmā'*. Some of the objections pertain to the conditions of *ijmā'* as stipulated by the jurists, while others relate to the possibility of its occurrence. Some practical difficulties have also been pointed out. *Ijmā'* is a source that is accepted by all the Sunnī schools, just as they accept the two primary sources, yet there is no established system for its transmission. The only transmission of *ijmā'* one finds is within the schools; in the books of each school. Further, some of the cases or instances of *ijmā'* that are cited do not meet the conditions stipulated for *ijmā'* when they are examined outside the schools of *ijtihād* and *fiqh*.

Due to these factors and objections, some modern scholars have said that *ijmā'* does not appear to be a practical principle and cannot operate as a source of law, at least in the modern times. The view of the present author is that the very fact that *ijmā'* has been accepted as a primary source of law for so many centuries by the leading jurists of Islam, it has to have a greater or deeper role than is exhibited by the external conditions imposed by jurists. In other words, the matter needs to be examined a little more deeply, perhaps, in the context of modern law.

An examination of the principle of *ijmā'* in a general way reveals that all it is saying is that if a rule or principle is upheld collectively by the highest legal forum in the land, then, such a principle or rule must be followed by those subordinate to this forum. This is exactly what the doctrine of *stare decisis* says in the English common law system. The deeper the examination of the principle of *ijmā'*, the greater is the conviction it requires that the decision of the higher forum, or the full bench of the highest court (en banc), so to say, must be followed and maintained by the lower courts.

In the earlier stages of the growth of Islamic law, the forum was confined to the jurist Companions. Later, when the schools of law emerged, the forum moved to the leading jurists of each school and operated within the schools. Today, when the *ummah* is composed of different jurisdictions in Muslim countries, the forum would automatically be the highest court in each Muslim country. In fact, the principle fits in perfectly with the legal system in those countries that have the English common law as the modern tradition.

Review Questions

1. What is the meaning of *ijmā'* and what are the conditions for its validity?
2. What are the different types of *ijmā'* and what is the legal force of *ijmā'* as a source of Islamic law?
3. What is the binding strength of tacit *ijmā'* or *ijmā' sukūtī*?
4. What do you understand by the term *sanad* of *ijmā'*? Is it necessary for the jurist to rely on *sanad* for purposes of *ijmā'*?
5. Describe the meaning of *ijmā'* and its role as a source of law in the modern times.
6. The Constitution of Pakistan does not recognize *ijmā'* as a source of Islamic law. Discuss.
7. Compare the activities of the Supreme Court, the Federal Shariat Court and the Council of Islamic Ideology with the activity of the jurists when arriving at a consensus (*ijmā'*).

Part III

The Secondary Sources of Islamic Law

13 *Maṣlaḥah* and the *Maqāṣid al-Sharī'ah*

The secondary sources of Islamic law are mostly rational. The term "rational" with respect to secondary sources means that these are not material sources in which the rules are stated. The rational sources are techniques of legal reasoning that the *mujtahid* employs during his *ijtihād*. The material sources used during this legal reasoning are the Qur'ān, *Sunnah* and *ijmā'*, and the rational secondary sources provide the means of extension for the law stated in these primary sources.

The secondary sources of Islamic law to be discussed in the chapters of this Part are: *qiyās* (analogy); *istiḥsān* (juristic preference of the stronger principle); *istiṣḥāb al-ḥāl* (presumption of continuity); *maṣlaḥah mursalah* (extended analogy); and *sadd al-dharī'ah* (blocking the lawful means to an unlawful end). Sources that are not considered rational, but transmitted are discussed in the last chapter of this Part. Accordingly, The first study taken up is that of *qiyās*, however, before we do so we would like to discuss the concept of *maṣlaḥah* and the *maqāṣid al-sharī'ah*.

A discussion of the *maqāṣid al-sharī'ah* (the purposes of Islamic law) as well as the principle of *maṣlaḥah,* before discussing the rational sources, becomes necessary due to several reasons. The first is that the principle of *maṣlaḥah* has grown to envelope all the rational sources. Each rational source is today considered part of the larger doctrine of *maṣlaḥah.* The second is that this principle is considered the most important and the most comprehensive instrument of *ijtihād* for the modern times; its discussion must therefore precede that of the rational sources. A third reason is that the larger doctrine of *maṣlaḥah* must be distinguished from the narrower principle of *maṣlaḥah mursalah,* which is considered one type of rational source within the broader doctrine.

In our book, *Theories of Islamic Law,* we have given most of the credit to Imām al-Ghazālī for developing the doctrine of *maṣlaḥah.* This is justified, but here we would like to acknowledge the contribution of the jurist who made the first clear statement about *maṣlaḥah* and the *maqāṣid al-sharī'ah.* It was non other than the great Imām al-Sarakhsī.

The meaning of *maṣlaḥah* is discussed first and is followed by a description of the purposes of Islamic law or the *maqāṣid al-sharī'ah.*

13.1 The Meaning of *Maṣlaḥah* (Interest) and the Doctrine of Utility

The words *maṣlaḥah* and *manfa'ah* are treated as synonyms. *Manfa'ah* means "benefit" or "utility," that is, it leads to some kind of benefit. In its literal meaning *maṣlaḥah* is defined as جلب المنفعه ودفع المضرّة (*jalb al-manfa'ah wa-daf' al-maḍarrah*) or the seeking of benefit and the repelling of harm.

13.1.1 The Meaning of Utility and Bentham

If this literal meaning is pursued further it will lead to something similar to the principle of utility expounded by Jeremy Bentham, which means securing the maximum human happiness. The seeking of human happiness in this sense may imply three things:

(*i*) That the happiness sought here is dependent upon human desires or reason. The pursuit of such happiness may or may not coincide with the form of benefit or *manfa'ah* intended by the *sharī'ah*.

(*ii*) The emphasis in this form of happiness will always be on the collective utility, that is, the happiness of the entire community and the interests of the individual may be given a back seat.

(*iii*) The pursuit of pure utility[231] may ultimately lead to the economic analysis of law (as expounded by Richard Posner and the Chicago School). In other words, all legal decisions must be reduced to a cost-benefit analysis either financial or economic. This may or may not suit the goals of the *sharī'ah*.

13.1.2 *Maṣlaḥah* in Islamic Law

Manfa'ah (benefit or utility), however, is not the technical meaning of *maṣlaḥah*. What Muslim jurists mean by *maṣlaḥah* is the seeking of benefit and the repelling of harm **as directed by the Lawgiver.** The seeking of utility in Islamic law is not dependent on human reason and pleasure. Al-Ghazālī, therefore, defines *maṣlaḥah* as follows:

> As for *maslaḥah*, it is essentially an expression for the acquisition of *manfa'ah* (benefit) or the repulsion of *maḍarrah* (injury, harm), but that is not what we mean by it, because acquisition of *manfa'ah* and the repulsion of *maḍarrah* represent human goals, that is, the welfare of humans through the attainment of these goals. **What we mean by *maṣlaḥah*, however, is the preservation of the ends of the *shar'*.**[232]

Three things are obvious from this statement:

231. See Edgar Bodenheimer, *Jurisprudence: The Philosophy and Method of the Law,* 84 for the details of the principles of utility and Richard Posner, *Economic Analysis of Law* for economic analysis.
232. Al-Ghazālī, *al-Mustaṣfā min 'Ilm al-Uṣūl*, Baghdad, 1294 (A.H.), vol. 1, 286.

(*i*) That the pursuit of human goals and the principle of utility based on human reason is not what is meant by *maṣlaḥah.*

(*ii*) That *maṣlaḥah* is the securing of goals or values that the Lawgiver has determined for the *sharī'ah.*

(*iii*) That the goals determined for the *sharī'ah* by the Lawgiver may or may not coincide with values determined by human reason. Thus, reasoning based upon the principle of utility or on economic analysis may sometimes be acceptable to the *sharī'ah,* but it may be rejected at other times when there is a clash of values.

13.2 The Classification of *Maṣlaḥah*

Muslim jurists classify *maṣlaḥah* in several ways. These classifications are expected to show us how this principle covers most of the rational sources and how the discussion of the sources is linked with the purposes of Islamic law. Some of the most important classifications are provided below.

13.2.1 First classification: *maṣlaḥah* acknowledged or rejected by the *sharī'ah*

For purposes of this classification, it is important to understand that the underlying causes of the *aḥkām* present a hierarchical structure of attributes. Sometimes the *sharī'ah* recognises a lower level attribute as the basis for the law, while at other times it accepts a higher level attribute. The level at which an attribute is acknowledged indicates the type of rational source being used. The classification that follows is based on the recognition of attributes at different levels.[233] Four types of *maṣlaḥah* are discussed under this heading:

1. ***Maṣlaḥah* acknowledged at the level of the lowest category.** The first type is *maṣlaḥah* acknowledged by the

233. The most lucid presentation of the different types of *maṣlaḥah,* in our view, is to be found in al-Rāzī, *al-Maḥṣūl,* vol. 6, 162–67.

Lawgiver at the level of the lowest category (*naw'*). Take the case of drinking *khamr* (wine). The underlying cause at the lower level could be "intoxication," that is, losing of one's senses. A higher level cause could be the "protection of the intellect." Recognition of a cause at the lower level means that the rational source invoked is analogy (*qiyās*). This means that the law can be extended to other things on the basis of analogy using the rule: whatever intoxicates is prohibited. Prohibiting intoxication is, therefore, the repelling of harm or the securing of an interest protected by the law (*maṣlaḥah*). All those cases where the Lawgiver has identified underlying causes at the lowest level fall under the first type of *maṣlaḥah*. Further, this tells us that using analogy (*qiyās*) is one type of *maṣlaḥah*.

2. ***Maṣlaḥah* acknowledged at the level of the genus.** The second type is *maṣlaḥah* that is acknowledged by the Lawgiver at the level of the genus, that is, at a level higher than the lowest category. Such a recognition takes us beyond the level of analogy into the realm of other rational sources, especially *maṣlaḥah mursalah*. This recognition of attributes can go up to the highest level of the purposes of law. The purposes of Islamic law at the highest level are five: Preservation of *dīn;* preservation of life; preservation of *nasl* (progeny); preservation of intellect; and preservation of wealth. The jurists illustrate the recognition of these attributes through a large number of examples. Thus, the Companions of the Prophet (peace be on him) were not sure whether the text of the Qur'ān should be compiled, because the Prophet had not done so during his lifetime. In the interest of "preservation of *dīn*" they decided that it should be gathered and compiled. The texts clearly mention that a life is to be taken for a life in the case of *qiṣāṣ* (retaliation). Where two or more persons participate in the murder of one person, should more than one life be taken for a single life? It was decided that in the interest of the "preservation of life" such a law should be made. The details of this type will be explained under the discussion of *maṣlaḥah mursalah* as well

as under the discussion of the third mode of *ijtihād.*

3. ***Maṣlaḥah* that is rejected by the *sharī'ah.*** The third type *maṣlaḥah* is one that is not acknowledged by the *sharī'ah,* because it clashes with a text. The jurists have found it difficult to give examples of this type. They provide hypothetical cases. Let us assume that the *ḥukm* for a person indulging in sexual intercourse during fasting is the freeing of a slave. A jurist may say that this provision gives a loophole to a very rich person, because setting free a slave is nothing for him. Such a jurist may say that this option should therefore not be available to a rich man in the interest of "the preservation of *dīn.*" The *sharī'ah,* however, does not recognise such a measure and the argument is without foundation and is rejected. In other words, a provision proposed in contradiction of what the *sharī'ah* has already provided will not be recognised as a *maṣlaḥah* that clashes with a text of the Qur'ān or *Sunnah* is rejected.

4. ***Maṣlaḥah* that is neither acknowledged nor rejected.** The fourth type is a *maṣlaḥah* that is neither acknowledged by the *sharī'ah* nor is it rejected. This type of *maṣlaḥah* is one that is strange (*gharīb*) for the *sharī'ah.* An example will be provided under the discussion of *maṣlaḥah mursalah* for ease of understanding.

13.2.2 Second classification: *maṣlaḥah* according to its inner strength

This classification is based upon the purposes of Islamic law and their types. The types of *maṣlaḥah* according to their inner strength are three: *ḍarūrāt* (necessities); *ḥājāt* (needs); and *taḥsīnāt* (complementary goals).

1. *Ḍarūrāt* (necessary interests). Necessary interests are those without the protection of which there would be anarchy and chaos in society. The absence of protection for these interests would mean the loss of everything that we hold dear. These prized social interests are five in number:

a) Preservation and protection of religion (*ḥifẓ 'alā al-dīn*).
b) Preservation and protection of life (*ḥifẓ 'alā al-nafs*).
c) Preservation and protection of progeny (*ḥifẓ 'alā al-nasl*).
d) Preservation and protection of intellect (*ḥifẓ 'alā al-'aql*).
e) Preservation and protection of wealth (*ḥifẓ 'alā al-māl*).

2. *Ḥājāt* (supporting needs). The second type of interests are called *ḥājāt* or supporting interests required by the necessary interests for their smooth operation and implementation. If these supporting interests are not protected by the law there would be hardship and loss in the performance of social functions. This means that the primary or necessary interests would not be lost, but there would be considerable friction and difficulty in their protection. The examples of these interests given by jurists pertain mostly to exemptions granted by the law. For example, the exemptions available due to illness or journey in case of worship serve these interests, just like the contract of *salam* (advance payment) works as an exemption to facilitate transactions. The necessary interests do not depend on these exemptions or supporting needs, but their operation is facilitated.

3. *Taḥsīnāt* (complementary interests). These interests provide additional rules that lead to the moral and spiritual progress of the individual and society. Examples are: voluntary *ṣadaqah* and many ethical and moral rules (like the command not cut trees or to kill animals during war). In reality, the *taḥsīnāt* tell us that there is a moral shell around the necessities and supporting needs provided by the *sharī'ah*. Thus, morality goes hand in hand with the law and there is no separation as may be found in Western law.

This classification shows the types of purposes of the Islamic law and the relationship between them.

13.2.3 Third classification: definitive and probable interests

Some jurists, and some later writers, have maintained that there are interests that are definitive (*qaṭ'ī*) and those that are probable (*ẓannī*). Jurists like al-Ghazālī and al-Shāṭibī have spent considerable time in showing that all the interests classified according to their inner strength above are definitive, because they have been constructed through a process of induction (*istiqrā'*) rather than deduction. Certain cases of interests that have been called strange or *gharīb* may, however, be deemed to be probable. Yet, the major area of probable purposes lies in the area called *ashbāh* by al-Ghazālī.[234] (See the figure below at p. 252, as well as the section on what lies beyond the *maqāṣid*.)

This issue is found in Western law as well when values are classified according to different types of rationality, with some legal philosophers, like Kelsen, maintaining that most interests or values preserved by the law do not meet the standards of rationality that can be called definitive.[235] These, however, are values identified by human reason. We shall have something more to say about this when we discuss the third mode of *ijtihād* in the next part of this book.

13.2.4 Fourth classification: public and private interests

The necessary interests, the supporting needs and complementary interests can all be divided into public interests and private interests. In fact, the settlement of legal disputes always involves some kind of conflict or clash between public and private interests or between two private interests.

The problem that arises, especially in modern times, is whether public interests are based on the rights of Allah (*ḥaqq Allāh*) or on the rights of the state (*ḥaqq al-salṭanah*) or are these the same thing?

---

234. See Al-Ghazālī, *Shifā' al-Ghalīl fī Masālik al-Ta'līl*, 142 as well as the chapter on the *ashbāh*.

235. Edgar Bodenheimer, *Jurisprudence*, 203.

13.3 The Doctrine of *Maṣlaḥah* and *Maslaḥah Mursalah:* Distinction

The principle of *maṣlaḥah mursalah* was first used by Imām Mālik, the founder of the Mālikī school. It was elaborated and developed in the works of al-Ghazālī.[236] Out of this discussion there emerged a larger doctrine of *maṣlaḥah,* which is much wider than the principle or source of Islamic law called *maṣlaḥah mursalah.*

The larger doctrine requires that during the use or employment of rational sources to discover the law, each derived law must be checked against the purposes of Islamic law or the *maqāṣid al-sharī'ah.* If there is some compatibility (*munāsabah*) between the derived law and the purposes, then the law is valid, otherwise it may be rejected. In this sense, all the rational sources fall under this larger doctrine. Thus, the larger doctrine covers *qiyās, istiḥsān* and *maṣlaḥah mursalah.* In other words, each of these rational sources has now become or is deemed a type of this larger doctrine. It is for this reason that the meaning of *maṣlaḥah* and the nature of the purposes of law has been discussed before the description of the rational sources.

13.4 *Maqāṣid al-Sharī'ah* or the Purposes of Islamic Law

The purposes of law are divided by al-Ghazālī into two types:

- *dīnī* or purposes of the Hereafter.
- *dunyawī* or purposes pertaining to this world.

Each of these is divisible into *taḥṣīl* or securing of the interest and *ibqā'* or preservation of the interest. *Taḥṣīl* is the securing of a benefit (*manfa'ah*) and *ibqā'* is the repelling of harm (*maḍarrah*). The phrase *ri'āyat al-maqāṣid* (preservation of the *maqāṣid*) is used to indicate both *taḥṣīl* and *ibqā'*.[237]

236. Especially in his book *Shifā' al-Ghalīl.*
237. Al-Ghazālī, *Shifā' al-Ghalīl,* 186–87.

The worldly purposes (*dunyawī*) are further divided into four types: the preservation of *nafs* (life), the preservation of *nasl* (progeny), the preservation of *'aql* (intellect), and the preservation of *māl* (wealth). Each worldly purpose is meant to serve the single *dīnī* purpose. When all types are taken together, we have five ultimate purposes of the law:

- *dīn* (religion),
- life,
- progeny (may be called the preservation of the Family),
- intellect, and
- wealth.

These five purposes are designated as *ḍarūrāt* (necessities) and are the primary purposes of the law. These are followed by the *ḥājāt* (needs), which are additional purposes required by the primary purposes, even though the primary purposes would not be lost without them. The third category is that of purposes that seek to establish ease and facility (*tawassu'* and *taysīr*) in the law; these are called the *taḥsīnāt* (complementary values).

The relationship of the purposes of Islamic law may be seen in the figure below.

13.4.1 What is beyond the purposes?

If we move beyond the ultimate values recognised as the purposes of the law, we reach the area of weaker attributes, which are also used by the jurists for extending the law. This is the area of the *ashbāh* (probable values). These too are organized in the form of the particular and the general. This is the area of the probable or *ẓannī maqāṣid*.

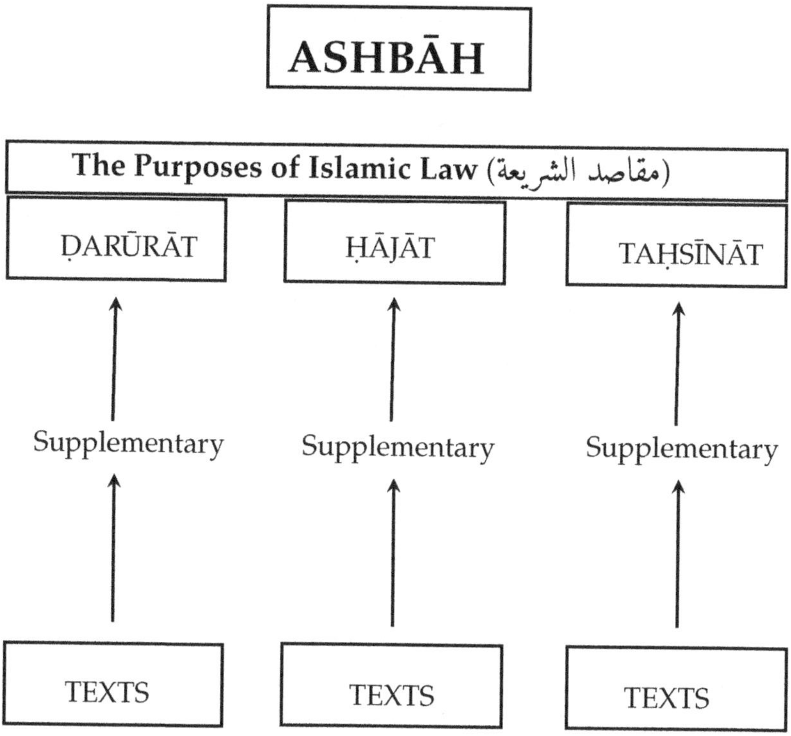

Thus, the purpose beyond these purposes could be the building of civilisation, security, the maintenance of equality, freedom, and many other values that are preserved and protected by each society and they are expressed as the aims of justice in Western law.[238] The Muslim jurists did not deal with such values, because they are probable and do not fall in the area of certain rationality. An attribute depicting such values is called *waṣf ba'īd* or a distant value; it is distant in comparison with the *ḍarūrāt*, each of which is a *waṣf qarīb* or near value.

13.4.2 *Maqāṣid al-sharī'ah* and the texts

The purposes of Islamic law have been determined from the texts through a process of induction (*istiqrā'*) rather than through deduction.[239] This is the reason why the *maqāṣid* are considered

238. Bodenheimer, *Jurisprudence*, 196.
239. Al-Shāṭibī, *al-Muwāfaqāt*, vol. 2, 7.

definitive (*qaṭ'ī*), and can be relied upon without a doubt, and the same pattern is to be found in the other details of the *sharī'ah*.[240] Al-Shāṭibī quotes a large number of verses of the Qur'ān to show how the ultimate purposes are indicated by the texts.

13.5 The Nature and Structure of the Purposes of the *Sharī'ah*

The structure of the *maqāṣid* is understood by appreciating the relationship of the primary purposes among themselves, and their relationship with the secondary and supporting purposes. As the *maqāṣid* are designed to ultimately serve the interests of the Hereafter, it is this relationship that may be examined first.

13.5.1 Primary purposes in the service of the Hereafter

The first purpose of the *sharī'ah* is to secure the interest of Man that pertains to the Hereafter. It is for this reason that the purposes are divided into *dīnī* or purposes of the Hereafter and *dunyawī* or purposes restricted to this world. The worldly purposes, in combination, seek to preserve and protect the interest of *dīn*.

Al-Ghazālī says that the second purpose, which is the preservation and protection of life, may be considered by some to have a higher priority than *dīn*, because without life there would be no religion. This argument takes collective life into consideration, and in this sense it would also hold true for the intellect too, because the existence of *'aql* is considered by jurists to be a condition of *taklīf* (legal obligation). He points out, however, that some provisions of the law clearly support the superiority of the interest of *dīn*. For example, the interest of *dīn* is preferred when the subject is asked to give up his life in the way of Allah, that is, for *jihād*. The relationship of the necessities or the primary purposes is seen through the following figure:

Al-Shāṭibī devotes three of the thirteen rules, in which he discusses the relationship among the purposes, to the discussion

240. Ibid.

of the Hereafter. The most important point he makes in this context is that the identification of the interests of Man has not been left to the whims and fancies of human beings, that is, to human reason, because all the purposes seek to establish and maintain life in this world to serve the interests of the Hereafter.

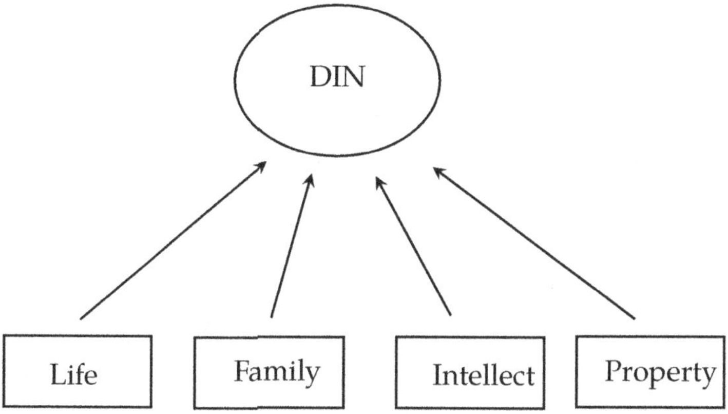

He also discusses the concept of utility and points out that benefits and harms are relative; they may vary from individual to individual, and from one situation to the other. If harm and benefit cannot be established directly from the texts, then, it is to be linked to what is usually considered beneficial or harmful. The general rule that he derives is that since the *maqāṣid* serve the interests of the Hereafter the determination of what is beneficial and what is harmful cannot be left to human reason. He seeks support from a number of Qur'ānic verses. One of these is:

ولو اتّبع الحقّ أهوآءهم لفسدت السّموات والأرض و من فيهنّ

> And if the Truth had followed their desires, verily the heavens and the earth and whosoever is therein had been corrupted. [Qur'ān 23 : 71]

In his view, the role of human reason begins after the *sharī'ah* has laid down the essential principles.[241] The first of the thirteen rules he expounds is devoted to this point.

The primary purpose of the *sharī'ah*, then, as indicated already, is to free Man from the grip of his own whim and fancy, so that

241. Al-Shāṭibī, *al-Muwāfaqāt*, vol. 2, 48.

he may become the servant of Allāh by choice, just as he is one without it.[242] The preservation and protection of *dīn* is intended by the Lawgiver to achieve this.

13.5.2 The two faces of the *maqāṣid*

Perhaps the most important feature of the *maqāṣid* is their dual thrust. Al-Ghazālī discusses this dual nature in detail in his book called *Jawāhir al-Qur'ān*.[243] This point has been ignored by almost all the later jurists, except for al-Shāṭibī.

The dual feature of the *maqāṣid* is evident in the use of the terms *ibqā'* and *ḥifẓ*, which we may call preservation and protection.[244] Al-Shāṭibī considers these the two aspects of *ḥifẓ*. The first he says is "what affirms its elements and establishes its foundations."[245] The second is "what repels actual or expected disharmony."[246] The focus of later jurists, and hence that of modern scholars, has been on the aspect of protection alone. Each purpose, however, has a positive or aggressive aspect and a negative or defensive aspect. From the positive aspect, the interest is secured by establishing what is required by the *sharī'ah* through each of its *maqāṣid*. Thus, the interest of *dīn* is secured by the creation of conditions that facilitate worship and establish the other essential pillars of Islam. The interest of life is secured by creating conditions for the existence of life. The interest of progeny is supported by facilitating and establishing family life. The interest of intellect is secured by promoting the means for the growth of the intellect. The interest of wealth is secured by creating proper conditions for the growth of wealth.[247]

242. Ibid., vol. 2, 38, 168.
243. Al-Ghazālī, *Jawāhir al-Qur'ān* (Beirut: Dār Ihyā' al-'Ulūm, 1985), 32-35
244. There may be a problem with the terminology adopted by the two jurists, because we noted above that al-Ghazālī has used the terms *taḥṣīl* and *ibqā'* where *ibqā'* means protection rather than preservation.
245. Al-Shāṭibī, *al-Muwāfaqāt*, vol. 2, 8.
246. Ibid.
247. Ibid., 2, 9.

	Dīn	Life	Family	Intellect	Wealth
+ve	Establish	Establish	Establish	Establish	Establish
-ve	Defend	Defend	Defend	Defend	Defend

From the defensive or the protective aspect, interests are secured by preventing the destruction or corruption of the positive aspect. Thus, *jihād* is prescribed for defending *dīn*, while prayer, fasting, pilgrimage, and *zakāh* help establish it. It is the duty of the *imām* to ensure proper conditions for both, while it is binding upon each subject to fulfil these duties, individually and collectively. Life is preserved through the provision of sustenance and the maintenance of good health, while it is protected or defended through the provision of penalties for those who destroy life without legal justification. *Nasl* is promoted through the maintenance of healthy family life and the institution of marriage, while penalties are provided for those who would corrupt it and destroy its values. The preservation of *'aql* is achieved through the provision of education and healthy conditions for its growth, while penalties are provided for the consumption of substances that destroy the intellect. Preservation of wealth is achieved by encouraging its growth, while theft or misappropriation of wealth is punished through penalties.

13.5.3 Primary and secondary purposes

The jurists break up the *maqāṣid* into three levels. This has already been pointed out. The first level is that of the necessities (*ḍarūrāt*), which have been maintained by all societies and without which the social structure will collapse. These are the primary *maqāṣid* and the jurists focus mostly on these. They are supported by the supporting needs (*ḥājāt*). The third level is that of complementary values and norms (*taḥsīnāt*).

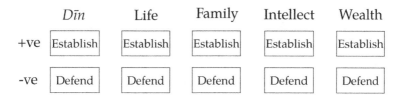

The important point made by jurists about the significance of each level is that the primary purposes are supported by the two other levels. However, if the last two levels are abolished the primary purposes will stand by themselves. This is not true for the lower levels. Thus, the existence of *ḥājāt* and the *taḥsīnāt* depends upon the primary purposes and they cannot be maintained on their own.

Dīn	Life	Family	Intellect	Wealth
Public	Public	Public	Public	Public
Private	Private	Private	Private	Private

The importance of the individual purposes within the *ḍarūrāt* is reflected in the order in which they are stated. Thus, *dīn* has precedence over life, life has precedence over *nasl*, *nasl* has precedence over *'aql*, and *'aql* has precedence over *māl*. This is not all. Each of the primary purposes may divided into public and private purposes. The public purposes seek to preserve the interests of the community as whole, while the private purposes protect the rights of individuals. Again, the purposes are divisible into those securing the rights of Allāh and those preserving or protecting the rights of the individuals. There is a fine distinction between the two kinds of divisions, though many modern scholars tend to consider them identical. The distinction lies in the fact that there are three kinds of rights to be identified rather than two. These are the right of Allāh, the right of the community as whole, and the right of the individual.

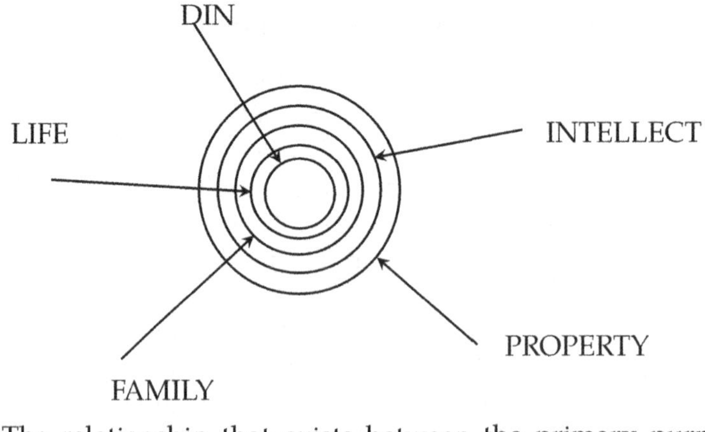

The relationship that exists between the primary purposes may be highlighted by visualising outer shells serving or protecting the inner shell or shells. Thus, the innermost shell is represented by the preservation and protection of *dīn*. This represents the foremost purpose of the *sharī'ah*. The shell surrounding it is that of life, which is itself surrounded by *nasl* and so on. The outermost shell is that of the preservation of wealth that serves all the inner shells and is subservient to them.

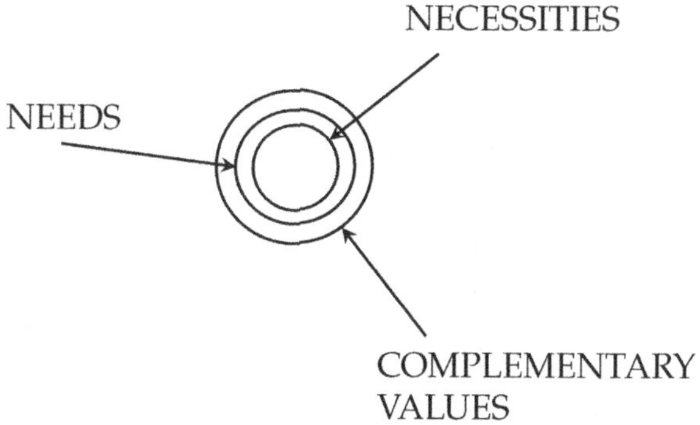

Each primary purpose considered to be a necessity has its own supporting needs and complementary norms. These are also to be viewed as shells, one inside the other. This relationship is explained by al-Shāṭibī through examples. Considering the example of prayer (*ṣalāt*), he says that the essential parts of the prayer are its *arkān* (elements) and *farā'iḍ* (obligations). Whatever is besides these is meant to complete and complement it.[248] The parts of prayer are distributed among the *maqāṣid* in such a way that each outer shell forms a protective boundary for the inner shell. One who crosses the outer shell or boundary will soon demolish the inner shell. Thus, the person who gives up the *nafl* (supererogatory) prayers will soon give up the *sunan*, and will finally demolish the *farā'iḍ*. There are many instances in the law, he says, that correspond with the analogy of *nafl* and *farā'iḍ*. For example, even a drop of wine or a small quantity of it is prohibited, because it leads to the consumption of larger quantities, though it does not intoxicate or damage the intellect. A severe penalty is provided for stealing a thing of small value as it leads to the stealing of larger amounts and to robbery.[249] In the same way, the

248. Al-Shāṭibī, *al-Muwāfaqāt*, vol. 2, 22.
249. Ibid., 22–23.

ethical and moral norms hover around and protect the main and essential legal norms. The *ḥājī* and the *taḥsīnī* are, therefore, to be considered the servants of the *ḍarūrī*.

13.5.4 Priorities within the *maqāṣid*

The relationships described above indicate that some purposes have a higher priority than others, that is, they would be preferred in case of a clash between two interests. This fact also highlights an important point that while deciding a legal case or while attempting to understand the position of Islamic law on an issue, one cannot look at one purpose or interest alone. There is always a clash of two or more interests. This is achieved through the machinery of organized political society that seeks to strike a compromise between the conflicting wants, desires, and claims of individuals and between the competing interests. Looking at the purposes of law alone and identifying the priorities that exist between them would present a simplistic view of things.

The *maqāṣid* are always used as a reference point for the general principles of the law, and this makes the situation highly complex. This will be illustrated in the third part of this book under the discussion of the third mode of *ijtihād* (see page 379). Nevertheless, the *maqāṣid* considered alone present a fair picture of the entire system even for the layman, who is not trained in the law. If he observes a few rules, he can easily determine the answer to a question that he may have about the law. For the present purposes, we shall describe three main rules that govern the employment of the *maqāṣid*. Some other minor rules can be stated, but the idea is to avoid too much detail and technicalities.

13.5.4.1 Rule 1: The stronger interest shall prevail

The inherent strength of the interests secured by Islamic law is reflected in the order in which the *maqāṣid* are listed by the jurists. Thus, the preservation and protection of *dīn*, as we have pointed out earlier, has preference over the preservation and protection of life; life has a higher priority than *nasl*; *nasl* is prior to *'aql*; and *'aql* is preferred over *māl*.

Dīn	Life	Family	Intellect	Wealth
First	Second	Third	Fourth	Fifth

In practice this would mean, for example, that *jihād* has priority over preservation of life, and if an individual is asked to participate in it and give up his life in the cause of Allāh, there is legal justification for it. Preservation of life has a higher priority than the protection of *'aql*. Therefore, if a person is facing death in a desolate place due to lack of water and the only thing available to him is wine, he is under an obligation to save his life by drinking the wine. Life has priority over *māl* too and it is permitted to take the property of another person without fear of penalty during a famine, if such taking results in the saving of life or lives.

In the same way, the *ḍarūrāt* have priority over the *ḥājāt*, which in turn have priority over the *taḥsīnāt*.

13.5.4.2 Rule 2: The public interest is prior to the private

The different categories of the purposes can be understood in terms of public and private interests. Whenever a public interest is in conflict with a private interest, the public interest will prevail. The example used by the jurists is that of material handed over to artisans and craftsmen. The original rule of deposit (*wadī'ah*) required that this material being a deposit would not be compensated by the craftsmen in case it was destroyed, and the burden of proving tort (*ta'addī*) or negligence would be upon the customer, the owner of the property. This rule was changed to conform with the public interest, because the craftsmen were misusing the facility. The burden of proof was shifted to the craftsman, who had to show the absence of negligence. The Ḥanafīs based this change on *istiḥsān*. The example is expected to show that the public interest requiring security of transactions and protection of property of the general public was given preference over the interest of individuals, that is, the craftsmen.

In this case, both interests, public as well as private, lie within the same category, that is, the preservation of wealth. Does the rule that the public interest prevails over the private cut across all the categories? Can a public interest in a lower category be preferred over a private interest in a category with a higher priority? Apparently it can. Yet, the matter is not that simple; it involves the discussion of the three kinds of rights mentioned above, individual rights guaranteed by the *sharīʿah*, and the exact meaning of public interest. We do not have space to discuss all these issues here. This discussion will be taken up in a separate study of justice and Islamic law.

Another example used by al-Ghazālī upholds justification of taxation by the *imām* when the public interest is at stake. He permits a ruler in need of money to levy taxes in order to organise *jihād*. Here what we are calling public interest is actually the right of God, which may not be the same as the right of the state.

13.5.4.3 Rule 3: The definitive interest prevails over the probable

This rule has been the cause of confusion for some jurists following al-Ghazālī, and the confusion is witnessed in the works of some modern scholars too. Al-Shāṭibī states very clearly that all the interests preserved and protected by the *sharīʿah* are definitive (*qaṭʿī*). He repeats this point over and over again, and it is in fact a fundamental assumption of his work. The question, therefore, arises that if all interests are definitive, where does the probable interest come from? The answer to this issue is that the probable goals of the law belong to the area that is beyond the purposes and has been discussed above. These purposes have not been discussed by the jurists in detail. Most of the goals like building of civilisation, maintenance of security, equality, freedom and others would come under this heading. From another perspective, these goals have neither been rejected by the Lawgiver nor have they been directly acknowledged. Two cases mentioned by al-Ghazālī have been mentioned under the discussion of *maṣlaḥah mursalah* in the following chapter. There are, however, other possibilities too for probable interests to exist within the structure discussed, but we would like to leave this topic for the researcher here and devote adequate space to it in a separate study mentioned in the previous section.

13.5.5 *Maṣlaḥah*, Public Interest and Human Rights

Uṣūlīs, like al-Ghazālī, maintain that the public interest (*maṣlaḥah 'āmmah*) is invariably to be preferred over the private interest. This is the conclusion that Jeremy Bentham arrived at for his doctrine of utility. The problem is that with such an approach the possibility of promoting human rights, which are private interests, is eliminated. In other words, human rights will have very little role within such a philosophy. For Bentham this was not a problem. First, he rejected the idea of human rights and called such rights "nonsense on stilts." Second, he rejected the idea of the purposes of law. It was, therefore, natural for him to prefer the public interest all the time.

For Islamic law the position is different. In fact, the purposes of the *sharī'ah* are a reliable guide for human rights and they help us evaluate these rights. We have discussed this topic in a later chapter dealing with the third mode of *ijtihād*.

Review Questions

1. Compare the meaning of utility as expounded by Jeremy Bentham with the meaning of *maṣlaḥah* as used in Islamic law.
2. Give the classification of *maṣlaḥah* that has been acknowledged or rejected by the *sharī'ah* and then explain what is meant by the larger doctrine of *maṣlaḥah*.
3. Elaborate the classification of *maṣlaḥah* on the basis of its inner strength and explain the relationship of this classification with the general principles of Islamic law.
4. Interests are classified into definitive and probable. What is the advantage or purpose of such a classification?
5. Distinguish the doctrine of *maṣlaḥah* from *maṣlaḥah mursalah*.
6. What do you mean by the purposes of Islamic law? What is their relationship with the texts?

7. What is the purpose of the purposes of law or what is beyond the purposes?

8. The primary purpose is the preservation of *Dīn*. Elaborate.

9. The purpose of the *sharī'ah* have an affirmative and a defensive posture. Elaborate.

10. All the purposes of the *sharī'ah* can be classified into public and private interests. Elaborate.

11. What do you understand by the primary and secondary purposes of the *sharī'ah*?

12. Explain how the priorities within the *maqāṣid al-sharī'ah* work.

13. The *uṣūlīs* have stated that *maṣlaḥah 'āmmah* is always to be preferred over the *maṣlaḥah khāṣṣah*. Do you see some problems with this statement?

14 *Qiyās* (Analogy)

The discussion of *qiyās* covers several topics. These are: definition; elements; conditions pertaining to the elements; types of analogy; and justification of *qiyās* as a source of law. Some topics that are of practical significance, like deriving the underlying cause (*'illah*), will be taken up under the second mode of *ijtihād* in the next part, where it will be shown how the *mujtahid* undertakes *ijtihād* based on analogy.

14.1 Definition of *Qiyās*

In its literal meaning, the word *qiyās* (قياس) means measuring or estimating one thing in terms of another. Thus, measuring cloth against the metre rod is *qiyās*. It also applies to making two things equal, that is, comparing. This comparison may be physical or it may be rational. Thus, mapping a shoe upon a shoe to see their equality is *qiyās*.[250] The word *qiyās* is sometimes used in its figurative sense, and not its actual sense, to mean examination (*naẓr*) or even *ijtihād*, which is its method,[251] by the application of the term used for the cause to the resulting activity.[252] The distinction between these terms needs to be maintained to avoid confusion.

In the technical sense, as defined by the jurists, it applies to "the assignment of the *ḥukm* of an existing case found in the texts of the Qur'ān, the *Sunnah*, or *ijmā'* to a new case whose *ḥukm* is not found in these sources on the basis of a common underlying attribute called the *'illah* of the *ḥukm*." Another definition is: "the equality of a case, whose *ḥukm* is not mentioned explicitly in the texts, with a case whose *ḥukm* is mentioned, on the basis of the equality between the underlying causes found in the two cases."

The definitions are stated in Arabic as follows:

١) إلحاق ما لم يرد فيه نص على حكمه بما ورد فيه نص على حكمه في الحكم، لاشتراكهما في علة ذلك الحكم ٢) تسوية واقعة لم يرد نص بحكمها، بواقعة ورد النص بحكمها في الحكم المنصوص عليه، لتساوي الواقعتين في علّة الحكم

If the texts of the Qur'ān or the *Sunnah*, or *ijmā'* contain a case whose *'illah* is known to the *mujtahid*, that is, the underlying reason because of which the *ḥukm* has been laid down, and he then sees a new case which has the same *'illah* in it, he will assign the *ḥukm* of the existing case to the new case. By such an assignment, he renders the two cases equal in terms of the *ḥukm*. This assignment or rendering equal is called *qiyās* in the terminology of the jurists.

14.2 Elements of *Qiyās*

The definitions of *qiyās* show that it has four ingredients or elements:

- the case (set of facts) mentioned in the text with its *ḥukm;*

250. Al-Bazdawī, *Uṣūl al-Bazdawī* in 'Abd al-'Azīz al-Bukhārī, *Kashf al-Asrār,* vol. 3, 395.
251. Ibid., vol. 3, 396.
252. Ibid.

- the *ḥukm* of the set of facts mentioned in the text;
- the *'illah* or the underlying cause that has led to the *ḥukm;* and
- the new case or the set of facts for which the *ḥukm* has not been explicitly mentioned and which needs a *ḥukm.*

The case mentioned in the text (the first element) is called the *aṣl,* that is, the root case or even the base. It is also called the *maqīs 'alayh* or the case upon which analogy has been constructed. The *ḥukm* of this case (the second element) is called the *ḥukm al-aṣl* or the rule to be passed on. The underlying cause of the *ḥukm,* which is determined by the jurist, is called the *'illah* or the *ḥukm.* The new case to which the *ḥukm* is extended is called the *far'* or the offshoot.[253] It is also called the *maqīs* or the case for which analogy is constructed. The *ḥukm* that has been established for the new case is called the *ḥukm al-far'* or the rule established.

14.3 Examples of *Qiyās*

We may now look at some examples to understand the operation of *qiyās*:

1. The prohibition of *khamr* (wine from grapes) is laid down in the Qur'ān.[254] The text prohibits *khamr* along with a statement of the disaster it leads to, that is, enmity and hatred among people. Now, *khamr,* according to some jurists (the Ḥanafīs), is the name of an intoxicating liquor made from grape juice, called wine in English. The Arabic term *khamr* in their view does not include other intoxicating

253. *Far'* (فرع) literally means branch.

254. O ye who believe! Intoxicants and gambling, (dedication of) stones, and (divination by) arrows, are an abomination,- of Satan's handwork: eschew such (abomination), that ye may prosper. Satan's plan is (but) to excite enmity and hatred between you, with intoxicants and gambling, and hinder you from the remembrance of God, and from prayer: will ye not then abstain? [Qur'ān 5:93, 94].

liquors like whiskey and beer that are made from other substances. The other intoxicants, according to the Ḥanafīs, are prohibited separately by the texts of the *Sunnah*. The Ḥanafīs, therefore, see no need to use analogy in this case. The majority, however, say that even if the word *khamr*, in its literal meaning, does not cover the other types of intoxicating liquors, the *ḥukm* of *khamr* can be extended to them through *qiyās* (analogy). Their reasoning takes the following form:

The jurists first decide that the *'illah*, or the underlying cause for which *khamr* has been prohibited is intoxication. On examining the other intoxicating liquors, they find that the property of being intoxicants is found in them. When it is verified that this property is found, they extend the *ḥukm* of *khamr*, which is prohibition, to the other intoxicating liquors as well.

Thus, *khamr* in this case is the *aṣl*, or the *maqīs 'alayh*, each one of the intoxicants, other than *khamr*, is the *far'* or the *maqīs*, and the property of being an intoxicant is the *'illah*. The prohibition of *khamr* is the *ḥukm al-aṣl*, while the prohibition of whiskey, say, is the *ḥukm al-far'*, which has been established through *qiyās*.

2. There is a tradition from the Prophet (peace be on him) that says: "The murderer will not inherit." This tradition prohibits the granting of inheritance to an heir who kills his predecessor from whom he is to inherit. The punishment for such an offender, in addition to the punishment for his crime, is deprivation from inheritance.

   What about a bequest (*waṣiyyah*)? The tradition mentions inheritance alone and not bequest. Supposing a legatee murders the testator, who has bequeathed his property to the legatee in his will. The offending legatee will be prevented from taking the bequeathed property on the basis of *qiyās*, because the *'illah* in the two cases is similar, which is "hastening the benefit prior to its appointed time through a criminal act or unjustified enrichment."

Murdering the predecessor in the case of inheritance mentioned in the tradition is the *aṣl* or the *maqīs 'alayh*, while murdering the testator is the *far'* or the *maqīs*. Hastening death prior to its appointed time through a criminal act is the *'illah*, because of which the *ḥukm* has been assigned. The *ḥukm al-aṣl* is prevention from inheritance, while deprivation from the bequest or legacy is the *ḥukm al-far'* established through *qiyās*.

3. A tradition from the Prophet (peace be on him) says: "A believer is a brother to his believer, therefore, it is not permitted for a believer to make a proposal (for marriage) where the proposal of his brother is still pending, or to make an offer of sale where his brother's offer is pending." This tradition proscribes proposals or offers to the same party till such time that similar offers made to this party by another person are pending and have not been refused or accepted. The underlying cause or *'illah* is causing harm to another's interest. This tradition does not mention the hiring of services or property. The proscription can be extended to hire through analogy.

4. Indulging in sale when the call for the Friday prayer is made is prohibited by the text of the Qur'ān. The underlying cause is reducing the incentive to offer the Friday prayer. This *ḥukm* can be extended to other contracts like pledging or marriage that may have been planned at such a time.

14.4 Conditions Pertaining to the Elements

As stated above, analogy has four elements: *aṣl; ḥukm al-aṣl; 'illah;* and *far'*. The conditions pertaining to the remaining three elements are stated below:[255]

255. For a systematic explanation of the conditions related to the elements of *qiyās*, see al-Sarakhsī, *Kitāb al-Uṣūl*, vol. 2, 149–74; al-Ghazālī, *al-*

14.4.1 Conditions of the *aṣl* or the case in the texts

A single condition is stipulated by the jurists for the *aṣl*. The condition is that the base case, on which analogy is being constructed, should not be an extension (*far'*) of another case mentioned in the texts. The reason is that if it is so, the analogy will be constructed upon the original case and not upon the extension.

14.4.2 Conditions pertaining to the *ḥukm* of the *aṣl*

The *ḥukm* has several conditions:

1. **It should be a *ḥukm* that has been established directly from the Qur'ān, *Sunnah* or *ijmā'*.** This means that it should not be the *ḥukm al-far'* or a *ḥukm* extended to a new case through analogy or some other method of legal reasoning.

   There is some disagreement among jurists whether a *ḥukm* established through consensus (*ijmā'*) can become a basis for extension through analogy. Those who oppose this say that it is difficult to determine the underlying cause for a *ḥukm* established through *'ijmā'*. In addition to this, each consensus has relied upon some evidence (which is called its *sanad*) in the texts. It is, therefore, better to rely upon the *ḥukm* in the *sanad* rather than upon *ijmā'*. Those who favour extension of the *ḥukm* from *ijmā'* maintain that there are several modes of discovering the *'illah*, and this can facilitate the extension of the *ḥukm* in *ijmā'*. They maintain that this is possible even when the *sanad* is not evident.

2. **That a determined *'illah* (cause) should be found for the *ḥukm* of the text.** The jurist should be able to determine an *'illah* for the *ḥukm*, and *'illah* that can be rationally understood to be the cause of the *ḥukm*.[256] It should not be *ḥukm* that has no understandable *'illah* and

Mustaṣfā, vol. 2, 87–99; al-Rāzī, *al-Maḥṣūl*, vol. 5, 331–76; Ṣadr al-Sharī'ah, *al-Tawḍīḥ*, vol. 2, 539–50.

256. 'Abd al-'Azīz al-Bukhārī, *Kashf al-Asrār*, vol. 3, 443.

is *ta'abbudī* (requiring ritual obedience). Thus, the setting of the sun is the cause for the evening prayer, but we cannot understand or are not required to understand why it has been determined as the cause. As compared to this "intoxication" as a cause for prohibition of wine is a cause that can be rationalised. Analogy is permitted where the *'illah* can be rationalised; in other cases there is no *'illah* and analogy fails.

3. **That the *ḥukm* should not have been abrogated.**[257] Analogy cannot be constructed on the basis of a *ḥukm* that stands abrogated. This depends upon the acceptance of the theory of abrogation. All four schools accept this theory.

4. **That the *ḥukm* should not be restricted to a specific case by another text.** If a *ḥukm* is specific for someone or some occasion it cannot be extended to other persons. Thus, the permission for the Prophet (peace be on him) of marrying more than four wives or the prohibition of marrying his wives after his death cannot be extended through analogy; these *aḥkām* were specific to him.[258]

5. **That the *ḥukm* should not pertain to an exemption.** The majority of the jurists maintain that analogy should not be constructed upon exemptions. The contract of *salam* (advance payment), for example, is an exemption from the rules of *ribā;* further analogy cannot be constructed upon it.

   Some of the Shāfi'īs maintain that once the exemption is granted through a text, it becomes a principle in its own right and may be used for further analogy. The pursuit of analytical consistency in the law and reasoning from principles would resist such a view. For how can you maintain two contradictory principles and still be able to extend them through legal reasoning; the results will be contradictory. It can be done, however, if one is using

257. Ibid., 445.
258. Ibid., 443.

a literal system of interpretation that has no room for reasoning for broad general principles. (See, for example, the discussion about the narrow definition of *fiqh* at page 55.)

6. **That the *ḥukm* should not pertain to the criminal law.**[259] This condition is imposed by the Ḥanafīs and pertains to the disagreement among the jurist about the meaning of *dalālat al-naṣṣ*. It may be mentioned here that this rule is observed in Western law as well. If the criminal law and crimes are permitted to be extended through analogy it will violate the principle of legality, which states that there can be no crime and no penalty without prior legislation.

14.4.3 Conditions pertaining to the *far'* or new case needing a *ḥukm*

The jurists lay down three conditions for the *far'*:

1. **That the texts should be silent about its *ḥukm*.** This means that it should not be expressly mentioned in the texts or in *ijmā'*. There is no *qiyās* for a case that is expressly mentioned in the text, because it has already been settled.

2. **The *'illah* of the *aṣl* should be found in the *far'*.** The jurist should be able to find the same *'illah* in the new case that he has found for the case mentioned in the texts.

   When this condition is not met fully and there is a difference between the *'illah* established for the *aṣl* and that for the *far'*, the analogy undertaken is called *qiyās ma' al-fāriq* or analogy with a distinctive attribute. An example is the division of the property through preemption between co-owners of the property from which the right emanated. Should the property be divided equally among them, or should it be divided in proportion to their shares? The Ḥanafīs maintain

259. Al-Sarakhsī, *Kitāb al-Uṣūl*, vol. 1, 242; Ṣadr al-Sharī'ah, *al-Tawḍīḥ*, vol. 2, 543. Cf. al-Ghazālī, *al-Mustaṣfā*, vol. 2, 92.

that they should be given equal shares irrespective of the proportion of their shares in the original property that gave them the right of preemption. The other jurists maintain that this right is similar to a partnership and they should be assigned the right of preemption in proportion to their property. The Ḥanafīs object that this is *qiyās ma' al-fāriq*, and the distinction is that in a partnership the revenue grows out of the property owned, while the right of preemption is not the result of a growth in property and cannot be compared with revenue.

14.4.4 Conditions pertaining to the *'illah* and meaning of *'illah*

The discussion of the *'illah* is, perhaps, the most important topic within the subject of rational sources. The limits and the conditions of the *'illah* not only determine the nature of analogy, but also determine the scope of other rational sources or techniques of legal reasoning like *istiḥsān* and *maṣlaḥah mursalah*. The larger doctrine of *maṣlahah* partly discussed in the previous chapter has also grown out of these discussions. This section is devoted to the conditions of the *'illah*. The modes of discovering the *'illah* called the *masālik al-'illah* will be discussed in the next part under the second mode of *ijtihād*.

Before the conditions pertaining to the *'illah* are discussed it is important to note certain distinctions. The first distinction is between *'illah* and *sabab*. This distinction was discussed in chapter 4 in the first part. The second distinction is between *'illah* (underlying cause) and *ḥikmah* (wisdom). These distinctions become obvious when the *'illah* is defined and its conditions are stated.

14.4.4.1 The meaning of *'illah* (the underlying cause)

The underlying cause of a *ḥukm* or its *'illah* is perhaps the most difficult concept in Islamic jurisprudence. Accordingly, many of the earlier jurists have avoided a definition. Instead, they try to focus on what it can be or what it cannot be. For example, al-Ghazālī begins the discussion of the *'illah* by saying: "It is permitted that the *'illah* be a *ḥukm* itself, like our saying that the sale of wine is void, because its utilisation has been prohibited...."[260] He then goes on to mention a large number of shapes that the *'illah* may acquire.

Modern jurists have tried to give definitions, but such definitions can be shown to be defective in the light of what the earlier jurists have said. In some of these definitions importance has been given to the securing of *maṣlaḥah,* while in others the importance has been given to the relationship between the cause and the *ḥukm.* We will extract the text of *al-Tanqīḥ* that is woven into the text of *al-Tawḍīḥ* to show how Ṣadr al-Sharī'ah describes it:

فصل العلة قيل المعرّف ويشكل بالعلامة وقيل المؤثر وهي في الحقيقة ليست بمؤثرة الا ان يقال بالنسبة الينا فان الاحكام تضاف الى الاسباب وقيل الباعث لا على سبيل الايجاب اي المشتمل على حكمة مقصودة للشارع في شرعه الحكم او دفع ضر وكون العلّة هكذا يسمى مناسبة والحكمة المجرّدة لاتعتبر في كل فرد لخفائها وعدم انضباطها بل في الجنس فيضاف الحكم الى وصف ظاهر منضبط يدور معها او يغلب وجودها عنده

We have given this text above to acknowledge the skill of this learned man, however, we will focus on the overlined part:

وصف ظاهر منضبط يدور معها او يغلب وجودها عنده

> An apparent and stable attribute that is either coterminous with the underlying rationale or the rationale is usually present when the attribute exists.[261]

In this definition we will focus on the words "apparent" and "stable," because they explain some important features of the underlying cause.

14.4.4.2 Conditions for the validity of the *'illah*

The analysis of this definition yields the following conditions for the *'illah:*

260. Al-Ghazālī, *al-Mustaṣfā*, vol. 2, 93
261. Ṣadr al-Sharī'ah, *al-Tawḍīḥ,* 551–54.

1. **That the *'illah* must be an apparent cause.** An apparent cause is one that can easily be perceived by the senses. It is an outward attribute and not something internal and concealed. This apparent attribute can be identified with ease both in the *aṣl* and in the *far'*. As compared to the *'illah,* the *ḥikmah* (wisdom) of the law is something internal and concealed and cannot be verified with ease. An internal or concealed reason does not qualify for becoming an *'illah.* The *ḥikmah,* according to al-Rāzī, is the *'illah* of the *'illah.* He maintains that the *ḥukm* can be based upon the *ḥikmah* as well.[262]

   In contracts, for example, the objective theory is favoured, because inner intention is something difficult to verify. It is difficult to verify what the contracting party really intends. The cause that makes a contract valid is, therefore, the outward expression of offer and acceptance (*'ījāb* and *qabūl*). Accordingly, the jurists maintain that the validity of contracts does not depend upon intention, but on the outward expression. In this case, verification of the intention is the *ḥikmah,* while offer and acceptance are the *'illah.* The *ḥukm* of validity is tied to the cause, offer and acceptance, in a way that the existence of the cause means the existence of the *ḥukm* and the non-existence of the cause its non-existence.

   In the case of curtailment of prayer on a journey, the *ḥikmah* is the hardship that a person will face. This is something internal and it cannot be verified whether the traveller is actually facing hardship. The *ḥukm* is, therefore, tied to the *'illah,* which is "journey" in this case.

2. **That the *'illah* should be a constant and stable attribute.** A constant and stable attribute is one that does not change with a change in circumstances and does not vary from person to person. In the example of curtailment of prayer on a journey, the *'illah* was "journey" itself. This attribute does not vary from person to person, that is, it does not matter whether the

262. Al-Rāzī, *al-Maḥṣūl,* vol. 5, 287 passim.

person going on a journey is young or old, strong or weak, healthy or ill. As compared to this, "hardship" is something that may vary from person to person: a strong person is not likely to face the same hardship as a weak person.

The *'illah* does change due to a change in circumstances either. In the same example, when "journey" is the cause of the *ḥukm,* it will not matter whether the subject is going on foot or on horseback, on a train or by car. The cause remains the same. If the wisdom, that is, "hardship" is deemed to be the cause, it will alter with the means adopted for travelling. A person going by car will suffer a lesser amount of hardship as compared to one going on foot.

3. **That the *'illah* should be extendible and not confined to the *aṣl.*** If the attribute determined by the *mujtahid* cannot be extended to other cases, the determination of such an *'illah* is futile and will not constitute a valid analogy. In the case of *ribā,* trading in gold and silver with an excess or with a delay is restricted. The *'illah* determined by Shāfi'īs here is "currency-value" (*thamaniyyah*). The Ḥanafīs maintain that this is an *'illah* that is *qāsirah* (confined to these two metals and coins made from them).[263] It cannot be extended to other things, therefore, it is not a valid *'illah.* It is for this reason that the Ḥanafīs determine "weight and measure" to be the *'illah* along with "genus."

4. **That the *'illah* should be an attribute that is compatible with the purposes of the law (*munāsib*).** The reason is that the purposes of Islamic law, in reality, provide the underlying rationale of all the rules. That is why the *ḥikmah* has been emphasised.

   Most of the attributes that have been determined as causes for the *aḥkām* are compatible with the purposes of Islamic law. The reason is that the purposes of the law have emerged from a collective consideration of the various *'ilal.* An *'illah*

263. Today we may agree that the *'illah* of "currency-value" has been extended to paper money.

derived by a jurist must, therefore, meet this condition. "Intoxication" as an *'illah* for the prohibition of *khamr* is compatible with the "preservation of the intellect." As compared to this, the colour of wine or its smell have no compatibility with this purpose and are not suitable causes.

There are different levels of compatibility and the concept of suitability (*munāsabah*) is not confined to *qiyās* alone. The concept covers other forms of legal reasoning, like *maṣlaḥah mursalah,* where it is not always the *'illah* that is relevant; the *ḥikmah* (wisdom) may also be used for determining the law.[264] The concept of *munāsabah* will be discussed within the second and third modes of *ijtihād* in the next part.

14.5 Types of Analogy (*Qiyās*)

The majority of the jurists classify *qiyās* into two broad types. The first type is determined by looking at the strength of the similarity of the two *'illahs* in the *aṣl* and in the *far'*. The second type is based on the manner in which the *ḥukm* is established in the new case. In addition to this, the Ḥanafīs classify analogy into *qiyās jalī* (manifest analogy) and *qiyās khafī* (concealed analogy). The classification according to the majority of the jurists is discussed first.

14.5.1 The first type: probable and definitive or *qaṭ'ī* and *ẓannī*

Qiyās is definitive when two conditions are met:

- That the *mujtahid* is fully convinced about the *'illah* he has discovered in the *aṣl.*
- That exactly the same *'illah* is found in the *far'*, that is, there are no distinctive attributes.

264. For a detailed analysis see Imran Ahsan Khan Nyazee, *Theories of Islamic Law,* 200–12.

The example of *qaṭ'ī* analogy is the proscription of saying "fie" to parents. The *'illah* discovered here by the *mujtahid* is "torment." In other words, saying "fie" to parents is something that causes grief or pain to them. This satisfies the first condition, because there is no doubt that the underlying cause is torment. When the *mujtahid* faces cases like abuse of parents or beating of parents, he is also sure that this underlying cause of torment is definitely found in such acts. This satisfies the second condition with certainty.

The underlying certainty in the discovery of the *'illah* and its application to the new case makes the analogy definitive or *qaṭ'ī*.[265]

The same conditions, when reversed, need to be fulfilled in the case of *ẓannī qiyās* or analogy with a probable strength. If the *mujtahid* is not certain about the *'illah* in either or both cases, the *qiyās* is said to be probable. An example of *ẓannī qiyās* is the assignment of the *ḥukm* of *ribā* from food items mentioned in a tradition to the water-melon on the basis of "food-value" as the *'illah*. The *'illah* of "food in general" is not a very convincing underlying cause; the Ḥanafīs and Mālikīs, therefore, reject it. Identifying it as a cause violates the first condition. The reason is that all the items mentioned in the tradition are basic foods with the significant attribute of being stored over long periods. This attribute is missing in the water-melon and, therefore, violates the second condition pertaining to the *far'*.

It may be noted here that even if the number of traditions in the case of *ribā* has reached a level that makes it *mutawātir ma'nawī*, which makes the *ḥukm* definitive, the *qiyās* in the above example is still *ẓannī* due to a weakness in the *'illah* both for the *aṣl* and the *far'*.

14.5.2 The second type: classification according to the strength of the *ḥukm* established in the *far'*

This classification is based on the nature of the *ḥukm* in the *aṣl*. It is a classification of analogy when the *ḥukm* in the *aṣl* is *ẓannī*.

265. It may be noted that the *ḥukm* in the text may not be *qaṭ'ī* here, that is, *qaṭ'ī al-dalālah*.

When the *ḥukm* in the *aṣl* is probable (*ẓannī*), the *qiyās* constructed upon it may be of three types. This is based upon the strength of the *ḥukm* established in the *far'*. Is the strength of the *ḥukm* of a higher order than that in the *far'*? Is the established *ḥukm* of the same order or strength? Is it of a lesser strength or order?

1. ***Qiyās* that is of a higher order is called *qiyās awlā*.** The example again is of constructing analogy for beating parents upon saying "uff" or "fie" to them. The *'illah* is torment and the torment inflicted in beating them is more than that in saying "uff." In another example, the consumption of the wealth of the minor, or even transferring it to one's own name, is proscribed by the Qur'ān. Consumption leads to the destruction of this wealth. By analogy it is said that destruction of any other type with respect to such wealth is also proscribed on the basis of the *'illah* of destruction (*itlāf*). Destruction by arson, for instance, is of a higher-order, because there is no chance of retrieval or recovery of the same wealth.

   This type of analogy is called *qiyās al-ma'nā* by Imām al-Shāfi'ī and is considered by him to be the strongest type of *qiyās*. According to the Ḥanafīs, this is not *qiyās* at all, but a literal mode for establishing the *ḥukm* called *dalālat al-naṣṣ*.

2. **The second type of *qiyās* is where the *ḥukm* established is of an equivalent order or of the same strength.** There is a tradition about the male slave jointly owned by two persons to the effect that if one of the co-owners sets him free, to the extent of his own share, he becomes liable to pay the value of the other co-owner's share to him. The case of the female slave is held to be identical on the basis of the *'illah* that is considered to be the "gifting of freedom by the *sharī'ah*" or freedom by operation of the law. The *ḥukm* for the male and female slave is deemed equal for this purpose.

   Another example given by some jurists is that of reducing the penalty of a married male slave, for extra-marital sexual intercourse, to half of 100 stripes on the analogy of the female slave whose case has been mentioned in the Qur'ān.[266]

Most of the cases of analogy will be covered by this type. It is called *qiyās al-'illah* and also *qiyās jalī* or manifest analogy.

3. **The third type is that of *qiyās adwan* or analogy of a lower order.** The example is that of extending the prohibition of *ribā* to all types of food on the basis of "food in general" as the *'illah.* This *'illah,* as stated earlier, is upheld by Imām al-Shāfi'ī. Imām Mālik disagrees with him by saying that the *'illah* in the food items mentioned in the tradition is food, but food that can be stored and preserved not all types of food. This attribute is missing from the water-melon, which lacks such attributes. Analogy if undertaken will be of a lower order due to a lesser number of attributes in the *far'*.

14.5.3 *Qiyās jalī* and *qiyās khafī* or manifest and concealed analogy

The term *qiyās jalī* (manifest analogy) has been used in various senses by the jurists, depending upon the school to which they belong. In the previous section, the term was used for the second type of analogy where the *ḥukm* established is of the same strength. Some have used it for the first type as well. Under this heading we are concerned with the way the Ḥanafī jurists have used it.

The Ḥanafīs use the term *qiyās jalī* to mean analogy for which the underlying cause is more or less apparent or can be discovered with relative ease. The jurist does not have to ponder too much over the attributes of the *'illah.* Almost all types of analogy are classified under this meaning. As compared to this, the real *'illah* may be less apparent and the jurist has to expend considerable

266. It is to be noted that the Ḥanafīs will use *dalālat al-naṣṣ* in this case, because analogy cannot be used in the law of crimes for assigning or even reducing penalties.

effort to discover it; the *'illah* is concealed so to say. This type of analogy is considered *qiyās khafī* or concealed analogy. In reality this is not analogy at all. In Islamic jurisprudence, according to the Ḥanafīs, concealed analogy is called *istiḥsān*. The next section deals with this form of analogy: *istiḥsān*.

14.6 Justification of *qiyās* as a source of Islamic law

The majority of Muslim jurists consider *qiyās* to be a valid evidence for proving the *aḥkām*. The Ẓāhirīs, some of the Mu'tazilah and the Ja'farī school (Shī'ahs) rejected it as a source and a form of legal reasoning. Both sides, those who accept it and those who reject it, give arguments in support of their view. Some of these arguments are recorded below:

14.6.1 Arguments of those who uphold *qiyās*

The arguments are provided from the Qur'ān, the *Sunnah*, from the practice of Companions and as rational propositions.

1. فاعتبروا يا أولي الأبصار (Consider, then, O ye with eyes (to see) [Qur'ān 59 : 2]). This verse asks those with eyes (intellect) to consider things, compare them, and ponder over them. The word *i'tibār* implies moving from one thing or place to another. In the present context it means moving one's thoughts between things in an effort to compare them. As *qiyās* is a method of legal reasoning that requires comparison between two things and moving the *ḥukm* from on to the other, it falls within the implications of this verse.

2. The famous tradition about Mu'ādh ibn Jabal when he was sent as a *qāḍī* to Yemen. He stated before the Prophet (peace be on him) that if he was not able to find a direct evidence in the Qur'ān and the *Sunnah*, he would use his considered opinion. This was approved by the Prophet (peace be on him). As considered opinion in the context of law is nothing

more than proper legal reasoning, and *qiyās* is the soundest method of legal reasoning, this amounts to an approval of *qiyās*.

3. There are many cases in which the Prophet (peace be on him) in response to the queries of the Companions tried to give answers in a form that was supposed to train them in legal thinking, and in many such cases the method is quite similar to analogy. For example, a person came to the Prophet (peace be on him) and said that his mother had resolved during her lifetime to perform *ḥajj*, but she died before she could fulfil this promise, and could he now perform it on her behalf? The Prophet (peace be on him) replied: "If she were under debt would you pay it back on her behalf?" The man said: "Yes." The Prophet replied: "Then pay the debts of Allah for these have the highest priority."

4. The Companions used to settle cases by performing analogy on already settled cases, that is, they followed precedents and performed analogy. In addition to such cases, there are instructions from the Companions to this effect. For example, the well known letter written by 'Umar, may Allah be pleased with him, to Abū Mūsā al-Ash'arī. In this letter he advised him: "Compare cases with settled precedents, and then select what you think will please Allah and is closer to the truth."

5. The cases in the texts of the Qur'ān and the *Sunnah* are limited and the cases that are faced by human beings are unlimited, therefore, there has to be some way of extending the law in these sources to cover new cases as well so that the new cases are settled according to Islamic legal norms. *Qiyās* is a very strict and tested method of extending the law, and in reality is nothing more than legal reasoning.

14.6.2 Arguments of those who reject *qiyās*

1. A verse of the Qur'ān says: "O ye who believe! Put not yourselves forward before God and His Apostle, but fear

God: for God is He Who hears and knows all things." [Qur'ān 49 : 1] The person who upholds analogy acts against the implication of this verse, because analogy means "putting yourself forward" before Allah and His Messenger when the Qur'ān and the *Sunnah* have not settled a case.

2. Another verse says: "And pursue not that of which thou hast no knowledge." [Qur'ān 17 : 36] Analogy is something that is probable (*ẓannī*) and doubtful, and acting upon it would amount to acting according to something of which we have no knowledge. This is particularly so when the Qur'ān says: "And We have sent down to thee the Book explaining all things, a guide and a mercy and glad tidings to Muslims." [Qur'ān 16 : 89] As everything is to be elaborated by the Qur'ān, there is no need for analogy.

3. There are many sayings of the Companions in which they have condemned the use of *ra'y* (personal opinion), and analogy is personal opinion.

4. Analogy leads to discord among the Muslims, because it does not lead to exactly the same opinion when different jurists are exercising it. The reason is that they may be trying to use a different precedent for solving the same problem. Something that leads to differences should be shunned.

5. It cannot be said that the *aḥkām* of the *sharī'ah* are based upon similarity and equality. For example, the thief who steals is to be given the penalty of cutting of the hand, while the embezzler is not punished in the same way, although there is no difference between them. Water and clean soil have both been considered means of ritual cleanliness when they are opposites.

The weaknesses in the arguments of those who reject analogy can be seen with ease. The main point here is that the judge has to give relief to the litigants who come to him. It is not possible for him to say to them that "I cannot find anything in the Qur'ān and the *Sunnah* to settle this case, therefore, I cannot help you."

The presumption is that a solution exists in the *sharīʿah* and the judge has to adopt some method of legal reasoning to extend the law from the limited number of texts that he can employ. As long as he is required to do so, analogy is a good and strict method of legal reasoning that maximises the chances of the discovery of the intention of the Lawgiver. The assertion that analogy is based on probable (*ẓannī*) knowledge is also without foundation, because there are many verses that are *ẓannī al-dalālah*, that is, there can be more than one way of interpreting them and understanding their meaning.

Review Questions

1. Define *qiyās* and explain why it is a strict method of extending the legal meanings in the texts.
2. What are the elements of *qiyās*? Explain the conditions associated with the *ʿillah* (underlying cause).
3. What do you understand by the *aṣl* of *qiyās*? What are the conditions pertaining to the *aṣl*?
4. What kind of new case becomes the object of *qiyās*.
5. Define the term *ʿillah* and explain the conditions pertaining to it.
6. What is the difference between an *ʿillah* and *sabab*?
7. Distinguish the meaning of *ʿillah* from that of *ḥikmah* as understood in *uṣūl al-fiqh*.
8. What do we mean when we say that the *ʿillah* must be compatible with the purposes of the *sharīʿah*?
9. Give the various classifications of *qiyās*.
10. *Qiyās* is either definitive or probable. Elaborate.
11. How is *qiyās* classified on the basis of the strength of the *ḥukm*?

12. Explain the terms *qiyās jalī* and *qiyās khafī*. What is the relationship of this classification with *istiḥsān*?

13. Justify *qiyās* as a source of law. What are the arguments of those who reject *qiyās* as a valid source.

15 *Istiḥsān* (Juristic Preference)

15.1 The Meaning of *Istiḥsān*

In its literal sense the word *istiḥsān* means "to consider something good." It is also applied to mean something towards which one is inclined or which one prefers, even if it is not approved by others. Al-Sarakhsī says: "*Istiḥsān* is the giving up of analogy and the adoption of what is easier for the people."[267]

Technically, it has been defined in several ways. Al-Bazdawī defines it as "moving away from the implications of analogy to an analogy that is stronger than it, or it is the restriction of analogy by an evidence that is stronger than it."[268] Al-Ḥalwānī defines it as "the giving up of analogy for a stronger evidence from the Book, the *Sunnah,* or *ijmā'*."[269] The Mālikī jurist, Ibn al-'Arabī

267. Al-Sarakhsī, *al-Mabsūt*, vol. 10, 151.
268. Al-Bazdawī, *Uṣūl al-Bazdawī* in 'Abd al-'Azīz al-Bukhārī, *Kashf al-Asrār,* vol. 4, 7–8.
269. Ibid.

defines it as "sacrificing some of the implications of an evidence by way of exception insofar as the exception opposes some of these implications."[270]

From all these definitions it is obvious that *istiḥsān* means the preference of a stronger evidence over analogy. In other words, it means:

- The preference of *qiyās khafī* over *qiyās jalī,* as explained in the previous section.
- It also means following the requirements of a stronger general principle that requires something different from strict analogy.
- It may also mean the creation of an exception to a general principle due to a stronger evidence when the general principle is based upon analogy.

Al-Sarakhsī points out that some jurists have criticised *istiḥsān* on the grounds that analogy is being given up for the personal opinion of the jurists.[271] He responds that this is totally misfounded for how can a jurist give up a *ḥujjah* (legally admissible authority) for something that has no authority.[272] In modern times, the words "juristic preference" may have implied something similar.[273] The reader should note that analogy is given up by the jurist only when he has a stronger evidence to rely on and this stronger evidence is one that is valid according to the *sharī'ah. Istiḥsān,* he says, is merely the comparison of two valid evidences (sources) and the preference of the stronger over the relatively weaker. It may also mean the restriction of one with the other. He concludes that "giving up of *qiyās* is sometimes due to the text, and at other times due to *ijmā'* or due to the principle of necessity."[274]

---

270. Ibid.
271. Al-Sarakhsī, *Kitāb al-Uṣūl,* vol. 2, 199.
272. Ibid., 200.
273. A term used by Abdur Rahim in his excellent book *Muhammadan Jurisprudence* (Lahore, 1908), section on *istiḥsān.*
274. Al-Sarakhsī, *Kitāb al-Uṣūl,* vol. 2, 202.

15.1.1 *Istiḥsān* is a method for looking at the consequences of a decision

Al-Sarakhsī explains that *istiḥsān* is a way of looking at the consequences of the application of two legal rules and the selection of one that creates ease and facility. He says that analogy is of two types. The first one is *jalī* or manifest where the strict rules of logic require a certain thing, but the consequences of implementing it are injurious.[275] On the other hand, the second type of legal reasoning called *qiyās khafī* may not appeal very much to the rules of logic, but its consequences are good and beneficial.[276] Al-Sarakhsī says that:

> *Qiyās* and *istiḥsān* are in reality two types of *qiyās*. One is *jalī*, but its effect is weak, therefore, it has been called *qiyās*. The other is *khafī* (concealed), but its effect is stronger, therefore, it has been called *istiḥsān*, that is, *qiyās mustaḥsan* (approved, preferrred). The preference is due to the effect and not because it is manifest or concealed. It is like this world and the hereafter: this world is manifest whereas the heareafter is concealed.[277]

He gives a number of examples to explain this, and some of these are given below.

15.2 Examples of *istiḥsān*

1. Abū Ḥanīfah on deciding the issue of the person who eats during a fast out of forgetfulness, is reported to have said: "Had it not been for the report by the people, I would have said that he should repeat his fast." What he meant by this was that strict application of the rules of fasting requires that

275. Ibid., 203.
276. This reminds us of the often quoted remarks of Oliver Wendell Holmes that the life of the law has not been logic, but experience.
277. Al-Sarakhsī, *al-Mabsūt*, vol. 10, 151.

anyone eating food has broken the fast. A report from the Prophet (peace be on him) says that "liability for three things has been lifted from my Ummah: forgetfulness; mistake; and duress." This is a case of *istiḥsān* where a text has been preferred over analogy, and by means of which an exception has been created.[278]

2. *Qiyās* prohibits the contract of *salam,* because it involves delay in the exchange of food items listed in the tradition of *ribā.* There is, however, the tradition from the Prophet (peace be on him) that says that "he made an exemption in the case of *salam.*"[279]

3. Similar to *salam* is the case of the contract of *istiṣnā'* or the manufacturing contract with advance payment. Analogy prohibits it on the basis of the same rules as in the case of *salam.* It is, however, permitted on the basis of *ijmā'* according to the Ḥanafīs.[280]

4. Analogy requires that ritually pure water should be used for ablution. In the case of wells in which dirt or carcasses of animals have fallen, following strict analogy would mean the non-use of these wells, and this would cause hardship to the people. The principle of necessity requires that use of these wells be permitted. This is done after observing formal cleaning methods.

5. The general principle of sale requires that a thing that does not exist cannot be sold. In the contract of hire (*ijārah*), the benefits or services that are being paid for do not exist at the time of the contract. The contract has been permitted on the basis of necessity, seeking support from the contract made by the Prophet Mūsā (Moses) as mentioned in the Qur'ān.[281]

---

278. 'Abd al-'Azīz al-Bukhārī, *Kashf al-Asrār,* vol. 4, 7.
279. Ibid.
280. Ibid.
281. Ibid.

In all these cases, the consequences of the application of strict analogy have figured significantly in the decision and the decision preferred was one that had more healthy consequences for the people.

15.3 Types of *Istiḥsān*

We may now list the various methods through which *istiḥsān* is employed in legal reasoning.[282]

1. ***Istiḥsān* through the text (*naṣṣ*).** A general principle emerging from the texts may not permit something, yet another text may provide an exception to this broad principle. An example of this is the contract of *salam* explained above; it has been permitted on the basis of a tradition when strict analogy would not permit it. Another example is that of *khiyār al-sharṭ* (stipulated option). The general principle requires that all contracts become binding on their conclusion. A tradition permits the stipulation of an option for three days as an exception to this principle.

2. ***Istiḥsān* on the basis of *ijmā'*.** The example is again the contract of *istiṣnā'* mentioned above. The general principle forbids transactions in things that do not exist at the time of contract. An exemption was made on the basis of consensus for the manufacturing contract seeking strength from the exemption made for the contract of *salam*.

3. ***Istiḥsān* on the basis of what is good (*ma'rūf*).** Some writers have used the word *'urf* (custom) to indicate that this one method of employing *istiḥsān*. Care has to be exercised in using such concepts. Al-Sarakhsī explains that one meaning of *istiḥsān* is where the *sharī'ah* is asking us to follow what is good and has left the determination of

282. The various types of *istiḥsān* have been explained by al-Sarakhsī, *Kitāb al-Uṣūl*, vol. 2, 202–208. See also 'Abd al-'Azīz al-Bukhārī, *Kashf al-Isrār*, vol. 4, 4–11.

this *ma'rūf* to our opinion. For example, the words of the Qur'ān: متاعا بالمعروف حقا على المحسنين (A gift of a reasonable amount is due from those who wish to do the right thing [Qur'ān 2:236]). So also the words: وعلى المولود له رزقهن وكسوتهن بالمعروف (But he (to whom the child is attributed) shall bear the cost of their food and clothing [Qur'ān 2:233]). In such cases, the principle is that we follow what the *sharī'ah* would consider to be good, that is, we determine it in accordance with the general principles of the *sharī'ah*. It does not mean following each and every custom in accordance with what the people have been practising. Even if it is an age old custom and is generally considered good, the ruling of *sharī'ah* must be given before it can be accepted. The point is explained under the discussion of custom as a source of law.

4. ***Istiḥsān* on the basis of necessity (*ḍarūrah*).** The example of wells has already been given above. So also Imām Mālik permitted slight uncertainty that will not lead to a dispute where the general principle requires the avoidance of uncertainty (*gharar*) that will lead to a dispute.

5. ***Istiḥsān* on the basis of *maṣlaḥah*.** This is attributed to Imām Mālik. The example, however, is from the time of the Companions and pertains to the liability of artisans. The general principle required that artisans were not to be held liable for things handed to them, unless it could be proved that they were guilty of negligence. In other words, the burden of proof of negligence was placed on the customer. 'Alī, may Allah be pleased with him, changed the rule, because the artisans were misusing the facility. He placed the burden of proof on the artisans who were required to show that there had been no negligence. The Ḥanafīs call this *istiḥsān* on the basis of necessity of the preservation of wealth, which again is similar to *maṣlaḥah*.

6. ***Istiḥsān* on the basis of *qiyās khafī*.** The general rule required that if beasts of prey had drunk from water it was no longer pure. Strict analogy required that the rule be

applied to domestic animals as well. Pondering over the issue the jurist finds that beasts of prey have soiled saliva, whereas domestic animals do not. The rule was not applied to such animals.[283]

15.3.1 Distinction between the various types

Al-Sarakhsī says that if *istiḥsān* is based upon the text or upon *ijmā,* the derived rule can serve as a further basis for analogy. In the other cases, like *istiḥsān* based upon necessity or concealed analogy, it is not possible to extend the new rule further.[284]

15.4 Justification of *Istiḥsān*

Some jurists, especially the Shāfi'īs, have objected to the use of *istiḥsān.* Imām al-Shāfi'ī said that *istiḥsān* is the following of one's personal whim and amounts to unjustified legislation. The dispute, however, appears to be around the literal meaning of the word *istiḥsān* rather than its technical meaning. The above examples show that many of the opinions stated above, especially those based on the texts, are held by the Shāfi'īs as well.[285] *Istiḥsān* is an efficient method of legal reasoning that ensures analytical consistency in the system and helps the jurist identify general principles and exceptions besides giving importance to the consequences of the decision.

Review Questions

1. *Istiḥsān* is the preference of *qiyās khafī* over *qiyās jalī.* Elaborate.
2. *Istiḥsān* is a method for adopting suitable consequences of a decision. Elaborate.

283. 'Abd al-'Azīz al-Bkhārī, *Kashf al-Asrār,* vol. 4, 9–11.
284. Al-Sarakhsī, *Kitāb al-Uṣūl,* vol. 2, 204.
285. See 'Abd al-'Azīz al-Bukhārī, *Kashf al-Asrār,* vol. 4, 18 for an explanation.

3. What are the different types of *istiḥsān*?
4. What are the various methods or evidences relied upon for employing *istiḥsān*?

16 *Istiṣḥāb* (Presumption of Continuity)

16.1 The Meaning of *Istiṣḥāb*

The word *istiṣḥāb* means the continuance of companionship. Technically it means the presumption of continuance of an earlier rule or its continued absence.[286] In this sense it means the maintenance of a status quo with respect to the rule. The previous rule is accepted, unless a new rule is found that goes against it. As an easy reference one may refer to *istiṣḥāb al-ḥāl* as the "accompanying rule." In reality, *istiṣḥāb al-ḥāl* is not a source of law nor is it a source for establishing new rules; it is merely a set of presumptions. This will be obvious from the discussion below.

286. Al-Sarakhsī, *Kitāb al-Uṣūl*, vol. 2, 223.

16.2 The Principles That Form the Basis of *Istiṣḥāb*

The following general principles form the basis of *istiṣḥāb:*

1. الاصل في الأشياء الإباحة—The original rule for all things is permissibility, that is, the presumption is that all things are permitted, unless prohibited by the *sharī'ah*. This rule applies to beneficial things alone, like food, drink and benefiting from all good things. It is known that spilling blood without justification is prohibited. The taking of wealth without a legal right is prohibited. Indulging in sex without lawful permission is prohibited. In general, the commission of any act that is injurious to another is prohibited, like defamation and all kinds of falsehood. This narrows down the scope of this principle. It is for this reason that some of the Ḥanafīs are considered to maintain the opposite principle: الاصل في الأشياء التحريم (the presumption is that all things are prohibited, unless the *sharī'ah* permits them). If we assume that most beneficial things are originally permitted, it means that they have been permitted by the Lawgiver. Can the state today prohibit some of these things? It is obvious that the evidence to do this must come directly from the sources of Islamic law. This shows that the principle may have some problems.[287] This is what Imām al-Ghazālī calls *nafī aṣlī* or the original vacuum. He maintains that this vacuum cannot be filled without a *dalīl* from the Qur'ān or the *Sunnah*.

2. الاصل براءة الذمة, also called *barā'ah aṣliyyah*. This principle means that there is no presumption of liability against anyone, and all liability has to be proved. This principle is more of a procedural nature and places the burden of proof on the person making a claim.

287. For further details, see Imran Ahsan Khan Nyazee, *Theories of Islamic Law*, 47–50.

3. اليقين لا يزول بالشك (certainty does not give way to doubt). This means that once a thing is established beyond doubt, it can only be set aside through an equally certain evidence. If a person is sure that he has performed ablution and later doubts this he is presumed to be ritually pure till he is certain that he is not.

The above principles highlight the different ideas associated with the principle of *istiṣḥāb.*

16.2.1 Types of *Istiṣḥāb* and Their Legal Validity

The principle of *istiṣḥāb* in certain forms was accepted by al-Shāfi'ī and in some of its forms by the Ḥanafīs as well. The following discussion by al-Sarakhsī is expected to throw light on the issue.

Al-Sarakhsī first discusses a broad principle in legal reasoning where there is no *dalīl*. The issue is whether "no *dalīl*" can be a form of legal proof. He says that some jurists lay down the following principle: "No-*dalīl* is an evidence for purposes of defence, but not for asserting a claim."[288] He maintains that an analysis of issues settled by the Shāfi'ī school shows that "it is a defensive presumption for the continuance of an existing rule, but not for establishing what was not there from the start." He then says that an analysis of cases in the Ḥanafī school shows that what al-Shāfi'ī states is valid only to the extent where the right of Allah is involved, but where the right of the individual is concerned it is not an evidence for either of the litigants, neither for purposes of defence and denial nor for purposes of establishing claims.

After dealing with this general approach, al-Sarakhsī states that "among the forms of reasoning without any *dalīl* is one called *istiṣḥāb al-ḥāl.*" This type of reasoning he states is *bāṭil.*[289] He then analyses the various types of *istiṣḥāb* to show what is acceptable and what is not. He divides *istiṣḥāb* into four types:

1. **Where the absence of *dalīl* is known with a certainty.** This type of certainty can come only from the texts themselves

288. Al-Sarakhsī, *Kitāb al-Uṣūl*, vol. 2, 215.
289. Ibid., 223.

and should be similar to the words: قل لا أجد فيما أوحي إلى محرما (Say: "I find not in the message received by me any (meat) forbidden" [Qur'ān 6:145]). When it is known with a certainty that there is no evidence that will change the existing rule, and the *dalīl* of the existing rule is known, the continuance of the *ḥukm* is valid. This rule requires a thorough examination of a new issue in the light of the general principles of the *sharī'ah*.[290]

2. **Where after pondering over the general evidences it is obvious to the jurist that there is an evidence that will change the existing *ḥukm*.** This means a negative *istiṣḥāb* where a jurist wishes to allege a change in an existing *ḥukm* established through valid evidences. In such a case, it can only be used as a defence and not for establishing a claim, because the opponent will say that in his opinion there is a contrary evidence.[291]

3. **Where the continuance of a *ḥukm* is alleged without making an effort for seeking an evidence that will change the rule.** According to al-Sarakhsī this is ignorance. The reason is that before searching for such an evidence the jurist cannot know whether the *ḥukm* has changed or an evidence is available for settling the case. This ignorance can in no way become an argument against others.[292]

4. ***Istiṣḥāb* for establishing a rule ab initio.** To use *istiṣḥāb* to establish a new rule is a grave mistake according to al-Sarakhsī. *Istiṣḥāb al-ḥāl,* he says, is the name for the continued following of a *ḥukm* that had been established through a valid evidence. Where there is no such *ḥukm,* the principle of *istiṣḥāb* does not apply.[293] Those who maintain

290. Ibid, 224.
291. Ibid., 224
292. Ibid.
293. Ibid. This is something to be noted by writers today who attempt in a haste to legalise modern institutions.

otherwise should examine the concept of *nafī aṣlī* elaborated by al-Ghazālī.

16.3 *Istiṣḥāb al-Ḥāl* Cannot Establish a New Rule

The above discussion shows that *istiṣḥāb* is a procedural rule that creates a presumption for denying something, but not for establishing a claim. As a source of law, the principle has little value as it cannot be used to establish a new rule.

16.4 *Istiṣḥāb al-Ḥāl* and the Islamisation of Laws

The law obtaining in Pakistan is based on the English law. It is the practice of some institutions to say that where a direct evidence is not found to show that the law is against the Qur'ān and the *Sunnah* it will be accepted as valid. According to this reasoning some people can be heard saying that only 5% of the laws need to be changed, because they clash with the texts and the rest should be accepted as Islamised. In the same spirit, perhaps, the Council of Islamic Ideology says that they have reviewed a large number of laws.

The principle of *istiṣḥāb* asserts that the continuance of a rule is conditional upon the fact that it was originally established by an evidence from the *sharī'ah*. Does the acceptance of existing Western laws, on the grounds that they are not repugnant to the Qur'ān and the *Sunnah*, enough to justify their validity? Will it not be better if each and every law on the statute book is justified *ab initio* on the basis of the sources of Islamic law? Will this not help in the application of these laws by the judiciary who deal in general principles as well as rules? It is, therefore, suggested that the CII should publish its legal reasoning underlying its recommendations and so should the Islamic Fiqh Academy of the OIC.

Review Questions

1. Elaborate the meaning of *Istiṣḥāb al-ḥāl*.
2. What are the principles associated with the "presumption of continuity"? What do you understand by the term *nafī aṣlī*?
3. *Istiṣḥāb* is not a valid method for laying down new rules. Comment.

17 *Maṣlaḥah Mursalah* (Extended Analogy)

17.1 The Meaning of *Maṣlaḥah Mursalah*

Maṣlaḥah is defined in its literal sense as "the acquisition of *manfa'ah* (benefit) or the repulsion of *maḍarrah* (injury, harm)." In the technical sense it means "the preservation of the the purposes of Islamic law in the settlement of legal issues."[294] The purposes of the law are interests recognised by the *sharī'ah*. *Maṣlaḥah mursalah* is also referred to as *istidlāl mursal.*

It was stated in the previous chapter that the jurists classify *maṣlaḥah,* in accordance with the acceptance and rejection by the *sharī'ah,* into four types:

1. The first type is *maṣlaḥah* acknowledged by the Lawgiver at the level of the lowest category (*naw'*). This is called *qiyās* (analogy).

294. Al-Ghazālī, *al-Mustaṣfā min 'Ilm al-Uṣūl*, vol. 1, 286.

2. The second type is *maṣlaḥah* that is acknowledged by the Lawgiver at the level of the genus (*jins*). This is called *maṣlaḥah mursalah.*

3. The third type of *maṣlaḥah* is one that is not acknowledged by the *sharī'ah*. This is called an interest that is rejected or *mulghā*.

4. The fourth type is a *maṣlaḥah* that is neither acknowledged by the *sharī'ah* nor is it rejected. This type of *maṣlaḥah* is called strange (*gharīb*).

In the present section the meaning of the second and the fourth types will be examined, that is, *maṣlaḥah mursalah* and *maṣlaḥah* that is strange or *gharīb*. The examination of the *gharīb* is expected to sharpen the understanding of *maṣlaḥah mursalah.*

17.2 The Conditions for the Validity of *Maṣlaḥah Mursalah*

Maṣlaḥah mursalah, sometimes referred to in the plural as *maṣāliḥ mursalah,* is a highly flexible and advanced type of analogy. It is employed when the jurist cannot find a rule for the case at hand through literal interpretation nor can he extend the meaning through strict analogy (*qiyās*), because there is no specific base (*aṣl*) from which he can extend the rule by analogy. In other words, individual or specific evidences do not control the law any more. The word *irsāl* means to "let go." We can say here that the individual or specific texts have "let go" of the issue or they have released their hold. The case now has to be settled by "looking at all the texts collectively." This is achieved by referring to the purposes of Islamic law or the *maqāṣid al-sharī'ah.*

The first thing that a jurist employing *maṣlaḥah mursalah* has to do is to "formulate a new principle that will control the problem being faced by him."[295] The new principle he has formulated must meet the following three conditions identified by al-Ghazālī:

1. He has to make sure that the new principle he has formulated does not clash with a text (*naṣṣ*) or attempt to alter the implication of a text.

2. He has to make sure that the principle does not clash with the existing principles and propositions of Islamic law. Al-Ghazālī calls these principles and propositions the *taṣarrufāt* (established practices) of the *sharī'ah*.[296]

3. The jurist must ensure that the principle he has formulated is not *gharīb* (strange) for the *sharī'ah*. This in reality means that the norm it promotes must be among the purposes of Islamic law recognised by the *sharī'ah*.

17.3 Illustrations of *Maṣlaḥah Mursalah*

The jurists provide a number of examples to elaborate the meaning of *maṣlaḥah mursalah*. Some of these are listed below:

1. The compilation of the Qur'ān after the death of the Prophet (peace be on him). Although the Prophet had indicated the order of the *sūrahs*, he had not given the orders for its compilation in the form of a book between two covers. The Companions were, therefore, not sure whether this should be done, because it was something that the Prophet had not done himself. They decided that it was essential to gather it and compile it in the "interest of the preservation of *dīn*." History has shown that this was a very wise decision.

2. The rule for murder (*qatl 'amd*) provided in the texts was that one life could be taken for one life by way of retaliation. It was not clear whether a number of persons could be

295. For the details see Imran Ahsan Khan Nyazee, *Theories of Islamic Law*, 282–87.
296. Ibid., 286.

subjected to *qiṣāṣ* when they participated in killing a single person. 'Umar decided that all of them should be put to death. This rule it is said was based on the "preservation of life," which is a purpose of Islamic law. This is strengthened by the words of the Qur'ān: "In retaliation there is life for you." 'Umar is reported to have said (in this decision) that if all the people of San'ā' had conspired to kill a single person he would put all of them to death.

3. The rule for artisans accepting goods from people for doing work on such things was that they were not required to show negligence if the thing was destroyed. The burden of proving negligence was on the customer. The artisans started misusing this facility. The Companions, therefore, decided to change the rule. After this decision, if a thing was destroyed in the hands of the artisans, the artisan would be required to show that there was no negligence on his part. The decision is based upon the need to "preserve the wealth of the community." This decision was given by 'Alī (R).

4. Al-Ghazālī has stated that on the basis of *maṣlaḥah mursalah* it is permitted to the ruler to impose taxes if the coffers are empty and he needs money for *jihād* or for preserving the security of the Muslim*Ummah*.

5. There is no penalty in the Qur'ān for drinking of wine. In the *Sunnah* the traditions vary, with some providing 80 lashes and others 40. 'Alī (R) fixed the penalty at 80 on the analogy of *qadhf*. This is the most elaborate and instructive of the examples and is explained below

These examples may appear simple in the identification of the rule, but the mental process required for employing it is somewhat complex. The process is quite similar to what is referred to in Western law as "reasoning from legal principles." This process is highlighted in the examples below. The first case is that of fixing of 80 lashes as a penalty for drinking wine. This is followed by two examples, one of *gharīb* and the other of *mulghā*. These two examples are hypothetical and have been constructed by al-Ghazālī to show the operation of the conditions.

17.4 The Process of Using *Maṣlaḥah Mursalah*

In this example it is shown that the jurist usually has a principle that is valid. He also has another principle about the validity of which he is not sure. The jurist makes a third broader principle that accommodates the two existing principles within it. In law this is considered to be a broad form of analogy and is called reasoning from legal principles.

The purpose of this example is also to show how the three conditions identified by al-Ghazālī above are satisfied. These conditions are that the new principle should not be *gharīb*, it should not conflict with a text, and it should not attempt to alter the implications of the text, that is, of other established principles, and that it should conform with the *maqāṣid*.

The case, as is well known, was decided by 'Alī (R). The drinking of wine is prohibited by the texts, however, no fixed penalty is prescribed. The penalties that appear in the traditions vary and are not fixed. He is reported to have said:

> He who drinks is intoxicated; he who is intoxicated raves; he who raves slanders; I (therefore) uphold the penalty of the slanderer for him.

This, according to al-Ghazālī, is based on *maṣlaḥah mursalah*. The principle quoted in the above statement is not mentioned in the texts, nor can it be derived from a specific rule. The first principle that the jurist possesses here and under which the penalty of slander *qadhf* is covered is that the "person who slanders is to be awarded the penalty of *qadhf* (slander)." This is explicitly mentioned in the Qur'ān, and the penalty is eighty stripes.

Al-Ghazālī says that this principle is *munāsib* (suitable), that is, it conforms with the purposes of the law. However, if we attempt to apply it to the case of the person who drinks, it does not appear to be *mulā'im* (compatible) with the general practices and principles (*taṣarrufāt*) of the law. The reason is that it would amount to giving him a penalty for an offence that he did not commit; namely, *qadhf*. Al-Ghazālī maintains that when probed deeply we find it to be *mulā'im* (compatible). This is based on the following legal reasoning.

The law, he says, often assigns the outward indication (*maẓinnah*)[297] of a thing the *ḥukm* of the underlying intended act or happening. Thus:

- penetration is considered to stand in place of actual ejaculation for purposes of bathing to achieve ritual purification;
- *bulūgh* (the age of puberty), which is the outward indication of discretion and maturity, is assigned the *ḥukm* of actual discretion to determine majority;
- sleep is assigned the *ḥukm* of ritual impurity, because one who sleeps is liable to becomes ritually impure.

Examining the last case, the reasoning would be:

> He who sleeps becomes ritually impure; he who becomes ritually impure performs ablution; therefore, he who sleeps is to perform ablution (for the next prayer).

This is the same as saying:

> He who drinks is intoxicated; he who is intoxicated raves; he who raves slanders; therefore, he who drinks is to be awarded the penalty for slander.

This reasoning leads to the conclusion that drinking of *khamr* is the outward indication of the loss of one's senses that leads to slander and finally to enmity and hatred. As a punishment for slander has been provided by the texts, it should be awarded for drinking wine, which is its outward indication. A new, and much

297. In the literal sense, it would be the outward location or incidence of the *ḥukm*.

wider, principle has now been formulated. The larger principle now includes both cases of *qadhf* (slander) and *shurb* (drinking).

Further, we notice that this case meets all three conditions prescribed by al-Ghazālī, that is, it is not *gharīb*, it does not conflict with an explicit text, and it does not alter the implications of the general propositions of law. The case, then, falls within the principle of *maṣlaḥah mursalah* proper.

It may be mentioned here that this illustration is not intended to show that a new rule was laid down. The penalties are provided in the texts of the *Sunnah*, and this legal reasoning was used as an aid to interpret the texts for choosing the appropriate penalty. Establishing a new rule for the criminal law through analogy or other forms of legal reasoning is not approved by all the jurists as it is against the principle of *nulla poena sine lege*, which is approved by Islamic law.

17.5 Identifying *Maṣlaḥah* That is *Gharīb*

The second example is being stated here to show the operation of the three conditions stipulated by al-Ghazālī, as well as further conditions on the basis of which a case that appears to be based on the *mursal* principle, but which is actually *gharīb*, may be accepted. The case is purely hypothetical.

Al-Ghazālī gives the example of Muslims besieged in a fort by the enemy. The enemy is attacking this fort and is using Muslim captives as shields in the hope that the Muslims in the fort will not fire at them. The question is should the Muslims fire at the enemy, even if the Muslims being used as human shields are killed?

This case violates all three conditions that al-Ghazālī has stipulated for *maṣlaḥah mursalah.*

- First, it conflicts with the texts that clearly lay down that no one is to be killed intentionally.
- Second, it violates the general propositions of the law, which prescribe that only those persons can be killed who have committed an offence. It is, therefore, not *mulā'im*

(compatible) with the general principles, which means it is *gharīb* or unacknowledged by the law.

- Third, by permitting the killing of Muslims under certain circumstances due to necessity, it attempts to alter the meaning of the implications of the texts, which is the third condition stipulated by al-Ghazālī.

Al-Ghazālī appears to be saying, although he does not say it explicitly, that even such a case may be drawn into the fold of the *istidlāl mursal,* which is *mulā'im,* but with additional conditions. These conditions are:

- that the case should lie in the area of the *ḍarūrat* (necessities), that is, it should be one of the five top purposes of the Islamic law;
- that it should be definitive (*qaṭ'ī*), that is, we should be certain about the resulting consequences;
- and it should be general (*kullī*), that is, it should affect the entire Muslim *ummah* and be a public interest.

This hypothetical case can be approved only if it assumes that the entire Muslim community is being attacked at once. If the entire community is destroyed or eliminated, Islam as a religion will disappear. If the entire Muslim *ummah* is threatened, this case would lie in the area of the *ḍarūrāt,* as it affects the first primary purpose of the law, that is, the preservation and protection of *dīn.* The second assumption is that we are certain that if we shoot at the disbelievers, who are using the Muslim captives as shields, they will be driven away and the Muslims, at least some of them, will be saved. This certainty about survival makes the case definitive (*qaṭ'ī*). The third assumption is the same as the first that the entire Muslim community is being attacked. Thus, there is the interest of a few Muslims pitted against the community as a whole, and the latter is to be preferred.

With these three conditions, then, this *mursal gharīb* may be accepted, however, it can be seen that the three conditions are impossible to meet in this case, even though they are hypothetically possible.

17.6 Identifying *Maṣlaḥah* That is Rejected (*Mulghā*)

As compared to the above hypothetical case, al-Ghazālī presents another hypothetical case. The case is that of a number of people in a boat who are cast out at sea and are about to die from hunger.[298] They cast lots to choose one of their companions who will be killed and his flesh will be eaten so that the others are saved. For legality, this requires a *gharīb* rule that is rejected by the *sharī'ah,* because it does not meet the three additional conditions imposed by al-Ghazālī.

- First, though it is obligatory on the people in the boat to save their lives even if they have to consume *ḥarām,* they cannot kill someone else to do so. The reason is that killing another person is prohibited without legal justification. Saving themselves by killing one whose life the *sharī'ah* protects is not a purpose defended by the *sharī'ah.* In other words, it is not *ḍarūrī.*

- Second, the people in the boat are not sure that they will be saved even if they consume the flesh of the person they kill. It is possible that they will stay at sea and will not be saved. The issue is, therefore, not *qaṭ'ī.*

- Third, and this is most important, the issue concerns only a few individuals in the boat and not the entire Muslim Ummah. It is, therefore, not *kullī* and, thus, cannot be a public interest.

298. It would be interesting to compare this with Lon Fuller, "The Case of Speluncean Explorers" in Davenport, *Voices in Court* (New York: The Macmillan Company, 1957), 514.

Killing of one individual here cannot be permitted by the *sharī'ah* as the issue fails to meet the additional conditions identified by al-Ghazālī. The interest of these individuals is thus rejected.

17.7 Justification of *Maṣlaḥah Mursalah*

The main objection against the use of *maṣlaḥah mursalah* in particular and the concept of *maṣlaḥah* in general is that it is based upon the *ḥikmah* (wisdom) of the rule rather than on the *'illah*.[299] The jurists have been very cautious in the use of *ḥikam* for the determination of laws. This argument is based on the use of strict analogy (*qiyās*) as the sole rational secondary source for the derivation of rules. The principle of *maṣlaḥah* is more flexible than strict analogy and is based on an interplay of general principles and the purposes of Islamic law. The general principles and the *maqāṣid* are based on the *ḥikmah* underlying the various rules.

Another argument that is sometimes advanced is that it will be misused by ignorant people. The response to this is that the legal system must ensure that its professionals observe the proper methodology that meets the conditions imposed above. Further, the principle is to be used mostly by the judges of the Higher Courts of the country and by the lawyers who assist these Courts. It is not upto every person to employ legal reasoning.

Review Questions

1. What is the meaning of *maṣlaḥah mursalah*? What is the meaning of the term *mursalah* within this term?
2. *Maṣlaḥah mursalah* is used when there is no supporting *aṣl*. Elaborate.
3. Describe the process of using *maṣlaḥah mursalah*?
4. How is a new rule justified by the jurist on the basis of *maṣlaḥah mursalah*?

299. For a detailed discussion see al-Rāzī, *al-Maḥṣūl*, vol. 5, 287 passim.

5. What is *maṣlaḥah* that is *gharīb*?

18 *Sadd al-Dharī'ah* (Blocking the Lawful Means to an Unlawful End)

The word *dharā'i'* is the plural of *dharī'ah* (means to an end). It is the means to an end irrespective of the end being lawful or unlawful, beneficial or harmful. The term *sadd al-dharī'ah,* however, means "blocking the lawful means to an unlawful end." As compared to this, the term *fatḥ al-dharī'ah* is also used, which means "permitting the unlawful means to a lawful end."

The principle of *sadd al-dharī'ah* is attributed to Imām Mālik. Some modern writers insist that its use can be seen in the rulings of most schools, however, the classical jurists have not acknowledged or even discussed it. It has been given attention by al-Shāṭibī.

The principle is not concerned with unlawful acts, because those are prohibited anyway. It is concerned with lawful acts that may be prohibited as they lead to unlawful results. For example, the cultivation of poppy has been banned in many countries, because it is leading in most cases to the production of opium and heroin, which is a deadly drug that is being misused. Here an act that was basically lawful has been declared unlawful. This prohibition in the terminology of the jurists would be called *sadd al-dharī'ah* or the "blocking of lawful means to an unlawful end." The question in each individual case would be: Is the end unlawful according to the *sharī'ah?*[300]

18.1 Types of Lawful Acts

For purposes of this principle, the jurists divide acts into three kinds:

1. **Those that rarely lead to harmful results.** The interest (*maṣlaḥah*) to be secured in such acts is greater than the injury (*mafsadah*) to be sustained. Examples are: looking at a woman to be proposed to and maintaining vineyards for grapes. The injuries that may arise from these acts are less than the benefits. Thus, the first usually leads to marriage and lawful relations, though it may sometimes lead to illicit relations as well. Grapes are used for a large number of purposes though they may also be used for making wine. The benefits in both are more than the harm.

2. **Those that usually lead to harmful results.** The injury in such acts is much more than the benefits to be derived. Examples are: the sale of arms during waves of terrorism and rebellion; renting out property to one who will use it for unlawful purposes, like maintaining a brothel; like the selling of grapes to a winery; like the sowing of poppy from which heroin will be made.

3. **Those in which there is an equal probability of harm and benefit.** This is a difficult area. Examples are: Marrying a woman with the intention of divorce so as to enable her to remarry her previous husband; prohibiting multiple transactions that may lead to *ribā* when combined, like *bay' al-'īnah.*

300. The reader will notice that this principle might clash directly with the principle of *istṣḥāb,* which implies that lawful acts can only be prohibited on the basis of a *dalīl* from the *sharī'ah.*

18.2 Disagreement of Jurists About the Legality of the Principle

Out of the three types of lawful acts discussed above, there is no dispute that the first type do not fall within the purview of the principle of *sadd al-dharīʿah.* The jurists disagree about the remaining two categories, that is, the second and the third. The Mālikīs and Ḥanbalīs say that acts in these two categories may be prohibited if they are leading to unlawful means. The Shāfiʿīs and the Ẓāhirīs[301] say that these are lawful acts and they cannot be prohibited.

Those who prohibit them argue that *sadd al-dharīʿah* is an acknowledged principle of *sharīʿah* and as long as these acts lead to unlawful results, they should be prohibited. For the last category of acts, the Mālikī jurists would say that "repelling of injury is to be accorded greater weight than the securing of benefit."

The root of the problem is based upon two theories in the law of contracts, because most of the acts mentioned above are contracts and are mostly lawful transactions (except for looking at a woman for purposes of marriage). These are the objective theory of contracts and the subjective theory of contracts. According to the objective theory, the law goes by the obvious meaning of the words used for offer an acceptance. It does not attempt to investigate the inner intention of the contracting parties. If the parties are entering into a contract that is lawful on the face of it, this theory will permit it. As compared to this, the subjective theory tries to investigate the inner intention of the parties as well. If it can be shown that the ultimate purpose is unlawful, the subjective theory will declare the contract unlawful. Take the case of *bayʿ al-ʿīnah* or the buy-back agreement, for instance. It consists of two separate transactions. If A sells a book to B for $100 in cash paid on the spot, and then after a few minutes B sells the book back to A for credit of one year for a sum of $120, the two

301. A Sunni school now extinct. As stated in the previous note, al-Shāfiʿī cannot accept this principle, because it will clash with the principle of *istiṣḥāb,* which he upholds.

separate transactions when combined are a transaction for lending on interest at 20%. Imām al-Shāfi'ī following the objective theory looks at them as two separate transactions having their own offer and acceptance; he does not bother about their real inner intention (which here appears to be the conclusion of an interest bearing transaction).

The principle of *sadd al-dharī'ah,* then, revolves around these theories. The Mālikīs and Ḥanbalīs favour the subjective theory and declare the principle of *sadd al-dharī'ah* to be lawful. The rest of the schools favour the objective theory and, therefore, find it difficult to accept this principle. As the bulk of the rulings in Islamic law are based upon the objective theory, it would be better to side with those who favour this theory.

The two sides provide detailed arguments for the acceptance or rejection of the principle. It is, however, suggested that the principle should not be rejected outright or even accepted outright. The principle should be linked with empirical evidence. If all the scientific and other evidence is pointing to the fact that an act is certainly leading to greater harm than benefit, the state should consider prohibiting the act in the greater public interest.

Although the jurists have deemed *sadd al-dharī'ah* to be an independent principle, there is no reason why it cannot be considered part of *maṣlaḥah mursalah.*

This brings to an end the study of the rational secondary sources in Islamic law. Some modern writers have also tried to include the use of legal fictions (*ḥiyal*) in such sources. Legal fictions, however, are procedural devices and part of the law of conveyancing. As such they cannot be considered a source of Islamic law.

Review Questions

1. What do you understand by the term *sadd al-dharī'ah*?

2. Analyze the type of lawful acts so as to identify those to which the principle of *sadd al-dharī'ah* can be applied.

3. The principle of *sadd al-dharī'ah* is disputed by some. Elaborate.

19 Other Secondary Sources

The previous chapters were devoted to the study of the rational sources or the rational secondary sources. There are a few other secondary sources that depend upon transmission (*naql*) and not on methods of reasoning. These will be considered in this chapter. The sources are the opinion of a Companion, earlier scriptures and custom.

19.1 Companion's Opinion (*Qawl al-Ṣaḥābī*)

A Companion, according to most jurists, is someone who saw the Prophet (peace be on him), believed in him, supported him and was in association with him for some time so that he could understand something of the ways of the *sharīʻah* from him.[302] After the death of the Prophet (peace be on him), it was the Companions who interpreted the law and developed it where

302. Al-Sarakhsī, *Kitāb al-Uṣūl*, vol. 2, 108–109.

needed. They undertook *ijtihād*, issued rulings, settled cases and became a source of guidance for later generations.

19.1.1 Views of those who accept it as a source

The main issue faced by the jurists under this source is whether *the opinion of a Companion is to be preferred over analogy (qiyās) undertaken by a later jurist?* In general, the Ḥanafīs maintain that if there is a clash between the opinion of a Companion and analogy, the analogy is to be given up and the opinion of the Companion is to be followed. The Shāfi'īs uphold that it is not binding on the jurist to give up analogy, he may or may not do so at his discretion.

Al-Sarakhsī, the Ḥanafī jurist, has the following to say:

> In the opinion of a Companion there is a chance that it is based on a narration of the revelation. It appears from their practice that if one of them possessed a text, he would either narrate it or he would base his opinion on it. There is no doubt that the opinion in which there is a chance of transmission from the Prophet (peace be on him) (the possessor of the revelation) is to be preferred over mere opinion. It is in this context that the preference of the opinion of the Companion over opinion is analogous to the preference of a *khabar wāḥid* over analogy. And even if their view was based upon analogy, their view is stronger than all who are not Companions. The reason is that they were witness to the practice of the Prophet (peace be on him) in the elaboration of the *aḥkām* and they saw the events that were the cause of revelation. It is on this basis that their view is to be preferred over the view of those who did not witness any of these things.[303]

The second area in which the Ḥanafīs maintain that it is binding to follow the opinion of a Companion is where the Companion is talking about quantities, numbers and periods.[304] The reason is that analogy has no role to play in this area, and most jurists are agreed that the opinion of a Companion is to be followed. Al-Sarakhsī points out that it is for this reason that we

303. Ibid., 108.
304. Ibid., 111.

have followed the opinions of Companions in the following cases (examples):[305]

- The rates of *zakāt*.
- The determination of the amount of dower.
- The determination of the minimum and maximum for the period of menstruation.
- The determination of the post-natal period.
- The determination of the maximum gestation period.

19.1.2 Views of those who do not consider it binding

Those who do not consider the opinion of a Companion to be binding maintain that they are under an obligation to follow the Qur'ān and the *Sunnah*, as well as those sources that are indicated by these two primary sources. These primary sources have not asked us to follow the opinion of a Companion as a source of law.[306]

19.1.3 Opinions of the Followers of the Companions (Tābi'ūn)

Al-Sarakhsī maintains that there is no dispute that the opinions of the Tābi'ūn are not binding in the sense that analogy should be given up in their preference. If one of them holds an opinion contrary to the consensus of the Companions, his opinion is not given weight in opposition to theirs.[307]

305. Ibid., 111–13.
306. Ibid., 106.
307. Ibid., 114–16.

19.2 *Shar' Man Qablanā* (Earlier Scriptures)

The meaning of *shar' man qablanā* is the body of rules ordained by Allah for the nations before the Muslim *ummah* through revelation to their Prophets and Apostles. Muslim jurists have differed somewhat about the relationship of such laws with the *sharī'ah,* as well as about their binding force for the Muslims. Some maintained that it was abrogated by our *sharī'ah,* while others said that those parts that were not abrogated are binding on us.

19.2.1 Types of earlier laws

1. **Rules that have been repeated in the Qur'ān or the *Sunnah* and made obligatory.** These texts themselves provide the evidence about the binding nature of the laws and we do not have to refer to the earlier scriptures. These laws are binding on us just as they were binding on the earlier nations. Example: Fasting during Ramaḍān [Qur'ān 2 : 183].

2. **Rules that have been described in the Qur'ān or in the *Sunnah,* but are considered abrogated.** Rules about carrion, blood, flesh of swine and the like.

3. **Rules that are not mentioned in the Qur'ān and the *Sunnah,* but are found in the earlier Scriptures.** There is no dispute that these are not binding on us.

4. **Rules that are mentioned in the Qur'ān and the *Sunnah,* but there is no evidence whether or not they are to be followed.** The example given by some jurists under this heading is that of *qiṣāṣ* (retaliation). There is, however, ample evidence in the texts that it is binding on us.

This shows that the real source for all such rules are the Qur'ān and the *Sunnah,* and they become binding on the Muslims when these primary sources grant the authority.

19.2.2 Reason why the earlier laws are not binding

To elaborate the basis for not accepting the rules in the earlier Scriptures, Al-Sarakhsī makes the following statement:[308]

> The most authentic statement in our view is that what is confirmed as an earlier law through the Book of Allah, or the elaboration by the Prophet (peace be on him), becomes a law for us, unless it is abrogated. As for what is transmitted by the People of the Book or is understood by the Muslims from their Scriptures is not binding on us, *because of the established evidence that they altered their Books.* Their transmission is, therefore, not accepted on the assumption that what is transmitted is entirely changed.

19.3 Custom (*'Urf*)

The earlier jurists make only a passing reference to custom, and they have never considered it as a source of law. In modern times, under the influence of Western jurisprudence, some writers have given more importance to custom as a source of law. Custom has been a source of law, but in a limited sense. This will be obvious from the discussion below.

The word *'urf* is usually associated with the word *ma'rūf* (good) in the texts. In this sense, it is what the *sharī'ah* considers to be good, and not what human reason or the prevalent practices consider to be good. If some of these practices are approved by the *sharī'ah,* then, they are acceptable to the law. The process of approval, prior to acceptance, is necessary.

19.3.1 Types of *'urf*

There are different ways of classifying *'urf,* and each classification is intended to bring out its nature.

19.3.1.1 Division into usage and practice

'Urf is divided first into *'urf qawlī* (usage) and *'urf fi'lī* (practice).

308. Ibid., 99–100

'Urf qawlī. The first type, or usage, may be analysed into the following types:

1. **The meaning of terms during the period of the Prophet (peace be on him).** This is the usage that was prevalent during the time of the Prophet. The meaning assigned to words at that period is used to understand the true intention of the Lawgiver.

2. **Technical terms of the law or *'urf shar'ī*.** The jurists usually employ the term *'urf shar'ī* to denote the technical sense that a term may have acquired in Islamic law. This technical meaning is usually different from the literal meaning in which the term is used. Thus, the word *ṣalāt* means any type of prayer or supplication, but in the technical sense it means the entire form of the prayer that has been transmitted from the Prophet (peace be on him). The word *ribā* literally means excess and in general usage it means "interest" in the sense of *sūd* in Urdu, but in the technical sense it has a much wider and comprehensive meaning assigned to it by the Qur'ān and the *Sunnah*. For legal purposes, it is the *'urf shar'ī* that has to be followed.

3. **Usage in a local area for purpose of transactions.** It is obvious that people using languages other than Arabic, undertake their transactions in their own language. Islamic law will recognise the meaning in such usage, but only if it conforms with the forms prescribed by the law, that is, if such use of words achieves the same purpose as the one prescribed. If it does not, the law will declare it *fāsid*. In other words, such usage has to be measured against the permitted rules before it can become permissible. It will not be recognised automatically.

It is obvious that none of these can be called a source of law in the sense that we understand custom to be a source in Western law.

***'Urf fi'lī* (practice).** This is of two types:

1. **The practices prevalent during the period of the Prophet (peace be on him).** These practices were either approved by the Prophet (peace be on him), either expressly or tacitly, or they were rejected. As such they became part of the *Sunnah.* The source of the law here was not custom, but the *Sunnah,* even though customs and practices did provide the raw material. Each practice was subjected to the norms of the *sharī'ah* by the Prophet himself, and was either accepted or rejected.

2. **Practices during the later periods.** These practices were faced by the jurists like new instances or cases and each one of them was subjected to scrutiny by the jurists. The jurists either justified these practices in the light of the principles of Islamic law or rejected them in the light of the same principles. No practice could automatically be approved just because it was a long standing custom.

We see from the above that though custom may provide the raw material to be considered by the jurist, no practice or custom can automatically be accepted as law. It has to be analysed and Islamised before it may be accepted. It may be noted that even in Western law, customs become law only when they are recognised by courts as such, and recognition means weighing them against the rest of the law for compatibility.

19.3.2 Can the Western laws obtaining in Pakistan be treated as custom?

It has been suggested by some that all the laws prevalent in Pakistan may be treated as *'urf* (custom) and thus declared valid. The idea behind this suggestion is that customs attain automatic validity just by being called customs. The idea is used by those who maintain that only five percent of the law needs to be changed for purposes of Islamisation and the rest should be left untouched. This is not correct. Each prevalent law must be treated as a new case and be analysed in the light of the principles of Islamic law. It is not sufficient to say that there is nothing in the Qur'ān and the *Sunnah* that clashes with a certain law, that is, the law has passed the repugnancy test. This way the law will not develop further on Islamic lines. Each law must be shown to be valid according to a principle of Islamic law. The Courts will then be able to develop the law and the principles further.

Review Questions

1. What is the status, among different schools, of the opinion of a Companion as a source of law?

2. Write a note on the earlier scriptures as sources of Islamic law.

3. Explain the meaning of *'urf* as a source of law. Compare it with custom as a source in English common law.

4. What are the different types of *'urf* and what is their significance for Islamic law?

5. Can the existing laws based on the English common law be treated as *'urf*? Answer the question by explaining the meaning of both *'urf* and custom in some detail.

Part IV

Ijtihād (Interpretation)

20 The Meaning of *Ijtihād* and its Modes

20.1 The Meaning of *Ijtihād*

The literal meaning of *ijtihād* is the expending of maximum effort in the performance of an act. Technically, it is the effort made by the *mujtahid* in seeking knowledge of the *aḥkām* (rules) of the *sharī'ah* through interpretation (بذل المجتهد وسعه في طلب العلم بالاحكام الشرعية بطريق الاستنباط). This definition implies the following:

- That the *mujtahid* should expend the maximum effort, that is, he should work to the limits of his ability so much so that he realises his inability to go any further.

- That the person expending the effort should be a *mujtahid*. An effort expended by a non-*mujtahid* is of no consequence, because he is not qualified to do so.

- The effort should be directed towards the discovery of the rules of the *sharī'ah* that pertain to conduct. All other types of rules are excluded.

- The method of discovery of the rules should be through interpretation of the texts with the help of the other sources. This excludes the memorisation of such rules from the books of *fiqh* or their identification by the *muftī*. Thus, the activity of the *faqīh* and the *muftī* cannot be called *ijtihād*.

20.2 *Ijtihād* is not Independent of the Qur'ān and the *Sunnah*

The word *ijtihād* is sometimes translated by those who have a superficial understanding of Islamic law as "independent reasoning." By this they mean that the *mujtahid* exercises his effort to derive laws in addition to those that have been laid down in the texts. Their statement also implies that *ijtihād* is independent of the texts of the Qur'ān and the *Sunnah*. This view is not only incorrect it is preposterous. There is no *ijtihād* outside the texts. All the modes of *ijtihād* described in this part operate within the texts. A consequence of such ideas is that when such people need to understand or refer to the laws in the texts they approach different *tafsīrs* rather than the manuals of law. Such a methodology is defective *prima facie*. The jurists were the only authorities for the interpretation of the **legal** texts of the Qur'ān and the *Sunnah* and their work is to be approached through manuals of *fiqh* and not *tafsīrs*.

20.3 The Task of the *Mujtahid*

The primary task of the *mujtahid*, as is evident from the above definition, is to discover the *aḥkām* of the *sharī'ah* from the texts. An important fact stated in the study of the sources is that the texts of the Qur'ān and the *Sunnah*, dealing with legal matters, are limited, while the new problems are unlimited. The task of the jurist, therefore, after a study of the primary sources, is to:

- discover the law that is either stated explicitly in the primary sources or is implied by the texts, that is, discover it through literal interpretation;

- extend the law to new cases that may be similar to cases mentioned in the textual sources, but cannot be covered through literal methods; and
- extend the law to new cases that are not covered by the previous two methods, that is, they are neither found explicitly or impliedly in the texts nor are they exactly similar to cases found in the texts.

The three tasks mentioned above not only tell us something about the nature of the sources, the way they point to legal rules, but also highlight the manner in which interpretation of the texts or *ijtihād* is to take place. In other words, these tasks tell us something about the different methods or the modes of *ijtihād* exercised by the jurist. An understanding of the modes of *ijtihād* helps draw a clear line between the literal methods of extending the law and the rational methods. Before the modes of *ijtihād* are studied, it is important to examine some basic assumptions in the light of which the jurist appears to be undertaking his task.

20.4 Basic Assumptions Made by the *Mujtahid*

The primary goal of all interpretation and *ijtihād* is to discover the intention of the Ultimate Lawgiver, Allah Almighty, with respect to the rules of conduct. The discovery of the intention of the Lawgiver in the texts leads to the assurance that the legal rules derived are truly Islamic. Obedience to such rules leads in turn to the formation of an Islamic legal system, a system based on norms determined by the Lawgiver. If the rules laid down are the result of human invention, the legal system cannot be called Islamic; all laws must conform with the intention of the Lawgiver.

Discovery of the true intention of the Lawgiver requires that the jurist interpreting the texts stay close to the literal and implied meanings of the texts and not give way to his own whims and fancies. The closer he stays to such meanings the greater the assurance that the norms are Islamic. In staying close to the texts and their literal as well as implied meanings, the jurist is guided by two main assumptions:

1. The first assumption in the words of al-Shāfi'ī is: "For those who follow the *dīn* of Allah there is guidance and evidence in the Book of Allah for each incident faced by them."[309] This means that the Qur'ān will provide guidance, either directly or indirectly, on all legal issues that the Muslims may face.

2. As already stated, the number of verses in the Qur'ān dealing with legal issues are limited, while the legal cases or issues faced by the Muslims, or to be faced by them, are unlimited. Even the texts of the *Sunnah* dealing with legal issues do not go beyond two thousand traditions. This means that there has to be some method, or methods, of extending the general principles in the Qur'ān and the *Sunnah* to cover all legal issues. These methods are evident through a study of the sources, but become even more obvious when the modes of *ijtihād* are examined.

20.5 Texts That are not Subject to *Ijtihād*

There are certain texts in which there is no need for the *mujtahid* to expend an effort. The reason is that these texts are the most authentic and the meanings found in them are most clear. The meaning of such texts can be discovered by anyone reading these texts.

In technical terms, the issue revolves around the meanings of the word definitive (*qaṭ'ī*) and probable (*ẓannī*). These words have a double meaning, as was explained in the discussion of the sources in Part 2. A text may be *qaṭ'ī al-thubūt,* that is definitive with respect to its transmission, and *qaṭ'ī al-dalālah,* that is, definitive with respect to its meaning.[310] All the verses

309. His assumption is based on the words of the Qur'ān: "And We have sent down to thee the Book explaining all things, a Guide, a Mercy and glad tidings to Muslims." Qur'ān 16:89.

310. We are using the term *qaṭ'ī al-dalālah* as an instructional device. In reality, this term is rather vague and is avoided by the earlier jurists who have a detailed system for describing the implications of words. This system will be examined in this part.

of the Qur'ān are definitive with respect to their authenticity or transmission and so are the texts of the *mutawātir sunnah.* There are very few of these texts that are definitive with respect to meaning. Being definitive with respect to meaning implies that only a single meaning is to be found from the text. For example, 100 stripes in the text pertaining to *zinā* (unlawful sexual intercourse) means 100 stripes, nothing more and nothing less; it is, therefore, definitive. There is no need for *ijtihād* to determine the number. As compared to this number, the meaning of "stripes" is not so clear. Are the stripes to be inflicted with a stick, a whip or something else? With what force are they to be applied? To what part of the body? All these questions require an interpretive effort by the *mujtahid.*

There can, therefore, be no *ijtihād* in texts that are definitive with respect to transmission as well as meaning. This meaning is also found in a principle that is stated by the Shāfi'ī jurists: "There is no *ijtihād* with the *naṣṣ.*" The word *naṣṣ* in this principle does not mean "text." *Naṣṣ* is the name for a word or text that gives a single or definitive meaning. Some writers have incorrectly interpreted this word to mean text for purposes of this rule, which has the effect of eliminating a major part of the activity called *ijtihād.* The reader should read such texts with caution.

Some of the cases that are considered to be outside the ambit of *ijtihād* are general obligations and proscriptions: the obligation of prayer; the obligation of fasting; the prohibition of *zinā* and so on. All such cases are those in which definitive texts with definitive meanings are to be found.

In short, *ijtihād* is relevant wherever there is a possibility of a text having more than one meaning. Such texts, whether they are definitive or probable with respect to transmission, are always probable with respect to meaning (*ẓannī al-dalālah*). *Ijtihād* in this context pertains to the discovery of the actual meaning by an examination of the strength of the meaning in various ways and in preferring such meaning over other likely meanings. It is in these methods that the jurists differ. They have adopted rules for interpretation and the application of these different rules may lead to a difference of opinion. This will be obvious in the next two chapters.

Sometimes, a meaning that may be probable is made definitive through consensus of opinion of the jurists. In such cases too, the jurists maintain that there is no possibility of *ijtihād,* and the meaning settled by *ijmā'* is to be followed by the *mujtahid.* This was explained in the study of *ijmā'* as a source of law. It is for this reason that jurists like al-Ghazālī have stated that the first thing a *mujtahid* must do when he begins interpreting is to find out if there is *ijmā'* on the issue.

Ijtihād also takes place in cases where no evidence, direct or indirect, can be found for an issue faced by the *mujtahid.* It is in these cases that some of the modes of *ijtihād* come into operation, as is explained below.

20.6 The Three Modes of *Ijtihād*

The jurists in general practice three types or modes of *ijtihād.* In reality, the activity of the jurist cannot be split up into separate modes. *Ijtihād* is a single seamless process, but for simplification and ease of understanding this activity is divided into three types as follows:

20.6.1 The first mode

In the first mode, the jurist stays as close as he can to the texts. He focuses on the literal meaning of the texts, that is, he follows the plain meaning rule. In doing so, he first tries to find explanations for difficult or unelaborated words from the texts themselves.[311] He moves to other sources, like the meaning of words in literature, later.[312] This also depends on whether the words have been used

311. He looks for such explanations in the texts of the Qur'ān as well as the *Sunnah.*

312. The jurist is equally concerned with the technical meanings that the words in the texts have been assigned by the texts themselves. Thus, words like *ṣalāt, zakāt,* and *ribā,* used in the Qur'ān have technical meanings assigned to them by the *Sunnah.* It is these technical meanings that are used in the law.

in the texts in their literal sense or their use is figurative (*ḥaqīqah* and *majāz*).

The text may not indicate the required meaning through a plain reading. In such a case, the jurist will use other techniques, called *dalālāt,* through which the implied meanings are ascertained. These techniques will be explained in the next chapter.

20.6.2 The second mode

When the first mode of literal construction is exhausted by the jurist, he turns to syllogism, which is called *qiyās.* This mode is confined to strict types of analogy. These are called *qiyās al-ma'nā* and *qiyās al-'illah.* Certain loose forms of analogy like *qiyās al-shabah* or analogy of resemblance are rejected by some jurists. The reason why only strict methods of analogy are approved is again the desire of the jurist to stay close to the intention of the Lawgiver. If very loose methods are adopted the Islamic colour of the legal system may be lost. *Qiyās* is, therefore, designed to be a strict type of analogy and may be said to apply to the process of finding an exact parallel. The second mode of *ijtihād* is confined to the use of *qiyās.*

20.6.3 The third mode

The second mode of *ijtihād* is confined to the extension of the law from individual texts, while in the third mode the reliance is on all the texts considered collectively. This means that legal reasoning is undertaken more in line with the spirit of the law and its purposes rather than the confines of individual texts.

The spirit of the law and its purposes can be witnessed clearly in the general principles of the legal system. The principles are used by methods like *istiḥsān* and *maṣlaḥah mursalah.* The third mode of *ijtihād* provides the jurist with the opportunity to generate new principles provided he observes a prescribed methodology and fulfils the conditions imposed for such legal reasoning.

20.7 The Complete Process of *Ijtihād*

It has been stated above that all three modes of *ijtihād* are practised as a single seamless activity. An understanding of these modes in not enough for visualising the total activity of *ijtihād*. There are some other processes involved that complete it. The following states and activities collectively depict the process of *ijtihād*.

- The *mujtahid* acquires the qualifications necessary for *ijtihād*.
- The *mujtahid* understands the different forms of *bayān* or elaboration of the texts, which is usually provided by the Lawgiver Himself, and also identifies the occasions on which such *bayān* is invoked.
- The *mujtahid* exercises all three modes of *ijtihād*, if necessary, in his effort to derive the law from the sources.
- The *mujtahid* understands abrogation (*naskh*) and identifies the occasions on which rules have been repealed by the Lawgiver.
- The *mujtahid* exercises preference (*tarjīḥ*) and reconciliation (*jam'*) among apparently conflicting sources.

All these activities when combined indicate the complete process of *ijtihād*. To understand *ijtihād* fully all these processes are to be understood.

20.8 The *Ḥukm* of *Ijtihād* and its Types

Ijtihād is obligatory (*wājib*) for the person who possesses the necessary qualifications for it and is equipped with the skills to perform it. The *mujtahid* is required to arrive at the *ḥukm shar'ī* through an examination of all the relevant evidences. Whatever rule he derives after such examination and investigation is the *ḥukm shar'ī* as far as he is concerned, and it is binding on him to follow it. He should not give up such a rule in favour of *taqlīd* of another *mujtahid*.

If a *mujtahid* is also the *qāḍī,* his opinion cannot be set aside by the *ijtihād* of another *mujtahid.* Even his own *ijtihād* on the same issue, arriving at a contrary opinion, will not upset his decision in the earlier case. The only way an opinion arrived at through *ijtihād* can be declared ineffective is when it is in clear conflict with a definitive text, because in such a case it was not *ijtihād ab initio.*

A *mujtahid* is not required to render opinions in all areas of the law, and he may specialise in one particular area if he so chooses. For example, a *mujtahid* may specialise in personal law alone, and even in this he may choose one area like inheritance. Some jurists have opposed the idea of specialisation in *ijtihād* and they do not permit it. The apparent reason is that Islamic law, like any other legal system, is a body of general principles that are interrelated and are internally consistent with each other. A *mujtahid* specialising in one particular area may not be able to maintain the internal consistency required by a legal system and thus his *ijtihād* may be prone to errors. The opinion of these jurists, who do not permit specialisation, appears to be based on a stronger reasoning.

20.9 The Qualifications of the *Mujtahid*

The qualifications for a *mujtahid* appear to be a later development in the history of Islamic law. No such qualifications were prescribed during the first two centuries of the Hijrah. It is only after the time of Muḥammad ibn Idrīs al-Shāfi'ī, the founder of the Shāfi'ī school, that such conditions were given greater importance. Prior to this, it was because of the performance of the jurist in the field of Islamic law and his acceptance by the people, who reposed their faith in him, that he came to be accepted as a *mujtahid.* Nevertheless, some conditions are deemed necessary and these are listed below:

1. *Knowledge of the Arabic language:* The texts are in Arabic and cannot be understood without a thorough understanding of Arabic. In fact, the Qur'ān, and even the texts of the *Sunnah,* are the standards that often determine the rules

of Arabic grammar. Interpreting the texts of the Qur'ān and the *Sunnah,* especially for purposes of deriving the law, is no easy job. The *mujtahid* has to have a very good command of the Arabic language to be able to undertake such interpretation.

2. *Knowledge of al-Kitāb:* The Qur'ān is the primary source of Islamic law. This means that it is a source for the law as well as the general principles of this law. Further, it is the source that validates all the other sources of the law. Though the legal texts are considered to be about 600, the jurists have often relied on the other verses as well for strengthening their opinions. The memorisation of the Qur'ān, or even the legal texts, is not considered necessary. It is sufficient if the jurist knows the location of the verses in the Qur'ān. It is for this reason that some jurists have devoted their lives to the writing of legal commentaries on the Qur'ān, often called *Aḥkām al-Qur'ān.* A condition within these conditions is that the *mujtahid* must know and understand all the occasions of abrogation, that is, the repealing and repealed laws, the *nāsikh* and the *mansūkh.* In addition, the jurist must have a knowledge of the *asbāb al-nuzūl* or the historical reasons why a certain verse was revealed, because this helps in the understanding of the intention of the Lawgiver; it provides the legislative history of the law.

3. *Knowledge of the Sunnah:* As the *Sunnah* provides a legal commentary on the laws in the Qur'ān and is also an independent source of the law, the *mujtahid* must be fully aware of all the precedents laid down by it. This entails a knowledge of the *mutawātir,* the *mashhūr* as well as the *khabar wāḥid.* Today, we have the *ṣaḥīḥ* compilations by the great traditionists like Imāms Bukhārī and Muslim. It must be noted, however, that the law that we read in *fiqh* books was derived and laid down by the schools of law before these compilations were made.[313] It is, therefore, necessary

313. Most of the law that was compiled by Imām Muḥammad al-Shaybānī

to understand the criteria laid down by the jurists for the classification and acceptance of *aḥadīth.* Although many of the rules are common, there are some differences too. Some very good books have been written in the present times that explain the criteria used by the jurists.

4. *Knowledge of Ijmāʿ:* As stated earlier, some jurists have laid down that the first source to be consulted, before a *mujtahid* begins his task of interpretation, is *ijmāʿ*. If there is *ijmāʿ* on an issue, the *mujtahid* cannot reopen such issue. In addition to this, knowledge of the principles upheld by *ijmāʿ* will guide the *mujtahid* on other issues.

5. *Knowledge of the maqāṣid al-sharīʿah:* This condition has been added by later jurists. In this book it has been shown in detail why a knowledge of the purposes of law is necessary for understanding and deriving the law. As these are ultimate values, a knowledge of Arabic is not essential for understanding the *maqāṣid al-sharīʿah* and their operation.

6. *Aptitude for ijtihād:* Another condition that some writers lay down is a natural aptitude for law and *ijtihād.* This is more like a God given gift than something that can be acquired. Just like a good knowledge of Arabic does not make a person a poet, the fulfilment of the above conditions will not make a person a *mujtahid.*

20.9.1 Who is a *mujtahid* today?

In the present times, possession of all the above qualifications is not likely to bestow the status of *mujtahid* on a person. The reason for this is that much depends on acceptance by the people. As there are established schools today, the need for such acceptance by the people does not exist. It is for this reason that jurists like al-Sarakhsī, al-Ghazālī, and many others who may be said to possess all the qualities of full *mujtahids* were not granted such a status.

---

around the middle of the second century was complete in his generation or even in the previous generation.

Ijtihād is primarily a legislative function, and today the state has a monopoly over legislation. An opinion issued by a *mujtahid* would have no significance unless it is accepted by the state and converted into law through legislation. In certain cases, the courts too may recognise an opinion and grant it weight in their decisions. The *mujtahid* in such a case would be the state and not the individual.

In Pakistan today, the Council of Islamic Ideology cannot be deemed to have the qualifications of a *mujtahid;* its status is more like that of a *muftī,* whose opinions are not binding. The CII itself is part of the state. At the international level, the Islamic Fiqh Academy of the OIC has a similar status as its opinions are mere recommendations and are not binding on anyone.

It was stated above that an opinion derived by a *mujtahid* is binding on him and he is supposed to act upon it. This is only possible today in private matters; in the rest of the law, he is bound to follow the law laid down by the state. This shows that there is limited scope of *ijtihād* by individuals today. There is, however, tremendous scope in modern times for the *faqīh.* This has been true for a sizable period of Islamic history. The role of the *faqīh* has been highlighted in Part 4 of this book.

20.10 *Ijtihād* a Legislative Function: The Need for an Islamic Theory of Legislation

After having said all this, we must recall what we said in the introduction to this book about the need for developing an Islamic theory of legislation. In the earlier structure of the legal system, the individual *mujtahids* and the schools of law had a big role to play. They dealt with almost the entire law leaving certain matters to the state. The *imām* or the state issued regulations under its *siyāsah* jurisdiction to raise taxes, to administer the *maẓālim* courts, to regulate the markets, to issue currency and to manage the institution of *iḥtisāb* among other things. With the passage of every century, the jurisdiction of the state kept on increasing and in the modern times many of the laws that were administered by the *qāḍī* in collaboration with the schools, or using the law laid down by the schools, have now been transferred to the exclusive domain of the state. Even the personal law is now administered by the state. The administration of the mosques and *waqfs*, the organisation of the pilgrimage and measures for the observance of the Ramaḍān are also the sole responsibility of the state. In short, the role of the schools and of the independent jurists has shrunk to the extent of becoming non-existent. The *'ulamā'* now act as advisors to courts and to the government, if they are invited to do so.

We also stated in the introduction that *ijtihād* is a legislative function, because it lays down the law for the first time, just as the modern legislature lays down the law in the form of statutes. All the rights and duties of the Muslims were determined by the decisions of the *mujtahid* or his school. All rights given, and taken away, depended on the version of the law issued by a school. All these functions now belong to the legislature (or in the case of Pakistan, to some extent, to the Federal Shari'at Court or the Shari'at Appellate Bench of the Supreme Court). During the earlier days, it was the theory of *ijtihād* that provided the basis for the legislative activity of the *mujtahid*. Today, it still contains the solid Islamic foundation that is necessary for all types of legislation, a foundation that must control, guide and determine the activity of the legislator in an Islamic state. Yet, it has been relegated to the background and is found to a minimal extent in various institutions that act as advisory bodies for the legislature.

The process of Islamisation will remain incomplete until the activity of the legislatures in Islamic states is brought fully under the purview of the institution of *ijtihād*. Even though the legislature cannot meet the requirements of *ijtihād* with respect to its individual members who will come from various professions and will have different levels of education, yet it must as an institution. The legislature must be supported as an institution for the performance of collective *ijtihād*. It is only when this is ensured that Islamic justice will be implemented and rights guaranteed by the Islamic legal system will be secured. The legislature in an Islamic state must have one and only one activity: *IJTIHĀD*.

All this will be possible when the Islamic Theory of Legislation based upon *ijtihād* is developed for the modern times. This places a very heavy burden on all the researchers and thinkers occupied with Islamic law. The theory must be alive to modern human problems and issues. It must engage the best minds in each Muslim country and move from these problems and issues back to the fundamental principles and norms of the Islamic system and then emerge to provide a humane and efficient legal system that Islamic law furnishes.

Review Questions

1. *Ijtihād* is always based upon the legal interpretation of the Qur'ān and the *Sunnah*. Argue.
2. What is the meaning of *ijtihād*?
3. What is the task of the *mujtahid* and what are the assumptions on which he works?
4. What are the three modes of *ijtihād* and how is the process of *ijtihād* completed?
5. What is the *ḥukm* of *ijtihād*, that is, what is obligatory for the *mujtahid*?
6. What are the qualifications of the *mujtahid* stipulated by the jurists? Can these qualifications be met today?
7. Who is the *mujtahid* in the modern Islamic state?
8. *Ijtihād* is primarily a legislative function. Elaborate.
9. How will *ijtihād* be carried out in the Islamic Republic of Pakistan?

21 The First Mode of *Ijtihād*: Interpreting the Texts

21.1 The Concept of *Bayān* (Elaboration)

In the study of the primary sources of Islamic law, we said repeatedly that the *Sunnah* acts as a commentary of the Qur'ān and elaborates the meanings in the texts in various cases. On occasions the Qur'ān also elaborates these meanings. Elaboration of these meanings implies that many terms that would otherwise be read in their literal sense acquire technical legal meanings. These terms are then used in the law in their technical meanings and are applied consistently for the interpretation of the texts. Terms like *ṣalāt, zakāt* and *ribā* are examples of such terms. The elaboration or explanation of the terms in the texts by the texts is called *bayān*. It is to be noted that *bayān* is not confined to the elaboration of technical terms; it works in various ways to reveal the rules of law. In this section it is our endeavour to explain the various types of *bayān*.

The importance of the meaning of *bayān* in *uṣūl al-fiqh* can be fully realised only when we examine the type of duty it places on the interpreter or the *mujtahid*. The method of the jurists and the teachings of *uṣūl al-fiqh* convey to us that the first task of the interpreter when determining the meanings of words and texts, especially technical terms, is to look for the meaning within the legal texts. The reason is that a term may have one or more literal meanings, but the texts may have used this term in a special way. This special way is called the *'urf shar'ī* (technical legal usage) and is the equivalent of the technical legal meaning of a term. It is only when the interpreter has failed to find an explanation of a term in the texts that he is to turn to other sources in literature, history or another discipline. It appears that modern interpreters turn to epistemology first and later, if they feel inclined towards it, to the texts of Islamic law. The glaring example in the modern age is that of the word *ribā*. Many interpreters have tried to discover the meaning of this term in literature, history and other religions first. Some have not even bothered to discover its technical meaning in the legal texts. As compared to them, the earlier jurists have been insisting all along that though the term *ribā* has many literal meanings, in the law it became a technical term and this technical meaning has to be discovered from the texts.

Bayān means to elaborate the meaning and make it evident.[314] Some jurists try to narrow down this general meaning to say that it is the elaboration of the meaning for the addressee so that he acquires the knowledge of the command contained in the text. Most jurists, however, prefer the more general meaning, that is, making the meaning of the text obvious. This meaning, they say, is to be found in the following texts: the saying of the Prophet (peace be on him): إنّ من البيان لسحر (Verily! In expression (style) there is magic); the words of the Exalted علّمه البيان (He has taught him an intelligent speech [Qur'ān 55:4]); and لتبيّن للناس ما نزّل إليهم (That thou mayest explain to men clearly what is sent for them [Qur'ān 16:44]). The last text gives the meaning of explaining or elaboration, whereas in the first two the meaning is different from mere elaboration. The first two texts both give the meaning of mode or expression or manner of speech. In reality, this is

314. Al-Sarakhsī, *Kitāb al-Uṣūl*, vol. 2, 26.

exactly what is meant by *bayān*. *Bayān* may, therefore, be defined as the distinctive manner or mode of expression and the style of elaboration employed by the Qur'ān or by the texts. Here we are concerned with the mode of expression that has a legal impact. It is obvious though that *bayān* applies to non-legal matters as well.

The majority of the jurists believe that *bayān* (elaboration) is accomplished through words as well as the acts of the Prophet (peace be on him).[315] Some of the Mutakallimūn state that elaboration cannot be accomplished through acts, because it must not be independent of or separate from the text being explained.[316] As acts have a separate existence they do not amount to *bayān*. The majority of the jurists do not give importance to this separation for purposes of elaboration of the texts.

The most important thing to note here is that *bayān* takes place through the texts—the texts of the Qur'ān and the *Sunnah*. The texts of *Sunnah* also contain the reports about the acts of the Prophet (peace be on him). The task of the jurist is to identify the occasions of *bayān* in the texts and to employ them in his interpretation.

The generally accepted types of *bayān* are five:[317] *bayān taqrīr; bayān tafsīr; bayān taghyīr; bayān tabdīl;* and *bayān ḍarūrah*. The meaning and description of each of these types is given below. It is to be noted that only the bare minimum explanations are provided; the jurists go into numerous details.[318]

21.1.1 *Bayān taqrīr* (complementary expression or elaboration)

This type of *bayān* involves the elaboration of meaning that is already evident. It has the effect of removing all doubt about some probable meanings that may also be implied by the text. The probable meanings are found in the text either due to the use

315. Ibid.
316. Ibid., 27.
317. According to some jurists there are seven types. They add *bayān ḥāl* and *bayān 'aṭf* to the five types listed above.
318. For the various types, see ibid., 26–53.

of a figurative term (*majāz*) or due to the use of a general word (*'āmm*) that could have been restricted. The *bayān* removes all such probabilities and sharpens the meaning. In the text of the Qur'ān, فسجد الملائكة كلّهم اجمعون (So the angels prostrated themselves, all of them together [Qur'ān 15:30]), the general word *al-malā'ikah* (angels) could also mean some of the angels, that is, the word could be restricted to some of its categories. The words كلّهم اجمعون (all of them together) remove this doubt. In the verse of the Qur'ān, ولا طائر يطير بجناحيه (Nor a being that flies on its wings [Qur'ān 6:38]), the word *ṭā'ir* (bird) may have been used in the figurative sense to include birds that do not fly, but the words *jināḥ* (wings) removes the possibility of the figurative meaning.

This type of *bayān* is valid when it accompanies the text as well as when it is separated from it.

21.1.2 *Bayān tafsīr* (enabling expression)

Bayān tafsīr is an elaboration that provides the details associated with the text and enables the subject to act upon the command in the verse. Prior to such elaboration acting upon the command in the text is not possible due to a lack of detail. The elaboration is meant for words that are *mujmal* (unelaborated) or *mushtarak* (equivocal). Once such words are elaborated through *bayān* they are called *mufassar* (elaborated).

Thus, the commands in the verse اقيموا الصلاة وآتوا الزكاة (observe prayer and pay the poor-due) are difficult to act upon, because the words *ṣalāt* and *zakāt* lack the detail required for praying as well as for paying *zakāt*. The elaboration for *ṣalāt* comes from the words and acts of the Prophet (peace be on him) when he says, "Pray as you see me praying." The detailed rates for payment of *zakāt* are also elaborated by the *Sunnah.*

Elaboration of this type may accompany the text or be separated from it. Some of the Mutakallimūn maintain that *bayān* for *mujmal* and *mushtarak* words should not be separate from the text, because without such elaboration it becomes difficult to act upon the text, and if such a *bayān* is permitted it means that an obligation for performing the impossible has been created. The majority of the jurists do not agree with them and maintain that there is no difficulty in waiting for a delayed *bayān*.[319]

21.1.3 *Bayān taghyīr* (elaboration by exception)

Taghyīr means change or alteration. This type of *bayān* is confined to exceptions (*istithnā'*) according to al-Sarakhsī. Some of the other jurists have made a different classification by placing texts depending upon contingent statements or the fulfilment of conditions in this as well. Al-Sarakhsī places this latter type into *bayān tabdīl*.

فلبث فيهم ألف سنّة إلّا خمسين عاما (And he tarried among them a thousand years less fifty [Qur'ān 29:14]). In this verse, the word *alf* (thousand) is the name of a number and would be construed as such if there were no exception. The exception alters the original number and makes it 950. In other words, if the exception had been missing a complete meaning would have been understood from the text, that is, staying for a thousand years. The exception has altered this meaning.

21.1.4 *Bayān tabdīl* (conditional expression)

According to al-Sarakhsī *bayān tabdīl* is the making of a *ḥukm* dependent upon the fulfilment of a condition. An example is the text: فإن أرضعن لكم فأتوهنّ أجورهنّ (And if they suckle for you (your offspring), give them their recompense [Qur'ān 65:6]). The meaning is that the payment of wages will not become due after the contract, unless suckling of the child is undertaken. The *ḥukm* does not come into existence without the completion of the condition. It comes into existence at the moment the condition is found. The contract when concluded requires payment of wages, but the stipulation of the condition is a change in such a requirement.

As indicated earlier, many jurists have classified texts associated with a condition under *bayān taghyīr*. Under the

319. Some even seek support from the story of Khiḍr and Moses, while discussing the merits of waiting for the *bayān*.

heading of *bayān tabdīl* these jurists place *naskh* or abrogation. Al-Sarakhsī maintains that *tabdīl* is different from *naskh* insofar as *naskh* is a change in a *ḥukm* that is already established by the text, whereas in *tabdīl* the *ḥukm* cannot come into being prior to the fulfilment of the condition. *Tabdīl* may also be distinguished from *taghyīr* insofar as the meaning is complete in *taghyīr* if the exception is not taken into account, but in *tabdīl* the meaning is not completed without the condition.

In both types of *bayān*, that is, *taghyīr* and *tabdīl*, an elaboration separated from the text is not accepted; it must accompany the text.

21.1.5 *Bayān ḍarūrah* (elaboration by necessity)

It is a type of elaboration that assigns a meaning to a text for which the text was not originally stated. In the verse وورثه أبواه فلأمه الثلث (And the parents are the (only) heirs, the mother has a third [Qur'ān 4:11]) it is clear that a third share is allotted to the mother. Through *bayān ḍarūrah* it becomes obvious that the father gets the rest.

The jurists further subdivide this type of elaboration into four types. The details can be gleaned from their books.[320]

21.2 Literal Interpretation of the Texts

The first mode of *ijtihād,* as already stated, is that of literal construction. In this mode the jurist stays very close to the texts in the effort to discover the true intention of the Lawgiver. This area of study is considered to be the most technical and difficult part of *uṣūl al-fiqh.* It would not be an exaggeration to say that the status of the *mujtahid* depends more or less on his expertise in this area along with the contribution he has made to literal interpretation of the texts.

A complete knowledge of this mode of *ijtihād* is not possible without a good knowledge of the Arabic language. Nevertheless, an idea of the broad methodology of the jurists can be grasped

320. See ibid., 50–53.

even in another language and this can facilitate further study, once a knowledge of Arabic is acquired.

A difficulty in acquiring a knowledge of the first mode of *ijtihād* is that there is not one but two broad and independent methodologies in this area. The first methodology is practised by the Ḥanafī school, and is called the method of the Ḥanafīs. The second method is followed by the majority schools, and is known as the method of the Mutakallimūn. Most writers on the subject first describe the Ḥanafī method and then deal briefly with the method of the Mutakallimūn. A similar method is adopted in this section; it is, however, difficult to practice both methodologies at the same time. In fact, it may be an error to do so.

The second difficulty is that later jurists, while describing these methods, inclined more and more towards a theoretical exposition. As jurists before them had interpreted and reinterpreted the texts in a variety of ways, the later jurists it appears never felt the need to apply these rules independently. The manner in which these methods were elaborated are, therefore, difficult to understand in the context of applied *uṣūl*. These expositions have been reproduced for centuries, and for this reason many modern Arab writers have also reproduced these methods in their theoretical expositions.

As compared to the later writers, some of the earlier jurists have dealt with the subject with an eye on actual application. Among the great jurists who elaborated these methods, and actually used them in their works, we find the names of al-Sarakhsī, al-Ghazālī, al-Rāzī and a few others. The best exposition, of course, is still considered to that of Imām al-Shāfi'ī himself in his book *al-Risālah*. If expertise in the first mode of *ijtihād* has to be revived there is a need to go back to the works of these writers. It is for this reason that the brief explanations that follow in this section are based on the works of al-Sarakhsī, for the Ḥanafī method, and on the works of al-Ghazālī, for the method of the Mutakallimūn.

21.2.1 The structure of interpretation

The primary task of the jurist is to discover the *aḥkām* from the texts. This is accomplished through a reading of the texts. Depending on the text, the jurist adopts several methods through which the *aḥkām* are established. According to al-Sarakhsī, these four broad methods are called the *dalālāt* or the implications of the text.[321] These are as follows:

1. The *aḥkām* are established through *'ibārat al-naṣṣ* or obvious meanings revealed through a plain reading of the text. We may call this the plain meaning rule.
2. The *aḥkām* are established through *ishārat al-naṣṣ* or the connotation of the texts.
3. The *aḥkām* are established through *dalālat al-naṣṣ* or through meanings implied by the texts.
4. The *aḥkām* are established through *iqtiḍā' al-naṣṣ* or through meanings required by the texts of a necessity.

In addition to these four methods there are some methods that are considered *fāsid* (not valid) by the Ḥanafīs, but are accepted by the other schools. The best known of these is the *mafhūm mukhālafah* or the contrary rule implied by the texts. Some of these will be discussed later within the methods practised by the Shāfi'īs.

The reading of the text to establish the *aḥkām* is supported by two types of underlying activity. These are as follows:

1. *Literal forms through which the ḥukm is indicated:* The *ḥukm* is indicated through commands (*amr*) and proscriptions (*nahy*) or through reports (*akhbār*) in the text conveying commands and proscriptions.

321. The rest of the chapter is based on al-Sarakhsī's elaboration of the structure of interpretation. It is for this reason that specific citations have been avoided.

2. *Literal forms through which the meaning is indicated:* There are different aspects of the meaning emerging from the texts. From one aspect the jurist is concerned with the number or categories that will be affected by the *ḥukm.* He classifies meaning from this aspect into *'āmm, khāṣṣ, mushtarak* and *mu'awwal.* From another aspect the jurist is concerned with the clarity with which words have been used. This clarity or ambiguity determines the strength with which the *ḥukm* is established, and the information is used to determine the *ḥukm* when two or more meanings are in conflict.

The broad methods of establishing the *aḥkām,* that is, the *dalālāt* will be taken up first followed by the determination of the *ḥukm* and meaning.

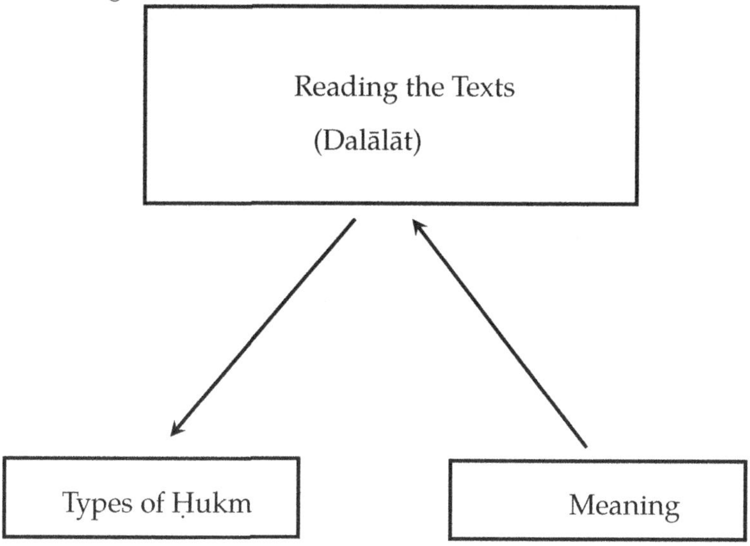

21.2.2 The four general literal methods of establishing the *aḥkām (dalālāt)*

21.2.2.1 *'Ibārat al-naṣṣ*—the plain meaning rule

'Ibārat al-naṣṣ is the method of looking at the text to determine the meaning that is **the main object of the text.** The *ḥukm* established through *'ibārat al-naṣṣ* is one for which the text is primarily laid

down and it is known without deep reflection that the apparent meaning of the text includes this *ḥukm.* A majority of the legal texts are covered by this rule. Such a reading may reveal primary as well as secondary meanings. The following examples illustrate the use of the plain meaning rule:

1. ولا تقتلوا النّفس الّتي حرّم الله إلّا بالحقّ (Take not life, which Allah hath made sacred, except by way of justice and law [Qur'ān 6:151]). This text indicates through a plain reading that homicide is prohibited. This is also a primary meaning and there is no secondary meaning.

2. The words واقيموا الصلاة وآتوا الزكاة indicate through a plain reading that it is obligatory to establish prayer and to pay the poor-due. This is also a primary meaning and there is no secondary meaning.

3. Sometimes a text may have more than one meaning; one meaning will be primary and the other will be secondary. In the verse of the Qur'ān
ذَٰلِكَ بِأَنَّهُمْ قَالُوٓا۟ إِنَّمَا ٱلْبَيْعُ مِثْلُ ٱلرِّبَوٰا۟ ۗ وَأَحَلَّ ٱللَّهُ ٱلْبَيْعَ وَحَرَّمَ ٱلرِّبَوٰا۟ (That is because they say: "Trade is like usury," but Allah hath permitted trade and forbidden usury [Qur'ān 2:275]), a plain reading or *'ibārat al-naṣṣ* indicates two meanings. The first is the negation of a similarity between *bay'* and *ribā,* while the second is the permissibility of *bay'* and prohibition of *ribā.* The first is the primary meaning and the second is secondary.

4. In the verse of the Qur'ān,
فَٱنكِحُوا۟ مَا طَابَ لَكُم مِّنَ ٱلنِّسَآءِ مَثْنَىٰ وَثُلَٰثَ وَرُبَٰعَ ۖ فَإِنْ خِفْتُمْ أَلَّا تَعْدِلُوا۟ فَوَٰحِدَةً
(Marry women of your choice, two, or three, or four; but if ye fear that ye shall not be able to deal justly (with them), then only one [Qur'ān 4:3]) there are three meanings. The first is permissibility of marriage. The second is the restriction of marrying more than four wives. The third is the restriction of marrying only one when there is fear of causing injustice.

All three meanings are grasped through a plain reading or *'ibārat al-naṣṣ* and all three are the main object of the text. The first meaning, however, is a secondary meaning and the last two meanings are primary meanings.

21.2.2.2 *Ishārat al-naṣṣ*—the connotation of the text

Ishārat al-naṣṣ is a method in which the *ḥukm* is established through an indication of the text by focusing on **a meaning accompanying** the primary meanings that are the main object of the text. Thus, the *hukm* established is not the main object of the text, but becomes evident in its complete form after a little reflection.

Al-Sarakhsī explains that a person looking up the road can see someone in the centre of the road coming straight towards him. In the same glance this person can also see, through the corners of his eyes, other persons on the road to the left and right of the person approaching in the centre, even though the intention is to look at the person in the centre alone. Again, if a person shoots an arrow at an animal, it is possible that the arrow strikes the main target and then hits another animal standing near the first. Likewise the *aḥkām* established by *'ibārat al-naṣṣ* and *ishārat al-naṣṣ*, that is, both are established by the same text.

1. وَعَلَى ٱلْمَوْلُودِ لَهُۥ رِزْقُهُنَّ وَكِسْوَتُهُنَّ بِٱلْمَعْرُوفِ (But he (to whom the child is attributed) shall bear the cost of their food and clothing [Qur'ān 2:233]). This verse indicates through a plain reading or *'ibārat al-naṣṣ* that the maintenance of a wife weaning a child is on the husband. By the indication of the text several *aḥkām* are established; two of these are mentioned below:

    a) That the child is attributed to the father. This is obvious from the words وَعَلَى المَوْلُودِ لَهُ.

    b) The same words also indicate indirectly that the father has a right over the child, his possessions and wealth. This is further affirmed by the words of the Prophet (peace be on him): اَنتَ وَمَالُكَ لِأَبِيكَ (You and your wealth are for your father). This also means that the father cannot be subjected to *qiṣāṣ* (retaliation) if he injures his child or even kills him.

2. فَسْـَٔلُوٓاْ أَهْلَ ٱلذِّكْرِ إِن كُنتُمْ لَا تَعْلَمُونَ (If ye realise this not, ask of those who possess the message [Qur'ān 16:43]). The verse indicates through a plain reading that it is obligatory to ask the *ahl al-dhikr,* because this is the main object of the verse, but it indicates through *ishārat al-naṣṣ* that it is necessary that such a group be in existence so that they can be asked.

3. وَشَاوِرْهُمْ فِى ٱلْأَمْرِ (And consult them in affairs (of moment) [Qur'ān 3:159]). The *'ibārat al-naṣṣ* indicates that the primary principle in Islam is consultation (*shūra*), but the *ishārat al-naṣṣ* indicates the the necessity of having such a consultative body, because consulting the entire population is not possible.

4. The verses وَحَمْلُهُۥ وَفِصَـٰلُهُۥ ثَلَـٰثُونَ شَهْرًا (The carrying of the child to his weaning is (a period of) thirty months [Qur'ān 46:15]) and وفصاله في عامين (And in years twain was his weaning [Qur'ān 31:14]) collectively indicate through *ishārat al-naṣṣ* that the minimum gestation period is six months.

The above examples indicate that the *aḥkām* available through *ishārat al-naṣṣ* are not readily available. They need some reflection over the implications of the text to ascertain, which means some aptitude for and training in *fiqh.*

21.2.2.3 *Dalālat al-naṣṣ*—the implication of the text

Dalālat al-naṣṣ is a method through which the *ḥukm* of a thing explicitly stated in the text is also established, on the basis of a common meaning, for a thing not mentioned in the text through the syntax and not through analogy (*qiyās*). In other words, this extension of the *ḥukm* is possible through a reading of the text and the rules of analogy are not needed. This is the viewpoint of the Ḥanafīs. The Shāfi'īs place this in the category of analogy and call it *qiyās al-ma'nā* or *qiyās jalī.* Some also call it the *mafhūm muwāfaqah.* In other places, in this book, it has been called a movement from a lower-order meaning to a higher-order meaning.

1. فَلَا تَقُل لَّهُمَآ أُفٍّ (Say not to them a word of contempt [Qur'ān 17:23]). The plain meaning of the text or *'ibārat al-naṣṣ* indicates that saying "fie" to parents is prohibited. The underlying cause is "harm to parents." The text itself implies that causing other more grievous types of harm is also prohibited, like abusing them, beating them and so on. In fact, abuse and beating have a higher priority for prohibition, because they are more grievous than saying "fie." In this case, the movement is from a lower-order meaning to a higher order meaning.

2. إِنَّ ٱلَّذِينَ يَأْكُلُونَ أَمْوَٰلَ ٱلْيَتَـٰمَىٰ ظُلْمًا إِنَّمَا يَأْكُلُونَ فِى بُطُونِهِمْ نَارًا ۖ وَسَيَصْلَوْنَ سَعِيرًا (Those who unjustly eat up the property of orphans, eat up a fire into their own bodies: they will soon be enduring a blazing fire [Qur'ān 4:10]). This verse indicates through a plain reading the prohibition of wrongfully consuming the wealth of orphans. By way of *dalālat al-naṣṣ,* however, it is implied that setting fire to the wealth of the orphan or unjustly destroying it in any other way is also prohibited, because these acts amount to the consumption of wealth. The underlying cause in all these cases is "wrongful destruction."

***Dalālat al-naṣṣ* and the criminal law.** The Ḥanafīs maintain that the provisions of the criminal law cannot be extended by analogy, but they can be extended through *dalālat al-naṣṣ.* The reason is that if analogy is permitted for extension of crimes it will widen the scope of such crimes and will work against that primary principle of Islamic law that there is no crime and no punishment without a text (*nullum crimen nulla poena sine lege* — لا جريمة ولا عقوبة بلا نص). For example, a tradition says لا قود الّا بالسيف (there is no retaliation unless the sword is used). The meaning apparent through *'ibārat al-naṣṣ* is that retaliation is prescribed where homicide is with the sword, because the sword is an instrument used for this purpose. The meaning implied through *dalālat al-naṣṣ* is that retaliation should be awarded by the judge as a penalty in all cases where an "instrument prepared for killing" like a spear or a gun has been used. A secondary meaning may be that the execution in the case of *qiṣāṣ* is carried out with the sword.

The Shāfi'īs, on the other hand, permit the determination of crimes through analogy. As they consider *dalālat al-naṣṣ* a type of analogy there appears to be no difference between their opinion and that of the Ḥanafīs. Analogy, however, has other types and permitting the determination of crimes through any type of analogy will widen the scope of the criminal law without there being prescribed texts. This will work against the principle of legality mentioned above.

21.2.2.4 *Iqtiḍā' al-naṣṣ*—requirement of the text by necessity

The word *iqtiḍā'* means demand or requirement. In this context, it is a meaning required by the text in addition to what is stated by the words. This requirement is a prerequisite to understanding the meaning of the text, for otherwise it would be difficult to act upon the *ḥukm* in the text. According to al-Sarakhsī, what is proved this way is similar in some ways to the *ḥukm* proved by *dalālat al-naṣṣ,* however, the latter provides a stronger proof, because it is proved through the syntax. *Iqtiḍā' al-naṣṣ*, on the other hand, is not proved through the syntax, **but is required by the law to complete the conceptual meaning.**

1. حُرِّمَتْ عَلَيْكُمْ أُمَّهَٰتُكُمْ وَبَنَاتُكُمْ (Prohibited to you (for marriage) are your mothers and daughters [Qur'ān 4:23]). The prohibition of mothers and sisters here means prohibition by way of marriage. The meaning of *nikāḥ* (marriage) is required by the text and by the law, though it is not mentioned in the text.

2. حُرِّمَتْ عَلَيْكُمُ ٱلْمَيْتَةُ وَٱلدَّمُ وَلَحْمُ ٱلْخِنزِيرِ (Forbidden to you (for food) are dead meat, blood and the flesh of swine [Qur'ān 5:3]). In

this text the meanings implied by necessity are "eating and making use of." The translation, therefore, does not give the complete meaning.

***Iqtiḍā' al-naṣṣ* and the *maḥdhūf* (missing text).** Al-Sarakhsī makes a distinction between a concept or meaning implied by a necessity of the law and the missing word that is implied by the text and is to be read into it to complete the meaning. He gives a number of examples, one of which is reproduced here: إِنَّ اللهَ رَفَعَ عَن أُمَّتِي الخَطَأَ وَالنِسيَانَ وَمَا اَستُكرِهوا عَلَيه (Allah has lifted from my *ummah* (the liability arising from) mistake, forgetfulness and what they have been coerced into doing). In these words of the Prophet (peace be on him), the meaning is complete if the word *ḥukm* is read into the text, that is, the *ḥukm* of forgetfulness, the *ḥukm* of mistake, and the *ḥukm* of duress. The meaning would then be that the *ḥukm* for such acts has been lifted. Al-Sarakhsī says that this is implied by necessity, that is, "liability for" acts done in such states is lifted.

He says that the *maḥdhūf* (missing) word is filled up by adding a word or words to the language, while the meaning implied by necessity is filled by the completion of the legal concept or meaning, without any addition to the language.

21.2.2.5 The strength of the *aḥkām* proved by the four methods and conflict between them

The strength of the *aḥkām* proved by each of the four methods is in the order in which they have been studied. Thus, a *ḥukm* proved by *'ibārat al-naṣṣ* is the strongest. This is followed by a *ḥukm* proved by *ishārat al-naṣṣ*, which in turn is followed by *dalālat al-naṣṣ*. The *ḥukm* proved by *iqtiḍā' al-naṣṣ* is comparatively the weakest. The significance of assigning these methods grades of strength is that the stronger will be preferred over the weaker in case of conflict. A few examples are given below:

Conflict between *'ibārat al-naṣṣ* and *ishārat al-naṣṣ*. In the words of the Allah, وَعَلَى ٱلْمَوْلُودِ لَهُۥ رِزْقُهُنَّ وَكِسْوَتُهُنَّ بِٱلْمَعْرُوفِ, the father has been given importance by way of *ishārat al-naṣṣ,* with respect to rights over the child, as explained above. As compared to this, when the Prophet (peace be on him) was asked, "Who has the best right for good treatment among relatives?" he replied, "Your mother!" He was asked, "And then?" He said: "Your mother!" He was asked: "And then?" He replied: "Your mother!" He was asked: "And then?" He said: "Your father!" This tradition, by way of *'ibārat al-naṣṣ* places the mother three grades above the father. When the two derived rules are compared, the verse by way of indication gives the father a greater right of maintenance from the child's wealth, whereas the tradition grants a greater right to the mother, or at least it makes their rights equal.

In the verse وَمَن يَقْتُلْ مُؤْمِنًا مُّتَعَمِّدًا فَجَزَآؤُهُۥ جَهَنَّمُ خَـٰلِدًا فِيهَا (If a man kills a believer intentionally, his recompense is hell, to abide therein forever [Qur'ān 4:93]), the plain meaning or *'ibārat al-naṣṣ* indicates that there are many penalties in the hereafter for the murderer. By *ishārat al-naṣṣ,* however, it indicates that there is no *qiṣāṣ* (retaliation) for him in this world. There is another verse كُتِبَ عَلَيْكُمُ ٱلْقِصَاصُ فِى ٱلْقَتْلَى (The law of equality is prescribed to you in cases of murder [Qur'ān 2:178]), which indicates through its plain meaning that there is *qiṣāṣ* for homicide. The plain meaning in the latter text is preferred over the indication in the former.

Conflict between *ishārat al-naṣṣ* and *dalālat al-naṣṣ*. In the words of the Allah, وَمَن يَقْتُلْ مُؤْمِنًا مُّتَعَمِّدًا فَجَزَآؤُهُۥ جَهَنَّمُ خَـٰلِدًا فِيهَا, the *ishārat al-naṣṣ* indicates that there is no *kaffārah* (expiation) in murder (*qatl 'amd*). In the words of the Exalted, وَمَن قَتَلَ مُؤْمِنًا خَطَـًٔا فَتَحْرِيرُ رَقَبَةٍ مُّؤْمِنَةٍ وَدِيَةٌ مُّسَلَّمَةٌ إِلَىٰٓ أَهْلِهِۦٓ (And whoever kills a believer by mistake it is ordained that he should free a believing slave and pay blood money to the deceased's family [Qur'ān 4:92]) however, it is implied through *dalālat al-naṣṣ* that there should be *kaffārah* in intentional homicide as well. The Ḥanafīs preferring *ishārat al-naṣṣ* over *dalālat al-naṣṣ* say that there is no liability of expiation in murder.

Conflict between *'ibārat al-naṣṣ* and *iqtiḍā' al-naṣṣ*. In the words of Allah, the Exalted, وَمَن قَتَلَ مُؤْمِنًا خَطَـًٔا فَتَحْرِيرُ رَقَبَةٍ مُّؤْمِنَةٍ وَدِيَةٌ مُّسَلَّمَةٌ إِلَىٰٓ أَهْلِهِۦٓ (And whoever kills a believer by mistake it is ordained that he should free a believing slave and pay blood money to the deceased's family [Qur'ān 4:92]) it is implied through *'ibārat al-naṣṣ* that there is liability in the case of *qatl khaṭa'* (involuntary manslaughter). The tradition from the Prophet (peace be on him), إنّ الله رفع عن أمّتي الخطأ والنسيان وما استكرهوا عليه (Allah has removed from my *ummah* (the liability arising from) mistake, forgetfulness and what they have been coerced into doing) implies through *iqtiḍā' al-naṣṣ* that there is no liability at all in the case of mistake. The former meaning is preferred over the latter.

21.2.2.6 Literal methods of proving the *ḥukm* considered *fāsid* (irregular) by the Ḥanafīs, but practised by the others

Al-Sarakhsī describes a number of methods that are practised by other jurists, but are not permitted by the Ḥanafīs. Some of these can be understood after the study of this section is complete. The most important of these is *mafhūm mukhālafah* or the opposite meaning of the *ḥukm* proved by a text. This is explained in the following section.

21.2.3 The literal methods of establishing the *aḥkām* practised by the Shāfi'īs

According to al-Ghazālī, the Shāfi'īs divide the methods for proving the *aḥkām* into two types:

1. Through the syntax and grammatical form of the text also referred to as *manṭūq* or explicit meaning.

2. Through implications other than the syntactical meaning also referred to as *ghayr manṭūq* or the implied meaning.

21.2.3.1 *Dalālat al-ṣīghah* or proving the *ḥukm* through the syntax

Dalālat al-ṣīghah as conceived by the Shāfiʿīs has the same meaning as *ʿibārat al-naṣṣ* or the plain meaning rule according to the Ḥanafīs. The majority of the *aḥkām* are proved through this method. This has been explained in detail above.

21.2.3.2 *Dalālat al-lafẓ bi-ghayr al-ṣīghah* or proving the *ḥukm* through means other than the plain meaning

According to the Shāfiʿīs, the *ḥukm* may be proved in six ways when the jurist is not focusing on the plain meaning rule or the meaning obvious through the syntax. These methods are as follows:

1. *Iqtiḍāʾ* (implicit meaning)
2. *Ishārah* (indication)
3. *Īmāʾ* (indication of compatibility)
4. *Mafhūm al-muwāfaq* (compatible higher-order meanings)
5. *Mafhūm al-mukhālaf* (opposite meaning)
6. *Maʿqūl* (rationalised meaning)

A brief description of each of these methods is given below.

Iqtiḍā. It is a meaning that is not explicit in the text, but is implicit. A word or meaning has to be implied in the text so as to make the text meaningful or to make its meaning complete for acting upon it. It is similar to the Ḥanafī method called *iqtidāʾ al-naṣṣ* with the difference that here the meaning of *maḥdhūf* or an implied word is also possible, unlike the Ḥanafī method.

Ishārah. This method again is similar to the Ḥanafī method of *ishārat al-naṣṣ*, and examples have been stated above.

Īmā'. This method is not used so much for the derivation of the *ḥukm* as for the understanding of the *'illah* or underlying cause of the text. For example, in the words of the Allah, السارق والسارقة فاقطعوا أيديهما (the thieves, male and female, cut off their hands), the plain meaning is that there is an obligation to apply the penalty of amputation. In addition to this meaning it is implied by the text that the underlying cause of such a *ḥukm* is the act of theft.

Mafhūm muwāfaq. It is a meaning not explicitly stated in the text, but which is understood from the intention and object of the Lawgiver. This method is more or less similar to the meaning of *dalālat al-naṣṣ*. It is referred to as *qiyās al-ma'nā*, a movement from a lower-order to a higher-order meaning, *qiyās jalī*, and *faḥwā al-khiṭāb* (implication of the address). According to the Shāfi'ī system, then, this is not a literal method of proving the *aḥkām* and really belongs to the area of analogy.

Mafhūm al-mukhālafah. This is a method of proving a *ḥukm* through the opposite meaning of the *ḥukm* explicitly mentioned in the text. It is also called *dalīl al-khiṭāb* or an indirect evidence of the communication (from the Lawgiver). As stated earlier, the Ḥanafīs reject this method of proving the *ḥukm*. The Shāfi'īs, on the other hand, classify it into several categories: *mafhūm al-ṣifah; mafhūm al-sharṭ; mafhūm al-ghāyah; mafhūm al-'adad;* and *mafhūm al-laqab*. Some examples are given below.

- *mafhūm al-ṣifah* means the opposite of an attribute that helps identify a category. In the tradition, في السائمة الزكاة (there is *zakāt* in pasturing animals) the plain meaning makes pasturing animals liable to *zakāt*. The opposite meaning is that there is no *zakāt* in non-pasturing animals. In the verse,

  ومن لم يستطع منكم طولا أن ينكح المحصنات المؤمنات فمن مّا ملكت أيمانكم
  من فتياتكم المؤمنات

  (If any of you have not the means wherewith to wed free believing women, they may wed believing girls from among those whom your right hands possess [Qur'ān 4:25]) the plain meaning is the permissibility of marrying believing slave girls when there is inability to marry free women, but the opposite meaning is that there is no permission for marrying non-believing slave girls.

- When a *ḥukm* is suspended on the fulfilment of a condition, the absence of the condition indicates the existence of the opposite *ḥukm*. This is called *mafhūm al-sharṭ*. In the same verse above, as the condition for marrying believing slave girls is the existence of the inability to marry free women, the rule would be that when an ability to marry free women exists believing slave girls cannot be married.

- *Mafhūm al-ghāyah* means that when a limit imposed by a *ḥukm* in the text is over the opposite *ḥukm* is invoked. For example, the command is to eat and drink during Ramaḍān till the white of the dawn is visible. As soon as this limit is reached the opposite *ḥukm*, that is, prohibition of eating and drinking is invoked.

- *Mafhūm al-'adad* means that if a determined number is mentioned in the *ḥukm*, the *ḥukm* for other than that number is not valid. Thus, if the specified *ḥadd* in the texts is 80 or 100 stripes, a number other than these numbers cannot be specified as *ḥadd*.

- *Mafhūm al-laqab*. If the *ḥukm* is associated with a proper noun, the *ḥukm* for all others is the opposite. For example, when the text says, "Muḥammad is the Messenger of Allah," it means that no one else can be a messenger of Allah. When the text says, "Prohibited for you are your mothers...," it means that all persons not mentioned are permitted.

The majority of the schools reject *mafhūm al-laqab;* it is only the Shāfi'īs who use it. All schools, other than the Ḥanafīs, accept the remaining four types of *mafhūm al-mukhālafah* mentioned above.

The *mafhūm al-mukhālafah* is linked with a rule of interpretation pertaining to the command (*amr*). The Shāfi'īs maintain that "a command (*amr*) to do something means the proscription (*nahy*) of its opposite." The Ḥanafīs reject this.

Ma'qūl. The term *ma'qūl* is used here to mean extension of the meaning in the text through all rational means. In this sense, it includes extension of the law in the text through analogy, *maṣlaḥah mursalah*, and all the other rational sources acceptable to the majority of the schools. These rational sources have been studied in *uṣūl al-fiqh*.

It should be obvious from the above discussion that three of the above six methods approved by the Shāfi'īs belong to the second mode of *ijtihād* and are not really literal methods; one of these overlaps with the third mode as well.

21.2.4 *Amr* (command) and *nahy* (proscription): the nature and type of *ḥukm* established

The main purpose of the jurist in interpreting the texts is to see if a *ḥukm* has been laid down. If a *ḥukm* is laid down what is its nature? Is it obligatory or recommended or permissible? Once this is known, the *ḥukm* can be followed by the subject. Most of the *aḥkām* are known through commands and proscriptions in the texts. The jurist has to recognise these commands and proscriptions and to gauge their exact implications, before he can say with assurance that such and such is the rule of Islamic law. The command (*amr*) is discussed first.

21.2.4.1 The command (*amr*) and its rules

A command is usually expressed in the form of the imperative, "do this (افعل)," or in the present tense or in the form of reports (predicate) in the text from which a command is construed. Thus, commands are like: "Establish prayer," "Obey Allah and obey the Messenger," "He who witnesses the month should spend it in fasting," "Mothers suckle their children for two complete years."

Does the command necessitate obligation? The jurists have to decide upon an initial presumption with respect to the command.

This means that when they read a command in the text does this command always create an obligation? Is the resulting *ḥukm* always a *wājib* (obligatory) or is it recommended (*mandūb*) or permissible (*mubāḥ*)? There are other possibilities too, like instruction, disciplining and so on.

Some jurists say that when we read a command we will always assume that initially an obligation is created, but we can change this obligation into a recommendation or permissibility if this is indicated by an accompanying text or some other evidence. There are others who say that we will initially assume a recommendation, but we will change it to obligation if another evidence indicates this. Others take the initial presumption to be permissibility.

From this a rule of interpretation is created, like الأمر للوجوب (The command necessitates an obligation). This is also known as the *ḥukm* or the *amr* or the rule to be followed for the command. The jurists who follow this rule mean that the initial assumption is obligation to be changed if another evidence indicates a different meaning. Whatever the rule adopted by the school, it is followed consistently by such school.

Does a command initially imply the repetition of an act? If an act is commanded in the text does it imply that the act has to be repeated, for example, the command for the evening prayer. Does it mean that the prayer has to be said every evening. In this case it is obvious that it has to be repeated, but there may be cases in which it may not be so clear. Here too the jurist is concerned with the initial presumption. Should the act commanded be assumed to be repetitive or for a single instance alone?

The general rule is that initially a command will be interpreted for a single performance, but if another evidence indicates that repetition is implied then such repetition will be construed.

Does a command imply immediate or delayed compliance? This pertains to commands for the performance of which an extended period is provided. For example, the *ẓuhr prayer* for which a period is provided that is more than that required for its performance, unlike the evening prayer for which the time provided is just sufficient. If the obligation created by the command is connected to the initial part of this extended time, a person leaving on a journey after the initial time cannot curtail his prayer, because he has already become liable for the complete prayer. If, on the other hand, the command is related to the last part of the period, then, he can curtail his prayer, because he is not yet liable for the complete prayer.

21.2.4.2 The proscription (*nahy*) and its rules

The rules for the proscription (*nahy*) are almost identical to those of *amr*. Thus, the rule for *nahy* may be: النهي للتحريم (The proscription necessitates prohibition). This is also called the *ḥukm* of the proscription or the rule to be followed for it. The other issues are also the same, that is, whether it requires immediate or delayed compliance and whether it requires a constant abstention from the act or a one time omission.

21.2.5 The number or categories affected by the *ḥukm*: *'āmm*; *khāṣṣ*; *mushtarak*; and *mu'awwal*

After determining that a *ḥukm* exists in the texts, the jurist is concerned with the number or categories of acts that are affected by the *ḥukm* or the categories of persons who are affected or even the categories of objects. This depends on whether the words used in the text are general (*'āmm*) or specific (*khāṣṣ*) or whether they are equivocal (*mushtarak*). The specific word has further types: *muṭlaq* (indeterminate) and *muqayyad* (determined). *Amr* and *nahy* are also treated as types of the specific word, but we have dealt with them separately.

21.2.5.1 The specific word (*khāṣṣ*), its types and rules

A word that is by design meant to be applied to a single thing, class, or genus is said to be a specific word. The main attribute of the specific word is that **a limit comes to the mind.** This shows that a specific word has three types:

- **Applied to proper nouns.** The specific word includes proper names or nouns like Zayd or Muḥammad. This is limited to a single person.

- **Applied to mean common collective nouns.** In this sense the specific word is applied to collective nouns like "man," "woman," "horse." All these are in very large numbers yet the word conveys a limit. Thus, "man" means all men, whatever their number.

- **Applied to mean generic nouns.** The specific word can also be applied to mean a genus or a generic noun. For example, the word *insān* in the meaning of "Man," that is, all mankind.

Whatever the type of noun used, in a specific word **the numbers are limited.** The *ḥukm* of the specific word is that it applies to the thing named definitively. According to most jurists, the *ḥukm* of the specific word (*khāṣṣ*) requires the identification of the meaning of the word and thereafter it requires that the subject act upon what it has been used for in the language, unless an evidence indicates that it has been used in the figurative sense.

Types of *khāṣṣ*: *muṭlaq* and *muqayyad*. A derivative noun or an adjective used as a noun is called the *sifah,* for example, the word murderer. This may be indeterminate, because we cannot answer the question: which murderer? The reason is that there are a number of murderers and we do not know which one is intended. Such a word is called an absolute word or an indeterminate word (*muṭlaq*). When the meaning of an indeterminate word is limited or determined it is called *muqayyad* or the determinate word. Thus, if we can limit the use of the word "murderer" to tall or short or old or young or the like, we will know which murderer is intended. Thus, when the words of the Qur'ān say, "Prohibited for you are carrion, blood, and the flesh of swine," it is not clear which type of blood is intended, because some blood is left inside an animal even after slaughtering. The word is *muṭlaq* in this sense. Another text, therefore, points out that it is "flowing blood," that is, blood that flowed out of the animal after slaughter.

21.2.5.2 The equivocal word (*mushtarak*)

The *mushtarak* (equivocal word) includes more than one meaning with the likelihood that it can apply to any of these meanings. It may be noted that Abdur Rahim has preferred the word "homonym" for the *mushtarak*. The term homonym does include the meaning of *mushtarak*, but it can also mean separate words with the same sound, like the words "bear" and "bare." The term is, therefore, being avoided here. When the jurist ponders over the meaning of the equivocal word, he comes to discover that it really applies to a single meaning. This single selected meaning is called *mu'awwal*, which literally means returning a thing to its origin.

According to the Ḥanafīs, the rule for the *mushtarak* is suspension of decision till such time that the meaning becomes obvious through elaboration—on the belief that what is intended is the truth. They stipulate that the search for the meaning is to be continued either through contemplation or through reliance upon another evidence, because the words of the Wise Lord are not devoid of meaning.

As regards the *mu'awwal* the Ḥanafīs say: the *mu'awwal* is to be acted upon in the same manner that the *ẓāhir* is acted upon, except that the obligation of acting upon a manifest (*ẓāhir*) meaning is established through a definitive implication, while the obligation to act upon the *mu'awwal* is established through an implication that also conveys the likelihood of its being wrong. Thus, it is not definitive and has the same weight as that of the *khabar wāḥid*.

21.2.5.3 The general word (*'āmm*)

According to the jurists, the general word is one that applies to all the things included in its meaning, and in such meaning **no limit on the number comes to mind.** Thus, the word "men" is general in the sense that it includes a large number of men, but no limit comes to mind. Likewise, the words "who (من)" and "what (ما)" convey general meanings, but no limit comes to mind. There are a large number of literal forms listed by the jurists that convey generality, and this can be understood from the form of words and the implications of meaning.

The Ḥanafīs say that the general word establishes a *ḥukm* for all that it includes (in its meaning) with a certainty, just as the particular word establishes the *ḥukm* for its meaning, except in those forms where the generality cannot be assigned due to the absence of the object; in such a case the *ḥukm* is suspended till the meaning is elaborated (through *bayān*) by making the undetailed meaning apparent.

According to al-Shāfi'ī the general word does not pass on the *ḥukm* to all its categories with a certainty, because when we use a general word it probably includes everything it is suitable for and not certainly. For example, if we say "the wind destroyed everything," we know that the wind cannot destroy everything.

Restriction (*takhṣīṣ*) of the general word. The general word, like the specific word, is definitive according to the Ḥanafīs. In other words, the application of the *ḥukm* to all its meanings is definitive. This makes its restriction more difficult. It requires an evidence as strong as the general word to restrict it. According, to the Shāfi'īs, the general word is *ẓannī*, therefore, it can be restricted with a probable evidence.

When the general word is restricted in meaning it remains a persuasive proof for the *ḥukm* in the meaning that remains after the restriction, irrespective of whether such remaining meaning is known or unknown, however, some doubt creeps into it so that its implication for the *ḥukm* is no longer definitive and certain.

21.2.6 The clarity or ambiguity with which the *ḥukm* is established

The types of words used for increasing clarity are four: *ẓāhir* (manifest); *naṣṣ* (explicit); *mufassar* (elaborated); *muḥkam* (unalterably fixed). These have opposites in the meaning of increasing ambiguity: *khafī* (obscure); *mushkil* (difficult); *mujmal* (unelaborated); and *mutashābih* (unintelligible). The information generated by these categories is employed by the jurists in *tarjīḥ* (preference) and in determining the strength of the *ḥukm*. Brief explanations of these meanings along with their rules are given below.

1. The *ẓāhir* (manifest) is a word whose meaning is apparent by a simple reading and no further effort is required to understand it. It is the first meaning that comes to mind on reading the text. The rule for the *ẓāhir* is that it is binding in nature and is definitive whether it is *'āmm* or *khāṣṣ*.

2. The explicit word or *naṣṣ* is one whose meaning becomes even more clear than the *ẓāhir*, because of the accompanying evidence from the speaker, and that such clarity would not be forthcoming but for the evidence. The impact is the same as the *ẓāhir*, but its meaning is clearer due to the speech of the speaker. Thus, it is stronger than the *ẓāhir* in conveying the *ḥukm*.

3. The *mufassar* is a word for an uncovered meaning whose content has been discovered in a manner that leaves no room for any further *ta'wīl* (interpretation). This gives it an even greater clarity than the *ẓāhir* and the *naṣṣ*. The *ḥukm* of the *mufassar* is an excess over *naṣṣ* and *ẓāhir*—it is definitive and does not admit of *ta'wīl*, but there is a possibility of abrogation.

4. The *muḥkam* is a word that is clearer in meaning than all the above and along with this it is not subject to abrogation or change. As a proof for establishing the *aḥkām* it is the strongest.

The types of meanings in order of obscurity are as follows:

1. The obscure word or *khafī* is one whose meaning is concealed and the intention is unclear due a deficiency in the form (in which it is used), which prevents the discovery of the meaning except by investigation. The *ḥukm* of *khafī* is the belief in the truth of the intended meaning and the obligation of investigating the intended meaning until it is elaborated.

2. The *mushkil* or the difficult word is the opposite of *naṣṣ*. It is a word whose meaning is difficult to discover except by another evidence that removes the remaining ambiguity. *Mushkil* is close to the *mujmal*. Its *ḥukm* is the belief in the truth of the intended meaning and the obligation to search for the meaning till such meaning is elaborated.

3. The *mujmal* or the unelaborated word is the opposite of *mufassar*. It is a word whose meaning is not known, except through a commentary of the elaborating evidences by way of *bayān* (see the meaning of *bayān* above) so that the meaning becomes known. *Hukm:* Belief in the truth of the meaning and suspension of decision in it till the elaborating evidence is found and the meaning is explained.

4. The unintelligible or the *mutashābih* is a term in which all hope of knowing the Lawgiver's intention is cut off. The *ḥukm* is belief in its being true, the giving up of further investigation, and the suspension of decision about its intention.

21.2.7 The effect of the use of words in the actual or metaphorical meanings

All words are first examined for whether they have been used in accordance with their actual application (*ḥaqīqah*) or they have been used in the figurative sense (*majāz*). Each such application may be clear in such application (*sarīḥ*) or it may be allusive (*kināyah*). It is not possible to go into the details here. The rules for such use alone are stated below.

Ḥaqīqah is a the application of a term for the known original thing to which it is usually applied. *Majāz* is the application of a term that is borrowed for application to a thing other than the thing for which it was designed. The *ḥukm* of *ḥaqīqah* is the acceptance of the existence of that to which it is applied whether it is *amr, nahy, khāṣṣ* or *'āmm*. The *ḥukm* of *majāz* is the acceptance of the existence of that for which it is borrowed whether this is *khāṣṣ* or *'āmm*.

The *ṣarīḥ* is every word whose meaning is laid bare and the intention behind its use is uncovered whether the intention is *ḥaqīqah* or *majāz*. *Kināyah* (allusion) is the opposite of this, and it is a word whose meaning is veiled, unless it is elaborated by a *dalīl*.

The actual (*ḥaqīqah*) application is given up in favour of five cases: *dalālat al-Isti'māl 'urfan* (technical legal usage); *dalālat al-lafẓ; siyāq al-naẓm* (syntax); the attribute of the speaker; and *maḥall al-kalām* (context).

It is to be noted that all speech is composed of names, verbs, and *ḥurūf*. *Ḥaqīqah* and *majāz* are operative not only in nouns and verbs, but also in *ḥurūf*.

Review Questions

1. Elaborate the concept of *bayān* as understood by the *uṣūlīs*.
2. The integral bond between the Qur'ān and the *Sunnah* can never be severed. Elaborate.
3. What are the different types of *bayān* and what do they mean with reference to interpretation?
4. Describe in general terms how the literal interpretation of the texts takes place.
5. Elaborate the structure of interpretion in the context of the *dalālāt*.
6. What is meant by the *dalālāt* and how do they reveal the *aḥkām*?
7. What is the strength of the *aḥkām* proved by the *dalālāt*?
8. Compare the *dalālāt* with the rules of interpretation (legislative presumptions) in law.
9. *Dalālat al-naṣṣ* is the same thing as *qiyās al-ma'nā*. Comment.
10. *Qiyās* cannot be undertaken for the criminal law, but *dalālat al-naṣṣ* can be used for it. Comment.

11. How is preference undertaken within the *dalālāt*?
12. What are the substitutes for the *dalālāt* according to the majority schools, other than the Ḥanafīs?
13. How are *amr* and *nahī* interpreted for establishing the *aḥkām*?
14. Define the terms *'āmm, khāṣṣ, mushtarak* and *mu'awwal.*
15. Define the terms relevant to the clarity and the ambiguity with which the *aḥkām* are established.

22 The Second Mode of *Ijtihād*: Reasoning by Analogy

The nature and meaning of *qiyās* has already been explained in Part Two. The purpose here is to understand it in relation to *ijtihād*. As stated earlier, the jurist employs the second mode of *ijtihād* when the first mode of literal interpretation does not cover the case faced by him. The first thing to understand, therefore, is the relationship between the first mode of *ijtihād* and the second, that is, how does the jurist move from the first to the second mode.

22.1 Moving From the First Mode of *Ijtihād* to the Second

The movement from the first mode of *ijtihād* to the second is understood through three types of meaning that a text may imply. The details have been explained by Ibn Rushd in his book *Bidāyat al-Mujtahid* and are summarised below.

Ibn Rushd says that the meaning of *qiyās*, and hence this mode of *ijtihād*, is understood in simple terms by examining three orders of meaning. These are: the higher-order meaning; the lower-order meaning; and the equivalent meaning. These meanings have already been explained as three types of analogy.

1. The example of a higher-order meaning is like saying "fie (أف)" to parents. If saying "fie" is prohibited, then, other higher-order acts like beating them and other forms of abuse are definitely prohibited. This is not *qiyās* according to the Ḥanafīs, because the meanings like beating and abuse are implied by the literal meaning of the text. We saw earlier that they called it *dalālat al-naṣṣ*. The Shāfiʿīs, however, consider it *qiyās al-maʿnā*, the strongest type of analogy.

2. The lower-order meaning may be explained through the example of *ribā* in food items. A tradition from the Prophet (peace be on him) mentions four food items. The question is can these meanings be extended to other things. If the attribute of food in wheat is to be found in a water-melon, there should be no problem in including a water-melon under the prohibition of *ribā* on the basis of "food-value" as the underlying cause of prohibition. We find, however, that wheat has other attributes that may serve as the *ʿillah,* like measure, weight, and the quality of being preserved. Some of these qualities are not found in the water-melon. Wheat, thus, has more attributes, and these attributes are missing in a water-melon. If the water-melon is included in the meaning of food for purposes of *ribā,* it would be a movement from a higher-order meaning to a lower order meaning, from more attributes to a lesser number of attributes. This is considered analogy by the Shāfiʿīs alone, but the others reject it. The others call it *qiyās maʿ al-fāriq,* that is, analogy in which a distinctive attribute is missing.

3. There may be cases where we can neither find a higher-order meaning or a lower-order meaning. What we do in such cases is that we extend the meaning to all equivalent meanings. This is the real meaning of *qiyās* and is sometimes

called *qiyās al-'illah.* Analogy is undertaken in this form by discovering an underlying cause for the *ḥukm* in the text and an identical cause in the case faced by the jurist. *Qiyās,* then, is the transference of the *ḥukm* not to higher-order meanings or lower-order meanings, but to equivalent meanings.

The method of discovering equivalent meanings is not based on literal methods. Equivalent meanings are those that serve as the underlying causes of the *ḥukm.* In technical terms, such a meaning is called the *'illah.* The underlying meaning for which a *ḥukm* has been laid down is first determined. The new case faced by the jurist is then examined to see whether it carries within it a similar meaning. If it does, the *ḥukm* is assigned to the new case. If we have two metals, say gold and platinum, there is no way we can say gold and also mean platinum. The underlying meaning in gold and silver may be determined as precious metal as far as the rules of *ribā* are concerned. If we say precious metal, however, the term covers gold, silver, platinum, and other precious metals. Take the case of salt among the food items mentioned in the tradition of *ribā.* One jurist may say that the common meaning is food, another may say that it is food that can be preserved, while a third may say that if salt is subject to *ribā* then other important foods should be subject to *ribā.* The first two jurists would be talking about equivalent meanings, while the third would be talking about extending a lower-order meaning to a higher-order meaning.

The Shāfi'īs, as already stated, consider the three types of extension, through different orders of meaning, as different types of *qiyās.* The Ḥanafīs, on the other hand, call the first *dalālat al-naṣṣ* or the implication of the text, the second as *qiyās ma' al-fāriq,* and the third as regular *qiyās.* **The second mode of *ijtihād,* according to the Shāfi'īs would include all three, but according to the Ḥanafīs it is confined to the equivalent methods alone.**

22.2 The Methods of Discovering the Underlying Cause (*Masālik al-'Illah*)

The first task for a jurist reasoning on the basis of analogy is to find the underlying cause or the *'illah.* Without the *'illah* analogy is not possible. The jurists have identified detailed methods for the identification of causes of the *aḥkām* in the texts. These are called *masālik al-'illah* or the methods for discovering the underlying cause. They are summarised below.

1. **The text (*naṣṣ*).** The text itself may indicate the underlying cause of the *ḥukm* it contains. This would be the strongest type of *'illah.* The indication in the text, however, may not be explicit. It may be indicated through pointer (*īmā'*) or other hint. The express words are usually "because of this (لأجل ذلك) or "so that (كي)" and many others. An example is:

   كي لا يكون دولة بين الأغنياء منكم

   So that it does not make a circuit between the rich among you. [Qur'ān 59 : 7]

   One case of *īmā'* is when the *'illah* is followed by "fā" (فاء) as in:

   السارق والسارقة فاقطعوا أيديهما

   The thief, male and female, cut off their hands.[Qur'ān 5 : 38]

   This shows that the cause of cutting of the hand is theft (*sariqah*).

2. ***Ijmā'.*** The underlying cause may be determined through consensus. For example, the *'illah* of guardianship over wealth is determined by consensus to be "minority." From this it was extended to other cases as well.

3. **Derivation of the *'illah* (*takhrīj al-manāṭ*).** When the underlying cause is not indicated directly by the text or by *ijmā'*, the jurist derives the cause through *ijtihād.* This is called the derivation of the *'illah* or *takhrīj al-manāṭ,* where *manāṭ* is something on which another thing is suspended or hung. The following methods are used for this:

   a) *Munāsabah* (suitability). The jurist may have a number of attributes in mind that can possibly be designated as the cause of the *ḥukm.* He checks these attributes against the *ḥikmah* of the *ḥukm* or even against the ultimate *ḥikam,* that is, the purposes of the law. If the cause does not clash with these values, or is complementary to them, he selects it as the underlying cause. For example, intoxication is deemed to be a suitable *'illah* for drinking wine, because it attacks the intellect and preservation of the intellect is a purpose of the *sharī'ah.* In reality, suitability or *munāsabah* takes us into the third mode of *ijtihād,* because it yields an underlying cause that is based on the *ḥikmah* (wisdom) and cannot possibly meet all the conditions that have been laid down for the underlying cause in its definition.

   b) *Dawrān.* This means the co-existence of the *ḥukm* and an attribute, that is, whenever the attribute is found the *ḥukm* is found too. Grapes and grape juice are consumed as food although wine is made from them. The jurist finds that whenever grape juice develops the attribute of intoxication it is prohibited. He, therefore, selects intoxication as the cause.

   c) *Sabr and taqsīm.* This is a process of elimination of attributes through division and testing of the attributes. *Sabr* means testing and *taqsīm* means splitting up or division. Taking the case of *khamr* again, assuming that the text "each intoxicant is *khamr*" is not known, the jurist finds that wine is a liquid, it is made of grapes, it gives off a peculiar smell, and it is an intoxicant. As the jurist is looking for a stable cause that does alter with circumstances and can be extended, he eliminates all the attributes one by one after testing them and is left with intoxication as the underlying cause. For example, the attribute of being made from grapes and peculiar smell cannot be extended to others, and being a liquid cannot be extended either, he is left with intoxication.

22.2.1 Discovering the cause in the new case: *taḥqīq al-manāṭ*

After the discovery of the underlying cause for the *ḥukm* in the *aṣl,* the jurist turns towards the underlying cause in the new case. This is called the verification of the *'illah* in the *far'* or *taḥqīq al-manāṭ*. Generally, the verification of the underling cause in the new case does not need a *mujtahid.* For example, if a new drink is invented and we need to find out whether it is an intoxicant or not, a pharmacist may perform a better job than a *mujtahid.* Some jurists, including al-Shāfi'ī, consider this as *ijtihād* too. Al-Shāṭibī says that this type of *ijtihād* can never stop. The reason is obvious: it does not need a *mujtahid.*

22.3 Analogy and the Modern Jurist

Qiyās al-'illah (syllogism) usually called analogy is a very strict method of interpretation. As compared to this *qiyās al-shabah* is a more flexible type of analogy that is used by some jurists and rejected by most. It does not involve the mapping of the *'illah* in two parallel cases with the precision that is required in *qiyās al-'illah.* In his introduction to *Bidāyat al-Mujtahid*, Ibn Rushd implies that though there is great emphasis on *qiyās al-'illah,* in practice one finds many jurists employing *qiyās al-shabah,* that is, basing their reasoning on a general resemblance rather than discovering the specific *'illah.*

Nevertheless, we find that the earlier jurists have worked very hard for discovering the underlying causes of the *aḥkām.* There is hardly a case in the texts whose underlying cause, where one is to be found, has not been derived by the earlier jurists. In fact, in many cases one will find not one but several underlying causes for a single *ḥukm*. The modern jurist, who plans to reinterpret the texts for his times, will find a tremendous task facing him in his search for new underlying causes. In many if not most cases, he will have to choose between the various underlying causes determined by the jurists. While we are not implying that the discovery of new underlying causes is impossible, we are definitely implying that this will not be an easy task. It would be very good if some able researcher were to catalogue all the established underlying causes (*'ilal*). The first mode of *ijtihād* is no different. It is for this reason that we find the modern jurists picking and choosing opinions out of the work of the earlier jurists. As compared to these two modes, the third mode of *ijtihād* has been used sparingly in Islamic law. The jurists do rely on the earlier precedents to justify its legality, but the truth is that by the time (of al-Shāṭibī when) it was refined as a methodology, the Muslim nations were ready to fall prey to colonialism. The field is lying wide open for the modern jurist.

Review Questions

1. What are the different orders of meaning in the texts as explained by Ibn Rushd?

2. What are the different methods for discovering the underlying causes (*'ilal*) in the texts?

3. What is the meaning of *taḥqīq al-manāt* and how is it related to *qiyās*?

4. What do you understand by *qiyās al-shabah*?

23 The Third Mode of *Ijtihād:* Employing the *Maqāṣid al-Sharī'ah*

Qiyās is the finding of an exact parallel and it cannot meet all the needs of the jurist in solving the multitude of cases faced by him. The jurist needs to move to a more flexible and broader methods to meet his needs. The nature of these broader methods is understood if we examine the difference between *qiyās* and the wider methods. To explain this difference, we have to understand how the jurist moves from the second to the third mode of *ijtihād*. The explanation is provided through the example of *khamr*[322] insofar as it takes us from the second mode of *ijtihād* to the third mode.

322. The reader may wonder why the example of *khamr* is used all the time. The reason is that it has been constructed for instructional purposes. In reality, many jurists would say that you cannot use analogy or another method for extending the criminal law, because it violates the principle of legality. The Ḥanafīs, for instance, do not permit the use of analogy in the criminal law. Yet, it must be noted that analogy has not been used by them for creating new offences, but it has been used for giving relief in existing offences.

23.1 Moving From the Second Mode of *Ijtihād* to the Third: the *'Illah* and the *Ḥikmah*

The word *khamr* in its literal sense means wine made from grape juice. If we stay with this literal meaning we may not be able to apply the *ḥukm* of prohibition to other intoxicants like whiskey, gin, beer and so on, things that have not been made from grape juice. This is true if we examine the texts of the Qur'ān alone and do not look at traditions. The problem of extending the *ḥukm* of *khamr* to other intoxicants is presented below in the form of a dialogue between a Shāfi'ī jurist and a Ḥanafī jurist. (The example is hypothetical, and it is to be noted that *qiyās* cannot be used to extend the law of crimes, as it is against the principle of legality upheld in the criminal law).

Shāfi'ī: The word *khamr* is a generic term whose meaning is either *khimār* (from *khimār al-mar'ah* or the veil of a woman). Thus, everything that puts a veil over the mind or beclouds the mind is covered by this term and is thus prohibited. On the other hand, the meaning could also be derived from *khamīr* or *takhmīr,* which means fermentation. The word, therefore, applies to every liquor prepared through fermentation. With this meaning the *ḥukm* can be extended either literally to all higher-order and lower-order meanings, and even to equivalent meanings, thus, prohibiting all liquors not mentioned in the *ḥukm* by name.

Ḥanafī: *Khamr* is not a generic term; it is just a name like any other name: Asad (lion), Shayr (lion) Khān[323] and so on. When names are given to things or persons, it is not because of some inherent quality or attribute in such things or persons; they are assigned only for identification and not for extension by law to other things with the same qualities.

Shāfi'ī: I disagree. Names can be extended through their underlying meanings, but even if it is conceded that they

323. A name very common in the northern parts of Pakistan, and used by Rudyard Kipling for the Bengal tiger; Shayr means lion/tiger.

cannot, we do not face a problem in the case of *khamr.* All we have to do is to discover the underlying cause (*'illah*) and extend it through analogy. The underlying cause is "intoxication" and this meaning enables us to extend the *ḥukm* to all intoxicants, that is, all things with an equivalent meaning or *'illah.* Each beverage that intoxicates can be given the *ḥukm* of *khamr.*

Ḥanafī: Intoxication or being an intoxicant is not a valid *'illah* for *khamr.* Had this been the *'illah,* only intoxication from *khamr* would be prohibited; drinking a drop or a small quantity would not have been prohibited, because this does not intoxicate. We see, however, that such small quantities are prohibited in case of *khamr* even though they do not intoxicate. The truth is that *khamr* is prohibited for itself, it has no *'illah.* Intoxication, on the other hand, is prohibited separately by other texts. As *khamr* is prohibited for itself we are not permitted to drink even a drop.

Shāfi'ī: We still think that intoxication is a valid *'illah* for *khamr,* and drinking of small quantities is prohibited, because it leads to addiction and the consumption of more and more.

Ḥanafī: Now you are not talking about the *'illah* (underlying cause) of *khamr,* but about the *ḥikmah* (underlying wisdom). *Ḥikmah,* as you know cannot be a valid *'illah,* because it cannot be a stable cause. It varies from person to person and with circumstances. (The Ḥanafī jurist is saying that you are no longer in the mode where *qiyās* or finding an exact parallel is used).

Shāfi'ī: We also know that wine and gambling lead to enmity, hatred and ultimate corruption. This appears to be a powerful and convincing reason to prohibit *khamr,* and even a drop of *khamr.* Intoxication, therefore, appears to be a suitable *'illah* that conforms with other practices of law.

Ḥanafī: You have now moved to the higher genera of causes and are no longer talking about regular *qiyās,* which we call *qiyās al-'illah.*

The dialogue shows that *qiyās* or the second mode of *ijtihād* is based upon reasoning from a determined stable cause that is suitable for becoming an *'illah.* The stable cause is used to extend the rule to an exact parallel. The third mode of *ijtihād,* on the other hand, is based on reasoning from general principles based on the *ḥikmah* or wisdom of the underlying rule.

23.2 The Interplay Between General Principles and the *Maqāṣid al-Sharī'ah*

The previous discussion shows that the moment the jurist starts using the *ḥikmah* or the wisdom underlying the texts for the extension of legal rules, he is not practising *qiyās,* but a much wider methodology. Most general principles are based on the *ḥikmah* of the laws and it is through these general principles that the jurist extends the law through a methodology that we have called the third mode of *ijtihād.*

To understand the third mode of *ijtihād* we have to understand fully the meaning of general principles. We also have to see how general principles are formed in Islamic law.

A general principle in Islamic law is a generalised explanation for the *'illah.* Take a simple example of the curtailment of prayer during journey. Islamic law permits the curtailment of prayer or even the postponing of the fast to anyone proceeding on a journey. The underlying cause (*'illah*) for this rule is "journey." This is a stable cause, which means that it will not change according to circumstances or vary with persons. It does not matter to this cause whether it is raining, or is very hot, or the weather is very pleasant. The rule will remain the same or stable for everyone. It also does not matter to this rule if someone is travelling by plane or railway or on horseback or on foot; the rule for journey will always remain the same.

A little reflection reveals, however, that the underlying wisdom of this rule of curtailment of prayer, while on a journey, is that a traveller usually faces some hardship (*mashaqqah*). Focusing on this wisdom, we can draw broad generalisation: *Whenever the subjects face hardship, the law will grant some exemption.* This generalisation is an explanation for the exemption given by the law. It tells us that on a journey a traveller is likely to face hardship and is, therefore, entitled to some exemption. A general principle is, thus, an explanation for the rule.

If the general principle we have derived above is used to extend the law it can cover many cases. All cases of hardship, whatever their nature, will be settled according to this principle. Using general principles makes the extension of the law very flexible and easy. An uncontrolled use of general principles, on the other hand, might mean that we are no longer sure whether the intention of the Lawgiver is being followed. For this reason, Muslim jurists usually avoid reasoning from the *ḥikmah* or wisdom underlying the texts.

Ignoring this *ḥikmah* completely, however, would also not be a practical solution, especially when there are numerous new cases requiring decision. The jurists have, therefore, devised a methodology or methodologies for the use of general principles in settling the law. These methodologies, for the sake of convenience, have been collectively called the third mode of *ijtihād*. Examples of this mode of *ijtihād* were provided during the study of *maṣlaḥah mursalah*.

23.3 A Value Oriented Jurisprudence

The third mode of *ijtihād* presents **an area of discretion** to the *mujtahid*. **He has the opportunity to formulate a new principle and to use it after verifying it against the purposes of Islamic law as well as its general principles.** This process of verification is, in fact, a methodology for controlling the absolute discretion of the jurist. The methodology may be designated as a theory of values or a theory of interests. In Western law too similar developments have taken place in the present (20th) century. It will be instructive to examine these developments briefly.

The idea of natural law has had a very powerful influence on Western jurisprudence. This idea signifies three things:

1. That there is a body of universal principles that are acceptable to most nations and their legal systems.

2. That the positive law of a country or the man-made law must conform to these principles in order to be valid. In other words, the content of the positive laws must conform to the ultimate universal principles.

3. That this body of laws is discoverable by human reason.

The idea of natural law has passed through many stages. In some stages it has been closely associated with religion, while in others it has been considered a pure invention of human reason. Natural law saw a decline with the rise of the scientific spirit and the growth of positivism. There has, however, been a revival of this law in the 20th century. In its modern form the idea of natural law is inclined more towards a value oriented jurisprudence. Even sociological jurisprudence, as developed by Roscoe Pound and others, has led to the development of several categories of interests. Each legal dispute is seen as a clash between interests, and it is the function of law to reconcile these interests or values.

Dias has devoted a whole chapter to values in his book on jurisprudence. In his view, the ultimate values that are identified by Western jurisprudence are: (1) national and social safety; (2) sanctity of the person; (3) sanctity of property; (4) social welfare; (5) equality; (6) consistency and fidelity to rules, principles, doctrine and tradition; (7) morality; (8) administrative convenience; and (9) international comity.

A closer examination shows that most of these interests are identical to the five purposes of Islamic law or the *maqāṣid al-sharīʿah.* What is interesting is that their use is also similar and so is the methodology.

Dias has shown that in statutory interpretation, in the use of precedents and the employment of customs, there is always an element of discretion. It is this element of discretion that enables the judge to extend the law to new situations. In the use of this discretion, however, the judge is not free. He is bound by standards that require him to do justice in accordance with the value structure and the reconciliation of interests.

A comparison of the judicial method in Western law with the methodology of the Muslim jurists based on the third mode of *ijtihād* shows that there are quite a few similarities in the two methods. Yet, there are several vital differences too and it is important to identify these differences.

23.3.1 Distinction between the value system in Islamic law and Western jurisprudence

1. The first distinction pertains to the discovery of good and evil or right and wrong through the use of reason. These are issues of morality. The question is whether reason can be a source of law independently of the *sharī'ah?* In other words, can we rely on natural law as a guide for lawmaking? *The majority of the Muslim jurists held that the guide for right and wrong is the sharī'ah and reason alone is not a reliable guide.* A brief comparison was made in the chapter on the *Ḥākim* in the first part of this book.

2. The second distinction flows from the first: *the values upheld by Western legal systems are based on human reason, while the values upheld by the sharī'ah have been determined by the Lawgiver.* This was explained in detail under the meaning of *maṣlaḥah* in the chapter on the purposes of Islamic law.

3. There are two concepts of rationality. The first gives us certain and infallible knowledge, which is called definitive (*qaṭ'ī*) in Islamic law. The second concept of rationality gives us reasonably reliable knowledge, but it does not reach the level of the first type. The values determined by the *sharī'ah* convey the first type of knowledge, because they have been determined by Allah, the ultimate Lawgiver. The values upheld by Western legal systems do not belong to the first

> category of rationality as their source is human reason. Hans Kelsen and Alf Ross have actually denied that justice can be based on such values, because a clash of these values reveals the irrationality of their structure. Bodenheimer, after analysing the views of such jurists, has tried to show that even the second concept of rationality presents a viable basis for such values, especially when they are supported by empirical or scientific evidence.
>
> Muslim jurists, on the other hand, do not find the conflict of values to be irrational. They explain this conflict through the operation of various types of rights and the rules of preference. These rules were explained under the discussion of the principle of *maṣlaḥah.*

The above discussion is intended to show that the third mode of *ijtihād* provides a viable methodology for the Muslim judges, especially those of the higher courts. This methodology, combined with the methodology of the *faqīh* discussed in the next part, can yield an efficient and modern legal system.

23.4 *Maṣlaḥah* and the Modern Jurist

We must add here that the writings of some modern scholars on *maṣlaḥah* and the *maqāṣid al-sharīʿah* imply that the purposes of law can be used for the derivation of the law all by themselves, that is, without reference to the general principles in the rest of the law. As pointed in this book under the discussion of the purposes of law and in an earlier work—(*Theories of Islamic Law*)—we have tried to show that there are various kinds of general principles in Islamic law. Al-Ghazālī has described them in detail. The jurist must use one of these principles to settle a case that comes to him for decision. If he cannot find an existing principle suitable for his needs in this case, he may formulate a principle that he thinks is applicable and which he believes to be compatible with the remaining principles of the law. Once he has done this, he is under a duty to justify this principle in the light of the *maqāṣid* showing which interest or value is preferred over others by this principle. In addition to this, he must show that it meets all the conditions that al-Ghazālī has stipulated for the justification of the principle.

While we are relying heavily on al-Ghazālī here, we do not mean that there can be no other methodology for justifying the principle formulated by the jurist. In fact, this area of interpretation offers vast opportunities to scholars occupied with the study of Islamic law of developing and refining this methodology. There are many grey areas that need to be clarified, especially those pertaining to the relationship between the rights of God, the fundamental rights of the individual granted by the *sharī'ah* and the interests of the state or public interest. This is also an area where the methodology of the *faqīh* discussed in the next part and that of the *mujtahid* appears to overlap.

Review Questions

1. What is the difference between *'illah* and *ḥikmah*? Are the *maqāṣid* based entirely on *ḥikmah*?
2. How are the general principles found in the texts related to the *maqāṣid al-sharī'ah*?
3. Compare the use of the *maqāṣid* in law with the use of the value system in law? (Both Dias and Bodenheimer have discussed this in detail)
4. The *maqāṣid* are made to work through general principles. Comment.

24 Abrogation (*Naskh*) and Preference (*Tarjīḥ*)

A discussion of *ijtihād* cannot be complete without an examination of the doctrine of *naskh* (abrogation) and the rules of *tarjīḥ* (preference and reconciliation of the different evidences on a single issue).

It may be mentioned at the outset that the issue of abrogation has been the subject of debate in modern times. When it is examined from the perspective of the layman, he finds it difficult to rationally accept that a verse of the Qur'ān can be abrogated, especially when this is claimed to have been done through the *Sunnah* on a few occasions. Accordingly, many Muslim scholars have denied this doctrine altogether. The Orientalists have their own view on the issue and they employ the doctrine for constructing the history of the Islamic texts. Some learned scholars have tried to show how the occasions where abrogation is claimed can be explained in other ways that do not rely on this doctrine. Notable among these scholars is Shāh Walī Allāh. Even some earlier jurists did not accepted it, but the Sunnī schools have accepted the doctrine unanimously. It is not possible for us to record here the debates over this issue, and we will present here the point of view of the vast majority of Muslim jurists who accept this doctrine. We will, however, note at the end some of the logical and methodological problems that can arise as a result of the rejection of the doctrine. The reader will obviously form his own opinion.

24.1 The Doctrine of Abrogation (*Naskh*)

The literal meaning of *naskh* is cancelling or transferring. In its technical sense it is used to mean the "lifting (*raf'*) of a legal rule through a legal evidence of a later date." The abrogating text or evidence is called *nāsikh,* while the repealed rule is called *mansūkh.*

All the four Sunnī schools unanimously accept the doctrine of abrogation, though they may disagree on the details. Most of the independent jurists also accepted this doctrine. It may, therefore, be assumed to be a kind of consensus. The concept of "repeal" and "overriding laws" is a necessity in a legal system and Islamic law acknowledges it. **Such repeal in the texts, though, could only occur during the lifetime of the Prophet (peace be on him), that is, abrogation where claimed comes from the Lawgiver; it is not the work of the jurists.**

According to al-Sarakhsī the Jews did not accept this concept in their legal system. Perhaps, the reason for this was that they had very little chance of implementing their system through a state, and their law has remained theoretical having been developed mostly during the diaspora. It is only in the modern times that they have been able to establish a state.

Although some modern Muslim scholars have tried to deny the doctrine of abrogation, the doctrine was firmly established within the Islamic legal system by the unanimous agreement of the schools of law and their jurists.

24.1.1 Examples of repealing and overriding laws

One of the earliest cases of repeal of an earlier command was the directive to change the direction of the *qiblah* from Bayt al-Maqdas to al-Masjid al-Ḥarām. The repealing verse is:

قد نرىٰ تقلّب وجهك في السّمآء فلنولّينّك قبلة ترضٰها فولّ وجهك شطر المسجد الحرام وحيثما كنتم فولّوا وجوهكم شطره

> We see the turning of thy face (for guidance) to the heavens: now shall We turn thee to a Qiblah that shall please thee. Turn then thy face in the direction of the Sacred Mosque: wherever ye are, turn your faces in that direction. [Qur'ān 2:144]

Naskh is total (*kullī*), where it may lift the entire law and substitute another one for it, or it may be partial (*juz'ī*), when the law is repealed for a certain class alone. This is what may be called the overriding of a general law by a special law. For example, a general law in the Qur'ān provides penalties for all those who falsely accuse chaste women of sexual intercourse. It then provides a special law in the case of spouses accusing each other of unchastity. The provisions of the general law are not applicable to spouses, because the special law overrides that provision.

24.1.2 The wisdom behind the doctrine of abrogation

It is generally acknowledged that Islamic law works for the interest (*maṣlaḥah*) of human beings. Interests may keep on shifting with a change in circumstances, and the law adjusts accordingly. The law was laid down in the period of the Prophet (peace be on him) gradually and in stages. The aim was to bring a society steeped in immorality to observe the highest standards of morality. This could not be done abruptly. It was done in stages, and doing so necessitated repeal and abrogation of certain laws.

24.1.3 Distinction between *naskh* (abrogation) and *takhṣīṣ* (restriction)

The concept of overriding laws (*naskh kullī*) is sometimes confused with restriction (*takhṣīṣ* or *naskh kullī*). The similarity between the two is that both annul a rule for a certain class of people. The difference between the two is that in the case of abrogation the rule has become applicable to all without distinction and a later evidence comes and removes it for certain people. In other words, the rule had become applicable and an obligation was created before it was removed. In the case of restriction, the general rule is not established for a class of people *ab initio*, because the restricting evidence was read with the general evidence; it did not become operative at a later date.

It is for this reason that some jurists stipulate that the abrogating evidence should be separate from the obligation creating evidence, while the restricting evidence should accompany the obligation creating evidence. Others do not consider this to be an effective distinction. The main difference is that an abrogating evidence operates after the obligation has been created, while a restricting evidence operates before the creation of the obligation.

24.1.4 Types of abrogation

Abrogation is of two types: explicit and implicit. Explicit abrogation takes place when the Lawgiver has explicitly stated that a rule is abrogated. For example, the Prophet (peace be on him) said "I used to forbid you from visiting graves, but you may do so now."

Implicit abrogation takes place when the Lawgiver has not expressly pointed out the abrogation, but has laid down a new rule that conflicts with an earlier rule and there is no chance of reconciling the two provisions. An example is the period of *'iddah* for a woman after the death of her husband. Verse 240 of al-Baqarah provides as under:

وَالّذين يتوفّون منكم ويذرون أزواجا وصيّة لأزواجهم متاعا إلى الحول غير إخراج

> Those of you who die and leave widows should bequeath for their widows a year's maintenance without expulsion. [Qur'ān 2:240]

This verse implies that a woman whose husband has died has to wait for a whole year. This was the rule in the early days of Islam, till the following verse was revealed:

والّذين يتوفّون منكم ويذرون أزواجا يتربّصن بأنفسهنّ أربعة أشهر وعشرا

> If any of you die and leave widows behind; they shall wait concerning themselves four months and ten days. [Qur'ān 2:234]

This verse indicates that the waiting period is four months and ten days. This verse, therefore, acts as an abrogating verse for the earlier rule, because it was revealed later.

24.1.5 The attributes of the abrogating and abrogated evidences

Abrogation always proceeds from the Lawgiver. It is, therefore, necessary that both types of evidences, the abrogated and abrogating, must have existed during the period of revelation. The jurist discovers the dates alone. The main rule for the evidences is that the abrogating evidence be of the same legal strength as the abrogated evidence. This leads to a number of sub-rules.

1. One text of the Qur'ān can abrogate another text.
2. The *mutawātir sunnah* can abrogate the rule in the Qur'ān, and vice versa, as both are definitive (*qaṭ'ī*) and the source of both is revelation.
3. A *khabar wāḥid* can abrogate another *khabar wāḥid.*
4. *Ijmā'* cannot abrogate the texts, and vice versa, as it always takes place after the death of the Prophet (peace be on him) and abrogation occurs before it.
5. Abrogation is not permitted through analogy, and one analogy cannot abrogate another analogy.

24.2 Justification for the Doctrine of Abrogation

The doctrine of abrogation has been described very briefly above. We have also tried to describe some fine distinctions, drawn by the jurists, between abrogation (*naskh kullī*) and *takhṣīṣ* (restriction), also called *naskh juz'ī* or partial abrogation. While the doctrine of abrogation is rejected by many modern scholars, very few object to *takhṣīṣ* (restriction). If we look that the issue in a non-technical and objective way, we find that there is no difference between the two processes, except in the quantum of the effect they have on an existing rule.

For example, one verse of the Qur'ān prescribes in general terms that any person, male or female, indulging in unlawful sexual intercourse is to be awarded a hundred stripes. This is a general command and in the absence of a restricting evidence it would apply to all those who commit this offence. After this, another verse says that the penalty for the same offence committed by a married slave-girl is half that for free women. The result is that the rule for the slave-girl is altered by restricting the general application of the first verse.

24.2.1 Comparing the Impact of Abrogation and Restriction

In this case, it does not really matter whether we call it abrogation or restriction. The result is that the earlier general rule, which applied to the slave-girl as well, is no longer applicable to her. It may be argued that the rule was not contained in the general meaning in the first place and we came to know about this on reading the second verse. In other words, the two texts are deemed to apply separately to two separate situations. The jurists would reply that this is how the rules will be applied and there is no conflict between the sources of the *sharī'ah*. Yet, the conflict remains in the minds of human beings when they try to rationalise these rules and relate them to each other for analytical consistency within a legal system. Thus, the jurist would say that the general rule is that one hundred stripes are to be applied to every fornicator, but in the case of the slave-girl the rule has changed. The latter is now a case exempted from the general rule and subject to a special rule. On the basis of this reasoning the jurists would say that those who do not accept abrogation will also have to give up the principle of *takhṣīṣ* or restriction of one text by another, because there is no fundamental difference between the two.

Can a system of interpretation work if it accepts neither abrogation nor restriction? To our mind this is possible theoretically, but it will give rise to a highly literal system of interpretation. Such a literal system may work for the *'ibādāt*, but when it comes to a modern legal system, requiring analytical consistency for the further development of rules, it is bound to fail.

We, therefore, conclude that the process of abrogation, when considered in a general way, without all the technical distinctions, appears to be the same as the restriction of the meaning of one verse by another, except in the extent of its impact. In our view, those who deny the doctrine of abrogation must logically deny the possibility of restriction of meanings (*takhṣīṣ*) in the texts as well. God knows best.

24.3 The Rules of Preference (*Tarjīḥ*)

There is no conflict between the texts or evidences of the *sharī'ah*. The conflict lies in the mind of the *mujtahid*. The primary reason for this is that he does not know the dates on which the evidences were revealed. Where the dates are known, the jurist follows the doctrine of abrogation. In case he does not know the dates, he adopts the methods of preference (*tarjīḥ*) and reconciliation (*jam'*). The rules of preference are as follows:

1. The explicit meaning (*naṣṣ*) is preferred over the manifest meaning (*ẓāhir*).

2. The elaborated meaning (*mufassar*) is preferred over the explicit meaning (*naṣṣ*).

3. The *muḥkam* is preferred over all other meanings.

4. The rule established through a plain reading of the text (*'ibārat al-naṣṣ*) is preferred over one proved through an indirect implication (*ishārat al-naṣṣ*).

5. The rule established through an indirect implication (*ishārat al-naṣṣ*) is preferred over one established through its implication (*dalālat al-naṣṣ*).

6. Preference is undertaken through the power of the argument rather than through the number of evidences. This has some sub-rules:

    a) The evidences from the Book and the *Sunnah* are preferred over analogy.
    b) *Ijmā'* is preferred over analogy. Consensus is definitive and will be preferred over probable evidences in case of conflict. It is for this reason that al-Ghazālī sates that the first thing a jurist must do is to find out if a consensus has occurred on the point under consideration.
    c) A *mutawātir* tradition will be preferred over a *khabar wāḥid*.
    d) A *khabar wāḥid* transmitted by a Companion who enjoys a reputation as a jurist will be preferred over another *khabar wāḥid* transmitted by a Companion who does not enjoy such reputation.

There are a large number of other rules, but the above should suffice as a representative sample.

24.3.1 Reconciliation (*jam'*)

Before preferring one evidence over another, the jurist tries his best to reconcile the conflicting evidences when the two texts are of the same strength. For example, in the case mentioned above under implicit abrogation regarding the waiting period of a woman whose husband has died, some jurists have maintained that there is no abrogation and the texts can be reconciled. They maintain that there are two periods mentioned for two separate cases. The longer period, of one year, is to be followed in case the woman is pregnant and she awaits delivery of the child.

Review Questions

1. It is maintained by some that there is no abrogation of the texts in Islam, while others say that this view is held by those who have a superficial understanding of Islamic law. Discuss.
2. What is the doctrine of *naskh* as elaborated by the jurists?
3. What is the distinction between abrogation and restriction?
4. Briefly describe the rules of preference (*tarjīḥ*?

Part V

Madhāhib, *Taqlīd* and *Fatwās*

25 The Meaning of "School of Law" and Following a Madhhab

25.1 The Views of Modern Scholars on Why a Particular School Should be Followed

The learned Taqī Usmani wrote a very comprehensive document on the issue. This has now been translated into English.[324] We will rely on this document alone as the learned Taqi Usmani has, as usual, dealt with the topic in a very comprehensive manner, and most other scholars offer the same arguments. We will attempt to organize the arguments given through excerpts from this text. No attempt will be made to correct or edit the words, except obvious errors. The learned scholar, presents the following arguments:

- **Islamic law is complex, therefore, requires specialists, and these specialists are the jurists:** The issues of Islamic law are very complex and such complexity requires specialization. The jurists are the specialists who deal with

324. Legal Status of Following a Madhhab. It is available on the Internet.

Islamic law. "So ask the people of remembrance if you know not."[325] This verse implies that the specialist be followed. A verse says: "O you who believe! Follow Allah; follow the Messenger and those of authority (Amr) amongst you."[326] A large number of authorities are quoted in the document to show that the term those in authority means the jurists. The words of the Qur'ān, "And if you dispute, then refer it to Allah and the Messenger if you really do believe in Allah and in the Last Day,"[327] are not directed at the layman. The verse is interpreted to mean that this is a command for the jurists.

- **The jurists were pious persons and such persons should be followed:** This meaning has also been derived from the the Quran where it means following prophets and good people in religious affairs: "They are the ones whom We guided, so follow their guidance."[328] Follow the good an pious people for some of them may be really guided.

- ***Taqlīd* or following the opinion of another was prevalent even in the time of the Companions (R), but later a need was felt for systematization:** *Taqlīd,* which means following someone else's opinion was to be found even in the time of the Companions (R), but a few generations later a dire need was felt for systematization. Opinion without knowledge was discouraged. It was the responsibility of a person who was not a scholar to ask someone who had knowledge of the Quran and Sunnah. If the knowledgeable person gave an erroneous *fatwā,* the burden of sin is on the *muftī* and not on the questioner. Certain historical changes occurred and these led to a need for systemization.

- **Ultimately, the jurists saw a need for drawing the boundaries of *taqlīd* and of the following of one school:**

325. Qur'ān 16:90.
326. Qur'ān 4:59.
327. Qur'ān 4:59
328. Qur'ān 6:90.

The scholars saw that there was a need to demarcate the practice of *taqlīd*. For reasons of administration and to avoid the possibility of contradictions amongst the scholars of differing *ijtihād* over a primary source, the people were encouraged to follow only one Imam and *mujtahid* instead of referring to several. This idea gained hegemony during the third and fourth century Hijrah. Hence, this has been the dictum of the vast majority of the Ummah for subsequent centuries, and scholars themselves have conformed to *taqlīd* of a particular Imam. The jurists were concerned at the decay of piety and devoutness amongst the Muslim populous, devoutness being the norm during the time of the Companions (R). They feared that the scruples of subsequent generations would not be as elevated as those of the first three generations (Salaf). If under these circumstances, the door of following an Imam in general were unconditional inadvertently desires would become the commanding principle. A person left freely to adopt the view which suited him best and abandon the *fatwā* which did not meet his "standards" of comfort begs the question upon what basis is the "non-scholar" to choose between two contrary *fatwās* if not one's own *nafs* (desires). It is clear that this line of action would result in people using Islamic law as a triviality to entertain the lower self. No Muslims scholar of any repute has validated this kind of practice.

- **Becoming a *mujtahid* was no longer possible:** The *taqlīd* of four Imams became popular throughout Muslim cities and the *taqlīd* of other scholars was forsaken. The doors of diverse opinions were closed because so many academic terms were being used to denote so many different concepts and because it had become so difficult to reach the stage of a *mujtahid*. There was the apprehension that the title of *mujtahid* be attributed to one who was not worthy, or someone who is inauthentic (and cannot be trusted) in his opinion and in his religious practice. Scholars declared that attaining the stage of a *mujtahid* was not possible and restricted people to follow a particular Imam. They prevented people from following Imams alternately as this was tantamount to playing [with Islam]. This discussion is based on the statement of Ibn Khaldūn, *Muqaddimah* (Egypt: Makatab Tijariyah Kubrah, n.d.), 448.

- **Following a school is not *bid'ah* (innovation):** A question might arise from this analysis: How can something that was not necessary during the times of the Companions and their followers become necessary for people who came after them? An eloquent reply has been offered by Shah Waliyullah:

  > It is mandatory that there should be someone in the community (Ummah) who knows details of particular rules and laws with their reasoning and proofs. The people of truth have unanimously agreed to this premise. A science or action which is necessary to fulfill a mandatory action also becomes mandatory in itself. For example, the predecessors did not write the sayings of the Prophet (sallalahu alaihi wa sallam). Today writing and documenting Hadith has become necessary, because the only way we can know and learn Hadith is by knowing the books of Hadith. Likewise, the predecessors did not engage in studying syntax and etymology, because their language was Arabic, and advanced study of these ancillary sciences was not required. Today, learning these sciences has become mandatory since the language has drifted considerably from the original language of Arabic. Based on this account, one must draw an analogy for proving that following one particular Imam and Mujtahid is sometimes necessary and sometimes not necessary. [Al-Insaaf fi bayan sabab Ikhtilaaf: 57/59. Published by Matba' Mujtabai, 1935. Ibid 69/71.]

Shah Waliyyullah hinted toward the chaos and corruption which was prevented by restricting *taqlīd* to one Mujtahid: "In short, following the Mujtahids was a subtle inspiration which Allah unveiled to the scholars. A consensus arose among the rightly guided scholars, to its indispensability. Knowingly or unknowingly, it was upon this inspiration which the vast majority of the ummah united." He wrote in another place: "The Ummah has unanimously agreed upon the validity of following one of the four schools of thought—which have been organized and documented. There are many obvious benefits in this, especially today where determination has dwindled; where desires have penetrated our consciousness and gloating with ones own opinion is seen as a virtue."

- **Why only four schools?** This begs the question: if following one particular Mujtahid is indispensable, why the need to restrict *taqlīd* to only the four schools of thought? Several great Imams and Mujtahids have occupied the pages of Islamic scholastic history such personages as Sufyaan Thauri, Imam Awzaa'i, Abdullah ibn Mubarak, Ishaq ibn Rahwaih, Imam Bukhari, Ibn Abi Layla, Ibn Sibrimah, Hasan ibn Saleh and many others. Are all Mujtahids not equally qualified to be followed? Such a contention is valid in principle, but rather, it is not effectively possible. The schools of thought of the Mujtahids mentioned above are not systematically documented. Had their schools been formally codified and structured similar to the major four schools, then there would be no hindrance to following them. Unfortunately, their schools do not exist formally, nor have the original sources of the schools survived. To follow such schools would therefore prove difficult.

- **Why one particular school and why not all?** Shah Waliyyullah, has allocated a whole chapter to this discussion in his book: "Iqdul Jeed" and called it: "The Chapter of Emphasising following one of these four schools of thought and denouncing the idea of forsaking them." He started the chapter by saying: "You should know that following these four schools has tremendous public advantages and benefits. Forsaking them is wrought with mischief and harms. We will explain this with many inferences ...."

Mawlana Taqi Usmani says: He then goes on to explain the many reasons which I will paraphrase in points instead of translating a very lengthy passage. It is incumbent to rely upon the early predecessors if one is to understand Islamic law. The only way for us to do this is either to determine that the statements of the predecessors have been transmitted to us via sound chain of narrators or to read their statements, which are documented in reliable books. It is necessary to establish that these statements have actually been trusted and used by other scholars. Finally, if their statements are open to several meanings, then the most preferred meaning be adopted. Occasionally the statement of a certain Mujtahid may appear to be general but in fact it may be quite specific, which would be recognised by the scholars who have studied his school of thought. Thus, it is necessary that the statements of this certain Mujtahid be documented, understood and explained such that the rationale is emphasised. If a certain Mujtahid has not had his statements codified then such a Madhab should not be relied upon. In our age, the four prominent schools of thought share this advantage whereas other schools do not.

Finally, if giving a Fatwa based on any of the earlier scholars and their schools of thought were to be made permissible, then corrupt scholars would take advantage of the Shari'ah and base their Fatwas on the statements of any of the predecessors. This would inevitably open the door to the abuse of their statements. Corrupt scholars would be asked to justify selfish desires by quoting pious predecessors. Relying upon following the vast majority of the community would arrest the drift to chaos within the Shari'ah.

The above arguments are good and the efforts of the learned Mufti Taqi Usmani have to be appreciated. We can raise some questions, but we will not as that will lengthen the description unnecessarily. The only point we will raise is that some people today may not find some of the arguments to be very convincing. For example, they may say that there are many pious scholars today who can be followed. Today, we have the means of checking the acts of corrupt scholars who plagiarize the work of other schools and present it as their own. The work of scholars who do not belong to the four accepted schools also stands documented. The general populace, with the spread of education, is quite capable of determining the chains of narrations from the published material. There may be benefits in not following a single school as it will provide freedom to deal with the multitude of problems faced by the Ummah today. Consequently, scholars can get together and decide that it is no longer necessary to follow a single school. In short, even a simple response may be enough to show that the very good arguments provided may not be sufficient to convince everyone. In reality, this is exactly what has happened and many educated people are approaching the *aḥadīth* on their own and concluding what the law must be on a particular point. The situation is rapidly becoming what may be called a "free for all." It is indeed a dangerous development for Islamic law.

The true argument must be discovered and for doing so we have to turn to *uṣūl al-fiqh* again.

25.2 The *Uṣūlī* Argument for Following a Single School

The true argument for following a single school, and also for not floating between schools, is to be found in the Discipline of *Uṣūl al-Fiqh* itself. In the introductory chapter, we have indicated that understanding the meaning of *'ilm uṣūl al-fiqh* is essential for many things. It is now time for the reader to test his understanding of the meaning.

25.2.1 The Nature of the *Qawā'id Uṣūliyyah*: the Basis of the Schools of Law

For the Uṣūlī, the term *uṣūl* implies "a body of principles" that he uses to interpret the texts.[329] As these *uṣūl* or rules contain within them the meaning of the "sources of Islamic law", he does not emphasise the meaning of *uṣūl* as sources, rather he focuses on the rules, which are the rules of interpretation. He hands over these rules to the jurists of the school (the *fuqahā'*), who use them to create the knowledge base of the law also called *fiqh*. It is better to call these *uṣūl* principles for reasons that should be obvious to the reader by now.

These principles of interpretation are formulated by the Muslim jurists in the form of general propositions. The major premise of these propositions serves as the principle. Such a principle is referred to as a *qā'idah uṣūliyah*. Thus, for example, a proposition may be stated as follows:

> The *aḥkām* of Allāh are established through the sources of Islamic law. **The Qur'ān is a source of law.** Thus [conclusion], each time a *ḥukm* is found in the Qur'ān it is proved as the *ḥukm* of Allāh.[330]

The major premise in the above proposition, which emerges as a principle is that **the Qur'ān is a source of law**. This is what is usually stated when we are talking about *uṣūl al-fiqh* as sources. The emphasis, however, is always on the last sentence; namely, **each time a *ḥukm* is found in the Qur'ān it is proved as the *ḥukm* of Allāh.** This latter statement focuses on the intention of the Lawgiver; it is the result of the effort that the *mujtahid* has made to understand the texts. It tells the *mujtahid* that if he is able to find a *ḥukm* in the texts of the Qur'ān that *ḥukm* stands proved or established as the *ḥukm* or rule laid down by Allah.

329. For a discussion on the nature of these rules see Ṣadr al-Sharī'ah, *al-Tawḍīḥ*, vol. 1, 41–45.
330. Ṣadr al-Sharī'ah, *Tawḍīḥ*, vol. 1, 45.

The same is the case with the *Sunnah* as well as *ijmā'*; when it is said that they are sources of law. The emphasis is identical. The same emphasis is applied by the Sunnī schools of law when they are formulating a principle for *qiyās*. Thus, when the jurist maintains that analogy (*qiyās*) is a source of law, the emphasis will always be on the fact that "each time analogy is successfully used to discover the law (from the Qur'ān and the *Sunnah*) a *ḥukm* of Allah is discovered or proved."[331] This is so as *qiyās* is merely a method of discovering a law laid down in the Qur'ān and the *Sunnah*. The law is actually being proved from the two primary sources.

We, therefore, have the following four unanimous principles for the Sunni schools:

1. Each time a *ḥukm* is discovered in the Qur'ān it is said to be proved. [Unanimous]

2. Each time a *ḥukm* is discovered in the *Sunnah* it is said to be proved. [Unanimous]

3. Each time a *ḥukm* is discovered though *ijmā'* it is said to be proved. [Unanimous, though al-Shāfi'ī had some reservations]

4. Each time a *ḥukm* is discovered through *qiyās* it is said to be proved. [Unanimous for the existing Sunnī schools]

The Sunni jurists are very strict about the acceptance of the above four principles. All those jurists who did not accept all the four principles are excluded from their fold. The opinions of the schools and/or scholars who do not accept all four are not binding; in fact, they have no legal value. The argument about the lack of documentation in these schools, therefore, fails. Today, when scholars quote such excluded schools or scholars must realize that those opinions have no legal strength.

When the meaning of *ijmā'* or consensus is confined to the consensus of the Companions (R), the first three rules become

331. Ibid.

essential for everyone to follow, that is, every Muslim. The reason is that it is through the Companions (R) that we came to know about the Prophet (pbuh), the Qur'ān that was revealed to him, and his noble Sunnah. The consensus of the Companions (R) is, thus, not to be taken lightly.

25.2.2 Additional *Qawā'id Uṣūliyyah* as the Basis of the Different Systems

The jurist, in this way, arrives at four fundamental principles of interpretation related to the four sources of the law. These four principles are not the only principles used in this discipline. Each school formulates principles for the additional sources that it accepts and acts upon them. The emphasis is the same as for the first four sources with respect to the resulting rule being the *ḥukm* of Allah.

We just mentioned the importance of the Companions (R) for the system. The first disagreement then will arise over whether the opinion of a Companion is binding for us as a precedent. Some have accepted it as binding, with certain conditions, while others have not.

A large number of such principles are derived from the rules of literal interpretation that are also part of *uṣūl*. The first question that may be raised here is: Why different rules when the rules of Arabic grammar are the same? The reality is quite different and if we were to say that each school has its own grammar, we would not be entirely wrong. In fact, it will be more apropriate to say that each schools is different grammar system, but this applies to what such grammar means in the legal sense; it is legal grammar. Those who have learned Arabic and know the rules of its grammar cannot just go ahead and read the texts of the Qur'ān and the Sunnah to say this is the law. They do not realize what they are talking about.

Then there are differences about the additional rational sources. Some schools accept some rational methods as valid, while others accept others. Together, the result is a huge body of rules, which we call the school of Islamic jurisprudence. A few examples of such *uṣūl* are given below:

1. Each time a *ḥukm* is discovered through the opinion of a Companion it is said to be proved. [Not unanimous; the Ḥanafīs consider it binding, but the Shāfiʿīs do not]
2. Each time a rule is proved through *istiḥsān*, it is said to be proved as a rule of Islamic law [Rejected by al-Shāfiʿī]
3. Each time a rule is proved through *istiṣlāḥ* or *maṣlaḥah*, it is said to be proved as a rule of Islamic law [Not unanimous]
4. Each time a rule is proved through *istiṣḥāb al-ḥāll*, it is said to be proved as a rule of Islamic law [Not unanimous]
5. Each time a command (*amr*) is found in the texts it conveys an obligation, unless another evidence indicates the contrary. [Not unanimous]
6. Each time a proscription (*nahy*) is found in the texts it conveys a prohibition, unless another evidence indicates the contrary. [Not unanimous]
7. Each time a *ḥukm* is expressed in general terms it applies to all its categories with a certainty (*qaṭʿī*), unless restricted by an equally strong evidence. [Not unanimous]
8. The *ḥukm* is proved through the persuasive power of the *dalīl* and not through the number of evidences. [Not unanimous]

These are only a few out of a large body of rules called the *qawānīn uṣūliyyah*, and we can go on and on and on; there are hundreds of such rules. A few have been stated so that the reader may get an idea of the tools employed by the jurists.

25.2.3 A School of Law Then is a Unique Body of Rules of Interpretation

We have seen above that some *qawānīn* are accepted unanimously by all schools, while others are not. The total body of such rules accepted by one school differs to some extent from the set adopted by another school. This is what makes them distinct schools of law. Within a school, the *uṣūl* adopted are analytically consistent, that is, they do not clash with each other rather they complement one another, like flowers in a bouquet. Across school boundaries there may be a clash among such *uṣūl*, with the colours showing incompatibility.

Theoretically, the body of such rules is adopted by the founder of a school. Thus, for the Ḥanafī school, the rules were adopted by Abū Ḥanīfah and those for the Malikī school by Imām Mālik. It is true that all the detailed rules may not have been laid down by the founder, but he did establish a base on which the details were constructed.

The body of rules adopted by each school amounts to the theory of interpretation or theory of law of that school. Each theory of law is somewhat different from that of another school and has an impact on the *aḥkām* derived. Understanding the nature of the *uṣūl* by relating them to each school is extremely important for understanding the discipline of *uṣūl al-fiqh*. It is also for this reason that picking and choosing opinions randomly across school boundaries is looked down upon and deemed inappropriate. We shall have more to say about this in the section of portability below.

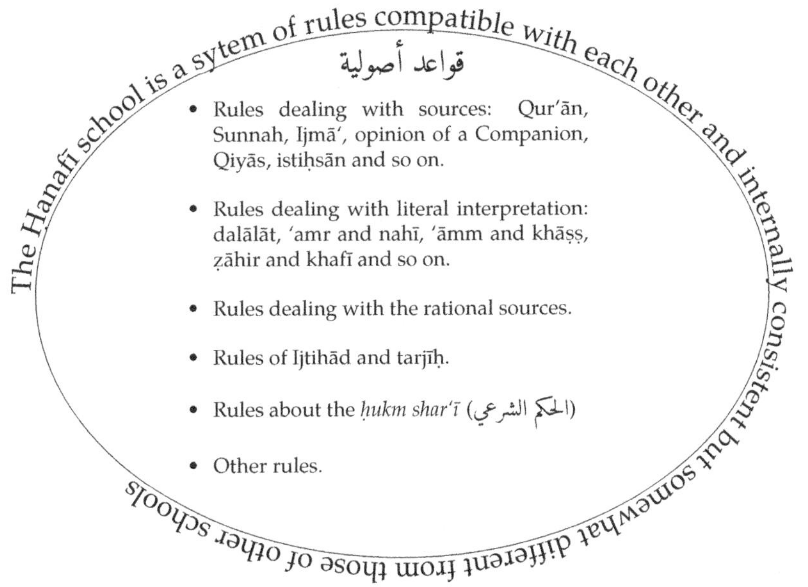

The Hanafī school is a sytem of rules compatible with each other and internally consistent but somewhat different from those of other schools
قواعد أصولية
• Rules dealing with sources: Qur'ān, Sunnah, Ijmā', opinion of a Companion, Qiyās, istiḥsān and so on.
• Rules dealing with literal interpretation: dalālāt, 'amr and nahī, 'āmm and khāṣṣ, ẓāhir and khafī and so on.
• Rules dealing with the rational sources.
• Rules of Ijtihād and tarjīḥ.
• Rules about the ḥukm shar'ī (الحكم الشرعي)
• Other rules.

Imagine each school as a vase; four identical vases. The base is the same, but the flowers arranged in them have different colours. The jurists of one school prefer one set of colours, while those of the other schools prefer other sets. There is an integral bond between the Sunni schools beyond this too, and we have explained that later.

25.2.4 The Analogy of Portability and Moving Between Schools

The distinctions mentioned above should have made matters clear about the necessity of following a school of law. We will, however, go ahead and use an analogy from the computer world as most people use computers today and will find the explanations easier. It may not be a perfect analogy, but will help.

There are different operating systems in which people work today: Windows, Unix (Linux), Macintosh OS and so on. Now there are certain files that can easily be read across all systems due to their portability. These may be like the PDF (portable document format), postscript files, image files and so on. Beyond this, a program file or even another file of one system may not open or work in another operating system. Thus, the Microsoft Office or Word program made for windows will not work on the Macintosh or even in Unix. The position in the schools of Islamic law is quite similar.

A person working in the Ḥanafī school should, therefore, remain in the Ḥanafī school. Choosing things from one school and pasting them into the other school will not work. Thus, taking an opinion based on *istiḥsān* and pasting it into the Shāfi'ī school will not work, because that school considers *istiḥsān* to be a nullity. Likewise, an opinion based on the rule that the opinion of a Companion is binding may not work in the Shāfi'ī school, which considers such an opinion not to be binding.

A person may say: what is the difference, when we follow one opinion we are following one acceptable school and when we follow another we are following another acceptable school? This question is excusable if it comes from a layman, but in the case of a jurist it is unpardonable. If the jurist, who knows the systems, says this he will be saying in one statement: *istiḥsān* is valid and not valid; opinion of a Companion is binding and non-binding; the general word is *qaṭ'ī* and *zannī*. This amounts to playing with the law, which is a sacred law. Thus, floating between schools is not pardonable.

If the layman, or a jurist for that matter, likes some opinions in the other school, he should move completely to the other school. Staying in one school and choosing pleasing opinions from other schools is not appropriate.

The learned Abu Zahrā, at the end of his book on *uṣūl*, attempts to lay down certain conditions for picking and choosing from different schools, or as some say floating between schools. The conditions reduced to the basics appear to say that the jurist must be a good man, he should do so honestly and not while pursuing his whims (*hawā*). It is difficult to accept such suggestions. The reason is simple: on what basis are you prefering an opinion of the other school? What are your rules of interpretation (assuming you are a great jurist) or technical standards on the basis of which you are carrying out the selection? Do you believe that *istiḥsān* is valid or not valid, and so on? If you have made a new operating system in which everything works, then this is marvellous. Making a new operating system means, you have set up a new school of Islamic law that has unique principles of interpretation. You have then turned into a *mujtahid muṭlaq* like the founders of the schools. In such a case, you do not have to choose, you must undertake fresh *ijtihād* for that is binding on you. And, you must declare the whole set of your principles of interpretation.

Selecting a whole new set of principles of interpretation is the real reason why we cannot have a *mujtahid muṭlaq* today. Maybe, a whole body of scholars can get together and set up a new system. The risk is that no one will follow them. Many modern scholars dream about introducing some kind of reform in Islamic law, and keep on making different suggestions. What they really need to do is to set up a new school. In our view, however, true reform will arise from within the established schools when we have mastered their rules; it cannot be done by breaking school boundaries.

Consequently, in our view, floating between schools, or picking and choosing from different schools amounts to blind *taqlīd*. It is quite different from *taqlīd* that is permitted, and which we will discuss below. The method of *talfīq* (or manufaturing a new opinion from parts of different rules of different systems) is even worse.

26 *Taqlīd* and its Implementation Within the School

Taqlīd, as generally understood, means following the opinion of the schools of Islamic law in matters of conduct. Thus, a Ḥanafī follows the opinion of the Ḥanafī school, while a Shāfi'ī follows the opinion of the Shāfi'ī school. As opposed to this, *ijtihād* means that the person in need of an opinion does not follow the opinion of any school, but derives the rule of conduct for himself directly from the sources of Islamic law. Such a person would obviously be designated as a *mujtahid*, and the *mujtahid* must have some basic qualifications. Further, the *mujtahid* must follow a system of interpretation: either an established system of a school or one that he has devised for himself, which will mean a new school. All persons who cannot lay claim to the status of a *mujtahid*, due to the lack of requisite qualifications and skills, must follow the opinion of some *mujtahid*, that is, they must perform *taqlīd*. Yet, we find that in modern times many scholars have condemned *taqlīd*, and have insisted on the necessity of *ijtihād*.

The reason for this is that in the writings of some of the earlier jurists *taqlīd* is considered mandatory for all jurists and independent *ijtihād* is not permitted. This is also termed as the "closing of the gates of *ijtihād*." There have been many discussions on this issue in modern *fiqh* literature, probably started by scholars like Rashīd Riḍā of Egypt. In the light of these discussions, many modern scholars maintain that the doors of *ijtihād* were never closed and this activity should be carried on in the modern world, and *taqlīd* should be shunned. Do these scholars mean that every layman should interpret the sources of Islamic law for himself and should avoid following the opinions of the schools of law? Do they mean that some scholars should undertake *ijtihād* and the rest should follow their opinions?

There is another form of *taqlīd* too, in which a layman does not follow one school, but chooses whichever opinion he likes from one of the schools. Thus, a scholar may choose an opinion from the Ḥanafī school today and tomorrow he may choose one from the Shāfi'ī school or from some other school for that matter. Is this *taqlīd* or *ijtihād*, or is it something else? We have already stated in the previous chapter that this is not proper.

Our purpose in this chapter will be to explain the exact meaning of *taqlīd* as it is understood by the jurists. This will be followed by the methods or structure through which this permitted form of *taqlīd* is implemented within a school.

26.1 Understanding the Meaning and Implications of *Taqlīd*

In the previous part, while discussing *ijtihād*, we stated that *ijtihād* is a legislative function, because it lays down the law for the first time. As compared to *ijtihād*, the purpose of *taqlīd* is to lay down a methodology for the *faqīh* for discovering and applying the law in the light of the already settled law. This is the function of the modern judge too, who discovers the law from the statutes and precedents to settle the disputes brought to him. It is not the task of the judge to legislate or lay down new law in his judgements. If he does this, he is encroaching upon the function of the legislature. Here we are following the generally accepted view and we are not concerned with the debate that questions whether the judge really discovers the law and applies it or whether he does legislate.

In Islamic law, the task of the *faqīh* appears to be the same as that of the modern judge who is settling issues of law and fact. The doctrine of *taqlīd* furnishes us the basic material for developing an Islamic theory of adjudication. In the introduction to this book we stated that the discipline of *uṣūl al-fiqh* provides us with the basic raw material and the structure through which work on the Islamic theory of adjudication can be carried out, just like it provides us with a methodology for the Islamic theory of legislation in the form of *ijtihād*. It would be naive to expect that *uṣūl al-fiqh* provides us with fully developed theories of legislation and adjudication that can be just picked up and implanted in a modern legal system. It does, however, provide us with substantial raw material with which we can easily build.

26.1.1 The Literal Meaning of *Taqlīd*

The word *taqlīd* is derived from *qalādah*, which means an ornament tied around the neck (like a necklace)[332] or it is the strap that holds the sheath of the sword and is usually swung around the shoulders. The word *qalādah* is also used to mean the strap by which a piece of wood is hung from the neck of an animal; it prevents the animal from running astray, because it strikes it on the knees when it tries to run. In this sense, the word *taqlīd* carries a restriction within it, and this restriction is found in the technical meaning of the term.

26.1.2 The Technical Meanings of *Taqlīd*

In its technical sense, *taqlīd* is defined by Ibn al-Ḥājj as "acting upon the word of another without *ḥujjah* (proof or lawful

332. Muḥammad ibn 'Alī al-Shawkānī, *Irshād al-Fuḥūl* (Cairo, 1327 AH) 246.

authority)."[333] There are two ways in which this definition has been understood, and has led to some confusion about the meaning and role of *taqlīd* in the present times.

The first meaning is assigned by modern writers. Abdur Rahim, for example, understands it to mean the following of the opinion of another without knowledge or authority for such opinion.[334] In other words, when a person asks a jurist for an opinion, he should not ask him about the basis for his opinion, whether it has been derived from the Qur'ān, the *Sunnah* or *ijmā'* or some other source; he should follow it without question. This meaning is accepted generally by most modern writers, and it is this form that they condemn. The earlier jurists do not understand the meaning of the definition in this way.

According to the earlier jurists, the word *ḥujjah* means permission given by the *sharī'ah*. *Taqlīd*, therefore, means following the opinion of another when the *sharī'ah* has not given permission to do so. This meaning makes *taqlīd* unlawful, that is, whoever follows the opinion of another without permission of the *sharī'ah*, is committing an unlawful act.

Following the opinion of a jurist does not fall within this meaning of *taqlīd*. The Muslim jurists maintain that following the opinion of a qualified jurist is permitted by the *sharī'ah*, and is not *taqlīd*. This means that there are two types of *taqlīd:* prohibited *taqlīd* and permitted *taqlīd*. To understand this thoroughly, the *ḥukm* of *ijtihād* as well as that of *taqlīd* needs to be examined.

To understand the meaning of *taqlīd* in law, let us examine the definition again. According to the jurists, the use of the word *ḥujjah* in the definition, "acting upon the word of another without *ḥujjah*," excludes this activity from the meaning of *taqlīd*. Al-Shawkānī explains that the use of the word *ḥujjah* excludes the following four types of activity from the meaning of prohibited *taqlīd:*

333. Ibn al-Ḥājj, *al-Taqrīr wa al-Taḥbīr* (Būlāq, 1316 AH) vol. 3, 340. This is the generally accepted definition and can be found in the works of al-Ghazālī and others.

334. Abdur Rahim, *Muhammadan Jurisprudence*, 171.

- Acting upon the words of the Prophet (peace be on him) is not prohibited *taqlīd*.
- Acting upon *ijmā'* is not prohibited *taqlīd*.
- Acceptance of the word of an upright (*'adl*) witness by the *qāḍī* is not prohibited *taqlīd*.
- The layman acting upon the word of a jurist is not performing prohibited *taqlīd*.[335]

The Ḥanafī jurists may add a fifth case to this: acting upon the opinion of a Companion of the Prophet is not prohibited *taqlīd*. These cases do not fall under condemned or prohibited *taqlīd*, because the *sharī'ah* has permitted all these forms; a *ḥujjah* (proof) exists for such permission. Some of these cases are obvious, but the case of the *faqīh* is explained by al-Ghazālī as follows:

> If it is said that you have condemned *taqlīd*, and this (layman's *taqlīd* of the jurist) is the very essence of *taqlīd*, we shall respond that *taqlīd* is the acceptance of an opinion without *ḥujjah*, but following the opinion of the *muftī* has been made obligatory (*wājib*) for the layman through the *dalīl* (evidence) of *ijmā'*, just as it is obligatory for the judge to accept the statement of (an *'adl*) witness.[336]

The authority permitting this activity, and excluding it from the meaning of *taqlīd* is *ijmā'*. Following the opinion of the jurist by the layman, therefore, cannot be called prohibited *taqlīd*, that is, condemned *taqlīd*.

Some jurists exclude some more cases from the meaning of condemned *taqlīd* on the basis of the principle of necessity (*ḍarūrah*). The founder of the Mālikī school, Mālik ibn Anas, is said to have permitted fourteen cases of *taqlīd*. A few of these are given below:

335. Al-Shawkānī, *Irshād al-Fuḥūl*, 246.
336. Al-Ghazālī, *al-Mustaṣfā min 'Ilm al-Uṣūl*, vol. 2, 384.

- It is permitted to the layman to accept the opinion of a doctor (*ṭabīb*).
- It is permitted to accept the opinion of a trader in the valuation of property (as an expert).
- The buyer is allowed to accept the opinion of the butcher that the meat he is buying has been properly slaughtered.
- The statement of a child bringing permission to the guest at the door that he is allowed to enter may be accepted by the guest.

This shows that *taqlīd* is a part of our daily lives and we are indulging in some form of *taqlīd* at each step. The truth of this claim is driven home when we examine our modern legal system.

26.1.3 *Taqlīd* in the Pakistani Legal System

The Constitution of Pakistan permits *taqlīd* in articles 189 & 201. These articles make the judgements of the Supreme Court binding on all courts and the judgements of the High Courts binding on courts subordinate to them. The doctrine of precedent and *stare decisis* are nothing more than institutionalised forms of *taqlīd*. When the lower courts follow the opinions of the higher courts they are undertaking *taqlīd*.

In addition to this, laymen accept the opinions of lawyers in their daily legal problems. Likewise, the courts accept the statements of witnesses, unless their veracity is challenged. The opinions of experts are accepted in a host of other matters.

The conclusion we may draw from this is that *taqlīd* is an essential principle of our daily lives and is based upon division of labour where some persons specialise in certain areas and become experts. The *muftī* or the *faqīh* is an expert in his area and there should be no hesitation in accepting his opinion by those who are laymen in his field of specialisation.

26.2 The Primary Function of a School of Law

In the Islamic legal system, the system of *taqlīd* or following precedents is implemented through the schools of law. The primary function of the school is, therefore, to make the law clear and evident for the people who follow the school, whether these are individuals, institutions or the rulers themselves.

One often hears people complaining that the Muslim jurists disagree about everything. There are multiple opinions in the school and one does not know which opinion to follow. These views are not expressed by laymen and students alone; one hears even some teachers saying this and the fact is reflected in their method of teaching as well. In other words, they indulge in what is called *qīla wa qāla*, that is, this jurist said this and the other said that, and yet another said something else.

How then can a person following a school know what the law is? Answering this question is the primary function of the school. From the multiple views exising within the school, a single opinion is preferred. The preferred opinion is the law. In fact, there is a special class of jurists who are assigned this function. They check many things including the sound narration of views within the school. In cases where there is some confusion, the school will issue a *fatwā* upholding one of many opinions as the law to be followed. It is due to this that one hears the phrase: the *fatwā* today is on such and such opinion.

The rule for this activity is well settled and has been observed for centuries by the school. In fact, this has been done from the very earliest times when the school started maturing. The rule is: there will always be a single **preferred** opinion within the school.

Ibn 'Ābidīn states this as follows:

> The preferred opinion of the school is to be followed, and the opinion not preferred is to be treated as non-existent (*al-marjūḥ ka'l-adam*). It is as if the preferred opinion has abrogated the other opinions.[337]

337. Ibn 'Ābidīn, *Rasā'il Ibn 'Ābidīn* (Lahore, 1976), 49.

There is, thus, no confusion about which opinion of the school is to be followed. This also sets aside the objection raised by some that there are so many opinions in Islamic law that one does not know which opinion to follow. The schools bring uniformity into their law through this method. The method through which the preferred opinion of the school is declared is discussed below.

26.3 The Resources of the School: Jurists, Issues and Texts

The rsources of a school of Islamic law are visualized in three hierarchies. There is a hierarchy of jurists, a hierarchy of issues and a hierarchy of texts. An understanding of these hierarchies provides a deep understanding of the structure and nature of a school of Islamic law. In this section, we will look at each hierarchy.

26.3.1 The Hierarchy of Jurists Within a School

The founder of a school has two functions: he lays down the *uṣūl* or the principles of interpretation and he uses these principles to settle the issues of the law (*furū'*). Thus, Abū Ḥanīfah laid down the principles of interpretation for the Ḥanafī school and he used these principles to derive the detailed rulings of the substantive law. The founders of the other schools did the same for their schools. This type of jurist is called the *mujtahid muṭlaq* or the absolute jurist. This jurist is completely independent insofar as he does not indulge in any type of *taqlīd*.

As compared to the founder, there are other jurists who are well qualified to undertake *ijtihād*. These jurists, however, follow the principles of interpretation laid down by their teacher. They use these rules of interpretation to derive the substantive law, and their opinions in this area may differ from those of their teacher. These jurists are performing *taqlīd* when they follow the opinion of their teacher about the principles of interpretation. This type of *taqlīd* is called *taqlīd fī al-uṣūl* or *taqlīd* in the principles of interpretation. The jurist who performs *taqlīd fī al-uṣūl* is called *mujtahid fī al-madhhab* or the *mujtahid* who is independent within the school.

There are other jurists in the school as well who are well qualified, but have not been granted the status of *mujtahid fī al-madhhab*. These jurists perform only one type of *taqlīd*, and this is called *taqlīd fī al-furū'* or following the decisions of the jurists of the higher grade. These jurists follow the opinions or decisions of the school laid down by the *mujtahid muṭlaq* and the *mujtahid fī al-madhhab*.

In a developed legal system, it is not possible that there be just two or three types of jurists. There are several types, and each developed school has determined the grades of the jurists based on these types. It is through these grades that Islamic law implements its system of following precedents. Ibn 'Ābidīn lists these grades for the Ḥanafī school as follows:

1. **The first grade:** *mujtahid muṭlaq* or *mujtahid fī al-shar'*. The *mujtahid muṭlaq* is usually the founder of the school, for example, Abū Ḥanīfah for the Ḥanafī school. He lays down the principles of interpretation for the school. We have already examined these principles in some detail above. The *mujtahid muṭlaq* uses his principles of interpretation to derive the law from the sources (for the *mujtahid*). In short, this type of independent jurist lays down the principles of interpretation as well as the law. In terms of our Islamic theory of legislation, this jurist is the legislator who also lays down the methodology of the legislator.

2. **The second grade:** *mujtahid fī al-madhhab* or the *mujtahid* within the school. The *mujtahid fī al-madhhab* performs *taqlīd fī al-uṣūl*, that is, he follows the principles laid down by the founder of the school, and using these principles derives the law himself. His opinion in the derived law may differ from that of his teacher. Jurists like Abū Yūsuf and Muḥammad al-Shaybānī are within this grade in the Ḥanafī school. They used the principles determined by Abū Ḥanīfah to derive the law. In the case of *muzāra'ah* (tenancy), for example, they differed with their teacher. Abū Ḥanīfah declared tenancy

to be illegal, while the two disciples (*ṣāḥibayn*) declared it legal. The opinion preferred by the school is that of the *ṣāḥibayn*. The jurists in this grade are independent in all respects, except the *uṣūl* (principles of interpretation). In terms of our theory of legislation, this jurist is also a legislator, but he follows the methodology of legislation determined by the full *mujtahid*.

3. **The third grade:** *mujtahid fī al-masā'il* or the *mujtahid* for new issues. The *mujtahid fī al-masā'il* determines answers to cases that are not settled by the jurists of the first two categories. In the Ḥanafī school, jurists like al-Khaṣṣāf, al-Ṭaḥāwī, al-Karkhī and al-Sarakhsī are placed in this grade. These jurists cannot question the cases that have been settled by the jurists of the first two grades. Their function is said to be the determination of new unsettled cases. A comparison of the methodology of these jurists with those in the next grade shows that the methodology is the same and is called *takhrīj*. These are the jurists whom we will should call the true *faqīhs*, along with those in the next grade. We now step into the area of adjudication, and this jurist is like the judge of the Supreme Court, so to say, who is filling the gaps left in statutes or earlier precedents.

4. **The fourth grade:** *aṣḥāb al-takhrīj* or those jurists who clarify the law of all the existing cases. The great jurist Abū Bakr al-Jaṣṣāṣ is placed in this category. The truth is that he was no less than any of the jurists in the previous category, and the methodology used by him was the same as that used by the *mujtahid fī al-masā'il*. This methodology will be explained at some length in the next chapter. For this purpose, we will combine these two grades into one, that is, the *mujtahid fī al-masā'il* and the jurist practising *takhrīj* and call both the *aṣḥāb al-takhrīj*.

5. **The fifth grade:** *aṣḥāb al-tarjīḥ* or those who preferred the stronger opinions in the school so as to bring uniformity into the law. Jurists like Abū al-Ḥusayn al-Qudūrī, al-Kāsānī,

al-Marghinānī (the author of *al-Hidāyah*) are placed in this grade.

6. **The sixth grade**. The rest of the well known jurists in the Ḥanafī school are placed in this grade. They are said to recognise the stronger opinions preferred by the jurists of the previous grade. Most well known jurists like Ṣadr al-Sharī'ah, Ibn al-Humām and the authors of the authoritative texts (*mutūn mu'tabarah*) would fall in this category. An examination of their method and their works reveals again that they were no less than the jurists in the previous category.

26.3.2 The Hierarchy of Issues Within a School

Some writers have erroneously stated that *ijtihād* is a source of Islamic law. For the *mujtahid*, it is a process, the effort that he expends, for the derivation of the law. For the *faqīh*, it is the result of the *ijtihād* that is a source, not the *ijtihād* itself. The output or the result of *ijtihād* is the record of the decisions given by the *mujtahid*. It provides the precedents required by the *faqīh*.

In the Ḥanafī school, the first such source are the books called the *Ẓāhir al-Riwāyah* written and compiled by Imām Muḥammad al-Shaybānī. These are followed by others as shown below:

1. *Masā'il al-Uṣūl* or the *Ẓāhir al-Riwāyah*. These are books that record not only the opinions of the leading jurists of the Ḥanafī school, but also those of other leading jurists like Ibn Abī Laylā and al-Awzā'ī. The first book is called *Kitāb al-Aṣl* or *al-Mabsūṭ*.[338] This is the first book on Islamic law, and

338. It is unfortunate that only three or four volumes of this book have been published so far in Egypt. The Islamic Research Institute, which should have taken the initiative, has not been able to edit and publish this important book so far. The complete book should make eight to ten volumes—the manuscript waits in vain at the Cairo Museum. According to our knowledge, some energetic private publishers are now making efforts to undertake the task.

most of the opinions recorded there are to be found today, either in the Ḥanafī school or even in other Sunni schools.

The other books under this heading are: *al-Ziyādāt* (with a huge commentary), *al-Jāmi' al-Ṣaghīr, al-Jāmi' al-Kabīr, al-Siyar al-Ṣaghīr,* and *al-Siyar al-Kabīr.* All these books have been called *Ẓāhir al-Riwāyah* as they represent the most authentic formulation of the school. What we mean by this is that the methodology used in these books is definitely that of the first jurists of the school.

2. *Masā'il al-Nawādir.* These are cases narrated in books other than the *Ẓāhir al-Riwāyah.*

3. The *fatāwā* and *al-wāqi'āt.* These are opinions of later jurists, or the *faqīhs* on cases not contained in the books listed at (1) and (2) above.

The rule for the above texts is that the issues in the first category are to be preferred over those in the second and third category, in case there is a contradiction.

The *Ẓāhir al-Riwāyah* were summarised under the title of *al-Kāfī.* It is on this summary that several important books by later jurists were constructed. For example, al-Sarakhsī wrote his famous 30 volume book *al-Mabsūṭ* as a commentary on this summary. Abū Bakr al-Kāsānī also relies on it for his *al-Badā'i' al-Ṣanā'i'.* Later books like *al-Hidāyah* by al-Marghinānī rely on the original as well as on later commentaries.

Books in the Mālikī and Shāfi'ī school that can be compared to the *ẓāhir al-riwāyah,* though written sixty to seventy years later, are *al-Mudawwanah al-Kubrā* by Saḥnūn for the Mālikī school, and the *Kitāb al-Umm* written by al-Shāfi'ī himself. The *Ẓāhir al-Riwāyah,* however, are much more extensive.

Ibn 'Ābidīn has given a few words of warning when it comes to consulting later books. His text is reproduced below:

> As you have known the obligation to follow the preferred opinion out of the various opinions...know then that most of the verdicts handed out today by

> merely referring to the books of the later jurists are not trustworthy, especially the unverified verdicts in books like *Sharḥ al-Nuqāyah* by al-Quhistānī, *al-Durr al-Mukhtār*, and *al-Ashbāh wa al-Naẓā'ir*...for they contain in many cases the preference of a rejected opinion and the preference of that which is the opinion of another school, not preferred by anyone in this school.
>
> The transmission of an opinion may occur in about 20 books of the later jurists and still the opinion may be incorrect as the first jurist has erred and those coming after him have transmitted the opinion from him.[339]

Ibn 'Ābidīn is trying to tell us that a case should first be traced in the earliest books, and then in the later. When a case is found it needs to be subjected to verification. This verification means determining the underlying rule. Without tracing the rule employed, the *faqīh* can never be sure how the new case is to be settled. The tracing of the rule is a process that is identical to tracing the rule and *ratio decidendi* from a series of cases in modern law and separating it from the *obiter dicta*. This process is the essence of the methodology of *takhrīj*. The rule once extracted is used to settle the new case.

26.3.3 The Hierarchy of Texts Within a School

The texts of the school are the different categories of works produced by the jurists. In the Ḥanafī school, these are the earliest case books of the school that consist of cases settled by Imām Abū Ḥanīfah and his colleagues. These were recorded by Imām Muḥammad. Another category is that of the precis or *mukhtaṣars*. These books record the law that is to be followed. A third category that developed later are called the *fatāwā*, which rely on the *mukhtaṣars*, but add additional cases not covered by the *mukhtaṣars*. Commentaries have been written on all three categories of books and may be said to form a separate class. The

339. Ibn 'Ābidīn, *Ḥāshiyah* (Quetta, 1399 AH), vol. 1, 57; *Rasā'il*, 49.

description that follows is excerpted from the introduction to our translation of al-Marghīnānī's *Hidāyah*. The detailed description may be more useful for those interested in the nature of the texts.

It is well known that the first works on Islamic law are those written by Imām Muḥammad (God bless him).[340] Some of these works were referred to as the *Ẓāhir al-Riwāyah*. Scholars assign several meanings to this term, however, the meaning we are interested in is that the *Ẓāhir al-Riwāyah* are "the preferred rules from among the different narrations of the rules." Imām Muḥammad's works, besides the rulings of Abū Ḥanīfah, Abū Yūsuf and Muḥammad al-Shaybānī (himself), include a large number of other views. The other views recorded are, for example, those of Zufar, Ibrāhīm al-Nakha'ī, Ibn Abī Laylā, Abū Thawr, and al-Awzā'ī (God bless them all). A system of law that presents such a variety of opinions is difficult to follow, unless some rules are chosen for practice. Accordingly, after recording the rulings of different jurists, Imām Muḥammad himself identified some of those rules that were to be followed by the people. These rules were referred to as the *ẓāhir* rules or the rules preferred for compliance. These rules were primarily recorded in *Kitāb al-Aṣl* or *al-Mabsūṭ*. The recording of preferred opinions does not mean that other rulings were not recorded in this book. It is in *al-Jāmi' al-Ṣaghīr*, however, that Imām Muḥammad focused entirely on the preferred rules that were to be followed by the worshipper as well as the *qāḍī*. In fact, he focuses mostly on rules that help deal with violations so that a ruling (*fatwā*), or a decision, can be given to one who seeks it. Thus, we do not find a description of *wuḍū'* or *ṣalāt* in *al-Jāmi' al-Ṣaghīr*. According to 'Allāmah al-Lakhnawī (God bless him), he did not mention those rules that were followed day in and day out by every Muslim. The book was directed entirely at practice

340. Imām Mālik's *al-Muwaṭṭa'* and *Kitāb al-Āthār* by Imām Abū Yūsuf cannot be treated as books of Islamic law proper. We do not wish to dwell on a list of Imām Muḥammad's works and the details associated with them. These are well known and have been recorded by us in our works on Islamic jurisprudence, and by others in similar works.

(of the jurist); the other details could be acquired from *Kitāb al-Aṣl*. *Al-Jāmi' al-Ṣaghīr* was the first summary or précis in Islamic law that listed only those statements of the rules that were to be followed.[341] The second such summary was *al-Siyar al-Ṣaghīr*, also by Imām Muḥammad. The creation of these summaries shows the essential task of a *madhhab* or school of law: the bringing of uniformity into the law by identifying those rules, the *ẓāhir al-riwāyah*, out of a host of rulings, that were to be followed in practice by the school. These early summaries were not very comprehensive, because these were also the early days of the school; it had not acquired sufficient maturity.

The term *mukhtaṣar* appears to have been used for a rule book first by al-Muzanī (God bless him). He died in 264 A.H., and it is possible that such books were written before his time. His *Mukhtaṣar* is usually published with Imām al-Shāfi'ī's *Kitāb al-Umm*. In the Ḥanafī school, therefore, it was natural that al-Muzanī's nephew, al-Ṭaḥāwī, should use the term first.[342] After this, the writing of *mukhtaṣars* became a regular feature, whether or not this title was used. Some of the well known *mukhtaṣars* of the Ḥanafī school are the following:

1. *Al-Jāmi' al-Ṣaghīr* and *al-Siyar al-Ṣaghīr* by Imām Muḥammad al-Shaybānī (d. 189 A.H.). These have been described above.

---

341. *Al-Jāmi' al-Ṣaghīr* was reported by Imām Muḥammad entirely on the authority of Imām Abū Yūsuf. This adds to its strength. Imām Muḥammad based the work on forty *kitābs*, however, he did not make *bābs* or chapters within these *kitābs*. This work was undertaken by Imām Abū Ṭāhir al-Dabbās. As to why this book was recommended for memorisation depended upon the nature of the cases mentioned. These represented some of the core issues settled by the school. According to some jurists, the issues of this book were held in very high esteem and it was deemed necessary that no one be allowed to become a *qāḍī* or permitted to issue a *fatwā*, unless he had understood the issues of this book. 'Allāmah al-Lakhnawī has listed about forty jurists who wrote commentaries on this book, and these are all the well known jurists whose works we study today.

342. His book is called *Mukhtaṣar al-Ṭaḥāwī*.

2. *Mukhtaṣar al-Ṭaḥāwī* by al-Ṭaḥāwī (d. 321 A.H.). He begins with the statement that the book contains rules that cannot be ignored or whose knowledge must be acquired.
3. *Al-Kāfī* by Ḥākim al-Shahīd (d. 334 A.H.). In these *mukhtaṣars*, the chain of transmission of *fiqh* coming down from the earlier Imāms was maintained. This was the text chosen by Imām al-Sarakhsī (God bless him) for his 30 volume commentary *al-Mabsūṭ*. Al-Marawazī created this book by summarising *Kitāb al-Aṣl* and the two *Jāmi's* through the elimination of lengthy narrations and some repetitions.
4. *Mukhtaṣar al-Karkhī* by Imām al-Karkhī (d. 340 A.H.), the famous Ḥanafī jurist, who is also the author of *Uṣūl al-Karkhī*. We have not had the opportunity to examine this book, but jurists often quote it in their works.
5. *Mukhtaṣar al-Jaṣṣāṣ* by al-Jaṣṣāṣ (d. 370 A.H.). He was al-Karkhī's student.
6. *Mukhtaṣar al-Qudūrī* by al-Qudūrī. This was the text chosen by al-Marghīnānī for his own *Mukhtaṣar*. Al-Qudūrī (d. 430 A.H.) ordered the chapters in his book according to al-Ṭaḥāwī's book and not according to Imām Muḥammad's *al-Jāmi' al-Ṣaghīr*. Al-Qudūrī is said to have written a commentary on al-Karkhī's *Mukhtaṣar*.
7. *Tuḥfat al-Fuqahā'* by al-Samarqandī (d. 538 A.H.). He was al-Kāsānī's teacher and his father-in-law. The book is highly organized and a strict application of the term *mukhtaṣar* will exclude this book from this category.[343]
8. *Bidāyat al-Mubtadi'* by al-Marghīnānī (d. 593 A.H.). This is the *matn* of which *al-Hidāyah* is the commentary.
9. *Al-Ḥāwī* by Najm al-Dīn al-Turkī (d. 652 A.H.).
10. *Al-Fiqh al-Nāfi'* by Nāṣir al-Dīn al-Samarqandī.

After this there was an abundance of such texts and what we mention below are just a few of the well known texts.

343. The Author, however, says that he has brought in additional issues that were not included by al-Qudūrī, and that he has tried to remove the difficulties encountered in studying al-Qudūrī. Further, he has provided the *adillah* (evidences) and arguments in brief.

11. *Al-Mukhtār lil-Fatwā* by al-Mawṣilī (d. 683 A.H.). The commentary on this *matn* is written by *al-Mawṣilī* himself and is called *al-Ikkhtiyār*. This text is used in al-Azhar.
12. *Majma' al-Baḥrayn* by al-Sā'ātī (d. 694 A.H.)
13. *Kanz al-Daqā'iq* by al-Nasafī (d. 710 A.H.).
14. *Wiqāyat al-Riwāyah fī Masā'il al-Hidāyah* by Burhān al-Sharī'ah Maḥmūd ibn Sadr al-Sharī'ah (d. 747 A.H.). As the title shows, it was a summary prepared from al-Hidāyah itself, not only its *matn*. Ṣadr al-Sharī'ah al-Thānī (d. 747 A.H.), the grandson and student of this author, summarised the summary further, calling it *al-Nuqāyah*, and wrote a commentary on it as well.

Some of the texts that are used by the *madāris* for teaching, referred to as the acknowledged texts (*mutūn mu'tabarah*), are those mentioned at (6), (11), (13) and (14). Some add (12) to this list. In the grades mentioned above, these jurists, the authors of the *mutūn mu'tabarah*, are referred to as *muqallids*. They cannot prefer opinions, but have the ability to identify the strong opinions that are to be followed, that is, opinions preferred by those in the higher grades. In our view, preference should be given to *Bidāyat al-Mubtadi'* as the *matn* for teaching purposes and thereafter *al-Hidāyah* should be used as a commentary to understand the rules, as we elaborate below. Further, *Mukhtaṣar al-Qudūrī* is included within *Bidāyat al-Mubtadi'*.

The *mukhtaṣars* listed above and even those that are not listed form a linked chain. Each *mukhtaṣar* borrows from the one that precedes it. In this chain, preference is usually given to those opinions that came first. The attempt being to commence the statement of the rules with the opinions of the earlier Imāms. This conforms with the system of precedents in Islamic law. *In Islamic law, the precedents assigned priority are those that were laid down first and not those that came later.* The reverse order is followed in the common law, with the latest decision being given precedence.[344] The presumption in Islamic law is that the decisions arrived at

344. This is a wonderful topic for research.

earlier are closer to the *uṣūl*,[345] while those that came later are to be handled with caution. Those who are interested in this topic may examine the writings of Ibn 'Ābidīn on the subject. This system of precedents attaches significance to chains coming down from the earlier *imāms*, so as to distinguish the authentic from the spurious and the strong from the weak.

There is yet another feature that we consider most important, and to explain that we have to go back to the great Imām (Abū Ḥanīfah) and his disciples. Roscoe Pound, in his five volume work on jurisprudence, quotes from Hamilton's translation of the *Hidāyah* and says that this is the beginning of the case method of studying law.[346] In our view, this was not the beginning of the case method, rather the beginning was made by Imām Muḥammad in his well known books, which in turn reflects the tremendous effort made by the learned Imām and his teachers. It is because of this contribution alone that he is rightly called the greatest (A'ẓam) Imām. Imām al-Sarakhsī after praising the Imām says the following:

> Al-Shāfi'ī (God bless him) is reported to have said, "The people (jurists) are all dependants of Abū Ḥanīfah (God bless him) in *fiqh*." Ibn Surayj (God bless him), who was a leader among the companions of al-Shāfi'ī (God bless him), has reported that a man criticised Abū Ḥanīfah, so al-Shāfi'ī called him and said to him, "O so and so, you criticise a person to whom the entire *ummah* concedes three-fourths of knowledge when he does not concede to them even one-fourth." The man said, "And how is that?" He replied, "*Fiqh* is questions and responses (through the formation of cases) and he is the one who alone

345. That is, they were derived by those who had greater knowledge of the evidences, as they were close to the period of the Prophet (God bless him and grant him peace) and were more proficient in the use of *uṣūl* that they had laid down themselves.

346. The introduction of the case method of study in American law schools is attributed to Langdell and Ames.

> formulated the questions, thus, half the knowledge is surrendered to him. Thereafter, he answered all the questions[347] and even his opponents do not say that he erred in all his answers. When that in which they agreed with him is compared with what they disputed with him, three-fourths is surrendered to him.[348] The remaining[349] is shared by him with all other jurists."[350] The person repented on what he had said.

Whatever the source of this story, its implication is true. The words "questions and responses" means the formulation of cases, either actual or hypothetical, for explaining the rules. It is this that the Imām did along with his disciples.[351] Without these cases, *fiqh* would not have been understood, neither by the Ḥanafī jurists nor even by those of the Mālikī and Shāfi'ī schools, but that is another story, which is recorded in the next section. It is because of these cases and the associated rules that all jurists are dependants of Abū Ḥanīfah, Nu'mān ibn Thābit ibn Zotah (God be pleased with him). It is not without reason then that 'Allāmah al-Lakhnawī says: *wa mā adrāka mā Abū Ḥanīfah?*

The way the rules are elaborated in these works through chains of related cases is simply outstanding and highly sophisticated. This method was developed into an art that reached its perfection in the works of jurists like al-Sarakhsī, who added a tremendous amount of supporting detail to these cases. Till this time, Islamic law was a practical law solving problems; it needed all this detail. Today, very few people appreciate these cases or even read and benefit from this unique method of elaborating the law. Credit for further organising the cases in the light of the rules must be given to Ḥākim al-Shahīd as well. Nevertheless, great significance was

347. That is, settled the cases.
348. One-half for framing the initial cases and another one-fourth for the right decisions.
349. One-fourth.
350. Due to the possibility that he may have issued the correct rulings even in some of these.
351. Those who design cases today, for case studies, know that this is not an easy task.

attached to the study of the detailed cases by the earlier jurists. The idea is captured in another story. Abū al-Faḍl Muḥammad ibn Muḥammad ibn Aḥmad, al-Ḥākim al-Shahīd, who was a *qāḍī*, wrote two books: *al-Muntaqā* and *al-Kāfī*. The latter is the précis prepared from Imām Muḥammad al-Shaybānī's *al-Mabsūṭ* and the two *Jāmi'*s. It is said that he died in the year 334 A.H. He was executed brutally by the Turks and is, therefore, referred to as Shahīd. As the story goes, he is reported to have said prior to his execution that this is the fate of a person who prefers this world over the next. As to why he said this, some add that when he prepared *al-Kāfī* by removing repetitions and details from Imām Muḥammad's books, the Imām appeared to him in a dream. In this dream, Imām Muḥammad asked him, "Why have you done this to my books?" He replied, "The *fuqahā'* have become lazy so I deleted the repetitions and stated what is essential." At this Imām Muḥammad became very angry and said, "May God cut you up like the way you have cut up my books." It is said that the Turks tied him between two tree-tops (by pulling them down) and he was split into two. In our view, this is not a very pleasing story for we feel that al-Ḥākim al-Shahīd, may God bless him, made a powerful contribution to the case method that we have mentioned above. It does, however, tell us that true *fiqh* can be acquired only by working through the detailed cases. There is no method more powerful than this for the teaching of *fiqh*. It is also the method that dominated the scene for a long time, until the appearance of the literalists.

26.4 The Integral Bond Between the Four Sunni Schools

There is a saying that was current among the Ḥanafī jurists: "The seed of the discipline of *fiqh* was sown by Ibn Mas'ūd (R), irrigated by 'Alqamah (R), harvested by al-Nakha'ī (R), threshed by Ḥammād (R), milled by Abū Ḥanīfah (R), kneaded by Abū Yūsuf (R), baked by Muḥammad (R), and all the jurists partake of this bread"—Ibn 'Ābidīn (God bless him). The truth of this statement cannot be denied by anyone. In fact, we would like to add to the following words to this quotation: "And garnished by al-Sarakhsī (R)."

As has already been explained, the schools of Islamic law are not sects; they are systems of interpretation. Each school has its own independent set of principles, which cannot be mixed up with the principles of other schools without causing inner contradictions and analytical inconsistency. The set of principles adopted by each school is followed by the jurists within the school. It is obvious that the use of one set of principles may lead to a different legal opinion on the derived law. Despite these differences, an integral bond exists between the schools both in the area of *fiqh* as well as *uṣūl al-fiqh*. In this section, we will explain the nature of this integral bond or organic link. The link shows that the schools developed through an initial effort by the Ḥanafī school and later by mutual cooperation of all the four schools.

We may recall from the history of Islamic law that Kufah, a city in Iraq, gradually turned into a centre of *fiqh* and learning. The reason for its being so is traced to the decision of 'Umar (R), who sent 'Abd Allāh ibn Mas'ūd (R) (d. 32 A.H.) as a teacher and *qāḍī* for this area. This learned Companion trained a large number of jurists, who in turn produced students many of whom attained great fame. Among these jurists were Alqamah al-Nakha'ī, his nephew Ibrāhīm al-Nakha'ī, Qāḍī Shurayḥ, and Ḥammād ibn Abū Sulaymān.

The founder of the Ḥanafī School was Abū Ḥanīfah Nu'mān ibn Thābit ibn Zūṭah, possibly of Afghan origin. Imam Abū Ḥanīfah was born in Kufah in the year 80 A.H. (699 A.D.) and died in 150 A.H. (767 A.D.). He is also called Imām A'ẓam or the Great Imām. He began his early education in scholastics (*kalām*) and later developed an interest for jurisprudence under the tutorship of his Shaykh, Ḥammād ibn Abū Sulaymān (d. 120 A.H.).

He was a textile merchant by profession and it is said that due to this reason his *fiqh* reflects his practical approach to legal problems. Abū Ḥanīfah was later given the title of the leader of the school of Ahl al-Ra'y. He is reported to have met some Companions (R) as well, foremost amongst them is Anas ibn

Mālik. In this sense, he was a Follower of the Companions (R).

Out of the pupils of Abū Ḥanīfah, four are famous; they were: Abū Yūsuf Ya'qūb ibn Ibrāhīm al-Anṣārī (113–182 A.H.), Zufar ibn Hudhayl ibn Qays (110–158 A.H.), Muḥammad ibn al-Ḥasan ibn Farqād al-Shaybānī (132–189 A.H.), and Ḥasan ibn Ziyād al-Lu'lū'ī. Through these disciples, the fame of the Ḥanafī school spread far and wide. Abū Yūsuf was appointed judge in Baghdad and later became the Chief Qāḍī with authority to appoint judges all over the kingdom. He, thus, had the opportunity to propagate the school of the great Imām.

Muḥammad ibn al-Ḥasan al-Shaybānī, who must have been 18 years old when Abū Ḥanīfah died, takes the credit for recording not only the first books of the Ḥanafī school, but also those of the entire Islamic legal system. The books written by him were of two types: the first were called *ẓāhir al-riwāyah* or books of the primary issues, while the second were called *al-nawādir* or unusual cases. In addition to the above, he wrote *Kitāb al-Ḥujjah 'alā Ahl al-Madīnah,* a book on the use of traditions, and another book on traditions called *al-Āthār.* His version of Mālik's *Muwaṭṭa'* is also considered highly reliable. Abū Yūsuf also wrote a book on traditions called *al-Āthār,* and his *Kitāb al-Kharāj* is very well known. The above books form the foundation of Ḥanafī *fiqh.*

The distinctive feature of Imām Muḥammad's books and hence those of the Ḥanafī school is that they record *fiqh* in the form of issues and cases. Some of these were what are today in law schools called hypotheticals. Hypotheticals are carefully prepared cases for imparting instruction. Imām Abū Ḥanīfah is credit with the creation of all the issues and cases, which run in hundreds of thousands. It is obvious that some of the cases had come down from his teachers, while others must have been brought up by his able disciples. Nevertheless, the arrangement, refinement and organization of these cases is the work of this great jurist, due to which he earned the title of Imām A'ẓam.

It is these cases and issues, and the related case-method, that has left to the development of *fiqh* and Islamic law. They were deemed so important that jurists not belonging to the Ḥanafī school also latched on to them and tried to give their own views according to the principles of interpretation preferred by them. To understand this process and how the link was established we may briefly note some points about how the development of the law took place.

1. The law as we know it today (and by that we really mean today) began to crystallise around the year 100 AH. It became an organized and mature system by the year 132 AH when the Ummayyads lost power. It was the Ḥanafīs who had developed this law. The other schools had not even come into existence as yet.

2. Imām Abū Yūsuf and companions collaborating with the rulers refined the system and recorded the opinions not only of their own school, but those of other well known jurists as well like al-Awzā'ī, Ibn Abī Laylā and others.

3. The development of the other schools followed over the next two centuries. The Mālikī school emerged into prominence with the writing of Sahnūn, while Imām al-Shāfī's school was given some shape by al-Muzanī. This happened one hundred years after Imām Abū Ḥanīfah's death in 150 AH.

4. Schools like those of al-Tabarī and the Ẓāhirīs became extinct.

5. The Ḥanbalī school became extinct, but was revived by Ibn Taymiyyah and Ibn Qayyim towards the middle of the 8th century of the Hijrah.

6. The sound compilations of traditions, like the Ṣaḥīḥ of Imām al-Bukhārī, started appearing almost one hundred and thirty years after finalization of the law of the Ḥanafī school.

7. The first compilation of traditions is that by Imām Mālik. The first book on *uṣūl al-fiqh* was written by Imām al-Shāfi'ī. *Qawā'id fiqhiyyah* was written by al-Karkhī although these were derived from the writings of Imām Muḥammad. Other

compilations of these *qawā'id*, it is said, existed much before that.

8. The theory of interests or the purposes of the law started emerging a little before al-Ghazālī's time and was fully developed by him.

9. The sixth and the seventh centuries were a period of great creativity. Some say that it was in these centuries that *taqlīd* set in. This is not true.

10. Some of the most powerful works were produced by the jurists of what are now called the Central Asian States.

The truth is that most of the earlier authoritative books of the other schools are a response to what is recorded in Imām Muḥammad's books. *Al-Mudawwanah al-Kubrā* of the Mālikī school compiled by al-Saḥnūn is a response to the rulings given in the above books. Much of al-Shāfi'īs work is also in response to these works. Imām al-Shāfi'ī, it is well known, stayed with Imām Muḥammad and acquired knowledge from him. This is reflected in his books where he refers again and again to the decisions of the Ḥanafī school, even when he disagrees with them. On many occasions, one finds him disagreeing with Abū Ḥanīfah, but adopting the views of the other jurists of the Ḥanafī school, especially those of Zufar. The Mālikī work *al-Mudawwanah al-Kubrā* expressly acknowledges that they are giving their own views on the Ḥanafī (Iraqi) cases. The figure below shows this link along with the dates of devolopment. We may list these points as follows:

1. The Hanafi School, as already explained, was the first to develop the law systematically on the basis of what they had inherited from the Companions and their students in the form of issues or cases.
2. The Ḥanafī school, with the exception of the Imām, worked in collaboration with the rulers. In some periods, such collaboration decreased, but it did continue in one form or another right up to the time of the Ottoman

Turks. Accordingly, this is the school with the maximum experience in the administration of justice.

3. An examination of the earlier sources of the other schools shows that they developed in reaction to, or in response to, the work done by the Ḥanafī school by giving rulings on the issues recorded in his works. It is said that Imām al-Shāfi'ī had memorised the entire *Kitāb al-Aṣl*. There is a constant reference to the Ḥanafī school in his works. In the case of the Mālikī school, *al-Muwaṭṭa'* is the first book to be written by any Muslim jurist, but it is not really a manual of *fiqh*. The first authoritative book of this school is *al-Mudawwana al-Kubrā* written by Saḥnūn. This book expressly mentions that it contains the rulings given by Ibn al-Qāsim on the issues raised by the jurists of Kufa, that is, the Ḥanafīs. These rulings were issued according to the principles of interpretation adopted by the Mālikī school. The Ḥanbalī school developed by borrowing from all three schools.

Similar develpments can be shown for *uṣūl al-fiqh* as well. Although it was Imām Shāfi'ī who wrote the first book the contributions of Ḥanafīs like Jaṣṣāṣ and Dabbūsī cannot be overlooked. It was Jaṣṣāṣ who really developed the concept of *bayān* in the light of the views of his teacher al-Karkhī, although we attribute the origin of the idea to Imām al-Shāfi'ī. It was al-Dabbūsī who really organized the discipline of *uṣūl al-fiqh* and set a pattern that is followed by all later books, even till today.

The conclusion we may draw is that the four Sunnī schools are actually like one large family, although they now live in separate houses due to the different set of rules of interpretation adopted by them. These rules are so crucial that people from one house can visit other houses, but cannot stay there or borrow from them. They can, however, move to the other houses permanently if they like.

THE ORGANIC LINK BETWEEN THE SCHOOLS OF FIQH

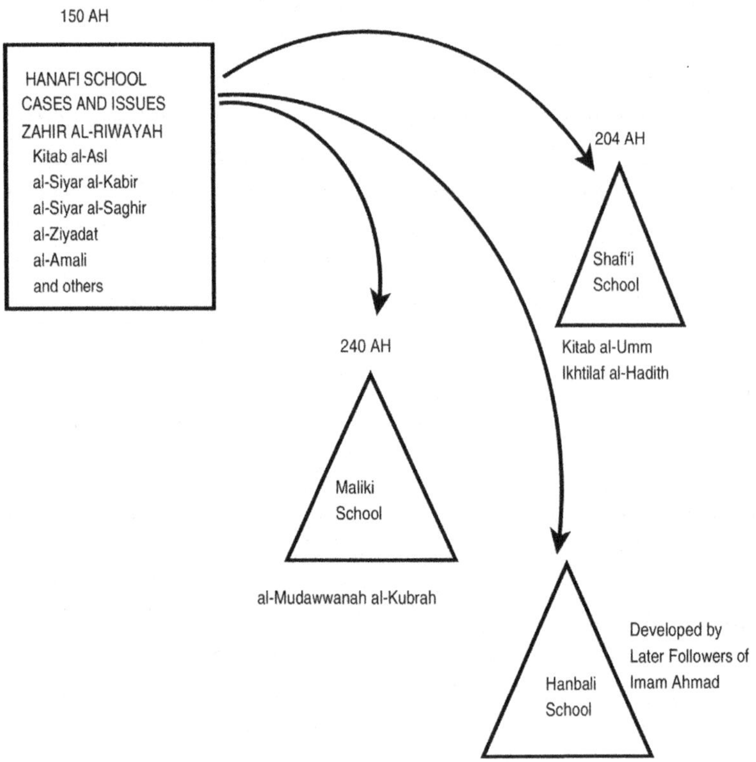

27 The Role of the Modern Muslim Jurist

After studying Islamic jurisprudence in some detail, most students are at a loss to discover how the system is to be implemented today. The asnwer is simple in some respects and very complex in other ways. The simple answer is that a legal system is implemented by the personnel who man the system. It is the quality of the persaonnel that will determine the success of the system in the present age. In this chapter, therefore, we will focus on the modern jurist, his qualifications and activity. We will try to identify the goals of such a jurist and how he can attain them. After doing so, we can hope that the complexities involved will be resolved gradually.

27.1 Is There a Possibility of Independent *Ijtihād* Today?

27.1.1 Independent *ijtihād* is Theoretically Possible Today, but the Reality is Different

It is theoretically possible today for a person to be a full *mujtahid*. Such a *mujtahid* can start from scratch and build the whole system of *fiqh* or part of it according to his *ijtihād*. This means that he can approach the texts of the Qur'ān and the *Sunnah* without the need of recourse to what the schools of Islamic law have said. He may even overturn some of the establihsed rulings of the established schools. What qualifications are required for such a *mujtahid* and what are the prerequisites before he can begin to undertake *ijtihād*?

In fact, we find today that certain learned scholars have arrogated this right to themselves without possessing the requisite qualifications or having met the basic requirements. The scholars do it with good intentions and we cannot doubt their intentions. They usually issue rulings that appeal to human reason. All we can say is that human reason must operate within the principles of the *sharī'ah* if the *ijtihād* has to have meaning.

What then are the qualifications? If a scholar has an excellent knowledge of Arabic, has studied *tafīrs* and the traditions very deeply, and possesses a very kind mind, he may have the basic qualfifications, but this is not all that is required. This scholar must lay down his principles of interpretation in detail. By this is meant the hundreds of principles that we have been trying to describe above and which are the foundation of any school or are the armour of the *full mujtahid*. They must then apply these rules of interpretation to the texts for the derivation of, at least, some rules. These rules of interpretation are not the rules used for *tafsīr*. The rules of *tafsīr* are only a fraction of what the jurist is required to work with. It is for the same reason that courts of law should not rely solely on *tafsīrs* for settling issues, while ignoring the rules of the establihsed schools laid down in their manuals. In short, this scholar must lay down his whole system of rules before some importance can be attached to his opinions, however pleasing they are in the rational sense. To do so, he has to first know what the existing principles are.

Establishing a whole system of rules, like the systems that are prevalent in the existing schools, is an impossible task for a single jurist. It has taken centuries for the rules of interpretation to be refined for the exisiting schools. Even if it is assumed that he can do it, the jurist will never be able to use them in his lifetime, because his entire life will be spent creating a new system. This is true even if he keeps all the rules of the schools in front of him and starts choosing rules to create a new system. Let us assume again that he can do it in a reasonably short time through the process of selection, what will be the result? Will he be able to use them? All that can happen is that it will result in a fifth Sunni school, and that too if his system is accepted to some extent. The conclusion is that there is no point in setting up a new system of legal interpretation when there is so much variety in the existing schools. It is exactly for this reason that jurists like Sarakhsī, Ghazālī, Dabbūsī, Karkhī and Jaṣṣāṣ did not set up their own schools, although they could have come up with a detailed and new system of interpretation. How then can an individual who does not even have a fraction of the ability of these great jurists come up with the new system and qualify for being a *mujtahid* with absolute authority?

What we have said above applies to all modern jurists, scholars, lawyers, judges and even to the state. In some law cases in Pakistan it has been suggested that the state is a *mujtahid* and *ijtihād* is a collective activity. This is not acceptable on the grounds that have been listed above.

On saying the above, we come to face another question: But *ijtihād* is an activity that cannot come to an end, and this requires that there be some *mujtahid* who can undertake this activity. The response is that this activity is not coming to an end; it will take place in a limited sense within the school and its sytem. There is no legal problem that cannot be solved through this activity within the school. We may now turn to the description of the nature of this activity.

27.1.2 The Highest Stature That a Modern Jurist Can Possibly Attain Today

Ijtihād in a limited sense has to be undertaken within the school and within the system set up by the school. There is no modern problem that cannot be solved with this activity. The reason is that the system set up by the jurists, despite the requirements of *taqlīd*, is so efficient and flexible that all problems can be solved.

For attaining the required qualifications, the jurist has to start at the lowest rung of the ladder described for the hierarchy of the jurists in the previous chapter. As he gains more expertise and moves up the ladder, he will be able to provide solutions for many problems. It is acknowledged that attaining the status of the *mujtahid fī al-masā'il* is also not possible for people today or even that of the *aṣḥāb al-takhrīj*. One look at the names of the jurists listed under these categories makes one shudder at the immense requirements for attaining that stage.

Nevertheless, the prospective jurist issuing rulings today must try to follow the methods of those jurists. Even if he cannot reach that stage, he will acquire a good knowledge of the methodology used by those jurists. It is, therefore, essential that we turn to a brief description of that methodology.

We may classify the modern jurist, once he has acquired the requisite skills, as a *faqīh*, and for this he may be anywhere in the last four grades of the jurists. The *faqīh* will use a methodology that is called *takhrīj*. In simple words, it will mean "discovering the law through the established general principles and extending it to new cases with the help of reasoning from principles." This methodology is evident in the works of jurists like al-Karkhī, al-Dabbūsī, al-Sarakhsī, al-Kāsānī, al-Marghīnānī and so on.

Today, the methodology of *takhrīj* is to be exercised by the higher courts in the country. In this work, jurists, law professors and lawyers will also participate using the same methodology. In other words, all cases in the law courts are to be settled through the methodology of *takhrīj*. The truth is that *takhrīj* is a methodology in which jurist, judges, professors and lawyers are already well versed; it is nothing new for them. What needs to be developed and refined, however, is the Islamic methods of undertaking adjudication. This method can be expressed simply in the statement: *judges do not legislate, they merely discover the law.*

It should also not be assumed that the *faqīh* cannot approach the sources that we have described in part two and called the sources for the *mujtahid.* He certainly can, but the system erected by the *fuqahā'* appears to be saying that there is no need to reinvent the wheel. The entire law, after analytical systematization, has been organized around a large body of principles, precedents and rules. This body of principles, precedents and rules provides enough flexibility for expansion and change. So why go through the whole process once again, a process over which centuries of labour has been expended by the *mujtahid?* Why not build on the work that has been done already; why lose the heritage?

The *faqīh* then is to perform the following tasks:

1. **To settle disputes in the light of the existing case law**. This means maintaining the decisions already settled by the *mujtahid.* It is an activity that is similar to the doctrine of *stare decisis* in the law. It makes the following of precedents necessary for the *faqīh.* The difference is that the Islamic precedents at the top have greater priority, as already explained.

2. **To extend the law, if necessary, from the existing general principles of Islamic law**. These principles are basically of two types: those that have been stated explicitly in the texts of the Qur'ān and the *Sunnah* and those that have been derived by the jurist through the existing law settled by the *mujtahid.*

3. If the new case faced by the *faqīh* cannot be settled on the basis of the two previous methods, **to formulate a new principle provided that this new principle meets the conditions laid down by the jurists**. Briefly, these conditions are that the new principle should not attempt to overturn the meaning or implication of a text of the Qur'ān or the *Sunnah;* it should not alter the meaning of

an established principle of the law; and it should be in conformity with the purposes of Islamic law (*maqāṣid al-sharī'ah*).

Finally, we may quote the great Imām al-Karkhī who laid down a comprehensive principle for the present context:

> The principle is that if for a new case, the seeker does not find an answer or a precedent in the books of our school, then, it is necessary for him to derive the answer from other sources, either from the Book or from the *Sunnah* or from other evidences, moving from the strongest to the stronger, **however, the *ḥukm* will not lie outside of these principles**. Al-Nasafī (the commentator) said: The settled issues have been derived from these principles, and new cases and incidents can be derived from them as well.

27.1.3 Inter-school Disputes

Such disputes arise mainly from contracts where citizens belonging to different schools will enter into transactions with each other. Commercial contracts may be dealt with through the uniform law made for the whole country. This leaves matters that we talk about under personal law. A method was laid down for these during the British times in India, but we would like to qualify that somewhat.

Marriages across school boundaries take place and are a fact of life. The same applies to all contracts and transactions. The courts in the Sub-Continent have held that in case of a dispute arising out of a marriage in which the husband and wife belong to different "sects," the rules of the sect of the defendant will apply.[352] "There can be no doubt that justice, equity and good conscience require that the question of the validity of the alleged marriage must be

352. This rule was settled in *Aziz Bano v. Ali Muhammad Ibrahim*, AIR (1925) Allahabad, at 720. The term "sect" in this case is inappropriate; the schools of law are not sects.

determined according to the personal law of the defendant, that is, the Shiah Law."[353] The statement clearly shows that the rule of following the defendant's law in case of marriage is based upon "justice, equity and good conscience," which basically means the principles and concept of justice of the English common law. This is not a valid basis for determining rules for Islamic law, nor can it be called "*ijtihād*" as some may assume.

This rule leads to uncertainty as the husband and wife can never be clear about their respective duties, and also about which law will apply when they disagree, when such knowledge is essential for the proper functioning of marriage and is not a question of always settling matters in court. Marriage is a contract and should be treated like all other conctracts. Consequently, the law to be applied for disputes that come before courts and for determining the duties of the spouses should be the law of the school under which the contract has been concluded. The law of the school must be identified at the time of the contract whether the marriage is solemnised by a registrar or by the civil court.

There are different schools within the Shi'ahs and also within the Sunnīs, and inter-marriages can adopt different forms. The above rule should be followed not only where the marriage is between a Shi'ah and Sunni, but also when it takes place, for example, between a Ḥanafī and a Shāfi'ī. Following the law under which the marriage contract is concluded will not amount to changing one's school and each spouse can continue to follow his or her school for all matters other than marriage and divorce.

27.2 Issuing *Fatwās* and Judgments

27.2.1 The Need for Recording Reasoning With the *Fatwā*

A modern *fatwā* and a judgment should have the same structure. The detailed responses given to issues by jurists like al-Sarakhsī have this format. The structure basically requires four things: the

353. *Aziz Bano v. Mohammad Ibrahim Husain*, 89 Ind Cas 690, at para. 5.

statement of facts of the case, the identification of the issues to be resolved, legal analysis in which the rules are applied to facts, and finally the conclusion (holding or ruling). As education spreads, questions are raised by persons who are well educated; some are scholars in their own right. They deserve adequate and well reasoned responses. Very short *fatwās* issued by learned Muftīs are, therefore, no longer the right thing to do. Every *fatwā* must be accompanied by a reasonable account of the legal reasoning adopted. There are several advantages in doing this:

- First, is the issue of qualification. A detailed and well reasoned *fatwā* will easily show whether the *muftī* is qualfied to issue a *fatwā*. If it is just a matter of reading the texts and mentioning the rule written in those texts, then anyone with a reading knowledge of Arabic can do this. In fact, a computer software can be designed that can easily reproduce such rules, and might perform the task better. Providing legal reasoning is, therefore, essential.

- Second, a well reasoned *fatwā* has great instructional value. If *fatwās* are issued for a few years according to this method, a huge knowledge-base will be created, which can be used by teaching institutes for building the case method of study. Legal education will improve considerably.

- Third, journals reviewing this knowledge base will be able to indicate the direction that changes and developments in the law are taking. It will help correct the errors that may have been made unintentionally. This can bring about a uniform and effective development of the law.

There are many good books written by jurists on how to issue *fatwās*. Well known among these are the works of Ibn 'Ābidīn (Ḥanafī), al-Nawawī, al-Qarāfī and Ibn al-Qayyim. It is not our purpose to reproduce the contents of these books here. We will just provide a few quotations from jurists that may prove helpful.

Imām Abu al-Ḥusayn al-Karkhī laid down the following rule for responding to a question: "When a person asks a question it is necessary for the responding jurist not to answer in absolute and general terms. He should examine the question to see whether it is a single category or may be divided into two or more. He should then examine each category word for word and give a suitable answer to the question. This principle is of immense benefit. The reason is that a reply in absolute terms can readily be ripped apart, because words are seldom employed in general terms." What he is saying is that the facts of the case should be clearly understood, and broken down into precise issues before giving an answer.

The learned author of *Fatāwā Qāḍī Khān* gave very precise advice to the person issuing *fatwās*, the *muftī*, as to how he is to conduct himself in searching for and issuing of the ruling. The advice is reproduced below:

> The *muftī* in our times, from among our (contemporary) companions, when he is asked for a *fatwā* on an issue, and is asked about an incident, should:
>
> (1) If the issue is related from our early companions through the *ẓāhir* transmissions, without a disagreement among them, is to incline towards them and issue the ruling according to their opinion. He is not to oppose them with his own opinion, even if he is a full *mujtahid*. The presumption is that the truth sides with our companions, and they are not to be opposed. His *ijtihād* cannot reach the level of their *ijtihād*. He is not to incline towards the opinion of a jurist who has opposed them. Nor is he to accept such a person's *hujjah* (proof), because they knew the *adillah* (evidences) and could distinguish between an evidence that was authentic and established and one that was the opposite of this.
>
> (2) If the issue is disputed by our companions, and one of his disciples is siding with Abū Ḥanīfah (God bless him), he is to adopt their view, due to the combining of the conditions (of *ijtihād*) and the gathering of sound *adillah* in their view. If both disciples oppose

Abū Ḥanīfah (through a common opinion), and if the difference is based upon a change in conditions due to the passage of time, like rendering a verdict on the basis of *prima facie* moral probity, he is to adopt the ruling of the two disciples, as the condition of the people has changed. Thus, in the case of *muzār'ah, mu'āmalah* and similar issues, he is to adopt the view of the two disciples. The basis is the unanimous agreement of the later jurists on these issues. In issues other than these, some have maintained that the *muftī* is to be given an option of choosing (between them) according to what his opinion guides him to. 'Abd Allāh ibn al-Mubārak has said that he is to adopt the opinion of Imām Abū Ḥanīfah (God bless him) in such a case. They discussed the question as to who is a *mujtahid*. Some said that if a person is asked about ten issues and he gives a sound ruling in eight of these and errs in the rest, he is a *mujtahid*. There are others who maintain that the *mujtahid* is one who has necessarily absorbed (memorised) *al-Mabsūṭ*, identified the abrogating and abrogated texts, knows the *muḥkam* and *mu'awwal*, and is aware of the practices and customs of the people.

(3) If the issue is found in books other than the *Ẓāhir al-Riwāyah*, then if it is compatible with the *uṣūl* (system of interpretation and *qawā'id*) of our companions, he is to act upon it.

(4) If there is no narration about the issue from our companions, but the later jurists have agreed about it to some extent, he is to act upon it. If they have disagreed, he is to undertake *ijtihād* and issue the ruling that appears sound to him.

(5) If the *muftī* is a *muqallid* and not a *mujtahid*, he is to follow the view of the person who has the greatest expertise in *fiqh* in his view, but he is to attribute the response to such a (knowledgeable) person. If the most

> learned person in *fiqh*, in his view, lives in a city other than his, he is to have recourse to him in writing, and is not to work on conjecture for fear of fabrication.

We may now turn to a sample *fatwā* in which an attempt was made to provide adequate reasoning.

27.2.2 Sample *Fatwā*

A question was sent to this writer by a person who appears to have a reasonable knowledge of the rules of *fiqh*. The question is detailed and consists of several issues. The question is first reproduced followed by the response:

27.2.2.1 Question

¶ **1.** I have a very unusual question concerning *uṣūl al-fiqh*. I am contacting you because you are an expert in this field, and I am sure that the average *mufti* would not be able to answer it. I will be sincerely grateful to you if you could help me in this regard.
¶ **2.** My question regards the cases in which the *asbāb* of the usual *aḥkām* are anomalous or missing. As an instance, I will consider the situation of a Muslim living within the polar circles, where the sun does not set at all for six months and does not rise for the following six months. I know that there are already *fatāwā* providing a solution to the related questions (for instance: one should follow the timings of the nearest country). But my question is quite different: I would like to know why the *fuqahā'* feel the need to devise special *aḥkām* for such cases, instead of simply applying the general rule.
¶ **3.** I further explain my question through an illustration: if the sun does not set for six months, as it happens at the poles, then during that long period the *sabab* for *salāt-ul-maghrib* is simply missing. Consequently, according to the general rule, there should be no *wujūb* for *ṣalāh*. Why do the *fuqahā'* have to devise an alternative line of reasoning to make the situation somehow similar to the "normal" cases? Of course, I do know that meanwhile in the rest of the world days and nights alternate, but

why should I care about that? If I am in a place where the *sabab* of *dukhūl waqt al-salaah* does not "happen," then the *shart of wujūb* for *ṣalāh* is not fulfilled, and that *ṣalāh* is not *wājib* for me. Any other considerations should be irrelevant for me, unless there is a *dalīl shar'ī* to that effect.

¶ **4.** I understand that this conclusion is very astonishing and that it raises misgivings, considering that the obligation of something as fundamental as *ṣalāh* would be suspended, but why should it be any different from the case of a menstruating woman, for whom the *wujūb* of *ṣalāh* is likewise suspended? Or from case of someone who does not have to pray *jumu'ah* because he lives in an small and isolated village where there is no mosque and only very few Muslims live? Or from the case of someone who does not pay the *zakāh* because his possessions do not reach the nisaab?

¶ **5.** No *mufti* raises an objection about these cases, or devises an alternative line of reasoning in order to establish the *wujūb*. That is because, due to the particular circumstances, the *wujūb* has been suspended by the *Shāri'* (Lawgiver) Himself. And yet, in other cases where applying the general rule leads to some strange result, as in the example of the polar circles, the *fuqahā'* make up new *aḥkām*, instead of accepting the logical conclusion of the general ruling as it is, however bizarre.

¶ **6.** What right do we humans have to change the *aḥkām* of *sharī'ah*? I already know about the *maqāṣid*, which should be taken into consideration and take priority over the general *aḥkām*, but how do we know that making the *ṣalāh* "regularly timed" in a geographical area where the Lawgiver Himself suspended the regularity of time-keeping would be according to the *maqāṣid*?

¶ **7.** As a side note, I would like to add that I really don't understand the reasoning of those who consider finding a solution to the "polar problem" as important for establishing that Islam is universal, fearing that it would not be universal if the *ḥukm* of *ṣalāh* would not be applicable to the polar regions. In my understanding, Islam IS universal, and its universality is not affected in the least by the fact that the *shurūṭ* of *ṣalāh* do not apply in the polar areas. It is simply the natural order of things established by Allah.

¶ **8.** I hope you will be able to provide me some clarification of this issue, on the basis of some *adillah shar'iyah.* I have a hard time accepting explanations like "it is just common sense," "it feels right" or other vague and subjective answers not supported by *adillah.* In the field of *sharī'ah,* as I understand it, the reasoning methodology should be based on *ẓāhiri asbāb* and the reasoning should be like that of Sayyidinā Musā ('alayhi al-salām), not on *bāṭini* argumentations like those of Sayyidina al-Khidr ('alayhi al-salām). I would be very much obliged if you could help me with this issue.

Jazaaka Allahu khairan.

27.2.2.2 Response

The Issues Raised

¶ **9.** The questioner is a very intelligent and a well read Muslim. He appears to have a good knowledge of the *sharī'ah*: both *fiqh* and *uṣūl al-fiqh.* We will first assess the issues he has raised and then try to answer them in a manner that should be satisfactory for him and for other readers. A number of issues have been raised and these are as follows:

- Whether in cases where the *asbāb* of the usual *aḥkām* are anomalous or missing—the requirements of the general rule imposing the obligation not being met—the jurists feel compelled, so to say, to bring such cases under the general rule and impose the obligation.

- Whether the jurists should restrict their reasoning to the verifiable causes expressly mentioned in the texts of the Qur'ān and the *Sunnah,* and when the causes are missing they should not extend the rules to new cases.

- Whether the attempt to extend the obligation, against the general rule, amounts to changing the *aḥkām* of the *sharī'ah,* a right that we as human beings do not have.

- Whether *maqāṣid* "take priority over the general *aḥkām*" or can overturn the regular *aḥkām.*

- Whether the *sabab* of *dukhūl waqt al-salaah* does not "happen" in the polar regions, and if so whether the *shart of wujūb* for *ṣalāh* is not fulfilled, thus, rendering *ṣalāh* as not *wājib* for people living there.
- Whether the universality of the noble *sharī'ah* comes into question in places where the apparent *asbāb* mentioned in the texts do not occur at all.

¶ **10.** These are some of the issues raised by the questioner. Some of these issues need comprehensive treatment, but the task of the *fatwā* is to indicate basic reasoning. The readers who wish to pursue the reasoning further may do so on their own. The first four issues have been taken up together in the first section, because they deal with fundamental matters of methodology and *uṣūl al-fiqh*.

Why Not Leave Peripheral Issues Alone

¶ **11.** A primary rule stated at the beginning of many books on *uṣūl al-fiqh* is that the legal texts of the Qur'ān and the *Sunnah* are to be acted upon to the extent possible.[354] This rule implies that the intention of the Lawgiver is to be given effect through our actions. The question then is what is the intention of the Lawgiver underlying each text, and in particular what are the limits to which such intention goes? We have to stay with this intention to the limits to which it extends. This is achieved by understanding the limits of the concepts that underlie these texts. These limits are first understood through literal means. Once these are exhausted, rational extensions are undertaken till we finally reach the level of the *maqāṣid al-sharī'ah*.

¶ **12.** Throughout the history of *uṣūl* it has been the fundamental position of the jurists that literal methods and rational methods are organically related and the intention of the Lawgiver is to be

354. See Abū Zayd 'Ubayd Allāh ibn 'Umar ibn 'Īsā al-Dabbūsi, *Taqwīm al-Adillah* (Beirut: Dār al-Kutub al-'Ilmiyyah, 2001), 13; al-Sarakhsī, *Uṣūl al-Sarakhsī* (Beirut: Dār al-Ma'rifah, 1973), 10.

discovered through all methods declared valid by the jurists.[355] The validity of each method is the subject-matter of *uṣūl*.

¶ **13.** The questions that may arise are: Should we limit our search for the intention of the Lawgiver and consequential actions to the literal meanings alone? If we have to extend our search, should it be confined to a strict method like *qiyās*? Should we delve into the area of the *ḥikmah* and thus adopt *istiḥsān, maṣlaḥah* and the *maqāṣid* as valid methods?

The Debate is Not New: To Extend Concepts or Not to Extend?

¶ **14.** Discussion about these questions is not new. It began with the Ẓāhirīs who wanted to confine the search to the literal meanings alone. There were others who argued that at the outer limits of literal interpretation, you cannot separate *qiyās* (syllogism) from the literal implications.[356] The well known example of not saying even "uff" (fie) to parents may be used here. It is a command of the noble Qur'ān. If we adopt the apparent literal meaning alone then the command becomes confined to uff. Mistreating parents by beating them or turning them out of the house is not covered in this literal meaning. The implied literal meaning includes them, however. The Ẓāhirīs may agree with this saying that this is actually a literal implication. The Ḥanafīs agree saying that this is done through *dalālat al-naṣ*, but the Ṣhāfi'ī jurists say that this extension is actually a form of syllogism called *qiyās al-ma'nā*. Now, if the Ḥanafī jurist want to extend the meaning through *qiyās* to the obligatory maintenance of parents thus providing them with shelter and subsistence, the Ẓāhirīs will definitely not agree.

¶ **15.** The extension of meanings in these ways is essential, because this is the only way Islam can be called a complete way of life. Attempting to limit the intention of the Lawgiver to literal methods alone will narrow down the meaning of Islamic law and

355. This has been discussed in great detail in our forthcoming work called *The Secrets of Uṣūl*.

356. For the same reasons syllogism is treated as a literal method by some in Western law as well.

its impact on the lives of people. This was not acceptable to the majority who maintain that there is no option other than *ta'līl*.

¶ **16.** As a result of trying to limit the intention of the Lawgiver, the Ẓāhirī school soon lost a following and became extinct. Its methods were rejected by the majority. The consequence is that their opinions have academic and historical value alone, and there is nothing binding in their opinion for anyone. Something similar to the Ẓāhirīs may be attributed to the Ahl al-Ḥadīth with the distinction that they try to follow everything without trying to check the derived literal meanings against the general principles derived through rational methods.

¶ **17.** Today, if we attempt to limit the intention of the Lawgiver to what is apparent from the texts and do not extend the intention to what is possible, we will be going against the stated position of the majority who maintain that we have no right to limit such intention. This also applies to limiting the rules of prayer timings to the apparent causes alone.

Some Scholars are Attempting to Revive the Debate in a New Form

¶ **18.** There are scholars, especially in the West, who are trying to revive the debate in a new form. We will not name names here and the Internet is loaded with their views for they have support from different quarters. They have come up with the assertion that the *sharī'ah* is one thing and *fiqh* is another thing. *Sharī'ah* is the law laid down by the Lawgiver, while *fiqh* is what the jurists think the law is. This assertion has two major implications.

¶ **19.** The first implication is that the *sharī'ah* is the literal meaning, and all the rest belongs to the minds of the *fuqahā'*. The *sharī'ah* is confined to the intention of the Lawgiver as is visible through the apparent literal meanings. The rest is the understanding of the *fuqahā'* pertaining to their own times. If the *fuqahā'* could have their own understanding of the law, so can we. We will, therefore, remove the work of the jurists and replace it with out own understanding based on our reason, modern ideas, human rights and international norms. When the work of the *fuqahā'* is set aside, and the intention of the Lawgiver is confined to the literal meanings alone, we will fill the vacuum with whatever pleases our reason.

¶ **20.** The second implication is that the schools continue to enjoy an overpowering authority over the masses. This authority must be shattered. It can only be done by setting aside the work of these jurists and labeling it as a creation of their own minds. The schools will automatically lose authority once this is done.

¶ **21.** Both implications, and the efforts behind them, have either failed or are bound to fail. It is not suggested, by any means, that the questioner belongs to this group of scholars, however, the very question as to why the jurists pursue rules that are not expressly implied follows similar reasoning.

The *Maqāṣid,* Deviant Particular Rules, and the Universality of the *Sharī'ah*

¶ **22.** The discussion about the *maqāṣid al-sharī'ah* (purposes of the *sharī'ah*) does not pertain to the core of the discussion on the topic addressed, but as the questioner has mentioned them, we will take up the matter very briefly here. The *maqāṣid* are organically linked to the concepts and meanings in the texts; they arise from such meanings. In this form, they are really broad general principles that highlight the general direction that the *sharī'ah* wants humans to take. General principles operate for usual cases (*aghlabiyyah*) and are subject to exceptions. This is the area of the *'azīmah* and *rukhṣah.* Likewise, the *maqāṣid.* An impression has been created by the writings of jurists like al-Shāṭibī that the *maqāṣid* are definitive (*qaṭ'ī*). Reading such works, some well known writers have suggested that the *maqāṣid* as universals can overturn some of the particular rules of the *sharī'ah.* This is preposterous and cannot be accepted. How can these purposes knock out the foundations on which they stand and from which they have emerged. In reality, the word *qaṭ'ī* has been misapplied in this context. Definitive here implies that it is definitely these five purposes that emerge from the texts. It does not mean that they are definitive in their implication to the extent that they can eliminate even the particulars (*juz'īs*). They are definitive to the extent that a general principle is definitive, which means that it is open to exceptions on the basis of a valid evidence.

¶ **23.** We may turn to the point that a deviation in the obligation of prayer at the poles or somewhere else, or in some special situation does not affect the universality of the *sharī'ah*. We will let Imam Shāṭibī answer this. He says: "A universal principle is not demolished by individual decisions nor rare opposing cases."[357] What he means is that rules are made for the usual cases, and the *shari'ah* keeps in view the existence of deviant cases. In other words, if I go to the North Pole, the obligation of prayer itself is not abolished, even though I cannot see the sun and am totally handicapped. He affirms again: "All these (exceptions) do not affect the legal basis, because the universal principle when it is established as a universal, the deviation of some individual rules from the requirement of the universal does not remove it from the status of a universal. Further, the rule that applies to a predominant majority is considered in the shari'ah as a general definitive rule, because individual deviations do not constitute a universal that conflicts with such an established universal."[358] This statement is in line with the assumptions of most schools. The universality of the *sharī'ah,* therefore, does not come into question due to such deviations.

¶ **24.** Having dealt with the first theoretical issues, we may turn to the issue of *wujub* of prayer in the polar regions where the sun is visible for six months.

The Obligation of Prayer and Prayer Timings in the Polar Regions

¶ **25.** *A Word About* Taḥqīq al-Manāṭ—There are two types of *ijtihad*: The first is called *tahqiq al-manat* and the other is reqular full blown *ijtihad* which may be called *takhrīj* to identify what we are about here.

¶ **26.** *Taḥqīq al-manāṭ* is not really *ijtihād* in the regular meaning of *ijtihād*. It is the ascertainment of legal facts insofar as facts affect

357. Al-Shāṭibī, *al-Muwāfaqāt*, vol. 1 (Beirut: Dār al-Kutub al-'Ilmiyyah, 2001), 185.
358. Ibid., vol. 2, 41.

legal rules. It has been called *ijtihād* out of respect for Imām al-Shāfi'ī, because he termed it *ijtihād* when he was discussing the determination of the direction of the *qiblah* on a cloudy night in the desert, in *al-Risālah*. We will, therefore, continue to refer to it as *ijtihād* and, in fact, try to show in a different work why it should be considered *ijtihād* of a type.

¶ **27.** This type of activity does not always need a jurist. For example, to determine if a beverage is an intoxicant, you will consult a pharmacist or chemist and not a jurist. Likewise when you are trying to determine the direction of the *qiblah* in a desert at night when there is a complete cloud cover; you need some kind of expert. The task of the jurist comes when the facts are reported to him, that is, what type of legal presumption is to be drawn from the reported facts. Some of our learned scholars are trying to undertake the activity of the expert when they try to figure out night and day at the poles even when the sun is visible or concealed for six months at a stretch. It is conveyed somewhere on the Internet that a learned scholar will visit some country in the polar regions to determine the timings of prayers there. How he will undertake *tahqiq al-manat* in a spaceship is beyond the burden of this document.

¶ **28.** Others ask us to follow the nearest land where day and night are visible. This is the task of the jurist. He draws a presumption from the reported facts and lays down the rule. The presumption, we believe, is that day and night are ocurring in the reckoning of the Almighty, even if we cannot figure out these changes even with our precise scientific instruments.

¶ **29.** *The Cause (Sabab) of Ṣalāt*—The crucial point to understand is that the cause of prayer is not the declining, or setting of the sun (*dulūk*), it is time. *Dulūk* is merely an indication of this time. Imām al-Sarakhsī says, "Know that prayer has been made obligatory due to its timings. Allah has said, 'Establish regular prayers—at the sun's decline till the darkness of the night, and the recital of the Qur'ān in the morning prayer,' for which reason the obligation recurs with the recurrence of time, and it is performed within its timings. Allah has said, 'For such prayers are enjoined on believers at stated times,' that is, an obligation linked to time."[359] He adds, "In the Book there is an indication about the timings, when it is said, 'So glory be to Allah, when ye reach eventide and when ye rise in the morning; Yea, to Him be praise, in the heavens and on earth; and in the late afternoon and when the day begins to decline.' "[360] He then explains that according to Ibn 'Abbās (God be pleased with him) *dulūk* means declining of the sun, while according to Ibn Mas'ūd (God be pleased with him), it is the setting of the sun upto the darkness of the night. Al-Kāsānī has recorded a similar discussion.[361]

¶ **30.** The important point to make is that the obligation of prayer does not go away if the sun is not seen or it is being seen, but the condition of *dulūk* is not met, because it is time or the timings that create the obligation for us. Of course, the real obligation is created by Allah Almighty Himself. Thus, if there is a dense cloud-cover that lasts for weeks, and the sun is not visible at all, it does not mean that the obligation of prayer itself has been removed; the timings are always there, for time moves on. We take a look at our clocks, or use some other method for knowing the time in the absence of clocks.

¶ **31.** The questioner, considering the visibility of sun as the cause rather than the prescribed timings as the cause, makes a point about a woman undergoing her periods for whom the obligation is lifted. He also mentions the absence of the obligation of *zakāt* in certain cases. These situations cannot be compared to the sun's visibility or its absence at the poles. They are cases where the evidences in the *sharī'ah* themselves have created the exceptions, therefore, the intention of the Lawgiver is clearly understood. We may, however, consider other cases where worshippers are handicapped in some ways, just as they are handicapped from assessing the time on the basis of the sun.

¶ **32.** The first is the case of the *istihadah* or a woman with irregular bleeding so that we cannot distinguish between menstrual and other bleeding. Does she give up prayer completely, because the

359. Al-Sarakhsī, *al-Mabsūṭ*, vol. 1, 141.
360. Ibid.
361. See, al-Kāsānī, *Badā'i' al-Ṣanā'i'*, vol. 1 (of 10), 455–56.

condition of *ṭaharah* is not established for her. Take another case called *salas* which means that one of the passages is never clean, like a person having no control over urination. In these cases, the jurists use estimates of what is normal and proceed to issue the ruling, as in the case of continuous bleeding. The reason is: who are we humans to limit the intention of the Lawgiver.

¶ **33.** In the case under examination too the cause is there at the poles in the reckoning of the Almighty, but the condition of our seeing it or assessing it is not established. We are handicapped. Time exists even there and the obligation cannot be removed.

¶ **34.** What if time itself changes, and the revolutions of the earth do not have the same meaning for us? In space even the cause may be different, but is not known to us; it is only known to the Almighty.

The Ruling

¶ **35.** The legal texts of the Qur'ān and the *Sunnah* are to be acted upon to the extent possible, and intention of the Lawgiver is to be given effect through our actions to the extent possibe by the use of rational evidences that have been accepted by the schools of Islamic law.

¶ **36.** Human beings have no right to limit or restrict the intention of the Lawgiver to the express statements in the Qur'ān and the Sunnah. Meanings must be extended on the basis of *'ilal* (underlying causes) and *ḥikmah* in accordance with the methods approved by the schools of Islamic law. This rule flows directly from the assumption that the *sharī'ah* is a complete code of life.

¶ **37.** An integral bond exists between *sharī'ah* and *fiqh*. *Sharī'ah* is the law and *fiqh* is its understanding; the *sharī'ah* cannot be understood without *fiqh* whose guardians are the schools of law.

¶ **38.** The *sharī'ah* is universal: it is meant for all mankind and for all places; its universality is not affected by exceptions or deviant individual cases.

¶ **39.** The residents of the polar regions are to be asked what they consider to be morning, afternoon, evening and night for purposes of their meals or work, and to estimate the timings accordingly. The Muslim community there can easily arrive at a consensus about the timings of prayer. Perhaps, they may seek help from neighbouring regions where conditions are different, as some scholars have suggested, but this does not appear to be necessary.

¶ **40.** In space, it is better to follow earth time as that is the only time we know. The time at the Ka'bah would be most suitable for this purpose.

Allah knows best.

Select Bibliography

Abū Dāwūd Sulaymān ibn al-Ashāth al-Sijistānī (817 or 18-889). *Sunan Abū Dawūd.* Trans. Ahmad Hasan. 1st Ed. 3 vols. Lahore, 1984.

Al-Āmidī, Sayf al-Dīn Abū al-Husayn ʻAlī ibn Abī ʻAlī ibn Muḥammad al-Thaʻlabī (d. 631 A.H./1233 C.E.). *Al-Iḥkām fī Uṣūl al-Aḥkām.* 4 vols. Beirut: Dār al-Kutub al-ʻIlmiyyah, 1985.

Austin, John. *Lectures on Jurisprudence.* 2 vols. London, 1911.

Al-Bazdawī, Fakhr al-Islām. *Usūl al-Bazdawī.* With its commentary by al-Bukhārī, ʻAlāʼ al-Dīn ʻAbd al-ʻAzīz ibn Aḥmad. *Kashf al-Asrār ʻan Usūl Fakhr al-Islām al-Bazdawī.* 4 vols. Beirut: Dār al-Kutub al-ʻIlmiyyah, 1418 A.H./1997 C.E.

Bodenheimer, Edgar. *Jurisprudence: The Philosophy and Method of the Law.* Cambridge, Massachusetts: Harvard University Press, 1974.

Coulson, N.J. *A History of Islamic Law.* Edinburgh, 1964.

_________. *Conflicts and Tensions in Islamic Jurisprudence.* Chicago, 1969.

Dias, R.W.M. *Jurisprudence.* London: Butterworths, 1985.

_________."The State and the Individual in Islamic Law." *The International and the Comparative Law Quarterly.* 6 (1957): 49–60.

Al-Dabbūsī, Abū Zayd ʻUbayd Allāh ibn ʻUmar ʻĪsā. *Taʼsīs al-Naẓar.* Cairo, n.d. 1-78. Followed by al-Karkhī. *Risālah fī Uṣūl.* 80–87 with comments by al-Nasafī.

Dworkin, Ronald. *Law's Empire.* Cambridge, Massachusetts: Harvard University Press, 1986.

_________. *Taking Rights Seriously.* London: Gerald Duckworth & Co., 1977.

_________."Hard Cases." *Harvard Law Review.* 8 (1975): 1057.

Eisenberg, Melvin A. *The Nature of the Common Law.* Cambridge, Massachusetts: Harvard University Press, 1988.

Al-Ghazālī, Abū Ḥāmid Muḥammad ibn Muḥammad (505 A.H./1111 C.E.). *Al-Mankhūl min Ta'līqāt al-Uṣūl.* Damascus, 1970.

_________. *Shifā' al-Ghalīl fī Bayān al-Shabah wa-al-Mukhīl wa-Masālik al-Ta'līl.* Baghdād, 1971.

_________. *Al-Mustaṣfā min 'Ilm al-Uṣūl.* 2 vols. Cairo, 1324.

_________. *Jawāhir al-Qur'ān.* Beirut, 1985.

_________. *Al-Iqtiṣād fī al-I'tiqād.* Ankara, 1962.

Hart, H.L.A. *The Concept of Law.* Oxford: Clarendon Press, 1961.

Ibn Nujaym, Zayn al-Ābidīn ibn Ibrāhīm. *Al-Ashbāh wa al-Naẓā'ir.* Cairo, 1387 A.H./1968 C.E..

Ibn Rushd, Abū al-Walīd Muḥammad ibn Aḥamad ibn Muḥammad (al-Ḥafīd). *Bidāyat al-Mujtahid wa Nihāyat al-Muqtaṣid.* 2 vols. Cairo, n.d.

Al-Jaṣṣāṣ al-Rāzī, Abū Bakr Aḥmad ibn 'Alī (370/981). *Aḥkām al-Qur'ān.* 2 vols. Istānbūl, 1355/1916.

_________. *Uṣūl al-Jaṣṣāṣ.* Lahore, 1989.

Al-Juwaynī, Imām al-Ḥaramayn. *Al-Burhān.* 2 vols. Cairo, n.d.

Al-Karkhi, 'Abd Allah ibn al-Ḥusayn (340/935). *Risālah fi al-Uṣūl.* On pp. 78–87 following al-Dabbūsī (430/1039). *Ta'sīs al-Naẓar.* Cairo, n.d.

Al-Kāsānī, Abū Bakr ibn Mas'ūd (d. 587 A.H./1191 C.E.). *Badā'i' al-Ṣanā'i' fī Tartīb al-Sharā'i'.* 7 vols. Beirut: Dār al-Fikr, 1417 A.H./1996 C.E.

Kelsen, Hans. *General Theory of Law and State.* Trans. Wedberg. 1945.

_________. *Pure Theory of Law.* Trans. Knight. 1967.

Al-Māwardī, Abū al-Ḥasan 'Alī ibn Muḥammad ibn Ḥabīb (450 A.H./1058 C.E.). *al-Aḥkām al-Sulṭāniyah.* Cairo, 1393/1973.

Nyazee, Imran Ahsan Khan. *Theories of Islamic Law: The Methodology of Ijtihād.* Islamabad: Federal Law House, 2007.

_________.*Partnership in Islam.* Islamabad: Federal Law House, 2007.

_________.*Corporations in Islam.* Islamabad: Federal Law House, 2007.

_________. *General Principles of Criminal Law: Islamic and Western.* Islamabad: Advanced Legal Studies Institute, 1998.

Pound, Roscoe. *Jurisprudence.* 5 vols. Minn: Paul West Publishing Co., 1959.

Al-Qarāfī, Muḥammad ibn Idrīs. *Kitāb Anwār al-Burūq fī Anwā' al-Furūq fī Uṣūl al-Fiqh.*, 4 vols. Bayrūt, 1343.

_________. *Sharḥ Tanqīḥ al-Fuṣūl.* Būlāq, n.d.

Rahim, Abdur. *Muhammadan Jurisprudence.* Madras, 1905.

Al-Rāzī, Fakhr al-Dīn ibn Muḥammad (d. 606 A.H./1210 C.E.). *Al-Maḥsūl fi 'Ilm Uṣūl al-Fiqh.* Ed. Ṭāhā Jābir Fayyāḍ al-'Alwānī. 6 vols. Riyāḍ, 1979.

Ṣadr al-Sharī'ah, 'Ubayd Allāh ibn Mas'ūd (d. 747 A.H./1346 C.E.). *Al-Tawḍīḥ fī Ḥall Jawāmid al-Tanqīḥ.* Karachi, 1979.

Al-Sarakhsī, Shams al-A'immah Abū Bakr Muḥammad ibn Abī Sahl Aḥmad (483 A.H./1090 C.E.). *Uṣūl al-Sarakhsī.* Ed. Abū al-Wafā' al-Afghānī. 2 vols. Cairo, 1372 A.H./1953 C.E..

_________. *Kitāb al-Mabsūṭ.* 30 vols. Cairo, 1324–31 A.H./1906-13 C.E.

Schacht, Joseph. *Origins of Muhammadan jurisprudence.* New York, 1940.

_________. *The Origins of Muhammadan Jurisprudence.* Rev. ed. Oxford, 1953.

_________. *Introduction to Islamic Law.* Oxford, 1964.

Al-Shāfi'ī, Muḥammad ibn Idrīs (150 A.H./768 C.E.–204 A.H./820 C.E.). *Kitāb Risālah fī Uṣūl al-Fiqh.* Ed. Aḥmad Muḥammad Shākir. Cairo, 1358 A.H./1939 C.E.

_________. *al-Umm.* 7 vols. in 4. Cairo, 1388 A.H./1968 C.E..

Al-Shāṭibī, Abū Isḥāq Ibrāhīm ibn Mūsā ibn Muḥammad al-Lakhmī (d. 790 A.H./1388 C.E.). *Al-Muwāfaqāt fī Uṣūl al-Sharī'ah*. Cairo: al-Maktabah al-Tijāriyyah al-Kubrā, 1975.

_________. *Kitāb al-I'tiṣām*. 2 vols. Beirut: Dār al-Kutub al-'Ilmiyyah, 1988.

Al-Taftāzānī, 'Alā' al-Dīn. *Al-Talwīḥ 'alā al-Tawḍīḥ*. In the margin of Ṣadr al-Sharī'ah, 'Ubayd Allāh ibn Mas'ūd (d. 747 A.H./1346 C.E.). *al-Tawdīḥ fī Ḥall Jawāmid al-Tanqīḥ*. Karachi, 1979.

Al-Zarkashī, Muḥammad ibn Bahādur (d. 794 A.H./1392 C.E.). *al-Baḥr al-Muḥīṭ fī Uṣūl al-Fiqh*. 6 vols. Kuwait: Wizārat al-Awqāf, 1413 A.H./1992 C.E.

Zaydān, 'Abd al-Karīm. *Al-Wajīz fī Uṣūl al-Fiqh*. Lahore, n.d.

Detailed Bibliography

The list of books and articles on Islamic jurisprudence that follows is by no means complete or exhaustive. It is to be hoped that some research institution in the Muslim world will publish a comprehensive bibliography on Islamic law and jurisprudence covering all the languages. Unfortunately this has not been been done so far.

Original Sources

Ḥanafī School

Abū Ḥanīfah, al-Nu'mān ibn Thābit ibn Zūṭā (d. 150/767). *Al-Fiqh al-Akbar.* Cairo, 1323.

Māturīdī, Muḥammad ibn Muḥammad, al- (d. 333/944). *Sharḥ al-Fiqh al-Akbar.* Ṣaydā: Manshūrāt al-Maktabah al-'Aṣriyyah, n.d.

Karkhī, 'Abd Allāh ibn al-Ḥusayn, al- (d. 340/951). *Risālah fī al-Uṣūl.* On pp. 78–87 following al-Dabbūsī (d. 430/1039). *Ta'sīs al-Naẓar.*

________. *Al-Aqwāl al-Uṣūliyyah.* Saudi Arabia: al-Jubūrī, 1989.

Shāshī al-Samarqandī, Abū Ya'qūb Isḥāq ibn Ibrāhīm, al- (d. 342/953). *Kitāb al-Uṣūl.* Delhi, 1264, 1310.

Jaṣṣāṣ al-Rāzī, Abū Bakr Aḥmad ibn 'Alī, al- (d. 370/982). *Uṣūl al-Fiqh al-Musammā bi-al-Fuṣūl fī al-Uṣūl.* 4 vols. Kuwayt: Wizārat al-Awqāf wa al-Shu'ūn al-Islāmiyyah, 1988.

Dabbūsī, Abū Zayd 'Ubayd Allāh ibn 'Umar 'Īsā, al- (d. 430/1039). *Ta'sīs al-Naẓar.* Cairo: al-Maṭba'ah al-Adabiyyah, 1320.

Bazdawī Fakhr al-Islam, 'Alī ibn Muḥammad ibn al-Ḥusayn, al- (d. 482/1089). *Kanz al-Wuṣūl ilā Ma'rifat al-Uṣūl.* On the margin of its commentary by 'Abd al-'Azīz al-Bukārī. *Kashf al-Asrār.* 4 vols. Beirut: Dār al-Kutub al-'Ilmiyyah, 1418 A.H./1997 C.E.

Sarakhsī, Shams al-A'immah Abū Bakr Muḥammad ibn Abī Sahl Aḥmad, al- (d. 483/1090). *Kitāb al-Uṣūl.* Title page *Uṣūl al-Sarakhsī.* Ed. Abū al-Wafā' al-Afghānī. 2 vols. Cairo, 1372.

Samarqandī, Abū Bakr 'Alā' al-Dīn al-Mansūr Muḥammad ibn Aḥmad, al- (d. 538/1144). *Mīzān al-Uṣūl fī Natā'ij al-'Uqūl*. Baghdād: Wizārat al-Awqāf wa al-Shu'ūn al-Dīniyyah, Lajnat Iḥyā' al-Turāth al-'Arabī wa al-Islāmī, 1987.

Nasafī, Ḥafīẓ al-Dīn Abū al-Barakāt 'Abd Allāh ibn Aḥmad ibn Maḥmūd, al- (d. 710/1310) *Matn al-Manār fi Uṣūl al-fiqh* [*Manār al-Anwār*]. Istānbūl, 1314–15.

________. *Kashf al-Asrār Sharḥ al-Muṣannaf 'alā al-Manār fī Uṣūl al-Fiqh 'alā Madhhab al-Imām Abī Ḥanīfah*. 1st. ed. Būlāq: al-Maṭba'ah al-Kubrā al-Amīriyyah, 1316.

Bukhārī, 'Abd al-'Azīz, al- (d. 730/1330). *Kashf al-Asrār* (commentary on al-Bazdawī's *Kanz al-Wuṣūl ilā Ma'rifat al-Uṣūl*). 4 vols. Beirut: Dār al-Kutub al-'Ilmiyyah, 1418 A.H./1997 C.E.

Ṣadr al-Sharī'ah al-Thānī al-Maḥbūbī, 'Ubayd Allāh ibn Mas'ūd (d. 747/1346). *Sharḥ al-Tawḍīḥ 'alā al-Tanqīḥ*. Cairo: al-Maṭba'ah al-Khayriyyah, 1322-24.

Ibn al-Malak, 'Izz al-Dīn 'Abd al-Laṭīf ibn 'Abd al-'Azīz ibn Amīn Firishtah (d. 797/1395). *Sharh Manār al-Anwār*. Istānbūl, 1314–15.

Ḥalabī, Zayn al-Dīn Abū 'Azzī Ṭāhir ibn al-Ḥasan ibn Ḥabīb, al- (d. 807/1405). *Mukhtaṣar al-Manār*. On pp. 2-26 and 155 in *Majmū' Mutūn Uṣūliyah*. Damascus, n.d.

Ibn al-Humām al-Siwasī al-Iskandarī, Kamāl al-Dīn Muḥammad ibn Humām al-Dīn 'Abd al-Wāḥid ibn 'Abd al-Ḥamīd (d. 861/1457). *Al-Taḥrīr fī Uṣūl al-Fiqh: al-Jāmi' bayn Iṣṭalāhay al-Ḥanafiyyah wa al-Shāfi'iyyah*. Cairo: Muṣṭafā al-Bābī al-Ḥalabī, 1351.

Mullā Khusraw, Muḥammad ibn Farāmurz ibn 'Alī (d. 885/1480). *Mirqāt al-Wuṣūl ilā 'Ilm al-'Uṣūl*. Cairo, 1320.

________. *Mir'āt al-Uṣūl fī Sharḥ Mirqāt al-Wuṣūl*. With al-Izmīrī. *Ḥāshiyat 'alā Mir'āt al-Uṣūl Sharḥ Mirqāt al-Wuṣūl*. 2 vols. Cairo, 1304.

Ibn Nujaym, Zayn al-'Ābidīn ibn Ibrāhīm (d. 970/1563). *Fatḥ al-Ghaffār bi Sharh Manār al-Anwār*. 3 vols. in 1. Cairo, 1355.

________. *Al-Ashbāh wa al-Naẓā'ir*. Cairo, 1387/1968.

Ibn al-Ḥalabī, Riyaḍ al-Dīn Muḥammad ibn Ibrāhīm (d. 971/1564). *Anwār al-Ḥālak 'alā Sharḥ al-Manār*. On the bottom margin in Ibn al-Mālik (797/1395). *Sharḥ Manār al-Anwār*. Istānbūl, 1315.

Amīr Bādshāh, Muḥammad Amīn (d. 987/1579). *Taysīr al-Taḥrīr*. 4 vols. Cairo, 1321.

'Azmī'zādah, Musṭafā ibn Muḥammad (d. 1040/1630). *Ḥāshiyah 'alā Sharḥ al-Manār*. On the top margin in Ibn al-Malak (d. 797/1395). *Sharḥ Manār al-Anwār*. Istānbūl, 1314–15.

Ḥaṣkafī, 'Alā' al-Dīn ibn Aḥmad ibn Muḥammad, al- (d. 1088/ 1677). *Ifāḍat al-Anwār*. Istānbūl, 1883 & 1300.

Kawākibī, Muḥammad ibn al-Ḥasan, al- (d. 1096/1685). *Manẓūmat al-Kawākibī fī Uṣūl Fiqh al-Sādah al-Ḥanafiyyah*. Al-Ṭab'ah 1. Cairo: Zāhid wa al-Khānjī, 1317/1899.

Ḥāmid ibn Muṣṭafā Effendī Qāḍī al-'Askar al-'Uthmāniyyah (d. 1098/1687). *Ḥāshiyah 'alā Mir'āt al-Uṣūl*. 2 vols. Cairo, 1280.

Izmīrī, Sulaymān ibn 'Abd Allāh, al- (d. 1102/1691). *Ḥāshiyat 'alā Mir'āt al-Uṣūl Sharḥ Mirqāt al-Wuṣūl*. 2 vols. Cairo, 1304.

Bihārī, Muḥibb Allāh ibn 'Abd al-Shukūr (d. 1119/1707). *Musallam al-Thubūt*. Hyderabad: Maṭba'at al-'Ulūm, 1297.

Mullā Jīwan, Aḥmad ibn Abī Sa'īd [Shaykh Mullā] (d. 1129/1717). *Nūr al-Anwār ma' Ḥāshiyah Qamar al-Aqmār*. Delhi: Kutub'khānah Rashīdiyyah, 1946.

Nābulusī, 'Abd al-Ghanī ibn Ismā'īl, al- (d. 1144/1731). *Khulāṣat al-Taḥqīq fī Bayān Ḥukm al-Taqlīd wa al-Talfīq*. Istānbūl: al-Maktabah 'Ishīq, 1978.

Bahr al-'Ulūm, Muḥammad 'Abd al-'Alī ibn Niẓām al-Dīn Muḥammad al-Anṣārī al-Lakhnawī (d. 1180/1766). *Fawātiḥ al-Raḥamūt Sharḥ Musallam al-Thubūt*. Būlāq, 1322.

Ibn 'Ābidīn, Muḥammad Amīn ibn 'Umar ibn 'Abd al-'Azīz (d. 1252/1837). *Nasmāt al-Asḥār Ḥāshiyah 'alā Ifāḍat al-Anwār*. Cairo, 1300.

'Abd al-Ḥalīm al-Lakhnawī, Aḥmad 'Abd al-Ḥalīm ibn Mawlānā Amīn Allāh (d. 1258/1842). *Qamr al-Aqmār 'alā Nūr al-Anwār*. Along with Mullā Jīwan. *Nūr al-Anwār*. Cairo, 1316 & Delhi, 1946.

Ṣafī al-Hindī, Muḥammad ibn 'Abd al-Raḥīm (d. 1315/1897). *al-Fā'iq fī Uṣūl al-Fiqh*. Cairo: Dār al-Ittiḥād al-Akhawī lil-Ṭibā'ah, 1411.

Maḥallawī al-Ḥanafī, Muḥammad ibn 'Abd al-Raḥmān, al-. *Taḥsīl al-Wuṣūl ilā 'Ilm al-Uṣūl*. Cairo, 1341.

Ruḥawī, Abū Zakariyā' Yaḥyā, al-. *Ḥāshiyah 'alā Sharḥ al-Manār*. At bottom center of page in Ibn al-Malak (d. 797/1395). *Sharḥ al-Manār*. 1315.

Shāfi'ī School

Shāfi'ī, Muḥammad ibn Idrīs, al- (d. 204/820). *Kitāb al-Risālah fī Uṣūl al-Fiqh*. Ed. Aḥmad Muḥammad Shākir. Cairo: Muṣṭafā al-Bābī al-Ḥalabī, 1358. Translated by Majīd Khaddurī. *Islāmic Jurisprudence: Shāfi'ī's Risālah*. Baltimore: Johns Hopkins Press, 1961.

_________. *Ikhtilāf al-Ḥadīth*. Beirut: Dār al-Kutub al-'Ilmiyyah, 1986.

Shāshī al-Qaffāl, Muḥammad ibn 'Alī, al- (d. 365/ 976). *Kitāb al-Uṣūl*. Luckhnow, 1277.

Khaṭīb al-Baghdādī, Abū Bakr Aḥmad ibn 'Alī, al- (d. 463/1071). *Taqrīb Kitāb al-Faqīh wa al-Mutafaqqih wa Uṣūl al-Fiqh*. Dimashq: Dār Iḥyā' al-Sunnah al-Nabawiyyah, 1970.

Shīrāzī, Abū Isḥāq Ibrāhīm ibn 'Alī ibn Yūsuf al-Fīrūz'ābādī, al- (d. 476/1083). *Al-Luma' fī Uṣūl al-Fiqh*. Cairo: Muṣṭafā al-Bābī al-Ḥalabī, 1377/1957.

_________. *Sharḥ al-Luma'*. Al-Ṭab'ah 1. Beirut: Dār al-Gharb al-Islāmī, 1988.

_________. *Al-Tabṣirah fī Uṣūl al-Fiqh*. Dimashq: Dār al-Fikr, 1980 & 1983.

_________. *Kitāb al-Ma'ūnah fī al-Jadal*. Beirut: Dār al-Gharb al-Islāmī, 1988.

_________. *Ṭabaqāt al-Fuqahā'*. Baghdād: al-Maktabah al-'Arabiyyah, 1356/1937.

Juwaynī Imām al-Ḥaramayn, Abū al-Ma'ālī 'Abd al-Malik ibn 'Abd Allāh, al- (d. 478/1085). *Kitāb al-Waraqāt*. Tunis, 1344. Translated by Leon Bercher. "Le 'Kitab al-Waraqat' Traite de Methodologie Juridique Musulmane." *Revue Tunisienne* (1930): 93-105, 1825-214.

________. *Al-Ta'līqāt 'alā Matn al-Waraqāt*. Beirut: al-Maktab al-Islā'ī, 1983.

________. *Sharḥ al-Waraqāt fī 'Ilm Uṣūl al-Fiqh*. Cairo: Muḥammad 'Alī Ṣubayḥ, 1965.

________. *Al-Burhān fi Uṣūl al-Fiqh*. Ed. 'Abd al-'Azīm al-Dīb. Doha: Maṭābi' al-Dawḥah al-Ḥadīthah, 1400.

________. *Kitāb al-Ijtihād min Kitāb al-Talkhīṣ li-Imām al-Ḥaramayn*. Dimashq: Dār al-Qalam, 1987.

Ghazālī, Abū Ḥāmid Muḥammad ibn Muḥammad, al- (d. 505/ 1111). *al-Mankhūl min Ta'līqāt al-Uṣūl*. Damascus, 1970.

________. *Shifā' al-Ghalīl fī Bayān al-Shabah wa al-Mukhīl wa Masālik al-Ta'līl*. Baghdād: Matba'at al-Irshād, 1971.

________. *Al-Mustaṣfā min 'Ilm al-Uṣūl*. Cairo: Matba'ah Muṣṭafā Muḥammad, 1937.

Rāzī, Fakhr al-Dīn ibn Muḥammad, al- (d. 606/1210). *Al-Maḥṣūl fi 'Ilm Uṣūl al-Fiqh*. Ed. Ṭāhā Jābir Fayyāḍ al-'Alwānī. 6 vols. Riyāḍ: al-Mamlakah al-'Arabiyyah al-Sa'ūdiyyah, Jāmi'at al-Imām Muḥammad ibn Su'ūd al-Islāmiyyah, Lajnat al-Buḥūth wa al-Ta'līf wa al-Tarjamah wa al-Nashr, 1979.

Āmidī, Sayf al-Dīn Abū al-Husayn 'Alī ibn Abī 'Alī ibn Muḥammad al-Tha'labī, al- (d. 631/1233). *al-Iḥkām fi Uṣūl al-Aḥkām*. 4 vols. Cairo: Matba'at al-Ma'ārif, 1332.

________. *Kitāb Muntahā al-Sūl fī 'Ilm al-Uṣūl* (Selections from *Iḥkām fī Uṣūl al-Aḥkām*). Cairo: Maṭba'at Muḥammad 'Alī Ṣubayḥ, n.d.

Zanjānī, Shihāb al-Dīn Maḥmūd ibn Aḥmad, al- (d. 656/1258). *Takhrīj al-Furū' 'alā al-Uṣūl*. Damascus, 1382.

Sulamī, Ibn 'Abd al-Salām, al- (d. 660/1262). *Qawā'id al-Aḥkām fī Maṣāliḥ al-Anām*. 2 vols. in 1. Cairo, 1388/1968.

Nawawī, Abū Zakariyā' Yaḥyā ibn Sharaf ibn Mūrī ibn Ḥasan ibn Ḥusayn ibn Jumu'ah ibn Ḥizām al-Ḥizāmī al-Ḥawrānī Muḥiy al-Dīn, al- (d. 676/1278). *Al-Uṣūl wa al-Ḍawābiṭ*. Beirut: Dār al-Bashā'ir al-Islāmiyyah, 1986.

Bayḍāwī, Abū Sa'd 'Abd Allāh ibn 'Umar ibn Muḥammad ibn 'Alī Abū al-Khayr Nāṣir al-Dīn, al- (d. 716/1316). *Minhāj al-Wuṣūl ilā 'Ilm al-Uṣūl*. 3 vols. in 1. Cairo, n.d.

'Alā'ī, Khalīl ibn Kaykaldī (d. 760/1359). *Talqīḥ al-Fuhūm fī Tanqīḥ Ṣiyagh al-'Umūm*. Beirut, 1983.

________. *Taḥqiq al-Murād fī anna al-Nahy Yaqtaḍī al-Fasād*. Beirut, 1975.

Fayyūmī, Aḥmad ibn Muḥammad (d. 769/1368). *Miṣbāḥ al-Munīr fī Gharīb al-Sharḥ al-Kabīr lil-Rāfi'ī*. Būlāq: al-Matba'ah al-Amīriyyah, 1906.

Ibn al-Subkī, 'Abd al-Wahhāb ibn 'Alī Tāj al-Dīn (d. 771/1370). *Al-Ibhāj fī Sharh al-Minhāj lil-Bayḍāwī*. 2 vols. Cairo, n.d. [He actually completed the commentary begun by his father Taqī al-Dīn as-Subkī who had reached the fourth issue under the discussion of *Wājib*].

________. *Jam' al-Jawāmi'*. Alongwith commentary by al-Maḥallī and al-Bannānī. 2 vols. Cairo, 1297. [Also *Ḥāshiyat al-'Allāmah al-Bannānī 'alā*

Sharḥ al-Jalāl Shams al-Dīn Muḥammad ibn Aḥmad al-Maḥallī 'alā Matn Jam' al-Jawāmi'. Beirut: Dār al-Kutub al-'Arabiyyah, 1975?]

_________. *Al-Ashbāh wa al-Naẓā'ir*. 2 vols. Beirut: Dār al-Kutub al-'Ilmiyyah, 1411/1991.

Isnawī, Jamāl al-Dīn, al- (d. 772/1371). *Al-Tamhīd fī Takhrīj al-Furū' 'alā al-Uṣūl*. Makkat al-Mukarramah: al-Maṭba'at al-Mājidiyah, 1353.

_________. *Nihāyat al-Sūl fī Sharḥ Minhāj al-Wuṣūl ilā 'Ilm al-Uṣūl*. 3 vols. Cairo: Maṭba'at al-Tawfīq al-Adabiyyah, n.d.

Taftāzānī, Mas'ūd ibn 'Umar ibn 'Abd Allāh, al- (d. 791/1398). *Al-Talwīḥ fī Kashf Ḥaqā'iq al-Tanqīḥ*. Commentary on Sadr al-Sharī'ah, *Tawḍīḥ fī Ḥall Jawāmid al-Tanqīḥ*. 2 vols in 1. Cairo: Maktabat wa Maṭba'at Muḥammad 'Alī Ṣubayḥ, 1957.

Imrītī, 'Abd al-Ḥamīd ibn Muḥammad, al-. *Laṭā'if al-Ishārāt ilā Tashīl al-Ṭuruq li-Naẓm al-Waraqāt fī al-Uṣūl al-Fiqhiyyah*. Cairo, 1330 & 1343.

Maḥallī, Jalāl al-Dīn Muḥammad ibn Aḥmad, al- (d. 864/1459). *Sharḥ 'alā Matn Jam' al-Jawāmi'*. In al-Bannānī (d. 1198/ 1784). *Ḥāshiyah 'alā Sharḥ al-Mahallī*. 2 vols. in 1. Cairo, n.d.

_________. *Sharḥ al-Waraqāt fī Uṣūl al-Dīn*. Cairo, 1959.

Ibn Amīr al-Ḥājj, Muḥammad ibn Muḥammad (d. 879/1474). *Kitāb al-Musammā bi-Taqrīr wa al-Taḥbīr*. 3 vols. Būlāq: al-Maṭba'ah al-Kubrā al-Amīriyyah, 1316–17/1898–1900.

Kirmāstī, Yūsuf ibn Ḥusayn (d. 906/1500). *Al-Wajīz fī Uṣūl al-Fiqh*. Cairo: Kassāb, 1984.

Suyūṭī al-Khuḍayrī, Abū al-Faḍl 'Abd al-Raḥmān ibn Abū Bakr ibn Muḥammad ibn Aḥmad Bakr Jalāl al-Dīn, al- (d. 911/ 1505). *Al-Ashbāh wa al-Naẓā'ir fī Qawā'id wa Furū' Fiqh al-Shāfi'iyyah*. Cairo, 1242/1826.

_________. *Taqrīr al-Istinād fī Tafsīr al-Ijtihād*. Al-Ṭab'ah 1. Al-Iskandariyyah: Dār al-Da'wah, 1983.

_________. *Radd 'alā man Akhlada ilā al-Arḍ wa Jahila anna al-Ijtihād fī Kull 'Aṣr Farḍ*. Beirut: Dār al-Kutub al-'Ilmiyyah, 1983.

_________. *Al-Ḥāwī lil-Fatāwī fī al-Fiqh wa 'Ulūm al-Tafsīr wa al-Ḥadīth wa al-Uṣūl wa al-Naḥw wa al-I'rāb wa Sā'ir al-Funūn*. Cairo: al-Maktabah al-Tijāriyyah al-Kubrā, 1959.

_________. *Ikhtilāf al-Madhāhib*. Cairo: Dār al-I'tiṣām, 1989.

Sumaykī al-Shāfi'ī, Zayn al-Dīn Abū Yaḥyā Zakariyā' ibn Muḥammad ibn al-Anṣārī, al- (d. 926/1520). *Lubb al-Uṣūl*. An abridgement of al-Subkī. *Jam' al-Jawāmi'*. Printed on the margin of its commentary by the author. *Ghāyat al-Wuṣūl: Sharḥ Lubb al-Uṣul*. Cairo, n.d.

Bannānī, 'Abd al-Raḥmān ibn Jād Allāh, al- (d. 1197/1783) *Ḥāshiyat al-Bannānī 'alā Sharḥ al-Jalāl al-Maḥallī 'alā Jam' al-Jawāmi' lil-Imām Ibn al-Subkī*. Cairo, 1285/1868.

Jawharī al-Ṣaghīr, Muḥammad ibn Aḥmad ibn Ḥasan al-Khālidī, al- (d. 1214/1799). *Ḥawāshī 'alā Ghāyat al-Wuṣūl*. On the bottom margin in Zakariyā' ibn Muḥammad ibn al-Anṣārī. *Ghāyat al-Wuṣūl*. Cairo, n.d.

Badakhshī, Muḥammad ibn al-Hasan, al-. *Manāhij al-'Uqūl*. Commentary on al-Bayḍāwī. *Minhāj al-Wuṣūl ilā 'Ilm al-Uṣūl*. 3 vols. in 1. Cairo, n. d.

Dimyatī al-Shāfi'ī, Aḥmad ibn Muḥammad, al-. *Ḥāshiyah*. At the bottom of pp. 16–79 in al-Juwaynī Imām al-Ḥaramayn (478/1085). *Kitāb al-Waraqāt*. Cairo, 1979.

Jawī al-Shāfi'ī, Aḥmad ibn 'Abd al-Laṭīf al-Khaṭīb, al-. *Ḥāshiyat al-Nafaḥāt 'alā Sharḥ al-Waraqāt*. Cairo, 1357/1938.

Shirbīnī, 'Abd al-Raḥīm, al-. *Taqrīr*. On the margin of al-Bannānī. *Ḥāshiyah 'alā Sharḥ al-Maḥallī*. 2 vols. in 1. Cairo, n.d.

Muḥammad Siddīq Ḥasan, Nawab of Bhopal (d. 1307/1890). *Ḥuṣūl al-Mā'mūl min 'Ilm al-Uṣūl*. Banāras, 19–?

_________. *Mukhtaṣar Ḥuṣūl al-Ma'mūl min 'Ilm al-Uṣūl*. Banāras: Idārat al-Buḥūth al-Islāmiyyah bi-al-Jāmi'ah al-Salfiyyah, 1982.

Mālikī School

Bājī, Abū al-Walīd Sulaymān ibn Khalaf, (d. 474/1081). *Iḥkām al-Fuṣūl fī Aḥkām al-Uṣūl*. Beirut: Dār al-Gharb al-Islāmī, 1986.

_________. *Kitāb al-Ishārah ilā Ma'rifat al-Uṣūl wa al-Wijāzah fī Ma'nā al-Dalīl* (Selections from *Iḥkām al-Fuṣūl fī Aḥkām al-Uṣūl*). Rabāṭ: Markaz Iḥyā' al-Turāth al-Maghribī, 1988?

_________. *Kitāb al-Ḥudūd fī al-Uṣul*. Beirut: Mu'assasat al-Zu'bī lil-Ṭibā'ah wa al-Nashr, 1973.

Ibn al-Ḥājib, 'Uthmān ibn 'Umar (d. 647/1249). *Kitāb Muntahā al-Wuṣūl wa al-'Amal fī 'Ilmay al-Uṣūl wa al-Jadal*. Cairo: Maṭba'at al-Sa'ādah, 1326/1908.

Qarāfī, Shihāb al-Dīn Abū al-'Abbās Aḥmad ibn Idrīs ibn 'Alī ibn 'Abd Allāh ibn Yāllīn, al- (d. 684/1285). *Sharḥ Tanqīḥ al-Fuṣūl fī Ikhtiṣār al-Maḥṣūl fī al-Uṣūl*. Cairo, 1393/1973.

_________. *Mukhtaṣar Tanqīḥ al-Fuṣūl*. Printed as *al-Muqaddimah al-Thāniyah* with the *Kitāb al-Dhakhīrah*. Cairo, 1381.

_________. *Kitāb Anwār al-Burūq fī Anwā' al-Furūq fī Uṣūl al-Fiqh*. 4 vols. Beirut, 1343.

Ishbīlī al-Shāṭ, Sirāj al-Dīn al-Qurashī ibn 'Abd Allāh ibn Muḥammad, al- (d. 725/1323). *Idrār al-Shurūq*. Commentary below text in al-Qarāfī (684/1285). *Kitāb Anwār al-Burūq fī Anwā' al-Furūq fī Uṣūl al-Fiqh*. 4 vols. Beirut, 1343.

Ījī, 'Aḍud al-Dīn 'Abd al-Raḥmān ibn Aḥmad, al- (d. 756/1355). *Al-'Aḍudiyyah (Sharḥ li-Mukhtaṣar al-Muntahā fī al-Uṣūl li-Ibn Ḥājib)*. 2 vols. in 1 (in the margin). Cairo: Maktabat al-Kulliyyāt al-Azhariyyah, 1973–1974.

Ibn Kathīr, Ismā'īl ibn 'Umar (d. 774/1373). *Tuḥfat al-Ṭālib bi-Ma'rifat Aḥādīth Mukhtaṣar Ibn al-Ḥājib*. Al-Ṭab'ah 1. Makkah: Dār Ḥirā', 1406/1986.

Shāṭibī, Abū Isḥāq Ibrāhīm ibn Mūsā ibn Muḥammad al-Lakhmī, al- (d. 790/1388). *Al-Muwāfaqāt fī Uṣūl al-Sharī'ah*. Cairo, 1922/1923.

_________. *Kitāb al-I'tiṣām*. 2 vols. Cairo, 1295.

Zarkashī, Muḥammad ibn Bahādur, al- (d. 794/1392). *al-Baḥr al-Muḥīṭ fī Uṣūl al-Fiqh*. 6 vols. Kuwait: Wizārat al-Awqāf, 1413/1992.

Ibn Farḥūn, Ibrāhīm ibn 'Alī (d. 799/1397). *Kashf al-Niqāb al-Ḥājib min Muṣṭalaḥ Ibn al-Ḥājib*.Beirut: Dār al-Gharb al-Islāmī, 1990.

'Irāqī, 'Abd al-Raḥīm ibn al-Ḥusayn, al- (d. 806/1404). *Takhrīj Aḥādīth Mukhtaṣar al-Minhāj fī Uṣūl al-Fiqh.* Cairo: Dār al-Kutub al-Salafiyyah, 1986.

Jurjānī (al-Gurgānī) al-Sayyid al-Sharīf, 'Alī ibn Muḥammad (d. 816/1413). *Sharḥ Sharḥ Mukhtaṣar.* Commentary in middle of page in al-Ījī (d. 756/1355). *Al-'Aḍudiyah (Sharḥ li-Mukhtaṣar al-Muntahā fī al-Uṣūl li-Ibn Ḥājib).* 2 vols. in 1. Cairo, 1393/1973 & 1394/1974.

Ibn al-Marḥūm, Muḥammad 'Alī. *Tahdhīb al-Furūq wa al-Qwā'id al-Saniyyah fī al-Asrār al-Fiqhiyyah.* Commentary in the margin in al-Qarāfī (682/1285) *Kitāb Anwār al-Burūq fī Anwā' al-Furūq fī Uṣūl al-Fiqh.* 4 vols. Beirut, 1343.

Ḥanbalī School

Abū Ya'lā al-Farrā' al-Ḥanbalī, Abū al-Ḥusayn Muḥammad ibn Muḥammad ibn al-Ḥusayn (d. 458/1066). *Al-'Uddah fī Uṣūl al-Fiqh.* Riyāḍ: al-Mamlakh al-'Arabiyyah al-Sa'ūdiyyah, 1980.

Kalwadhānī, Maḥfūẓ ibn Aḥmad (d. 510/1116). *Al-Tamhīd fī Uṣūl al-Fiqh.* Makkah: Jāmi'at Umm al-Qurā, 1985.

Ibn Barhān, Aḥmad ibn 'Alī (d. 518/1124). *Al-Wuṣūl ilā al-Uṣūl.* Riyāḍ : Maktabat al-Ma'ārif, 1983-1984.

Ibn Qudāmah al-Maqdisī, Muwaffaq al-Dīn Abū Muḥammad 'Abd Allāh ibn Aḥmad ibn Muḥammad (d. 620/1223). *Rawḍat al-Nāẓir wa Jannat al-Munāẓir fī Uṣūl al-Fiqh 'alā Madhhab al-Imām Aḥmad ibn Ḥanbal.* Cairo: al-Maṭba'ah al-Salafiyyah wa Maktabatuhā, 1385/1965.

Ibn Taymiyyah, Taqī al-Dīn, Abū al-'Abbās Aḥmad ibn 'Abd al-Ḥalīm ibn 'Abd al-Salām ibn 'Abd Allāh (d. 728/1328). *Al-Qiyas fī al-Shar' al-Islāmī.* Cairo: al-Matba'ah al-Salafiyyah, 1346.

_________. *Raf' al-Malām 'an al-A'immah al-A'lām.* Hijaz: al-Maktabat al-'Ilmiyyah, n.d.

Ibn Taymiyyah Taqī al-Dīn, Abū al-'Abbās Aḥmad ibn 'Abd al-Ḥalīm ibn 'Abd al-Salām ibn 'Abd Allāh (d. 728/1328); Ibn Taymiyyah, Shihāb al-Dīn Abū al-Maḥāsin 'Abd al-Ḥalīm ibn 'Abd al-Salām (d. 682/1283); Ibn Taymiyyah al-Ḥarrānī, Majd al-Dīn Abū al-Barakāt 'Abd al-Salām ibn 'Abd Allāh (d. 652/1245). *al-Musawwadah fī Uṣūl al-Fiqh.* Cairo, 1384.

Baghdādī al-Ḥanbalī, 'Abd al-Mu'min ibn Mas'ūd, al- (d. 739/1339). *Qawā'id al-Uṣūl fī Ma'āqid al-Fuṣūl.* Eds. Aḥmad Shākir and 'Alī Shākir. Cairo, n.d.

Maqqarī, Muḥammad ibn Muḥammad (d. 759/1358). *Al-Qawā'id.* Makkah : al-Mamlakah al-'Arabiyyah al-Sa'ūdiyyah, Jāmi'at Umm al-Qurā, Mahad al-Buḥūth al-'Ilmiyyah wa Iḥyā' al-Turāth al-Islāmī, Markaz Iḥyā' al-Turāth al-Islāmī, 1988.

Ibn Rajab al-Ḥanbalī, Zayn al-Dīn Abū al-Faraj 'Abd al-Raḥmān ibn Aḥmad (d. 795/1393). *Al-Qawā'id fī al-Fiqh al-Islāmī.* Cairo: Maktabat al-Kulliyyāt al-Azhariyyah, 1972.

Ibn al-Laḥḥām, 'Alī ibn 'Abbās al-Ba'alī al-Ḥanbalī (d. 803/1401). *Al-Qawā'id wa al-Fawā'id al-Uṣūliyah.* Cairo, 1357.

Ibn al-Najjār, Taqī al-Dīn Muḥammad ibn Aḥmad (d. 972/1564). *Sharḥ al-Kawkab al-Munīr al-Musammā bi-Mukhtaṣar al-Taḥrīr aw al-Mukhtabar al-Mubtakar*

Sharḥ al-Mukhtaṣar fī Uṣūl al-Fiqh. Makkah: Jāmi'at al-Malik 'Abd al-'Azīz, Markaz al-Baḥth al-'Ilmī wa Iḥyā' al-Turāth al-Islāmī, 1980.

Ẓāhirī School

Ibn Ḥazm, Abū Muḥammad 'Abd Allāh ibn Sa'īd (d. 456/1064). *Kitāb al-Iḥkām fī Uṣūl al-Aḥkām*. Cairo: Maktabat al-Khānjī, 1345-1347/1926-29.

________. *Mulakhkhaṣ Ibṭāl al-Qiyās wa al-Ra'y wa al-Istiḥsān wa al-Taqlīd wa al-Ta'ṭīl*. Dimashq: Maṭba'at Jāmiāt Dimashq, 1960.

________. *Al-Nubadh fī Uṣūl al-Fiqh al-Ẓāhirī*. Cairo, 1360/1940.

Independent Jurists

Ibn al-Mundhir al-Nīsābūrī, Muḥammad ibn Ibrāhīm (d. 309/921). *Al-Ijmā'*. Riyāḍ: Dār Tayyibah, 1982.

Ṭabarī, Abū Ja'far ibn Jarīr, al- (d. 311/923). *Ikhtilāf al-Fuqahā'*. Cairo: al-Maktabah al-Khidiwiyyah, 1902.

________. *Kitāb al-Jihād wa Kitāb al-Jizyah wa Aḥkām al-Muḥāribīn min Kitāb Ikhtilāf al-Fuqahā'*. Leiden: E. J. Brill, 1933.

Baṣrī, Abū al-Ḥusayn Muḥammad ibn 'Alī, al- (d. 436/1048). *Kitāb al-Mu'tamad fī Uṣūl al-Fiqh*. Dimashq: al-Mahd al-'Ilmī al-Faransī lil-Dirāsāt al-'Arabiyyah bi-Dimashq, 1964-1965.

Shāh Walī Allāh al-Dihlawī, Ibn 'Abd al-Raḥmān (d. 1175/1762). *al-Inṣāf Fī Bayān Sabab al-Ikhtilāf fī al-Aḥkām al-Fiqhiyyah*. Cairo: al-Maṭba'ah al-Salafiyyah wa Maktabatuhā, 1965.

________. *'Iqd al-Jīd fī Aḥkām al-Ijtihād wa al-Taqlīd*. Cairo: al-Maṭba'ah al-Ṣalafiyyah, 1965.

Secondary Sources: Arabic Titles

'Abajī, Muḥammad As'ad. *Sullam al-Wuṣūl ilā 'Ilm al-Uṣūl*. 1953.

'Abd Allāh, Maḥmūd Aḥmad Muḥammad. *Al-Amr wa Dalālatuhu 'alā al-Aḥkām al-Shar'iyyah*. Cairo: Dār al-Manār, 1986.

'Abd al-Barr, Muḥammad Zakī. *Taqnīn Uṣūl al-Fiqh*. Cairo: Maktabat Dār al-Turāth, 1989.

'Abd al-Ghaffār, al-Sayyid Aḥmad. *Al-Taṣawwur al-Lughawī 'inda al-Uṣūliyyīn*. Alexandria: Dār al-Ma'rifah al-Jāmi'iyyah, 1981.

'Abd al-Ḥamīd, 'Umar Mawlūd. *Ḥujjiyyat al-Qiyās fī Uṣūl al-Fiqh al-Islāmī*. Benghazi: Jāmi'at Qār Yūnus, 1988.

'Abd al-Ḥakīm, Muḥammad Ḥusnī. *Al-Ijmāl wa al-Bayān wa Atharuhumā fī Ikhtilāf al-Fuqahā'*. Cairo, 1982.

'Abd al-Qādir, Ālī Ḥasan. *Naẓrah 'Āmmah fī Tārīkh al-Fiqh al-Islāmī*. Cairo: Maktabat al-Qāhirah al-Ḥadīthah, 1956.

'Abd Rabbih, Muḥammad al-Saīd 'Alī. *Buḥūth fī al-Adillah al-Mukhtalaf fīhā 'inda al-Uṣūliyyīn*. s.l.: s.n., 1977-1978.

'Abd al-Raḥmān, Jalāl al-Dīn. *Ijtihād*. Cairo, 1986.

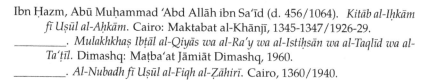

________. *Al-Ijmāl wa al-Bayān wa Waḍūhumā fī Nuṣūṣ al-Aḥkām*. Cairo, 1984.

________. *Al-Maṣāliḥ al-Mursalah wa Makānatuhā fī al-Tashrī'*. Cairo: Dār al-Kitāb al-Jāmi'ī, 1983.

________. *Al-Qāḍī Nāṣir al-Dīn al-Bayḍāwī wa atharuhu fī Uṣūl al-Fiqh*. Cairo: Dār al-Kitāb al-Jāmi'ī, 1981.

Abū al-Ḥasan 'Alī ibn al-'Abbās al-Ba'lī. *Al-Mukhtaṣar fī Uṣūl al-Fiqh 'alā Madhhab al-Imām Aḥmad ibn Ḥanbal*. Dimashq: Dār al-Fikr, 1980.

Abū al-Fatḥ, Aḥmad. *Kitāb al-Mukhtārāt al-Fatḥiyyah fī Tārīkh al-Tashrī' wa uṣūl al-Fiqh*. Cairo: Maṭba'at al-Nahḍah, 1924.

Abū al-Futūḥ, Abū al-Ma'āṭī Ḥāfiẓ. *Al-Madkhal li-Dirāsat al-Tashrī' al-Islāmī*. Casablanca: Abū al-Futūḥ, 1980.

Abū 'Īd, al-'Abd Khalīl. *Mabāḥith fī Uṣūl al-Fiqh al-Islāmī*. Aman: Dār al-Furqān, 1983.

Abū al-Īlā, 'Abd al-Qādir Muḥammad. *Buḥūth fī al-Ijtihād*. Cairo, 1987.

Abū Jayb, Sa'dī. *Mawsūāt al-Ijmā' fī al-Fiqh al-Islāmī*. Dimashq: Dār al-Fikr, 1984.

Abu al-Najā Muḥammad 'Abd Allāh. *'Ilm Uṣūl al-Fiqh*. Cairo: Muḥammad 'Alī Ṣubayḥ, 1966.

Abū al-Rushtah, 'Aṭā'. *Taysīr al-Wuṣūl Ilā al-Uṣūl*. Jordan, 1990.

Abū Sa'd, Muḥammad Shitā. *Mustaqbal al-Tashrī' al-Islāmī*. Cairo, 1986.

Abū Sulaymān, 'Abd al-Wahhāb Ibrāhīm. *Al-Fikr al-Uṣūlī*. Jeddah: Dār al-Shurūq, 1983.

Abū Yaḥyā, Muḥammad Ḥasan. *Ahdāf al-Tashrī' al-Islāmī*. Aman: Dār al-Furqān, 1985.

Abū Zahrah, Muḥammad. *Muḥāḍarāt fī Tārīkh al-Madhāhib al-Fiqhiyyah*. Cairo: Jam'iyyat al-Dirāsāt al-Islāmiyyah, 1977.

________. *Uṣūl al-Fiqh*. Cairo: Dār al-Fikr al-'Arabī, 1973.

Aḥmad, Abū al-Majd. *Al-Ijtihād al-Dīnī al-Mu'āṣir*. Constantinople: Dār al-Ba'th, 1985.

'Ālim, Yūsuf Ḥāmid. *Al-Ahdāf al-'Āmmah lil-Sharī'ah al-Islāmiyyah*. Herndon, VA: International Institute of Islamic Thought, 1991.

'Alwānī, Ṭāhā Jābir Fayyāḍ. *Uṣūl al-Fiqh al-Islāmī*. Herndon, VA: International Institute of Islamic Thought, 1988. [See also English Ed. Herndon, VA: International Institute of Islamic Thought, 1990.]

________. *Al-Ijtihād wa al-Taqlīd fī al-Islām*. Cairo: Dār al-Anṣār, 1979.

Āmrī, Nādiyah Sharīf. *Al-Qiyās fī al-Tashrī' al-Islāmī*. Cairo: Hajar, 1987.

________. *Al-Takhṣīṣ 'inda 'Ulamā' al-Uṣūl*. Cairo: Hajar, 1987.

________. *Al-'Āmm wa Dalālatuhu bayna al-Qaṭ'iyyah wa al-Ẓanniyyah*. Cairo: Hajar, 1987.

As'adī, Muḥammad 'Ubayd Allāh. *Al-Mūjaz fī Uṣūl al-Fiqh*. Cairo: Dār al-Salām, 1990.

'Ashmāwī, Muḥammad Sa'īd. *Uṣūl al-Sharī'ah*. Cairo: Dār al-Kitāb al-Miṣrī, 1979.

'Atīq, al-Ṣuḥbī. *Al-Tafsīr wa al-Maqāṣid 'inda al-Shaykh Muḥammad al-Ṭāhir Ibn 'Āshūr*. Tunis: Dār al-Sanābil lil-Thaqāfah wa al-'Ulūm, 1989.

'Atrabī Allāh, Sa'īd Muṣayliḥī. *Ijmā' al-Ummah*. Cairo:, 1987

________. *Al-Istiṣḥāb wa Atharuhu fī al-Fiqh al-Islāmī*. Cairo, 1987.

________.*Madhhab al-Ṣaḥābī wa Atharuhu fī al-Fiqh al-Islāmī*. Cairo, 1987.

'Awwāmah, Muḥammad. *Athar al-Ḥadīth al-Sharīf fī Ikhtilāf al-A'immah al-Fuqahā' Raḍiya Allāh 'Anhum*. s.l.: Maktabat Muḥammad Hāshim al-Kutubī, 1978.

Ayyūbī, Muḥammad Hishām. *Al-Ijtihād wa Muqtaḍayāt al-'Aṣr*. Aman: Dār al-Fikr, 1986.

Badakhshānī, Muḥammad Anwar. *Taysīr Uṣūl al-Fiqh*. Karachi: Idārat al-Qur'ān wa al-'Ulūm al-Islāmiyyah, 1990.

Badrān, Badrān Abū al-'Aynayn. *Uṣūl al-Fiqh*. Cairo: Dār al-Ma'ārif, 1965 & 1973.

________.*Adillat al-Tashrī' al-Muta'āriḍah wa Wujūh al-Tarjīḥ baynahā*. Alexandria: Mu'assasat Shabāb al-Jāmi'ah, 1974.

Baḥr al-'Ulūm, 'Izz al-Dīn. *Al-Taqlīd fī al-Sharī'ah al-Islāmiyyah*. Beirut: Dār al-Zahrā', 1978.

Baḥr al-'Ulūm, Muḥammad ibn 'Alī. *Al-Ijtihād, Uṣūluhu wa Aḥkāmuh*. Beirut: Dār al-Zahrā', 1977.

________.*Maṣdar al-Tashrī' li-Niẓām al-Ḥukm fī al-Islām*. Beirut: Dār al-Zahrā', 1977.

Ba'lī, 'Alī ibn Muḥammad. *Al-Mukhtaṣar fī Uṣūl al-Fiqh 'alā Madhhab al-Imām Aḥmad ibn Ḥanbal*. Makkah: Jāmi'at al-Malik 'Abd al-'Azīz, Markaz al-Baḥth al-Īlmī wa Iḥyā' al-Turāth al-Islāmī, 1980.

Al-Bannā, Muḥammad. *Min Maṣādir al-Fiqh al-Islāmī*. Cairo: Mahd al-Dirāsāt al-Islāmiyyah, 1969.

Barrī, Zakariyyā. *Maṣādir al-Aḥkām al-Islāmiyyah*. Cairo, 1975.

________.*Uṣūl al-Fiqh al-Islāmī*. Cairo: Dār al-Nahḍah al-'Arabiyyah, 1974.

Barzanjī, 'Abd al-Laṭīf 'Abd Allāh Āzīz. *Ta'āruḍ wa al-Tarjīḥ*. 1977.

Batashtī, Fawzī Muḥammad 'Abd al-Qādir. *Ḥujjiyyat al-Mursal 'inda al-Muḥaddithīn wa al-Uṣūliyyīn wa al-Fuqahā'*. Cairo:, 1982.

Bayānūnī, Aḥmad 'Izz al-Dīn. *Al-Ijtihād wa al-Mujtahidūn*. 1968.

Bayānūnī, Muḥammad 'Ad Allāh Abū al-Fatḥ. *Al-Ḥukm al-Taklīfī fī al-Sharī'ah al-Islāmiyyah*. Dimashq: Dār al-Qalam, 1988.

________.*Dirāsāt fī al-Ikhtilāfāt al-Fiqhiyyah*. Halab: Maktabat al-Hudā, 1975.

Bulayhī, Ṣāliḥ al-Barāhīm. *Al-Salsabīl fī Ma'rifat al-Dalīl*. Cairo: al-Sharikah al-Miṣriyyah lil-Ṭibā'ah wa al-Nashr, 1976.

Bultājī, Muḥyī al-Dīn 'Abd al-Salām. *Mawqif al-Imām al-Shāfi'ī min Madrasat al-'Irāq al-Fiqhiyyah*. Cairo, 1973.

Burhānī, Muḥammad Hishām. *Sadd al-Dharāī' fī al-Sharī'ah al-Islāmiyyah*. Beirut, 1985.

Būrnū, Muḥammad Ṣidqī ibn Aḥmad. *Al-Wajīz fī Īḍāḥ Qawā'id al-Fiqh al-Kulliyyah*. Beirut: Muāssasat al-Risālah, 1983.

Būṭī, Muḥammamad Sa'īd Ramaḍān. *Ḍawābiṭ al-Maṣlaḥah fī al-Sharī'ah al-Islāmiyyah*. Dimashq: Maṭbaāt al-'Ilm, 1966-67.

Darīnī, Fatḥī. *Al-Manāhij al-Uṣūliyyah fī al-Ijtihād bi-al-Ra'y*. Dimashq: Dār al-Kitāb al-Ḥadīth, 1975.

Dasūqī, Muḥammad al-Sayyid. *Al-Imām Muḥammad ibn al-Ḥasan al-Shaybānī wa Atharuhu fī al-Fiqh al-Islāmī*. Doha: Dār al-Thaqāfah, 1987.

Dawālībī, Muḥammad Ma'rūf. *Al-Madkhal ilā 'Ilm Uṣūl al-Fiqh*. Damascus: Maṭba'at Jāmi'at Dimashq, 1959.

Dāwūd, Muḥammad Sulaymān. *Naẓariyyat al-Qiyās al-Uṣūlī*. Alexandria: Dār al-Da'wah, 1984.

Dhahabī, Muḥammad ibn Aḥmad. *Manāqib al-Imām Abī Ḥanīfah wa Ṣāḥibayhi Abī Yūsuf wa Muḥammad ibn al-Ḥasan*. Karachi: Mīr Muḥammad Kutub Khānah, 1982.

Dharawī, Aḥmad Ibrāhīm 'Abbās. *Naẓariyyat al-Ijtihād fī al-Sharīāh al-Islāmiyyah*. Jeddah : Dār al-Shurūq, 1983.

_________.*Ithbāt al-Īllah al-Shar'iyyah bi-al-Adillah al-'Aqliyyah*. Jeddah: Dār al-Shurūq, 1982.

Dirīnī, Fatḥī. *Al-Manāhij al-Uṣūliyyah fī al-Ijtihād bi-al-Ra'y fī al-Tashrī' al-Islāmī*. 1975.

Faḍl Allāh, Mahdī. *Al-Ijtihād wa al-Manṭiq al-Fiqhī fī al-Islām*. Beirut: Dār al-Ṭalīāh, 1987.

Fākhūrī, 'Ādil. *Al-Risālah al-Ramziyyah fī Uṣūl al-Fiqh*. Beirut: Dār al-Ṭalī'ah, 1978.

Farghalī, Muḥammad Maḥmūd. *Buḥūth fī al-Qiyās*. Cairo: Dār al-Kitāb al-Jām'ī, 1983.

_________.*Ḥujjiyyat al-Ijmā' wa Mawqif al-'Ulamā' minhā*. Cairo: Dār al-Kitāb al-Jāmi'ī, 1971.

Fāsī, 'Allāl. *Maqāṣid al-Sharī'ah al-Islāmiyah wa Makārimuhā*. Al-Dār al-Bayḍā': Maktabat al-Waḥdah al-'Arabiyyah, 1963.

Faṭimī, Aḥmad. *Tajrīd al-Uṣūl*. 1974.

Fawdah, 'Abd al-Āẓīm. *Al-Ḥukm bi-mā Anzala Allāh*. Kuwait: Dār al-Buḥūth al-Īlmiyyah lil-Nashr wa al-Tawzī', 1987.

Fayḍ Allāh, Muḥammad Fawzī. *Al-Ilmām bi-Uṣūl al-Aḥkām*. Kuwait: Dār al-Taqaddum lil-Nashr wa al-Tawzī', 1989.

Fīfī, Yaḥyā ibn Ḥusayn. *Al-Nisyān wa atharuhu fī al-Aḥkām al-Shar'iyyah*. Beirut: Mu'assasat al-Risālah, 1981.

Ghiryānī, al-Ṣādiq 'Abd al-Raḥmān. *Al-Ḥukm al-Shar'ī bayna al-Naql wa al-'Aql*. Beirut: Dār al-Gharb al-Islāmī, 1989.

Hādī, 'Alī ibn Muḥammad Riḍā. *Kitāb Adwār 'Ilm al-Fiqh wa Aṭwāruh*. Beirut: Dār al-Zahrā', 1979.

Hajawī, Muḥammad ibn al-Ḥasan. *Fikr al-Sāmī fī Tārīkh al-Fiqh al-Islāmī*. Madinah: al-Maktabah al-'Ilmiyyah, 1976.

Ḥamādah, 'Abbās Mutawallī. *Uṣūl al-Fiqh*. Cairo: Dār al-Nahḍah al-'Arabiyyah, 1965.

Ḥamad, Aḥmad. *Al-Ijmā' bayna al-Naẓariyyah wa al-Taṭbīq*. Kuwait: Dār al-Qalam, 1982.

Ḥāmid, 'Abd al-Sattār. *Al-Imām Zufar ibn Hudhayl*. Baghdad: Wizārat al-Awqāf wa al-Shu'ūn al-Dīnī. 1980.

_________.*Al-Ḥasan ibn Ziyād wa Fiqhuhu bayna Mu'āṣirīhi min al-Fuqahā'*. Baghdad: Dār al-Risālah lil-Ṭibā'ah, 1980.

Ḥammūdah, Ṭāhir Sulaymān. *Dirāsat al-Ma'nā 'inda al-Uṣūliyyīn*. Alexandria: al-Dār al-Jāmi'iyyah, 1983.

Ḥanbalī, Shākir. *Uṣūl al-Fiqh al-Islāmī.* Dimashq: Maṭba'at al-Jāmiāh al-Sūriyyah, 1948.
Ḥasab Allāh, 'Alī. *Uṣūl al-Tashrī' al-Islāmī.* Cairo: Dār al-Ma'ārif, 1971.
Ḥasan, Khalīfah Bā Bakr. *Mānāhij al-Uṣūliyyīn fī Ṭuruq Dalālāt al-Alfāẓ 'alā al-Aḥkām.* Cairo: Maktabat Wahbah, 1989.
________.*Al-Adillah al-Mukhtalaf fīhā 'inda al-Uṣūliyyīn.* Cairo: Maktabat al-Wahbah, 1987.
Ḥasanayn, Ḥasanayn Maḥmūd. *Maṣādir al-Tashrī' al-Islāmī.* Dubai: Dār al-Qalam, 1987.
________.*Tafsīr al-Nuṣūṣ.* Dubai: Dār al-Qalam, 1986.
Ḥassān, Ḥusayn Ḥāmid. *Al-Ḥukm al-Shar'ī 'inda al-Uṣūliyyīn.* Cairo: Dār al-Nahḍah al-'Arabiyyah, 1972.
________.*Uṣūl al-Fiqh.* Cairo: 1979.
________.*Naẓariyat al-Maṣlaḥah fī al-Fiqh al-Islāmī.* Cairo: Dār al-Nahḍah al-'Arabiyyah, 1971.
Hawīsh, Muḥammad ibn Ibrāhīm. *Al-Ijtihād fī al-Sharī'ah al-Islāmiyyah.* Riyad: al-Jam'iyyah al-'Arabiyyah al-Sa'ūdiyyah lil-Thaqāfah wa al-Funūn, Idārat al-Thaqāfah, 1979.
Ḥifnāwī, Muḥammad Ibrāhīm Muḥammad. *Al-Ta'āruḍ wa al-Tarjīḥ 'inda al-Uṣūliyyin wa Atharuhumā fī al-Fiqh al-Islāmī.* Al-Manṣūrah: Dār al-Wafā', 1985.
________.*Naẓarāt fī Uṣūl al-Fiqh.* Cairo: Dār al-Ḥadīth, 1985.
Hītū, Muḥammad Ḥasan. *Al-Ijtihād wa Ṭabaqāt Mujtahidī al-Shāfi'iyyah.* Beirut: Mu'assasat al-Risālah, 1988.
________.*Al-Wajīz fī Uṣūl al-Tashrī' al-Islāmī.* Beirut: Mu'assasat al-Risālah, 1983.
Ḥuṣarī, Aḥmad Muḥammad. *Ikhtilāf al-Fuqahā' wa al-Qaḍāyā al-Muta'alliqah bihi fī al-Fiqh al-Islāmī al-Muqāran.* Cairo: Maktabat al-Kulliyyāt al-Azhariyyah, 1989.
________.*Istinbāṭ al-Aḥkām min al-Nuṣūṣ.* Benghazi: Jāmi'at Qaryunis, 1981.
Ḥusayn, Aḥmad. *Uṣūl al-Fiqh al-Islāmī.* Beirut: al-Dār al-Jāmi'iyyah, 1986.
Ḥusayn, Aḥmad Farrāj. *Tārīkh al-Fiqh al-Islāmī.* Beirut: al-Dār al-Jāmi'iyyah, 1988.
Ḥusayn, Muḥammad Ṣāliḥ Mūsā. *Al-Ijtihād fī al-Sharī'ah al-Islāmiyyah.* Dimashq: Dār Ṭalās lil-Dirāsāt wa al- Tarjamah wa al-Nashr, 1989.
Ibn 'Abd Allāh, Muḥammad ibn Yāsīn. *'Ilm Uṣūl al-Fiqh.* Mawṣil: Manshūrāt Maktabat al-Bassām, 1987.
Ibn 'Āshūr, Mu.hammad al-Ṭāhir. *Maqāṣid al-Sharīāh al-Islāmiyyah* Tunis: al-Sharikah al-Tūnisiyyah lil-Tawzī', 1978.
Ibn Bādīs, 'Abd al-Ḥamīd. *Mābādi' al-Uṣūl.* Al-Jazā'ir : al-Sharikah al-Waṭaniyyah lil-Nashr wa al-Tawzī', 1980.
Ibrāhīmī, 'Abd al-Riẓā Khān. *Risālah fī 'Ilm Uṣūl al-Fiqh.* Wiesbaden: Harrassowitz, 1981.
'Īd, Khālid 'Abd Allāh. *Mabādi' al-Tashrī' al-Islāmī.* Rabat: Sharikat al-Hilāl al-Ārabiyyah, 1986.
________.*Al-Madkhal li-Dirāsat al-Fiqh al-Islāmī.* Rabat, 1979.

Ismā'īl, 'Abd al-Ḥamīd Abū al-Makārim. *Al-Adillah al-Mukhtalaf fīhā wa atharuhā fī al-Fiqh al-Islāmī*. Cairo: Dār al-Muslim, 1983.

Ismāīl, Sha'bān Muḥammad. *Uṣūl al-Fiqh*. Riyad: Dār al-Marrīkh lil-Nashr, 1981.

_________.*Dirāsāt Ḥawla al-Ijmā' wa al-Qiyās*. Cairo: Maktabat al-Nahḍah al-Miṣriyyah, 1988.

_________.*Maṣādir al-Tashrī' al-Islāmī wa Mawqif al-'Ulamā' minhā*. Riyad: Dār al-Marrīkh, 1985.

_________.*Al-Imām al-Shawkānī wa Manhajuhu fī Uṣūl al-Fiqh*. Doha, Qatar: Dār al-Thaqāfah, 1989.

Jābir, Amīnah Muḥammad ibn Yūsuf. *Ibn Rajab al-Ḥanbalī wa Athāruhu al-Fiqhiyyah*. Qatar: Dār Qaṭarī ibn al-Fujā'ah, 1985.

Jabrī, 'Abd al-Muta'āl Muḥammad. *Al-Nāsikh wa al-Mansūkh bayna al-Ithbāt wa al-Nafy*. Cairo: Maktabat Wahbah, 1987.

Jamāl al-Dīn, Muḥammad Muḥammad 'Abd al-Laṭīf. *Qiyās al-Uṣūliyyīn bayna al-Muthabbitīn wa al-Nāfīn*. Cairo: al-Maktabah al-Tawfīqiyyah, 1985.

Jīdī, 'Umar ibn 'Abd al-Karīm. *Al-'Urf wa al-'Amal fī al-Madhhab al-Mālikī wa Mafhūmuhumā Ladā 'Ulamā' al-Maghrib*. Rabat, Morocco: Ṣundūq Iḥyā' al-Turāth al-Islāmī, 1982.

Jubūrī, Abū al-Yaqẓān Āṭiyyah. *Imām Zufar wa Ārā'uhu al-Fiqhiyyah*. Baghdad, 1980.

Kabīsī, Maḥmūd Majīd ibn Sa'ūd. *Al-Ṣaghīr bayna Ahliyyat al-Wujūb wa Ahliyyat al-Adā'*. Qatar: Idārat Iḥyā' al-Turāth al-Islāmī, 1982.

Kawtharī, Muḥammad Zāhid ibn al-Ḥasan. *Ta'nīb al-Khaṭīb 'alā mā Sāqahu fī Tarjamat Abī Ḥanīfah min al-Akādhīb*. Quetta: Maktabah Islāmiyyah, 1983.

_________.*Al-Ḥāwī fī Sīrat al-Imām Abī Ja'far al-Ṭaḥāwī*. Karachi: M. Sa'īd Kampanī, 1983.

_________.*Ḥusn al-Taqāḍī fī Sīrat al-Imām Abī Yūsuf al-Qāḍī wa Ṣafḥat min Ṭabaqāt al-Fuqahā'*. Karachi, 1983.

_________.*Al-Nukat al-Ṭarīfah fī al-Taḥḥaduth 'an Rudūd ibn Abī Shaybah 'alā Abī Ḥanīfah*. Cairo: Maṭba'at al-Anwār, 1946.

Khallāf, 'Abd al-Wahhāb. *Maṣādir al-Tashrī' al-Islāmī fī mā lā Naṣṣa fīh*. Cairo: Jāmiāt al-Duwal al-Ārabiyyah, Maḥd al-Dirāsat al-'Arabiyyah al-'Āliyah, 1955

_________.*'Ilm Uṣūl al-Fiqh*. Cairo, 1972.

_________.*Khulāṣat Tārīkh al-Tashrī' al-Islāmī*. Cairo: Dār al-Ansār, 1980.

Khān, 'Abd al-Karīm 'Alī. *Ma'ālim al-Wuṣūl ilā Kifāyat al-Uṣūl*. Beirut: Dār al-Zahrā', 1985.

Khaṭīb, 'Abd al-Karīm. *Sadd Bab al-Ijtiḥād wa mā Tarattaba 'alayh*. Beirut: Mu'assasat al-Risālah, 1984.

Khaṭīb al-Mawṣilī, Rashīd. *Usūl al-Fiqh al-Islāmī*. Iraq: Wizārat al-Awqāf wa al-Shu'ūn al-Dīniyyah, 1980.

Khayyāṭ, 'Abd al-'Azīz 'Izzat. *Naẓariyyat al-'Urf*. Aman: Maktabat al-Aqṣā, 1977.

_________.*Shurūṭ al-Ijtihād*. Cairo: Dār al-Salām, 1986.

Khinn, Muṣṭafā Sa'īd. *Athar al-Ikhtilāf fī al-Qawā'id al-Uṣūliyyah fī Ikhtilāf al-Fuqahā'*. Damascus, 1972.

________. *Dirasah Tārīkhiyyah lil-Fiqh wa Uṣulih wa al-Ittijāhāt Allatī Ẓaharat fīhimā*. Dimashq: al-Sharikah al-Muttaḥidah lil-Tawzī', 1984.

Khuḍrī Bey, Muḥammad. *Tārīkh al-Tashrī' al-Islāmī*. Cairo: Maṭba'at Dār Iḥyā' al-Kutub al-'Arabiyyah, 1926.

________. *Uṣūl al-Fiqh*. Cairo: al-Maktabah al-Tijāriyyah al-Kubrā, 1962.

Kirrū, al-Hādī. *Uṣūl al-Tashrī' al-Islāmī*. Tripoli: al-Dār al-'Arabiyyah lil-Kitāb, 1976.

Kubaysī, Ḥamad 'Ubayd. *Al-Madkhal li-Dirāsat al-Sharīāh al-Islāmiyyah*. Baghdad: Wizārat al-Ta'līm al-'ālī wa al-Baḥth al-'Ilmī, 1980.

Lakhmī, Ramaḍān 'Abd al-Wadūd 'Abd al-Tawwāb Mabrūk Muḥammad. *Al-Ta'līl bi-al-Maṣlaḥah 'inda al-Uṣūliyyīn*. Cairo, 1987.

Ma'ārik, Ṣabrī Muḥammad. *Al-Amr wa Dalālatuhu 'alā al-Aḥkām al-Shar'iyyah*. Cairo, 1987.

________. *Al-Ijmā' fī al-Tashrī' al-Islāmī*. Cairo, 1987.

________. *'Awāriḍ al-Ahliyyah 'inda al-Uṣūliyyīn*. Cairo: al-Maktabah al-Tawfīqiyyah, 1981.

Madkūr, Muḥammad Sallām. *Al-Ijtihād fī al-Tashrī' al-Islāmī*. Cairo: Dār al-Nahḍah al-Ārabiyyah, 1984.

________. *Al-Wajīz lil-Madkhal lil-Fiqh al-Islāmī*. Cairo: Dār al-Naḥah al-'Arabiyyah, 1978.

________. *Uṣūl al-Fiqh al-Islāmī, Tārīkhuhu wa Ususuhu wa manāhij al-Usūliyyīn fī al-Aḥkām wa al-Adillah*. Cairo: Dār al-Nahḍah al-'Arabiyyah, 1976.

________. *Mabāḥith al-Ḥukm 'inda al-Uṣūliyyīn*. Cairo: Dār al-Nahḍah al-'Arabiyyah, 1960.

________. *Al-Ḥukm al-Takhyīrī*. Cairo: Dār al-Nahḍah al-'Arabiyyah, 1963.

Mahdī, al-Wāfī. *Al-Ijtihād fī al-Sharī'ah al-Islāmiyyah*. Al-Dār al-Bayḍā', al-Maghrib: Dār al-Thaqāfah, 1984.

Maḥmaṣānī, Ṣubḥī Rajab. *Falsafat al-Tashrī' fī al-Islām*. Beirut: Dār al-'Ilm lil-Malāyīn, 1961. [English translation by Farhat J. Ziadeh, see below.]

Maḥmūd Ḥamzah. *Kitāb al-Farā'iḍ al-Bahiyyah fī al-Qawā'id al fiqhiyyah*. 1880/1881.

Ma'mūn, 'Abd al-Rashīd. *Durūs fī al-Madkhal lil-Fiqh al-Islāmī*. Morocco: Jāmiāt Muḥammad al-Awwal, Kulliyyat al-'Ulūm al-Qānūniyyah wa al-Iqtiṣādiyyah wa al-Ijtimā'iyyah bi-Wajdah, 1980.

Maṣrī, Zakariyyā 'Abd al-Razzāq. *Ma'rifat 'Ilm al-Khilāf al-Fiqhī*. Beirut: Mu'assasat al-Risālah, 1990.

Mayhūb, 'Abd al-Ḥamīd. *Uṣūl al-Fiqh*. Cairo: Dār al-Ṭibā'ah al-Muḥammadiyyah, 1987.

________. *Wujūh Bayān al-Ijmāl fī al-Sunnah wa al-Qur'ān*. Cairo: Dār al-Kitāb al-Jāmi'ī, 1985.

Muḥammad, 'Abd al-Qādir Shiḥātah. *Mabāḥith fī al-Amr bayna al-'Ulamā'*. Cairo: Dār al-Hudā, 1984.

________. *Mabāḥith fī al-Mujmal wa al-Mubayyan min al-Kitāb wa al-Sunnah*. Cairo, 1984.

Muḥammad Rashīd Riḍā. *Yusr al-Islām wa Uṣūl al-Tashrī' al-'Āmm fī Nahy Allāh wa Rasūlihi 'an Kathrat al-Su'āl*. Cairo: al-Mu'tamar al-Islamī, 1956.

Mūsā, Muḥammad Yūsuf. *Tārīkh al-Fiqh al-Islāmī*. Cairo: Dār al-Ma'rifah, 1964-66.

Nabhān, Muḥammad Fārūq, al-. *Al-Madkhal lil-Tashrī' al-Islāmī*. Kuwait: Dār al-Qalam, 1977.

Nadwī, Salmān al-Ḥusaynī. *Ārā' al-Imām Walī Allāh al-Dihlawī fī Tārīkh al-Tashrī' al-Islāmī wa Asbāb al-Ikhtilāf fī al-Madhāhib al-Fiqhiyyah wa bayna Ahl al-Ra'y wa Ahl al-Ḥadīth*. Lucknow: Dār al-Sunnah lil-Nashr wa al-Tawzī', 1986.

Nadwī, 'Alī Aḥmad. *Al-Qawā'id al-Fiqhiyyah*. Dimashq: Dār al-Qalam, 1986.

Najjār, 'Abd al-Mun'im Muḥammad. *Baḥth fī Uṣūl al-Fiqh 'an Ḥājat al-Muslimīn ilā al-Qiyās ka-Aṣl li-Istinbāṭ al-Aḥkām al-Shar'iyyah*. Cairo: Dār al-Hudā lil-Ṭibāāh, 1984.

_________.*Al-Iqnā' fī Bayān mā Qīla fī Ḥujjiyyat al-Ijmā'*.Cairo, 1989.

Nayfar, Muḥammad al-Ṭāhir. *Uṣūl al-Fiqh: al-Nahḍah al-'Ilmiyyah wa Atharuhā fī Uṣūl al-Fiqh*. Tunis: Dār Bū Salāmah, 1974.

Nimr, 'Abd al-Mun'im. *Al-Ijtihād*. Cairo: Dār al-Shurūq, 1986.

Qāḍī, Muḥammad Mukhtār. *Al-Ra'y fī al-Fiqh al-Islāmī*. Cairo, 1949.

Qaraḍāwī, Yūsuf. *Al-Ijtihād fī al-Sharī'ah al-Islāmiyyah*. Kuwait: Dār al-Qalam, 1985.

Qaṭṭān, Mannā' Khalīl. *Tārīkh al-Tashrī' al-Islāmī*. Riyad: Dār al-Mirrīkh, 1988.

Rabī'ah, 'Abd al-Āzīz ibn 'Abd al-Raḥmān. *Al-Sabab 'inda al-Uṣūliyyīn*. Riyad: Jāmi'at al-Imām Muḥammad ibn Sa'ūd al-Islāmiyyah, 1980.

Raḍwān, Fatḥī. *Min Falsafat al-Tashrī' al-Islāmī*. Beirut: Dār al-Kitāb al-Lubnānī, 1975.

Raḥmūnī, Muḥammad al-Sharīf. *Al-Rukhaṣ al-Fiqhiyyah min al-Qur'ān wa al-Sunnah al-Nabawiyyah*. Tunis: Nashr wa Tawzī' Mu'assasāt 'Abd al-Karīm ibn 'Abd Allāh, 1987.

Sa'dī, 'Abd al-Ḥakīm 'Abd al-Raḥmān. *Mabāḥith al-'Illah fī al-Qiyās 'inda al-Uṣūliyyīn*. Beirut: Dār al-Bashā'ir al-Islāmiyyah, 1986.

Sa'dī, Muḥammad Ṣabrī. *Tafsīr al-Nuṣūṣ fī al-Qānūn wa al-Sharī'ah al-Islāmiyyah*. Cairo: Dār al-Nahḍah al-'Arabiyyah, 1979.

Ṣadr, Muḥammad Bāqir. *Durūs fī 'Ilm al-Uṣūl*. Beirut: Dār al-Kitāb al-Lubnānī ; 1978-.

_________.*Ghāyat al-Fikr fī Uṣūl al-Fiqh*. Beirut: Dār al-Ta'āruf lil-Maṭbū'āt, 1988.

_________.*Uṣūl al-Fiqh*. Beirut: Dār al-Ta'āruf lil-Maṭbū'āt, 1990.

Ṣadr, Muḥammad Ṣādiq. *Al-Ijmā' fī al-Tashrī' al-Islāmī*. 1969

Ṣadr, Riẓā. *Al-Ijtihād wa al-Taqlīd*. Beirut: Dār al-Kitāb al-Lubnānī, 1976.

Sāhī, Shawqī 'Abduh. *Al-Madkhal li-Dirāsat al-Fiqh al-Islāmī*. Cairo: Maktabat al-Nahḍah al-Miṣriyyah, 1989.

Ṣa'īdī, 'Abd al-Muta'āl. *Fī Mīdān al-Ijtihād*. Cairo: Jam'iyyat al-Thaqāfah al-Islāmiyyah, 19–.

Ṣāliḥ, Muḥammad Adīb. *Tafsīr al-Nuṣūṣ fī al-Fiqh al-Islāmī*. Dimashq: Maṭba'at Jāmi'at Dimashq, 1964 & 1972.

Ṣāliḥ, Ṣubḥī. *Ma'ālim al-Sharī'ah al-Islāmiyyah*. Beirut: Dār al-'Ilm lil-Malāyīn, 1975.

Sālim, 'Aṭiyyah Muḥammad. *Tasḥīl al-Wuṣūl ilā Fahm 'Ilm al-Uṣūl*. Banaras: Idārat al-Buḥūth al-Islāmiyyah wa al-Da'wah wa al-Iftā' bi-al-Jāmi'ah al-Salafiyyah, 1983.

Salīm, Muḥammad Faraj. *Mabāḥith al-Qiyās al-Uṣūlī*. Cairo: Dār al-Ṭibā'ah al-Muḥammadiyyah, 1973.

Sarḥān, Muḥyī Hilāl. *Al-Qawā'id al-Fiqhiyyah wa Dawruhā fī Ithrā' al-Tashrī'āt al-Ḥadīthah*. Baghdad, 1987.

Sayyābī, Khalfān ibn Jumayyil. *Fuṣūl al-Uṣūl*. Muscat: Salṭanat 'Umān, Wizārat al-Turāth al-Qawmī wa al-Thaqāfah, 1982.

Sayyid, al-Ṭayyib Khuḍarī. *Buḥūth fī al-Ijtihād fī mā lā Naṣṣ fīh*. 1978-1979.

Sāyis, Muḥammad 'Alī. *Nashāt al-Fiqh al-Ijtihādī wa Aṭwāruh*. 1970.

_________. *Tārīkh al-Fiqh al-Islāmī*. Beirut: Dār al-Kutub al-Īlmiyyah, 1990.

Sha'bān, Zakī al-Dīn. *Uṣūl al-Fiqh al-Islāmī*. Cairo: Maṭba'at Dār al-Ta'līf, 1961-1962.

Al-Shahāwī, Ibrāhīm Dasūqī. *Kitāb al-Shahāwī fī Tārīkh al-Tashrī' al-Islāmī*. Cairo: Sharikat al-Ṭibā'ah al-Fanniyyah al-Muttaḥidah, 1968.

Shahrastānī, Muḥammad Ḥusayn. *Ghāyat al-Mas'ūl fī īlm al-Uṣūl*. Amman: Mu'assasat Āl al-Bayt li-Iḥyā' al-Turāth, 1982.

Shalabī, Aḥmad. *Tārīkh al-Tashrī' al-Islāmī wa Tārīkh al-Nuẓum al-Qaḍā'iyyah fī al-Islām*. 1976.

Shalabī, Muḥammad Muṣṭafā. *Uṣūl al-Fiqh al-Islāmī*. Beirut: Dār al-Nahḍah al-'Arabiyyah, 1974.

Sharaf al-Dīn, 'Abd al-'Aẓīm. *Maṣādir al-Tashrī' al-Islāmī*. Cairo: Sharaf al-Dīn lil-Tijārah, 1988.

Sharīfī, al-'Īd ibn Sa'd. *Asbāb Ikhtilāf al-Fuqahā' fī al-Akhdh bi al-Ḥadīth*. 1987.

Shaykh, 'Abd al-Fattāḥ Ḥusaynī. *Al-Ijmā' Maṣdar Thālith min Maṣādir al-Tashrī' al-Islāmī*. Cairo: Dār al-Kitāb al-Jāmi'ī, 1979.

Al-Shaykh, al-Ḥusaynī Yūsuf. *Buḥūth fī Uṣūl al-Fiqh li-ghayr al-Ḥanafiyyah*. Cairo: Dār al-Ittiḥād al-'Arabī lil-Ṭibāah, 1972.

Shinnāwī, Sa'd Muḥammad. *Madā al-Ḥājah lil-akhdh bi-Naẓariyyat al-Maṣāliḥ al-Mursalah fī al-Fiqh al-Islāmī*. Cairo, 1981.

Shinqīṭī, Muḥammad al-Amīn ibn Muḥammad al-Mukhtār. *Mudhakkirah fī Uṣūl al-Fiqh*. Cairo: Maktabat ibn Taymiyyah, 1989.

Shithrī, Muḥammad ibn Nāṣir ibn 'Abd al-'Azīz. *Al-Amr*. Saudi Arabia, 1988.

Shumrūkh, Ḥāmid Maḥmūd. *Tārīkh al-Tashrī' al-Islāmī*. Cairo, 1986.

Al-Sibā'ī, Muṣṭafā. *Al-Sunnah wa Makānatuhā fī al-Tashrī' al-Islāmī*. Beirut: al-Maktab al-Islāmī, 1976.

Sirāj, Muḥammad Aḥmad. *Naẓarāt 'Āmmah fī Tārīkh al-Fiqh al-Islāmī*. Cairo: Dār al-Thaqāfah lil-Nashr wa al-Tawzī', 1990.

Sulaymān, Jād al-Mawlā. *Fuṣūl fī Uṣūl al-Tashrī' al-Islāmī*. Cairo: Maktabat wa Maṭba'at Muṣṭafā al-Bābī al-Ḥalabī, 1949.

Ṣuway'ī, 'Abd Allāh Muḥammad. *Ijtihād al-Rasūl wa ba'ḍ Aṣḥābih*. Tripoli: al-Munsha'ah al-'Āmmah lil-Nashr wa al-Tawzī' wa al-I'lān, 1986.

Ṭanṭāwī, Maḥmūd Muḥammad. *Al-Madkhal ilā al-Fiqh al-Islāmī*. Cairo: Maktabat Wahbah, 1987.

Tawānā, Sayyid Muḥammad Mūsā. *Al-Ijtihād wa madā Ḥajatinā Ilayhi fī Hadhā al-Āṣr.* Cairo: Dār al-Kutub al-Ḥadīthah, 1973.

Taymūr, Aḥmad. *Naẓrah Tārīkhiyyah fī Ḥudūth al-Madhāhib al-'Arba'ah al-Ḥanafī, wa al-Mālikī, wa al-shāfi'ī, wa al- Ḥanbalī wa Intishārihā.* Cairo: al-Maṭba'ah al-Salafiyyah, 1931.

Thaqafī, Sālim 'Alī. *Al-Ziyādah 'alā al-Naṣṣ.* Cairo, 1985.

Tuffāḥah, Aḥmad Zakī. *Falsafat al-Tashrī' al-Islāmī.* Beirut: Dār al-Kitāb al-Lubnānī, 1979.

_________.*Maṣādir al-Tashrī' al-Islāmī wa Qawā'id al-Sulūk al-'Āmmah.* Beirut: Dār al-Kitāb al-Lubnānī, 1985.

Turābī, Ḥasan. *Tajdīd Uṣūl al-Fiqh al-Islāmī.* Beirut: Dār al-Jīl, 1980.

Turkī, 'Abd Allāh ibn 'Abd al-Muḥsin. *Asbāb Ikhtilāf al-Fuqahā'.* [s.l. : s.n.], 1974.

_________.*Uṣūl Madhhab al-Imām Aḥmad ibn Ḥanbal.* Cairo, 1974.

Turkī, 'Abd al-Majīd. *Munāẓirāt fī Uṣūl al-Sharī'ah al-Islāmiyyah bayna Ibn Ḥazm wa al-Bājī.* Beirut: Dār al-Gharb al-Islāmī, 1986.

'Ubādah, Muḥammad Anīs. *Tārīkh al-Fiqh al-Islāmī.* Cairo, 1980.

_________.*Uṣūl al-Fiqh lil-Ḥanafiyyah.* Cairo, 1980.

'Ulwān, Fahmī Muḥammad. *Al-Qiyam al-Ḍarūriyyah wa Maqāṣid al-Tashrī' al-Islāmī.* Cairo, 1989.

'Umarī, Nādiyah Sharīf. *Nashāt al-Qiyās al-Uṣūlī wa Taṭawwuruh.* Egypt: Hajar, 1987.

_________.*Al-Naskh fī Dirāsāt al-Uṣūliyyīn* Beirut: Mu'assasat al-Risālah, 1985.

_________.*Al-Ijtihād fī al-Islām.* Beirut: Mu'assasat al-Risālah, 1981.

Wafā, Muḥammad. *Aḥkām al-Naskh fī al-Sharī'ah al-Islāmiyyah* Cairo: Dār al-Ṭibā'ah al-Muḥammadiyyah, 1984.

_________.*Dalālat al-Awāmir wa al-Nawāhī fī al-Kitāb wa al-Sunnah.* Cairo: M. Wafā, 1984.

_________.*Dalālat al-Khiṭāb al-Shar'ī 'alā al-Ḥukm al-Manṭūq wa al-Mafhūm.* Cairo: M. Wafā, 1984.

Zaghlūl, al-Shaḥḥāt al-Sayyid. *Adillat al-Aḥkām fī 'Ahd al-Nubūwah wa 'Aṣr al-Khulafā'.* Alexandria: Dār al-Ma'rifah al-Jāmi'iyyah, 1989.

Zakkār, Suhayl. *Fī Tārīkh al-Tashrī' al-Islāmī.* Fās: Jāmi'at al-Qarawiyyīn, Kulliyyat al-Sharīāh, 1979.

Zalamī, Muṣṭafā Ibrāhīm. *Falsafat al-Sharī'ah.* Baghdad, 1979.

_________.*Asbāb Ikhtilāf al-Fuqahā' fī al-Aḥkām al-Shar'iyyah.* Baghdad, 1986.

_________.*Dalālāt al-Nuṣūṣ wa Ṭuruq Istinbāṭ al-Aḥkām fī Ḍaw' Uṣūl al-Fiqh al-Islāmī.* Baghdad, 1983.

Zarqā, Muṣṭafā Aḥmad. *Al-Istiṣlāh wa al-Maṣāliḥ al-Mursalah fī al-Sharī'ah al-Islāmiyyah wa Uṣūl Fiqhihā.* Dimashq: Dār al-Qalam, 1988.

Zarqā, Aḥmad. *Sharḥ al-Qawā'id al-Fiqhiyyah.* Beirut: Dār al-Gharb al-Islāmī, 1983.

Zaydān, 'Abd al-Karīm. *Madkhal li-Dirāsat al-Sharī'ah al-Islāmiyyah.* Beirut: Maktabat al-Quds, 1976.

_________.*Al-Wajīz fī Uṣūl al-Fiqh.* 1967.

Zaydān, Ṣalāḥ. *Ḥujjiyyat al-Qiyās.* Cairo: Dār al-Ṣaḥwah, 1987.

_________.*Al-Ḥukm al-Shar'ī al-Taklīfī.* Cairo: Dār al-Ṣaḥwah, 1987.

Zayn, Samīḥ 'Āṭif. *'Ilm Uṣūl al-Fiqh al-Muyassar.* Beirut: Dār al-Kitāb al-Lubnānī, 1990.

Zuḥaylī, Wahbah. *Mabāḥith al-Ḥukm al-Shar'ī.* Kuwait: Maktabat al-Falāḥ, 1989.

_________.*Uṣūl al-Fiqh al-Islāmī.* Dimashq: Dār al-Fikr, 1986.

Secondary Sources: English Titles

'Abd al-Wahhāb, Salāḥ al-Dīn. *An Introduction to Islamic Jurisprudence.* Cairo, al-Azhar, 1963.

'Abd-Allah, Umar F. *Mālik's Concept of 'Amal In The Light of Mālikī Legal Theory.* 1978 (Doctoral Dissertation).

Adams, Charles C. "Abu Hanifah, Champion of Liberalism and Tolerance in Islam." *The Moslem World* 36 (1946): 217–227.

Afchar, Hassan "Equity in Musulman Law." in *Equity in the World's Legal Systems: A Comparative Study.* Edited by R. Newman. Brussels, 1973. 111–23.

Aghnides, Nicolas Prodromou. *Mohammedan Theories of Finance.* New York, Columbia University, 1916.

Ajijola, Adeleke Dirisu *Introduction of Islamic Law.* Karachi, Pakistan: International Publishers, 1981 & 1983.

_________.*The Islamic Concept of Social Justice.* Lahore, 1977.

Amīnī, Muḥammad Taqī. *Fundamentals of Ijtehad.* Delhi: Idarah-I Adabiyat-I Delli, 1986. [Translation of *Ijtihād Kā Tārī'khī Pas-I Manẓar*].

Anderson, J. N. D. (James Norman Dalrymple), Sir. *The Study of Islamic Law.* Ann Arbor: University of Michigan, 1977.

_________.*Islamic Law in The Modern World.* New York: New York University Press, 1959.

_________."Is the Shari'a Doomed to Immutability?" *The Muslim World* 56 (1966): 10–13.

Anderson. Norman. *Islamic Law in the Modern World.* New York, 1959.

_________. "Law as a Social Force in Islamic Culture and History." *Bulletin of the School of Oriental and African Studies* 20 (1957): 13–40.

_________. "Recent Developments in Shari'a Law." *The Muslim World* 40 (1950): 244–256; 41 (1951): 34–48, 113–126, 186–198, 271–288; (1952): 33–47, 124–140, 190–206, 257–276.

_________. "The Shari'a and Civil Law." *The Islamic Quarterly* 1 (1954): 29–46.

_________. "The Significance of Islamic Law in the World Today." *The American Journal of Comparative Law* 9 (1960): 187–198.

Anderson, Norman & Coulson, Noel. "The Moslem Ruler and Contractual Obligations." *New York University Law Review* 33 (1958): 917–933.

Anderson, Norman & Coulson, Noel J. *Islamic Law in Contemporary Cultural Change.* Lahore, 1979?.

Ansari, Zafar Ishaq "Islamic Juristic Terminology Before Shafi'i, A Semantic Analysis with Special Reference to Kufa." *Arabica* 19 (1972): 255–300.

Arberry A. J. *Revelation and Reason in Islam.* London 1957.

Arnold, Thomas W. *The Caliphate.* Reprint, 1967. London, 1965.

Asad, Muhammad. *The Principles of State and Government in Islam.* Berkeley, 1961.

Audah, Abdul Qader. *Islam Between Ignorant Followers And Incapable Scholars.* Gary, Ind. : I.i.f.s.o., 1971.

Awa, Mohamed el-. "The Place of Custom ('Urf) in Islamic Legal Theory." *The Islamic Quarterly* 17 (1973): 177–182.

A'ẓamī, Muḥammad Muṣṭafā. *On Schacht's Origins of Muhammadan Jurisprudence.* Riyadh, Saudi Arabia: King Saud University, 1985.

Al-Azhari, Alauddin. *The Theory and Sources of Islamic Law for Non-Muslims.* Dacca, 1962.

Aziz, Ahmad. *Islamic Modernism in India and Pakistan 1857–1964.* London, 1967.

Aziz Ahmad. *Islamic Law In Theory And Practice.* Lahore: All-Pakistan Legal Decisions, 1956.

Badr, Gamal Moursi. "Islamic Law: Its Relation to Other Legal Systems." *The American Journal of Comparative Law* 26 (1978): 187–198.

Bagby, Ihsan Abdul-Wajid. Utility In Classical Islamic Law [Microform] : (1986.) (Dissertation submitted to the University of Michigan, Ann Arbor, U.S.A)

Bahnasi, Ahmad. F. *The Theory of Social Defence in the Light of Islamic Jurisprudence.* translated by S. M. Saad, Cairo, 1974.

Baroody, George. "Shari'ah: Law of Islam." *Aramco World,* Nov.–Dec. 1966.

Ba'th, Mikal Huda. *Islam Jurisprudence.* Washington, D.C.: Foundation The America Judicial System, [c1979]

Bin Mat, Ismaīl. *Adat And Islam In Malaysia.* Philadelphia, Pa., 1985.

Bishop, Eric E. F. "Al-Shāfi'ī (Muhammad Ibn Idris) Founder of a Law School." *The Moslem World* 19 (1929): 156–175.

Bonderman, David. "Modernization and Changing Perceptions of Islamic Law." *Harvard Law Review* 81 (1968): 1169–1193.

Brunschvig, Robert. "Logic and Law in Classical Islam." In *Logic in Classical Islamic Culture,* edited by G. E. Von Grunebaum, 9–20. Wiesbaden 1970.

Burton, John, 1929- *The Collection of The Qur'ān.* Cambridge: Cambridge University Press, 1977.

________.*The Sources of Islamic Law.* Edinburgh: Edinburgh University Press, 1990.

Calder, Norman. "Ikhtilaf and Ijmā' in Shāfi'i's Risāla." *Studia Islamica* 58 (1983): 55–81.

Chambers, Richard L. "The Ottoman Ulema and the Tanzimat." In *Scholars, Saints, and Sufis.* edited by Nikki Keddie, 33–46. Berkeley, 1972.

Chehata, Chafik. "Islamic Law." In *International Encyclopedia of Comparative Law.* Vol. 2, *The Legal Systems of the world: Their Comparison and Unification.* Chap. 2, *Structure and the Divisions of the Law,* edited by R. David, 138–142. Tubingen, 1971.

Coulson, Noel J. (Noel James). *A History of Islamic Law.* Edinburgh: University Press, 1978, 1964.

________. *Conflicts and Tensions in Islamic Jurisprudence.* Chicago: The University of Chicago Press, 1969.

_________. "Islamic Law." In *The New Encyclopaedia Britannica*. Vol. 9, *Macropaedia*, 938–943. 15th ed. Chicago, 1974.

_________. "Islamic Law." In *An Introduction to Legal Systems*, 54–79. Edited by J. Duncan Derrett. New York/ Washington, 1968.

_________. "Law and Religion in Contemporary Islam." *Hastings Law Journal* 29 (1978): 1447–1457.

_________. "Doctrine and Practice in Islamic Law: One Aspect of the Problem." *Bulletin of the School of Oriental and African Studies* 18 (1956): 211–226.

_________. "The State and the Individual in Islamic Law." *The International and Comparative Law Quarterly* 6 (1957): 49–60.

Crone, Patricia, 1945- *Roman, Provincial, And Islamic Law.* Cambridge: Cambridge University Press, 1987.

Daura, Bello. "A Brief Account of the Development of the Four Sunni Schools of Law, and Some Recent Developments." *Journal of Islamic and Comparative Law.* 2 (1968): 1–12.

David, Rene & Brierley, John. "Muslim Law." In *Major Legal Systems in the World Today: An Introduction to the Comparative Study of Law*, 421–446. 2d ed. London, 1978.

Diwan, Paras, 1924- *Muslim Law in Modern India.* Allahabad: Allahabad Law Agency, 1977, 1982, 1985.

Doi, A. Raḥmān I. *Sharīāh.* London: Ta Ha, 1984.

_________.*Basis of Sharī'ah.* Zaria, Nigeria, 1980.

_________.*Shari'ah In The 1500 Century of Hijra.* London: Tā-Hā Publishers, 1981.

Eliash J. "The Ithna'Ashari-Shi'ī Juristic Theory of Political and Legal Authority." *Studia Islamica* 29 (1969): 17–30.

Faruki, Kemal. *Ijma and the Gate of Ijtihad.* Karachi 1954.

_________. *Islamic Jurisprudence.* Karachi: Pakistan Publishing House, 1962. [Also Vanity Books, 1988].

_________. *The Evolution of Islamic Constitutional Theory and Practice from 610 to 1926.* Karachi/Dacca, 1971.

_________. *The Constitutional and Legal Role of The Umma.* Karachi: Ma'aref, 1979.

_________. "The Islamic Resurgence: Prospects and Implications." in *Voices of Resurgent Islam.* edited by John Esposito, 277–291, Oxford, 1983.

_________.*Five Schools of Islamic Fiqha (Jurisprudence).* 1st Ed. Karachi: Peermahomed Ebrahim Trust, 1976.

Forte, David F. "Islamic Law: The Impact of Joseph Schacht." *Loyola of Los Angeles International and Comparative Law Annual* 1 (1978): 1–36.

Fyzee, A. A. A. (Asaf Ali Asghar). *Outlines of Muhammadan Law.* Calcutta, Indian Branch, Oxford University Press, 1949, 1955, 1964, 1974, 1983.

_________. *An Introduction to The Study of Mahomedan Law.* London, 1931.

_________.*The Importance of Muhammadan Law in the Modern World.* Ahmedabad, 1965.

_________. "Shi'ī Legal Theories." in *Law in the Middle East.* Vol. 1, *Origins and Development of Islamic Law.* Edited by M. Khadduri & H. Liebesny, 113–131, Washington D.C. 1955.

________. "The Reinterpretation of Islam." *University of Malaya Law Review* 1 (1959): 39–57.

________. "Islamic Law, and Theology in India: Proposals for a Fresh Approach." *The Middle East Journal* 8 (1954): 163–183.

________. "The Relevance of Muhammadan Law in the Twentieth Century." *The Cambridge Law Journal* (1963): 261–269.

Ghanem, Isam. *An Outline of Islamic Jurisprudence.* Zairia: Ahmadu Bello University, 1975.

Gibb, H. A. R. & Kramers, J. H., eds. *Shorter Encyclopaedia of Islam.* Ithaca, 1953.

Glauber, Anne. "Religious Law in Changing Societies: Interpreting Islamic and Jewish Law." *New York University Journal of International Law and Politics* 12 (1979): 201–203.

Gloster, Patricia Carolyn. *The Evolution of Mālikī Law In Northern Nigeria, 1930-1960.* [Microform]. 1987.

Goitein, S. D. "The Birth-Hour of Muslim Law?" *The Muslim World* 50 (1960): 23–29.

Goldziher, Ignāc (Ignaz), 1850-1921. *The Zahiris: Their Doctrine and Their History.* translated by Wolfgang Behn, Leiden, 1971.

________.*Introduction To Islamic Theology and Law.* Translated by A. & R. Hamori. Princeton, 1981.

Habil, Abdurrahman, 1951- The Methodology of Abrogation and Its Bearing On Islamic Law and Qur'ānic Studies. [Microform]. 1989.

Hallaq, Wael B. *The Gate of Ijtihad: A Study in Islamic Legal History.* Ann Arbor Mich.: University Microfilms Inernational, 1983.

Hamidullah, Muhammad. "Influence of Roman Law on Muslim Law." Reprint from the *Journal of the Hyderabad Academy.* Madras, 1943.

________."Sources of Islamic Law—A New Approach." *The Islamic Quarterly.* I (195J): 205–211.

Hasan, Ahmad. *The Doctrine of Ijmā' in Islam.* Islamabad: Islamic Research Institute, 1978.

________.*The Early Development of Islamic Jurisprudence.* Islamabad: Islamic Research Institute, 1970.

________.*Analogical Reasoning In Islamic Jurisprudence.*

________.*Islamic Jurisprudence: The Ḥukm Shar'ī.* Islamabad: Islamic Research Institute, 1993.

________.Hassan, Ahmad. "Al-Shāfi'ī's Role in the Development of Islamic Jurisprudence." *Islamic Studies* 5 (1966): 39–273.

Hassān, Husayn Hāmid. *Introduction to Islamic Law.* Islamabad, 1996.

Hassan, Riazul. *The Reconstruction of Legal Thought in Islam.* Lahore, 1974.

Hicks, Stephen C. "The Fuqaha and Islamic Law." *The American Journal of Comparative Law* 30 (Supp.) (1982): 1–13.

Hourani, George F. "The Basis of Authority of Consensus in Sunnite Islam." *Studia Islamica* 21 (1964): 13–60.

________. "Joseph Schacht, 1902–69." *Journal of the American Oriental Society* 90 (1970): 163–167.

Hurgronje, C. Snouck. *Selected Works of C. Snouck Hurgronje.* Leiden: Brill, 1957.

Islahi, Amin Ahsan. *Islamic Law: Concept and Codification*. Lahore, 1979.

Jah, 'Umar. "The Importance of Ijtihad in the Development of Islamic Law." *Journal of Islamic and Comparative Law* 7 (1977): 31–40.

Kamali, Mohammad Hashim. *Principles of Islamic Jurisprudence*. Petaling Jaya, 1989.

Khadduri, Majid. "The *Maṣlaḥa* (Public Interest) and *'Illa* (Cause) in Islamic Law." *New York University Journal of International Law and Politics* 12 (1979): 213–217.

_________.Khadduri, Majid. *The Islamic Conception of Justice*. Baltimore, 1984.

_________.*Law in the Middle East*. vol . 1, *Origin and Development of Islamic Law*. Edited by M. Khadduri & H. Liebesny, 179–202. Washington D.C., 1955.

Khadeer, Mohammed Abdul. *Ijma and Legislation in Islam*. Hyderabad: Shivaji Press, 1974.

Khoja, Ali Muhammad. *Elements of Islamic Jurisprudence: An Outline of the Evolution & Principles of Islam*. Karachi, 1977.

Liebesny, Herbert. Review of *An Introduction to Islamic Law* & *A History of Islamic Law*. In *Journal of the American Oriental Society* 86 (1966): 239–40.

MacDonald, Duncan B. *Development of Muslim Theology, Jurisprudence and Constitutional Theory*. Reissued 1966, Lahore 1903.

Madina, Maan Zilfo. *The Classical Doctrine of Consensus in Islam*. Chicago: Dept. of Photoduplication University of Chicago Library, 1957.

Mahmasani, Subhi. "Adaptation of Islamic Jurisprudence to Modern Social Needs." in *Islam in Transition: Muslim Perspectives*. Edited by John Donohue & John Esposito, 181–187, Oxford, 1982.

_________.*Falsafat al-Tashrī' fī al-Islam: The Philosophy of Jurisprudence in Islam*. Translated by Farhat J. Ziadeh. Leiden, 1961.

Makdisi, George. *Religion, Law, and Learning in Classical Islam*. Hampshire, 1991.

_________."Law and Traditionalism in the Institutions of Learning of Medieval Islam." in *Theology and Law in Islam*. Edited by G.E. von Grunebaum, 75–88, Wiesbaden, 1971.

_________."Madrasa and University In the Middle Ages." *Studia Islamica* 32 (1970): 255–264.

_________."Muslim Institutions of Learning in Eleventh-Century Baghdad." *Bulletin of the School of Oriental and African Studies* 24 (1961): 1–56.

_________."The Significance of the Sunni Schools of Law in Islamic Religious History." *International Journal of Middle East Studies* 10 (1979): 1–8.

_________.*The Rise of Colleges: Institutions of Learning in Islam and the West*. Edinburgh, 1981.

Mansour, Mansour Hasan. *The Spread and The Domination of the Maliki School of Law in North And West Africa, Eighth-Fourteenth Century*. 1981.

Mardin, Ebul'ula. "Development of the Shari'a Under the Ottoman Empire." in *Law in the Middle East*. Vol. 1, *Origin and Development of Islamic Law*. Edited by M. Khadduri & H. Liebesny, 279–291, Washington, D.C., 1955.

Masud, Muhammad Khalid. *Islamic Legal Philosophy: A Study of Abū Isḥāq al-Shāṭibī's Life and Thought*. Islamabad: Islamic Research Institute, 1977.

Meron, Ya'akov. "The Development of Legal Thought in Hanafi Texts." *Studia Islamica* 30 (1969): 73–118.

Musleh-ud-Din, Mohammad. *Islamic Jurisprudence and the Rule of Necessity and Need*. Islamabad: Islamic Research Institute, 1975.

_________.*Philosophy of Islamic Law and the Orientalists*. Lahore: Islamic Publications, 1980.

_________.*Islamic Law and Social Change*. Lahore: Islamic Publications, 1982.

Nawaz, M. K. *A Re-Examination of Some Basic Concepts of Islamic Law And Jurisprudence*. Durham, NC: World Rule of Law Center, Duke University School of Law, 1963.

_________."Some Aspects of Modernization of Islamic Law." *Texas Quarterly* 9 (1966): 183–192.

Nour, A. M. Haj. "The Schools of Law: Their Emergence and Validity Today." *Journal of Islamic and Comparative Law* 7 (1977): 54–71.

_________."Qias as a Source of Islamic Law." *Journal of Islamic and Comparative Law* 5 (1969–76): 18–50.

Nyazee, Imran Ahsan Khan. *Theories of Islamic Law: The Methodology of Ijtihād*. Islamabad: Federal Law House, 2007.

_________."The Scope of *Taqlīd* in Islamic Law." *Islamic Studies*. (1983): 1–32.

_________. *Outlines of Islamic Jurisprudence*. Islamabad: Advanced Legal Studies Institute, 1998.

Paret, R. "Istiḥsān and Istiṣlāh." in *The Encyclopaedia of Islam*. vol 4. IRAN–KHA. Edited by E. von Donzel, B. Lewis & Ch. Pellat. 255–259, Leiden 1978.

Powers, David Stephan. *Studies in Qur'ān and Ḥadīth*. Berkeley: University of California Press, 1986.

_________."On the Abrogation of the Bequest Verses." *Arabica* 29 (1982): 246–295.

Qadri, Anwar Ahmad. *Islamic Jurisprudence in the Modern World*. Varanasi, U.P., 1963.

_________.*Justice in Historical Islam*. Lahore, 1968.

Rahim, Abdur. *The Principles of Muhammadan Jurisprudence*. London, 1911.

Rahman, Fazlur. *Islamic Methodology in History*. Karachi, Central Institute of Islamic Research, 1965.

Rahman, Hafeezur. *The Origin and Development of the Sunni School of Muslim Jurisprudence*. Aligarh, 1952.

Ramadan, Said. *Islamic Law: Its Scope And Equity*. London: P. R. Macmillan, 1961.

Rosen, Lawrence. "Equity and Discretion in a Modern Islamic Legal System." *Law & Society Review* 15 (1980–81): 217–245.

Schacht, Joseph. *Origins of Muhammadan jurisprudence*. New York, 1940, 1953, 1959, 1979

_________. *Introduction to Islamic Law*. Oxford: Clarendon Press, 1964, 1982.

_________.*Sociological Aspects of Islamic Law*. Berkeley: Center For The Study of Law And Society, University of California, 1963.

_________."Fikh." in *The Encyclopaedia of Islam*. Vol. 2, C–G. Edited by B. Lewis, Ch. Pellat & J. Schacht, 886–891. New ed. Leiden/ London, 1965.

_________."Foreign Elements in Ancient Islamic Law." *Journal of Comparative Legislation and International Law* 32, Parts 3 & 4 (1950): 9–17.

_________."Islam in Northern Nigeria." *Studia Islamica* 8 (1957): 123–146.

_________."Islamic Law in Contemporary States." *The American Journal of Comparative Law* 8 (1959): 133–147.

_________. "Modernism and Traditionalism in the History of Islamic Law." *Middle Eastern Studies* 1 (1965): 388–400.

_________."Pre-Islamic Background and Early Development of Jurisprudence." in *Law in the Middle East.* Vol. 1. *Origin and Development of Islamic Law.* edited by M. Khadduri & H . Liebesny. 28–56, Washington D.C, 1955.

_________."Problems of Modern Islamic Legislation." *Studia Islamica* 12 (1960): 99–129.

_________."The Schools of Law and Later Developments of Jurisprudence." in *Law in the Middle East.* Vol. 1, *Origins and Development of Islamic Law.* edited by M. Khadduri & H. Liebesny, 57–84, Washington D. C., 1955.

_________."Theology and Law in Islam." in *Theology and Law in Islam.* edited by G. E. von Grunebaum, 3–23. Wiesbaden, 1971.

Semaan, K. 1. "Al-Nāsikh wa al-Mansūkh: Abrogation and its Application in Islam." *The Islamic Quarterly.* 6 (1961): 11–29.

_________.*Ash-Shafiī's Risalah, Basic Ideas.* Lahore: Sh. M. Ashraf, 1974.

Shabbir, Mohammad. *The Authority and Authenticity of Hadith As A Source of Islamic Law.* New Delhi: Kitab Bhavan, 1982.

Al-Shafi'ī. *Al-Imān Muḥammad ibn Idris al-Shāfiī's al-Risāla fī 'Uṣūl al-Fiqh.* English tr. by Majid Khadduri. Cambridge: Islamic Texts Society, 1987.

Shehaby, Nabil. "Illa and Qias in Early Islamic Legal Theory." *Journal of the American Oriental Society* 102 (1982): 27–46.

Smith, Percy."The Ibadhites (*El-lbadhiya* or *el-Abadhiya*)." *The Moslem World* 12 (1922): 276–288.

Smith, Wilfred C. "The Concept of Shari'a among Some Mutakallimun." in *Arabic and Islamic Studies in Honor of Hamilton A. R. Gibb.* Edited by G. Makdisi, 581–602. Leiden, 1965.

Snouck Hurgronje, C. *Selected Works of C. Snouck Hurgronje.* Edited by G. H. Bousquet & J. Schacht. Leiden, 1957.

Tritton, A.S. "Reason and Revelation." in *Arabic and Islamic Studies in Honor of Hamilton A. R. Gibb.* Edited by G. Makdisi. 619–630. Leiden, 1965.

Udovitch, A. L. "Theory and Practice of Islamic Law: Some Evidence from the Geniza." *Studia Islamica* 32 (1970): 289–303.

Vesey-Fitzgerald, S. G. "Nature and Sources of the Sharī'a." in *Law in the Middle East.* Vol. 1 *Origin and Development of Islamic Law.* edited by M. Khadduri & H. Liebesny. 85–112. Washington, D.C., 1955.

_________."The Alleged Debt of Islamic to Roman Law." *The Law Quarterly Review* 67 (1951): 81–102.

Watt, W. Montgomery. "The Closing of the Door of Ijtihad." in *Orientalia Hispanica.* edited by J. 11. Barral. Vol. 1, 675–678. Leiden, 1974.

Weeramantry, C. G. *Islamic Jurisprudence.* Basingstoke: Macmillan, 1988.

Wegner, Judith R. "Islamic and Talmudic Jurisprudence: The Four Roots of Islamic Law and Their Talmudic Counterparts." *The American Journal of Legal History* 26 (1982): 25–71.

Weiss, Bernard G. *The Search For God's Law*. Salt Lake City: University of Utah Press, 1992.

_________. "Interpretation in Islamic Law: The Theory of Ijtihad." *The American Journal of Comparative Law* 26 (1978): 199–212.

Yusuf, S. M. *An Essay on the Sunnah: Its Importance, Transmission, Development and Revision*. Lahore, 1966.

_________."The Supremacy of Shariah Law in Islamic Society. *The Islamic Quarterly* 20–22 (1978): 15–23.

Ziadeh, Farhat. "Urf and Law in Islam." in *The World of Islam: Studies in Honor of Philip K. Hitti*. Edited by James Kritzeck & R. Bayly Winder, 60–67, London, 1960.

Glossary

adillah ijmālīyah: The general evidences for the law that contain within them the specific evidences. The Qur'ān, for example, is a general evidence, while a verse of the Qur'ān pointing to a *ḥukm* is a specific evidence or the *dalīl tafṣīlī*.

adillah tafṣīlīyah: Specific evidence. See also *adillah ijmālīyah*.

aḥkām: Plural of *ḥukm* (rule).

ahlīyah: Legal capacity.

ahlīyat al-adā': Legal capacity for execution.

ahlīyat al-wujūb: Legal capacity for the acquisition of rights and obligations.

'amal: Conduct. The principle used by Mālik ibn Anas to refer to the practice of the people of Medina.

'amalīyah: Pertaining to conduct or acts.

'āmm: General. A general word or textual evidence, as distinguished from a specific word (*khāṣṣ*).

amr: Command.

aṣl: Origin; root; foundation. Source of law. The established case that forms the basis of the extension of the *ḥukm* in *qiyās* (analogy). A principle of law. The principal amount in a debt.

āthār: Traditions reported from the Companions of the Prophet (God's peace and blessings be upon him).

'azīmah: A rule initially applied as a comprehensive general principle to which exceptions or provisos are provided by the law later. The exception is called *rukhṣah*.

bayān: Explanation. Technically, the explanation (*bayān*) refers to the elaboration of meanings in the texts.

dalālāt: The different ways in which the *aḥkām* are proved through the interpretation of texts.

dalālat al-naṣṣ: The implication of an explicit text.

dalīl: Evidence. In a literal sense the term means guide, but in technical terms it refers to an evidence that points to or indicates a rule (*ḥukm*).

ḍarūrī: Necessity. The term has particular significance for the purposes of law, the preservation of which is a necessity.

dhimmah: The equivalent of legal personality in positive law. A receptacle for the capacity for acquisition.

duyūn al-maraḍ: The debts that become due during death-illness. They restrict the power of disposal of the person suffering from death-illness.

fāsid: Vitiated; irregular. It is also used in the sense of voidable in the positive law. A contract, however, is voidable at the option of the parties, while the *fāsid* contract can become valid only if the offending condition is removed. It is an unenforceable contract.

furūq: The art of distinguishing apparently similar cases.

gharīb: A principle or rule that is alien to the generally acknowledged propositions of the law.

ḥadīth: Saying. The written record of the *Sunnah*. One *ḥadīth* may contain more than one *Sunnah*.

ḥājāt: Needs; necessities. Used for the secondary purposes of the law that are complementary to the five primary purposes or the *ḍarūrāt*.

ḥaqq al-salṭanah: The right of the state as distinct from the right of Allāh.

ḥawl: One year. The prescribed period after which payment of *zakāt* becomes due.

hazl: Jest. Refers to cases where utterances made in jest may have legal effects. The examples are marriage, divorce, and manumission.

ḥifẓ: Preservation. The word was used by al-Ghazālī with reference to the purposes of law.

ḥujjah: Proof; demonstrative proof. An evidence in the sources that forms the basis of persuasive legal reasoning.

ḥukm: Rule; injunction; prescription. The word *ḥukm* has a wider meaning than that implied by most of the words of English deemed its equivalent. Technically, it means a communication from Allāh, the Exalted, related to the acts of the subjects through a demand or option, or through a declaration.

ḥukm shar'ī: See *ḥukm*. The term *ḥukm shar'ī* is used to apply to its three elements: the Lawgiver (Ḥākim); the *maḥkūm fīh* or the act; and the subject or *maḥkūm 'alayh*.

ḥukm taklīfī: The obligation-creating rule. The primary rule of the legal system.

ḥukm waḍ'ī: The declaratory *ḥukm*. A secondary rule of the system that facilitate the operation of the primary rules.

ījāb: Obligation-creating command.

ijmā': Consensus of opinion. In the parlance of the jurists it is the agreement upon a *ḥukm shar'ī* by the *mujtahids* of a determined period. This definition would exclude the employment of this principle by a political institution, unless it is composed of *mujtahids*.

ijtihād: The effort of the jurist to derive the law on an issue by expending all the available means of interpretation at his disposal and by taking into account all the legal proofs related to the issue.

'illah: The underlying legal cause of a *ḥukm*, its *ratio decidendi*, on the basis of which the accompanying *ḥukm* is extended to other cases.

ishtirāk: Equivocality.

isnād: The chain of transmission of a tradition.

istidlāl mursal: Legal reasoning that is based on a principle freed from the hold of individual texts, that is, it is let go into the realm of the purposes of the law. It is also called *maṣlaḥah mursalah*.

istiḥsān: The principle according to which the law is based upon a general principle of the law in preference to a strict analogy pertaining to the issue. The principle is used by the Ḥanafīs as well as the Mālikīs. This method of interpretation may be employed for various reasons including hardship.

istiṣḥāb: Presumption of continuity of a rule or of its absence. A principle within the Shāf'ī system, which in general terms means: the status quo shall be maintained. In a more technical sense, it means that the original rule governing an issue shall remain operative. In such a case, the primary rule assigned to all issues is that of permissibility.

istiṣlāḥ: As distinguished from the broader principle of *maṣlaḥah*, it is a principle that permits a more flexible type of analogy as compared to *qiyās*.

istiqrā': Induction.

khāṣṣ: Particular; specific; specific word.

khabar wāḥid: It is a report from the Prophet that does not reach the status of *tawātur*, or of *mashhūr* according to the Ḥanafīs, that is, there are one or two narrators in its chain in the first three generations: Companions, *Tābi'ūn*, and their followers. As compared to this, the *mashhūr* report has one or two narrators among the Companions, but it reaches the status of *mutawātir* in the generation of the *Tābi'ūn*.

mafhūm al-mukhālaf: The implication contrary to the actual meaning of a text.

makrūh: Reprehensible; disapproved.

makrūh karāhat al-taḥrīm: Disapproval that is akin to prohibition.

makrūh karāhat al-tanzīh: Disapproval that is closer to permissibility.

manāṭ: The support or place of suspension of another thing. The underlying cause on which the *ḥukm* is suspended.

mandūb: Recommended.

manfa'ah: Utility.

maqāṣid al-sharī'ah: The purposes of the *sharī'ah*, whose preservation and protection amounts to the securing of an interest (*maṣlaḥah*).

maraḍ al-mawt: Death-illness; terminal illness. It may sometimes apply to states of mind that have not arisen due to illnesses, for example, a soldier in the battle field or a person on a ship threatened by a storm.

maṣāliḥ: Interests preserved and protected by the *sharī'ah*.

maṣlaḥaḥ mursalah: An interest that is not supported by an individual text, but is upheld by the texts considered collectively.

maṣlaḥah: The principle that the *sharī'ah* has determined goals or purposes and the securing of these purposes is an acknowledged interest (*maṣlaḥah*).

maẓinnah: Location. The outward indication of an actual cause of a *ḥukm*, like puberty for maturity and discretion, or sleep for the actual acquisition of impurities, or penetration for actual ejaculation in the offence of unlawful sexual intercourse.

mubāḥ: Permissible.

mujmal: The word whose meaning has not been elaborated by the text. The elaboration requires recourse to other texts.

mujtahad fīh: A matter that is subject to interpretation.

mujtahid muṭlaq: The absolute jurist—usually the founder of a school, who follows his own opinion even with respect to the rules of interpretation.

naṣṣ: Text; definitive implication of the text.

qaḍā': The judicial office. Also used for delayed performance of an act.

qaṭ'ī: Definitive.

qiyās: Analogy; syllogism. The extension of the *ḥukm* of a specific case established in the texts to a new case awaiting decision on the basis of a common underlying cause.

rukhṣah: Exemption. See *'azīmah.*

rushd: Discretion; maturity.

sadd al-dharī'ah: The plugging of lawful means to an unlawful end.

samāwīyah: Natural; pertaining to the heavens.

sanad: The evidence relied upon. The *sanad* of *ijmā'*.

Sunnah: The precedents laid down by the Prophet to be followed as binding law. These may be through statements, acts, or approvals.

ṭabaqāt: The grades of the jurists.

taḥqīq al-manāṭ: The verification of the attributes of an established case in a new case offered for examination. This process does not need a jurist. For example, a beverage may be examined to see if it is an intoxicant. This may need a chemist or pharmacist not a jurist.

taḥrīm: Prohibition.

taḥsīnāt: The third category of purposes that are complementary to the first two categories.

takhrīj: Methodology of a *faqīh* based on reasoning from general principles.

taklīf: Obligation.

taqlīd: Following the opinion of another without questioning the *dalīl* on which reliance is placed or without lawful authority from the *sharī'ah.*

tarjīḥ: Preference of one evidence over the other.

tawātur: Authentic transmission of reports and texts. A text or tradition reported by so many people in the first generation that its authenticity cannot be doubted.

'urf: Custom; usage. The usage during the period of the Prophet, which helps in discovering the original intent of the lawgiver.

ẓāhir: The apparent or literal meaning.

Index

Made in the USA
Columbia, SC
23 August 2020

17511361R00280